D0078673

TUDOR FRONTIERS AND NOBLE POWER

Tudor Frontiers and Noble Power

The Making of the British State

STEVEN G. ELLIS

CLARENDON PRESS · OXFORD
1995

Oxford University Press, Walton Street, Oxford OX2 6DP

Oxford New York

Athens Auckland Bangkok Bombay
Calcutta Cape Town Dar es Salaam Delhi
Florence Hong Kong Istanbul Karachi
Kuala Lumpur Madras Madrid Melbourne
Mexico City Nairobi Paris Singapore
Taipei Tokyo Toronto

and associated companies in
Berlin Ibadan

Oxford is a trade mark of Oxford University Press

Published in the United States
by Oxford University Press Inc., New York

British Library Cataloguing in Publication Data
Data available

Library of Congress Cataloging in Publication Data
Ellis, Steven G., 1950–
Tudor frontiers and noble power: the making of the British state
/ Steven G. Ellis.
p. cm.
Includes bibliographical references (p.).
1. Great Britain—Politics and government—1485–1603. 2. Power
(Social sciences)—Great Britain—History—16th century.
3. Nobility—Great Britain—History—16th century.
4. Tudor, House of. I. Title.
DA315.E54 1995
942.05—dc20 94-49540

ISBN 0–19–820133–8

1 3 5 7 9 10 8 6 4 2

Typeset by Best-set Typesetter Ltd., Hong Kong
Printed in Great Britain
on acid-free paper by
Biddles, Ltd., Guildford & King's Lynn

To Wallace MacCaffrey and John Morrill,
who provided inspiration and support, and to my landlord,
Patrick Collinson, who laid on the facilities

Preface

THE subject of this study is in many ways a very traditional one. The process of state formation is, however, a topic which has recently had a new lease of life. Partly this reflects contemporary interest in European integration, the Single European Act for instance. And it is manifested historiographically in such programmes as the European Science Foundation's collaborative project on 'The Origins of the Modern State in Europe, 13th–18th Centuries'. From a more insular perspective, it also constitutes an historiographical response to the problems of the modern British state, reflecting a heightened perception of its multinational character.

If the subject is traditional, the approach is perhaps less so. It reflects an attempt to combine the best features of two very different historiographical traditions, in England and Ireland. Most commonly, the process of state formation in the British Isles has been analysed from a nationalist perspective, in terms of the growth of modern nations, with modern national boundaries. This approach has certain advantages in explaining how the United Kingdom and the Republic of Ireland in their present forms came into being, but it is perhaps less useful as a means of analysing the political interests and ambitions of earlier societies. When I first began research on the early-Tudor period, over twenty years ago now, I was intrigued by the contrast between the ways in which historians of England and Ireland wrote about the Tudors and the peoples and territories over which they ruled. Tudor England was then an extremely lively field, with a very vigorous debate about Professor Sir Geoffrey Elton's theory of a 'Tudor revolution in government', and the equally important and fruitful controversy concerning the causes of the English Reformation and the advance of Protestantism. In the neighbouring island, however, these debates had then had very little impact, although the historiographical implications were no less important for Ireland. As later events proved, there were in fact some straws in the wind blowing across St George's Channel; but if there was then a debate in Irish historiography, it centred on relations between the Gaelic and English peoples within the island and on the origins of Catholic nationalism.

Twenty years on, many of the new insights into Tudor politics, society, and ecclesiastical history which were then being developed by English specialists have since been assimilated into Irish historiography. The subject has been further enlivened by the impact of colonial perspectives on Irish history. Undoubtedly too, the island's modern partition between Northern Ireland and the Irish Republic, and the growing violence and the political polarization between two communities since 1969, have fuelled historiographical controversy. Historians of Ireland have faced the further difficulty of relating developments to the separate formation of two modern states, two very different views of the present and of the significance of the past. The result is that, despite the comparatively small number of historians working in the field, Tudor Ireland is now an extremely lively and demanding topic on which to research and write.

The same can hardly be said of the development of English historiography over the past two decades. Although the area of Reformation studies remains quite lively, it seems to me that Tudor historiography in England since the 1970s has become increasingly introverted: English specialists have largely contented themselves with piecemeal additions and alterations to the inherited picture of the Tudor state. No doubt this is in many ways a credit to the breadth of vision of the generation of Tudor historians now in retirement, that the insights and perspectives which they devised and developed should have remained the orthodoxy for so long. Yet traditional Tudor perspectives are now increasingly out of step with the latest developments in the historiography of other periods of British history. Indeed if one compares Tudor historiography with recent work on the seventeenth century—written under the impact of multiple-kingdom perspectives—it is not too much to say that Tudor studies is in crisis, as is evident from the continuing decline in the numbers of established scholars and research students active in the field. Admittedly, the Tudor state was not a multiple monarchy (even if it did create a second kingdom in 1541). And controversy for controversy's sake is hardly a profitable exercise: it has to be said that in Ireland, at least, the recent debate about Revisionism has in many ways generated more heat than light. The fact remains, however, that it was the Tudors who laid the foundations for the dynastic union of 1603 and for a multinational state comprising the whole of the British Isles. It was Tudor strategies of incorporation and assimilation which exercised a formative influence on the process of state formation in later centuries and on the character of the modern British state.

In this context, then, the failure of Tudor specialists to develop perspectives along the lines of the new British history must be accounted an important missed opportunity. Of course the historian does need to beware the danger of projecting the problems and preoccupations of the present back into the past. (It remains to be seen, for instance, how much of the present preoccupation with British history will, in a putative United States of Europe in the next century, seem like a passing trend.) But it is not as if the problems faced by British monarchs from 1603 onwards were wholly unprecedented. The Tudors and indeed earlier English kings had faced very similar problems in establishing and consolidating their control over non-English peoples in territories remote from the centre of power. The essence of the dilemma faced by King James VI and I was precisely this—that the instruments and strategies inherited by Henry Tudor and revised and refined by his successors from the 1530s onwards for this very purpose could not be applied to the independent kingdom of Scotland after 1603. A new approach was needed. Thus a major weakness of modern Tudor historiography is its continued reliance on a perspective which is more appropriate to the governance of Anglo-Saxon England than to the diverse, multinational state which the Tudors actually ruled.

The present study constitutes an attempt to move towards a broader, less anachronistic perspective on the development of the Tudor state. And it will be as well to state at the outset some of the assumptions from which the discussion proceeds. Three propositions should be noted. The first is that the Tudors had a collective view of the dominions which they ruled. They saw them as one unit which they attempted to weld together into an English nation-state. As we shall see, the historian's practice of dividing the Tudor state into neat national territories—England, Ireland, Wales—although it reflects in some degree contemporary administrative divisions, obscures some of the more central and fundamental problems of Tudor government. Second, the Tudor state consisted of a core region, roughly coinciding with lowland England, where conditions were comparatively favourable to the exercise of royal authority, and a number of more remote, predominantly upland territories which were more difficult to rule. A balanced assessment of Tudor government, its successes and failures, must therefore pay much more attention to how the Tudors tackled the more intractable problems presented by these outlying territories which were less fully integrated into the state. Finally, the embryonic state which the Tudors ruled was an English one. Although the Tudors accounted among their subjects many Irish, Scots, Welsh, and even French, the various political communities which exercised power under the Tudors regarded themselves as English, were English-speaking and of English culture, and ruled through English structures of government. Perceptions of Englishness, it is true, sharpened considerably under the later Tudors—for instance, under the impact of the concept of England as an elect nation—but the political élites in the Tudor provinces were expected to conform to these changing norms. Thus the various Englishries need to be considered in an English context, even in those regions like Ireland where later developments imposed a very different outcome to the process of state formation and national identity. Indeed, a central argument of this study is that the problem of Ireland, which English historians habitually dismiss as a special case, is fundamental to the question of Tudor state formation.[1]

On the basis of these propositions, a further argument is advanced: that the Tudor experience of state formation powerfully influenced the response of English officials to the problems of multiple monarchy created by the Union of the Crowns in 1603. How the Tudors ruled their internal peripheries shaped their approach to the outward parts of the archipelago and the somewhat different problems of British state formation after 1603. Unfortunately, a complete historiographical reintegration of the Tudor state along the lines suggested would require almost a lifetime's

---

[1] For further discussion of these points, see R. A. Griffiths, 'The English realm and dominions and the king's subjects in the later middle ages', in John Rowe (ed.), *Aspects of government and society in later medieval England: essays in honour of J. R. Lander* (Toronto, 1986); S. G. Ellis, 'Crown, community and government in the English territories, 1450–1575', in *History*, 71 (1986), 187–204; id., '"Not mere English": the British perspective, 1400–1650', in *History Today*, 28 (1988), 41–8.

work. What is here attempted is a much more modest undertaking, but one which hopefully will establish a framework for the completion of the wider project. The study attempts to alter the usual perspective from which Tudor rule is viewed—London and the south-east—by focusing on the administration and defence of the two main frontier regions of the early-Tudor state, the far north of England and the English lordship of Ireland, roughly in the period 1485–1540. This is done by a detailed investigation of Tudor policy there, as manifested particularly in the careers of the successive Lords Dacre and Kildare who were the crown's chief representatives in the two borderlands for most of the period. The first part of the study sets the problems of the borderlands in context. The introduction briefly outlines the problems inherited by the Tudors in ruling their dominions; it assesses the way in which historians have traditionally analysed the borderlands; and it identifies some of the wider implications of the approach pursued here. The first two chapters discuss the creation of the northern and western frontiers as they existed in the early-Tudor period, problems of defence and policing, and the extent to which these problems were typical or otherwise of the whole Tudor state.

In the second section of the book the focus is on the two magnates who were normally entrusted by the crown with the rule of these marches. This part examines how they responded to the challenge by reorganizing their estates and deploying their tenantry and political connexion for the defence of their respective regions. In Ireland, the political manifestation of this combination of magnate power and delegated royal authority is comparatively familiar to historians as the Kildare ascendancy.[2] Rather than cover the same ground again, I have attempted in Chapter 5 to apply similar insights and perspectives to the study of the political ascendancy of a magnate whose control of a key border office was even longer and more secure than that of the so-called Great Earl. The last part of the book examines the causes and consequences of the crisis of 1534. Chapter 6 analyses the interaction between royal policies, court faction, and local politics in the two regions which led to the disgrace of the two magnates. Chapters 7 and 8 examine,

---

[2] This subject is treated in my *Tudor Ireland: crown, community and the conflict of cultures, 1470–1603* (London, 1985), chs. 3–5. Another recent and reliable account is by Professor David Quinn in Art Cosgrove (ed.), *A new history of Ireland*, ii. *Medieval Ireland, 1169–1534* (Oxford, 1987), chs. 21–4.

individually, the different responses of Dacre and Kildare to their disgrace: they also assess the way in which their reactions obliged the crown to rethink its policies towards the borderlands and to pursue separate strategies in each. In consequence, royal perceptions of the essential character of the problem in the two regions eventually came to differ. In conclusion, the book addresses the problem of the ways in which the early-Tudor experience of the borderlands coloured the government's attitude to order and good rule more generally in the Tudor state and so exercised a continuing influence on the problems of British state formation in the aftermath of 1603.

During research and writing for this book I have availed myself of occasional opportunities to try out my ideas in three exploratory papers. My appointment as O'Donnell Lecturer in the National University of Ireland for 1986 facilitated an exploratory survey of the similarities and contrasts between the two borderlands in a public lecture which was subsequently published as *The Pale and the Far North: government and society in two early Tudor borderlands* (Galway, 1988). An early version of Chapter 5 was read at one of the last of Professor Sir Geoffrey Elton's Tudor Seminars, in Cambridge in February 1988, and later appeared in the *Historical Journal*, 35 (1992), 253–77. And a paper discussing the military aspects of the 1534–5 campaign was written for a forthcoming collection of essays on *The Irish military tradition*, which is being edited by my colleague, Professor Tom Bartlett, and Dr Keith Jeffrey. Arising from these papers I received much advice and encouragement, and I should particularly like to thank Sir Geoffrey Elton, Dr Anthony Goodman, Dr Richard Hoyle, Professor Wallace MacCaffrey, Dr John Morrill, Dr Henry Summerson, and Dr Anthony Tuck in this regard. Among fellow historians of Ireland, my ideas and writings have been particularly influenced—not always in ways of which they would approve—by the work of Dr Brendan Bradshaw, Professor Robin Frame, Dr David Hayton, Professor James Lydon, Professor David Quinn, and my colleagues Professor Nicholas Canny and Professor Gearóid Ó Tuathaigh, all of whom very kindly discussed aspects of the project with me. My College very generously allowed me a sabbatical year in 1987–8, during which I undertook much of the research and a little of the writing for the book, and a further period of leave from September 1993, during which the study was completed. I am also particularly grateful to the Master and Fellows of Churchill College, to the President and Fellows of Clare Hall, and to the Cambridge History Faculty for the hospitality extended to me and the use of their facilities during my leave periods. The award of a Royal Irish Academy-British Academy Exchange Fellowship in 1985 and again in 1989, and grants by the Foundation Fund, Clare Hall, and the British Council, Dublin, funded many of the research trips, and I should also like to thank the staff of the libraries and record offices in which I worked. Documents in the Castle Howard Archives were consulted by kind permission of the Howard family. The Deputy-Keeper of the Public Record Office of Northern Ireland, Dr Anthony Malcolmson, also gave special permission for me to consult the original deeds in the Leinster collection. Finally, I should like to thank my colleague, Professor Gearóid Mac Niocaill, whose leadership of the UCG History Department since 1977 was instrumental in creating the kind of harmonious scholarly environment necessary for the completion of a work of this sort.

S. G. E.

Halifax, February 1994

Contents

Note on punctuation, coinage and dates

I have modernized the punctuation of quotations and silently expanded abbreviations. From 1460, a separate coinage for Ireland circulated there alongside sterling, and I have distinguished between pounds sterling (£) and pounds Irish (IR£): IR£1 was generally worth 13s. 4d. sterling. With regard to dating, the year has been taken to begin on 1 January rather than on 25 March, as was the custom in the Tudor territories.

List of maps

List of abbreviations

Alen's reg.	*Calendar of Archbishop Alen's register, c.1172–1534*, ed. C. Mc Neill (Dublin, 1950)
Anal. Hib.	*Analecta Hibernica*
BL	British Library
C. & W.	*Transactions of the Cumberland and Westmorland Archaeological and Antiquarian Society*
Cal. Carew MSS, 1515–74 [etc.]	*Calendar of the Carew Manuscripts preserved in the archiepiscopal library at Lambeth, 1515–74* [etc.], 6 vols. (London, 1867–73)
Cal. close rolls, 1485–1500 [etc.]	*Calendar of close rolls, Henry VII*, i. *1485–1500*, ii. *1500–09* (London, 1954–63)
Cal. doc. Scotland	*Calendar of documents relating to Scotland.* ed. J. Bain, 5 vols. (Edinburgh, 1881–1987)
Cal. inq. Co. Dublin	*Calendar of inquisitions formerly in the office of the Chief Remembrancer*, ed. M. C. Griffith, i. *Co. Dublin* (Dublin, 1991)
Cal. inq. p.m., Hen. VII	*Calendar of inquisitions post mortem, Henry VII*, 3 vols. (London, 1898–1956)
Cal. pat. rolls, 1232–47	*Calendar of patent rolls, 1232–47* [etc.] (London, 1906–)
Cal. pat. rolls Ire., Hen. VIII–Eliz.	*Calendar of patent and close rolls of chancery in Ireland, Henry VIII to 18th Elizabeth*, ed. J. Morrin (Dublin, 1861)
Cal. SP Spain	*Calendar of state papers, etc. relating to negotiations between England and Spain,*

ed. G. A. Bergenroth *et al.* (London,
1862–1954)

Christ Church deeds	'Calendar to Christ Church deeds, 1174–1684', ed. M. J. McEnery, in *Reports of the Deputy Keeper of the Public Record Office of Ireland, 20th report* (1888), *23rd* (1891), *24th* (1892), *27th* (1895)
CRO	Cumbria Record Office [Carlisle, etc.]
Durham	Durham University, Department of Palaeography and Diplomatic
EHR	*English Historical Review*
Ellis (ed.), *Original letters*	Henry Ellis (ed.), *Original letters illustrative of English history*, 11 vols. in 3 ser. (London, 1824–6)
Handbook Brit. chron.	F. M. Powicke and E. B. Fryde (eds.), *Handbook of British chronology* (3rd edn., London, 1986)
Hist. Jn.	*Historical Journal*
Hodgson, *Northumberland*	John Hodgson, *A history of Northumberland*, 3 parts in 7 vols. (Newcastle, 1820–5)
Holinshed, *Chronicles*	R. Holinshed, *The . . . chronicles of England, Scotlande and Irelande*, ed. H. Ellis, 6 vols. (London, 1807–8)
Hore and Graves, *Southern & eastern cos.*	H. F. Hore and J. Graves (eds.), *The social state of the southern and eastern counties of Ireland in the sixteenth century* (Dublin, 1870)
IHR Bull.	*Bulletin of the Institute of Historical Research*
IHS	*Irish Historical Studies*
Inq. p.m. Hen. VII	*Calendar of inquisitions post mortem, Henry VII*, 3 vols. (London, 1898–1956)

Ir. Sword	*The Irish Sword: The Journal of the Military History Society of Ireland*
Lambeth	Lambeth Palace Library, London
L. & P. Hen. VIII	*Letters and papers, foreign and domestic, Henry VIII*, 21 vols. (London, 1862–1932)
New hist. Ire.	*A new history of Ireland*, ii. *Medieval Ireland, 1169–1534*, ed. Art Cosgrove (Oxford, 1987); iii. *Early modern Ireland, 1534–1691*, ed. T. W. Moody, F. X. Martin, and F. J. Byrne (Oxford, 1976)
NLI	National Library of Ireland
Ormond deeds, 1172–1350 [etc.]	*Calendar of Ormond deeds, 1172–1350* [etc.], ed. E. Curtis, 6 vols. (Dublin, 1932–43)
Otway-Ruthven, *Med. Ire.*	A. J. Otway-Ruthven, *A history of medieval Ireland* (2nd edn., London, 1980)
PRO	Public Record Office, London
PROI	Public Record Office of Ireland, Dublin
PRONI	Public Record Office of Northern Ireland, Belfast
Red bk. Kildare	*The Red Book of the earls of Kildare*, ed. G. Mac Niocaill (Dublin, 1964)
RIA Proc.	*Proceedings of the Royal Irish Academy*
RSAI Jn.	*Journal of the Royal Society of Antiquaries of Ireland*
SHR	*Scottish Historical Review*
SP Hen. VIII	*State papers, Henry VIII*, 11 vols. (London, 1830–52)
Stat. Ire.	*The statutes at large passed in the parliaments held in Ireland*, 20 vols. (Dublin, 1786–1801)
Stat. Ire., Edw. IV	*Statute rolls of the parliament of Ireland . . . reign of King Edward IV*, ed.

	H. F. Berry and J. F. Morrissey, 2 vols. (Dublin, 1914–39)
Stat. Ire., Hen. VI	*Statute rolls of the parliament of Ireland, reign of King Henry VI*, ed. H. F. Berry (Dublin, 1910)
Stat. Ire., Hen. VII & VIII	'The bills and statutes of the Irish parliaments of Henry VII and Henry VIII', ed. D. B. Quinn, in *Anal. Hib.*, 10 (1941)
Statutes of the realm	*The statutes of the realm*, 11 vols. (London, 1810–28)
Summerson, Carlisle	Henry Summerson, *Medieval Carlisle: the city and the borders from the late eleventh to the mid-sixteenth century* (Carlisle, 1993), ii
TCD	Trinity College, Dublin
TRHS	*Transactions of the Royal Historical Society*
VCH Cumberland	*The Victoria History of the Counties of England. A history of Cumberland*, i–ii (London, 1901–5)

Map 1. The Lordship of Ireland c.1525

Clandeboy O'Neill

O'Neill

MacMahon

Carrickfergus

Strangford
Down
Dundrum
ULSTER
Ardglass
Greencastle
Carlingford
Dundalk
LOUTH
Ardee

Kells
Fore
Slane
Navan
Athboy
MEATH
Drogheda
Duleek
Skerries
Garristown
Kilkenny
West
Mullingar
Rathwire
Trim
Skreen
Ratoath
Swords
Malahide
Loughsewdy
Cloncurry
Dunboyne
Leixlip
DUBLIN
Athlone
Carbury
Maynooth
Newcastle
Lyons
DUBLIN
Dalkey

O'Connor Faly
KILDARE
Rathmore
Rathangan
Naas
Powerscourt
Fassaroe
Galway
Athenry
CONNAUGHT
Lea
Kildare
Kilcullen
O'Toole
Loughrea
Moret
Norragh
Bridge
Ballymore
Eustace
Castlekevin

O'More
Athy
Baltinglass
Wicklow
Roscrea
Castledermot
O'Byrne
O'Brien
O'Carroll
Rathvilly
Clonmore
Arklow
Nenagh
Carlow
CARLOW
Tullow

Limerick
Leighlinbridge
MacMurrough
Kilkenny
Gowran
O'Nolan
TIPPERARY
Callan
Duiske
Ferns
Adare
Cashel
Knocktopher
Thomastown
LIMERICK
Knockgaffon
Kilcash
KILKENNY
Killmallock
Cahir
Carrick-on-Suir
New Ross
Wexford
KERRY
Clonmel
Waterford
WEXFORD
Durbard's Island
Tralee
WATERFORD
Dingle
CORK
Youghal
Dungarvan
Cork
Kinsale

Baltimore

0   20   40   60 miles

Approximate
area of the English
marches

.... Boundary of the
march with the
maghery of the
Pale

County boundaries

O'Brien Gaelic chiefs

Map 2. The Anglo-Scottish border region

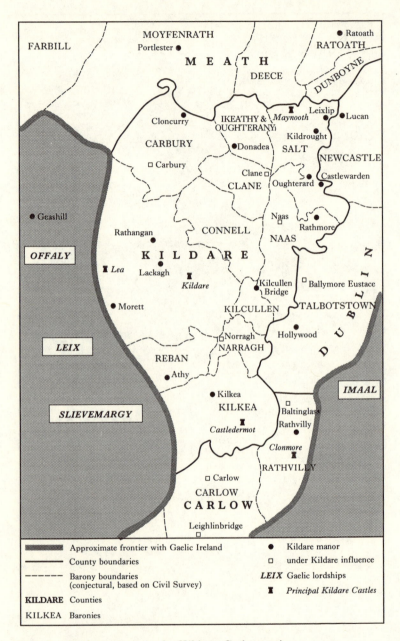

Map 3. Kildare estates in the Kildare–Carlow region

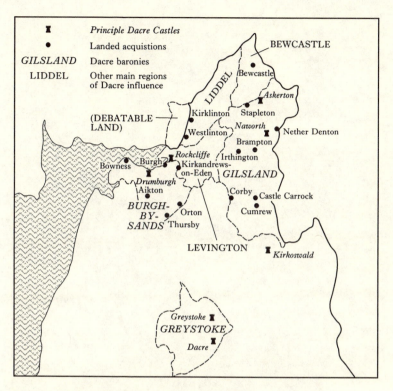

✠	Principle Dacre Castles
●	Landed acquistions
GILSLAND	Dacre baronies
LIDDEL	Other main regions of Dacre influence

BEWCASTLE

LIDDEL

Bewcastle

Askerton

Kirklinton   Stapleton

(DEBATABLE LAND)

Westlinton   *Naworth*   Nether Denton

Brampton

Rockcliffe   Irthington

Bowness   Burgh   Kirkandrews-on-Eden   *GILSLAND*

Drumburgh

Aikton   Corby   Castle Carrock

BURGH-BY-SANDS   Cumrew

Orton

Thursby

LEVINGTON   *Kirkoswald*

Greystoke ✠

GREYSTOKE

Dacre ✠

Map 4.   Dacre estates in northern Cumberland

Map 5. Gaelic Lordships, *c*.1534 with prominent English Marchers

PART I

The problem of the marches

❖

Introduction
The Tudor borderlands in context

IN 1485, after Henry Tudor had defeated King Richard III at the battle of Bosworth, he assumed control not just of England but of a disparate collection of territories and lands which had been annexed piecemeal to the crown of England over the previous four centuries. The extent and location of these lands were very little altered on the death of his son and successor, Henry VIII, over sixty years later; but the intervening period—and particularly the 1530s—had witnessed a number of attempts to weld them together as an unified nation-state. The territories may be divided into two groups. To the south there were the Channel Isles and the military outpost of Calais, which were all that remained of the French territories of medieval English kings after the loss of Normandy and Gascony in the mid-fifteenth century. Henry VIII made several attempts to recover the lost territories and so to add substance to his claims to the French crown; but in the event his efforts produced only two short-lived occupations of continental towns— Tournai between 1513 and 1518, and Boulogne from 1544 to 1550— and other fruitless invasions of French territory. None the less, the ostensible recovery of Henry V's continental empire was the great military objective of the reign, on which millions of pounds were spent.[1]

To the north and west another group of territories, of much greater geographical extent, had also formed part of the ring of strategic posts and buttresses maintained by England's medieval monarchs as a first line of defence against foreign invasion. This second group was the product of intermittent attempts by Anglo-Norman kings between the eleventh and fourteenth centuries to extend their control throughout the British Isles.[2] Yet here the

[1] John Guy, *Tudor England* (Oxford, 1988), 84–5, 99, 102–9, 190–2.
[2] Robin Frame, *The political development of the British Isles 1100–1400* (Oxford, 1990).

English military effort had been much more sporadic and small-scale, reflecting the comparative weakness and disunity of the opposition, the region's relative unimportance strategically, and the poor quality of much of the land there. The band of territory to the north and west of the English lowland zone has traditionally been marginalized by British historians as 'the Celtic fringe', although those parts which were under English control in the early sixteenth century actually comprised over half the geographical area of the Tudor state. Disregarding a few small islands, they comprised three regions. The land of Wales was divided into a large number of marcher lordships in the eastern half of the country closest to England, and the principality established by Edward I. This division reflected an earlier military frontier between the original areas of Anglo-Norman settlement in Wales and that part still controlled by the native Welsh princes before the Edwardian conquest; but in the early-Tudor period its significance was chiefly administrative. And even this distinction largely disappeared after 1536, when the crown finally got around to rationalizing administratively the consequences of Edward I's military victory 250 years earlier.[3]

By contrast, the *raison d'être* of the other two regions was still primarily a military one. The far north of England formed a buffer zone between lowland England and the independent kingdom of the Scots to the north. The English lordship of Ireland served a similar purpose with regard to the independent Gaelic chieftaincies there.[4] Yet more significant than its role in counteracting the relatively minor military threat presented by Gaelic Ireland, the lordship gave the crown control over the more fertile and strategically more important eastern and southern parts of Ireland opposite England and Wales, thus denying the use of the island to any foreign prince. After the loss of English Gascony and Normandy in the mid-fifteenth century, these two regions enjoyed an unique position within the English territories. They included

---

[3] On the constitutional position of the English borderlands, see Griffiths, 'English realm and dominions', 83–105.

[4] For the purposes of the present study, the far north is defined as the four most northerly counties of England. The lordship of Ireland is defined as that part of Ireland inhabited by the English of Ireland and under English rule: this was a normal contemporary usage, even though in English constitutional theory, the land or lordship of Ireland comprised the whole island. Similarly, such phrases as 'early-Tudor Ireland' refer to those districts under English rule and, by extension, its inhabitants.

the only extended land frontiers of the Tudor state, and as border-lands they presented particular problems of government to the Tudor régime. Thus, even though historians have traditionally treated the Tudor borderlands in isolation from each other, as different aspects of separate national historiographies, it is important to ask how far the very existence of the frontiers created common problems for the Tudor régime and elicited a similar response.

The nature of the administrative problems posed by the border-lands stemmed not just from the nature of the frontiers but from their very existence. The kingdoms of continental Europe were normally divided from each other by land boundaries, and the administrative structures which their princes developed to govern them took account of this fact—reflected in the sixteenth century, for instance, in the growth of standing armies and more elaborate professional bureaucracies. For the English monarchy, however, the fall of Lancastrian France had eliminated the most obvious need for the maintenance of a standing army. England was bureau-cratically underdeveloped, but had an unusually centralized and uniform structure of government very suited to the administration of southern and central England. This reflected the fact that con-ditions in these parts, the original area of the Anglo-Saxon monar-chy, were uniquely favourable to the exercise of royal authority. The region was quite exceptional within the British Isles, being predominantly lowland, with a rich soil and climatic conditions which were more favourable to agriculture than the areas to the north and west. These geographical advantages were exploited by successive waves of settlers from Roman to Norman times to build up a heavily manorialized and well-populated kingdom of towns and nucleated villages, from which to dominate the more frag-mented upland regions, with their dispersed patterns of settle-ment. The structures of government devised for lowland England were, however, much less suited to the administration of the out-lying territories where social structures were often more egalitarian and power decentralized.

Tudor officials were accustomed to think of England as an island—Shakespeare's 'scept'red isle'. Certainly, the distinctive-ness of its history and traditions derived in large measure from its separation from continental Europe.[5] Yet the Tudor state not only

[5] See especially R. A. Griffiths, ' *"This royal throne of kings, this scept'red isle"* ': *the English realm and nation in the later middle ages* (Swansea, 1983), 30; Guy, *Tudor*

had landed frontiers, but also particularly troublesome and untypical ones which the government could not afford to neglect. Although many parallels to the English borderlands existed elsewhere,[6] the normal relationship between European states with common boundaries was one of equality and co-operation. Each recognized the sovereignty of the other and was able, by and large, to control its own subjects and exercise good rule on its own side of the frontier. In the later middle ages English claims to empire throughout the British Isles meant that this normal relationship rarely existed in the case of the Anglo-Scottish frontier and never with regard to Ireland.[7]

Specifically, English kings claimed an overlordship over Scotland and tended to treat their Scottish counterparts as disobedient vassals. Their conduct in dealing with Gaelic Ireland was even more contemptuous: Gaelic chiefs were scarcely even considered the king's subjects, were usually denied access to the king's courts, while their titles to land and property went unrecognized. Not surprisingly, therefore, relations with Scotland and Gaelic Ireland were usually poor, with few extended periods of peace. Moreover, even the comparatively stable Scottish monarchy was frequently too weak to control its subjects effectively so as to maintain peace on the borders. Thus in Scotland, and much more so in Gaelic Ireland, the English government was encouraged to interfere in the internal affairs of what were in practice independent polities. It sought to secure its own ends by promoting discord in the neighbouring territories and by supporting one faction against the other, rather than by promoting peace and good neighbourliness. And because its relations with Scotland and Gaelic Ireland were so poor, the English government neglected to develop the necessary administrative structures to promote peace and good rule on its own side of the frontier.

The difficulty in defending these frontiers did not simply stem from bad neighbours, however, but from their sheer length, combined with the topography of the regions through which they ran,

England, 354; Hugh Kearney, *The British Isles: a history of four nations* (Cambridge, 1989), 1–9.

  [6] Cf. Robert Bartlett and Angus MacKay (eds.), *Medieval frontier societies* (Oxford, 1989).

  [7] Two works which address this problem are R. R. Davies, *Domination and conquest: the experience of Ireland, Scotland and Wales 1100–1300* (Cambridge, 1990); Frame, *Political development of the British Isles*.

and their remoteness from the centre. The Anglo-Scottish border was over 110 miles long from Berwick-on-Tweed to the Solway Firth; less than half of it was marked by rivers and streams; and it was around 300 miles distant from London as the crow flies. The Anglo-Gaelic frontier in Ireland lay still further from London, and was also longer and more discrete. Thus the vast scale of these frontiers meant that they could not be defended as a military outpost, like the Pale of Calais, with a system of fortifications manned by a permanent garrison. The costs of an elaborate system of defences of the kind necessary for these extended frontiers would have been far beyond Tudor resources. Certainly, garrisons were from time to time established to guard the main routes of entry, or as military staging posts in a diversified system of defences. Yet the defence of the frontier relied chiefly on the march itself—the strip of territory protected by castles and fortified towers and extending many miles inland—and the local population of the region. The system of defences and the obligation to maintain watch and ward and to do military service in defence of one's country, as laid down in the Statute of Winchester of 1285, was sufficient to exclude petty raiders from the interior. And in the case of major incursions, the intruders were held up for long enough for the authorities to concentrate a superior force to repel invasion. The troops available for the defence of the march were not, in the technical sense, professional soldiers, but the king's English subjects of the region; and despite the peculiar conditions in the march and the special arrangements made for defence, the inhabitants of the region expected to be governed, like Englishmen everywhere, by the course of the common law and the normal institutions of English government. It was the tensions between this principle, accepted by crown and community alike, and the constraints imposed by the more unsettled conditions in the march which lay at the heart of the problem of the borderlands.[8]

Clearly, therefore, the rule and defence of these remote frontiers were of central significance to the development of the modern state and also of considerable concern to the Tudor kings and their

---

[8] See especially Anthony Goodman, 'The Anglo-Scottish marches in the fifteenth century: a frontier society?', in R. A. Mason (ed.), *Scotland and England, 1286–1815* (Edinburgh, 1987), 18–33; id. (ed.), *War and border societies in the middle ages* (Gloucester, 1992); J. F. Lydon, 'The problem of the frontier in medieval Ireland', in *Topic, 13* (Washington, DC, 1967), 5–22.

officials. How have historians responded to the challenge posed by
the problem of the Tudor frontiers? Broadly, the response has
been to divide the borderlands up in accordance with more modern
politico-administrative units and to attempt to integrate them into
the prevailing nationalist historiographies. Thus the English lordship of Ireland is traditionally combined with Gaelic Ireland as
'Irish history', but seldom properly integrated into accounts of the
English nation and state. By contrast, there have been many fine
studies of the far north as a region of England,[9] but exceedingly
few which attempt any kind of comparison with English Ireland.[10]
Undoubtedly this kind of nationalist history makes it easier for us
to understand, from a modern standpoint, how the past turned into
the present, but the question arises as to how accurately it portrays
problems and change as seen by contemporaries. A short examination of the ways in which the particular individuals and societies
which form the content of this study have been evaluated by
historians will help to clarify this point.

With regard to English historiography, the major studies of
Henry VIII's reign have comparatively little to say about either
the Dacre ascendancy in the west marches or the Kildare ascendancy in Ireland.[11] For instance, the best biography of Henry VIII
largely overlooks developments in Ireland and neglects Kildare
completely, while an otherwise useful survey of Tudor rebellions
ignores the very region in which such protest movements were
most prevalent.[12] Dacre and the west marches have figured mar-

[9] Notably, for the Tudor period, the work of Mervyn James. See especially,
*Family, lineage and civil society: a study of society, politics, and mentality in the
Durham region, 1500–1640* (Oxford, 1974); *Society, politics and culture: studies in
early modern England* (Cambridge, 1986).
[10] Agnes Conway, *Henry VII's relations with Scotland and Ireland, 1485–98*
(Cambridge, 1932) offers some insights of this nature.
[11] Very recently, there have been signs of a change. See especially, Guy, *Tudor
England*, ch. 13 (the more surprisingly in view of the book's title); Peter Gwyn, *The
king's cardinal: the rise and fall of Thomas Wolsey* (London, 1990), ch. 7. Sir
Geoffrey Elton also devoted a chapter to the borderlands in his *Reform and Reformation: England, 1509–1558* (London, 1977), ch. 9.
[12] J. J. Scarisbrick, *Henry VIII* (London, 1968); Anthony Fletcher, *Tudor rebellions* (3rd edn., London, 1983). Another aspect of Tudor history which would
certainly benefit from a broadening of traditional nationalist perspectives is the
development of parliament. Recent surveys of Tudor parliaments ignore those in
Ireland and thus neglect the important insights into parliamentary history which
might be afforded by a more comparative approach. M. A. R. Graves, *The Tudor
parliaments: crown, lords and commons, 1485–1603* (London, 1985); Jennifer Loach,
Parliament under the Tudors (Oxford, 1991); T. E. Hartley, *Elizabeth's parliaments:
queen, lords and commons 1559–1601* (Manchester, 1992).

ginally more prominently in the traditional Tudor surveys, but even so interest has centred on Dacre's celebrated acquittal for treason in 1534 and the futile rising of Leonard Dacre in 1570. And general studies of Tudor nobles have stressed the emergence of a service nobility in England, in contrast to the territorial magnates of continental Europe. Dacre is thus marginalized as a feudal anachronism, a medieval robber baron, and the central problem of the family's long occupation of the wardenship is largely ignored.[13] Unlike Ireland, of course, it can hardly be denied that the far north formed part of England's national history, but Tudor surveys stress how 'backward' and untypical the region was of English provincial society as a whole. This presumably explains why some important studies of northern society, notably the work of Mr Mervyn James,[14] have had comparatively little impact on the wider picture. Until the mid-1530s at least, it would seem, marcher society and noble power there were relatively uninfluenced by those 'progressive' socio-political forces which were gradually transforming Tudor society in lowland England. The traditional historiographical response to the problem of the borderlands seems well captured by Professor Sir Geoffrey Elton's contention that in the 1530s 'the normal setting of government action' was England south of the Trent, and perhaps Wales at times, but that the north during the Pilgrimage constituted a 'highly special case', and that Ireland and Calais were 'special for different reasons'.[15] Thus by ignoring developments in Ireland and marginalizing the far north, the real pattern of change within the Tudor state is obscured by a smokescreen of success in southern England. Even so, the fact that Dacre and Kildare, who were two of the most powerful Tudor magnates and who, for half a century, dominated offices which were among the most onerous and sensitive in the Tudor state, should be so neglected is surely cause for concern. It suggests that perspectives on Tudor politics and government may need to be rethought—if well-worked themes like the court, administrative change, and the development of parliament in

---

[13] The best survey remains Penry Williams, *The Tudor regime* (Oxford, 1979), 4–5, 428–51, which also allows that noble power remained more entrenched in the borderlands. For the characterization of Dacre, see J. A. Guy, *The Cardinal's Court: the impact of Thomas Wolsey in Star Chamber* (Hassocks, 1977), 123.

[14] See above, n. 9.

[15] *Policy and police: the enforcement of the Reformation in the age of Thomas Cromwell* (Cambridge, 1972), p. viii.

England were so marginally relevant to the political realities of the border.

In a purely Irish context, by contrast, Kildare rule in the period before the family's rebellion and attainder in 1534 has received far more extensive and sympathetic consideration at the hands of historians. Yet it is doubtful whether this alternative perspective has permitted a more realistic appraisal of the career and political ambitions of the earls themselves, or of the kind of society in which they lived. Traditional perspectives on Irish history in the two centuries or so down to 1534 focus on interaction and assimilation between native and settler in the island and on the decline of English lordship there. Within this context, two related developments have been highlighted, both because of their apparent impact on late medieval politics and society and also because of their perceived relevance to developments from early modern times onwards. The first of these concerns the process by which the medieval Englishry gradually acquired an Irish identity, so that in particular circumstances clashes could occur between 'the English born in Ireland' and 'the English by birth', particularly royal officials sent over from England. One view of this development would argue that the English of Ireland were 'a middle nation', or Anglo-Irish, neither fully English nor fully Irish; and that this separate identity manifested itself politically in the phenomenon known as 'Anglo-Irish separatism'.[16] Second, it is argued, a powerful influence on the English of Ireland in the formation of this separate Irish identity was the phenomenon loosely described as 'gaelicization'; the aspect of cultural assimilation by which the English adopted the customs, language, and law of the Gaelic Irish.[17] Together, these two developments have been used to explain why the English of Ireland became so estranged from the English crown and the English of England that their loyalties were transposed to Ireland and they eventually came to make common cause with the Gaelic Irish as a distinct Irish nation.

From this perspective, the earls of Kildare apparently played a key role in advancing the process of integration and assimilation.

[16] James Lydon, 'The middle nation', in id. (ed.), *The English in medieval Ireland* (Dublin, 1984), 1–26.

[17] Art Cosgrove, 'Hiberniores ipsis Hibernis' in id. and Donal Macartney (eds.), *Studies in Irish history presented to R. Dudley Edwards* (Dublin, 1979), 1–14.

According to one recent assessment, the earls' establishment of a 'personal lordship over many Irish and Anglo-Irish leaders living beyond the bureaucratic control of the Dublin government' was comparable to the powers 'wielded by Ruaidhrí Ó Conchobhair [Rory O'Connor, high king of Ireland] on the eve of the Norman invasion'. Its destruction by the Tudors not only put an end to the long-established 'tendency towards assimilation' of the two communities which had 'culminated in the Deputyships of the earls of Kildare'; it also halted 'for a second time the long-drawn process of development from overlordship to centralised government' which was thus 'aborted before unity was achieved'.[18]

Ironically, therefore, from an Irish perspective the fall of Kildare is seen as ending the very process of centralization and unification which from a Tudor perspective it appeared to advance! Of course much depends on context. We may well accept that, so far as Gaelic Ireland was concerned, the Kildare ascendancy closely resembled a traditional overlordship of the kind which native chiefs like O'Neill and MacMurrough had sometimes built up. And it was in the earls' interests to cultivate this impression as a means of extending their influence. Yet no English king was so ignorant or neglectful of events in their lordship as to maintain as their deputy there a magnate who tolerated the gradual collapse of that lordship in the interests of Irish unity. And it is scarcely conceivable that the earls could even have imagined the kind of centralized Irish state which might have emerged from this process of Anglo-Gaelic assimilation. Overall, therefore, neither of the traditional perspectives from which the Kildare ascendancy has been approached by historians has proved very helpful in elucidating its essential character.

Before addressing the question of how the lordship and the far north might be integrated into a more balanced history of the Tudor state, some consideration is necessary of the so-called Revisionist Debate in Irish historiography, as it relates to this topic. The present study seeks to elaborate and develop an approach which was outlined in two earlier works, that is, to set Irish developments within a Tudor context. Necessarily, this approach

[18] Katharine Simms, *From Kings to Warlords: the changing political structure of Gaelic Ireland in the later middle ages* (Woodbridge, 1987), 20. An older study from this perspective is Donough Bryan, *Gerald FitzGerald, the Great Earl of Kildare, 1456–1513* (Dublin, 1933).

involved engaging with more traditional historiographical perspectives in Ireland. The Revisionist Debate has perhaps
now been pursued as far as conventional historical methods permit. Thus, despite the new evidence discussed here, I have deliberately avoided overloading the footnotes with a running
commentary of an historiographical nature in the chapters which
follow, although the question is taken up again in the conclusion.
For the benefit of English specialists, however, it may be helpful
to offer a brief summary and commentary on the arguments developed in my previous books and on the criticisms they have
attracted.

The first of these works, in point of research and writing, was a
detailed study of the operation of English government and of the
revival of English power and influence in Ireland in the period
1470–1534. The other book examined relations between crown and
communities in Tudor Ireland and the progress of the Tudor
conquest down to 1603.[19] In essence, my conclusions were twofold:
first, that the early-Tudor lordship of Ireland was a stable, recognizably English society, with interests and preoccupations which
were much like those of other English provincial communities,
especially those outside lowland England. In addition, I argued
that the range of problems faced by Tudor government in
Ireland—particularly marcher conditions and differences of law,
language, and culture—were not qualitatively different from those
successfully resolved in other Tudor borderlands. Admittedly,
from the mid-Tudor period onwards, politics and society in
English Ireland increasingly diverged from the pattern of development on the English mainland. It seemed to me, however, that this
divergence was chiefly the product of the novel and radical strategy
of conquest pursued by the Tudors in order to extend and consolidate English rule over the formerly independent Gaelic parts of
the island. Thus, I concluded, the side-effects of the strategy of
conquest, rather than qualitative differences in the inherited range
of problems, were one of the basic reasons why Ireland was never

[19] *Reform and revival: English government in Ireland, 1470–1534* (London, 1986);
Tudor Ireland. See also the related articles, 'Crown, community and government in
the English territories', 187–204; 'England in the Tudor state', in *Hist. Jn.*, 26
(1983), 201–12; 'Nationalist historiography and the English and Gaelic worlds in the
late middle ages', in *IHS* 25 (1986–7), 1–18.

properly assimilated after 1603 into the emerging British state.

The effect of these studies was to open the possibility of examining in relation to the other Tudor territories developments which had traditionally been approached in terms of the making of modern Ireland. Indeed Tudor specialists seemed to find the arguments advanced there and in a number of related papers unexceptionable,[20] and since the focus was on the changing English identity of the Tudor state they ran no danger of being labelled 'revisionist'. In Irish historical circles, however, the response was more critical. This approach to Tudor Ireland attracted adverse comment largely, it seems, because it was seen as ignoring or depreciating central themes in traditional Irish history-writing, particularly in relation to the continuing debate about a national past, the concept of a native race, and the claim to a national territory. The argument that early-Tudor Ireland comprised a stable English community, rather than an increasingly gaelicized Anglo-Irish colony artificially supported by English subventions, allegedly had implications for the relationship between medieval and modern Ireland: apparently, it lent support to modern theories of two nations in the two states of Ireland today and about the origins of partition. Specifically, it was characterized as an attempt to 'normalise' the 'catastrophic dimensions of the Irish past', and 'to extrude national consciousness as a dimension of the Irish historical experience from all but the modern period'.[21] A more general critique of this kind of history-writing added the charge that practitioners of revisionist history 'treat Gaelic sources as unimportant', even though Gaelic was 'the native language of a majority of people on the island until the nineteenth century', so that the majority population is portrayed 'as a foreign people or aliens'.[22] Finally, the use of the term 'nationalist' to describe traditional perspectives on this period apparently also irked some of those who had thought that—in the rather different sense in which these terms have been used in Irish historiography—they were in the revisionist camp. Predictably perhaps, it prompted the ques-

[20] They figure prominently, for instance, in John Guy's account of 'The making of the Tudor state': *Tudor England*, ch. 13.

[21] Brendan Bradshaw, 'Nationalism and historical scholarship in modern Ireland', in *IHS* 26 (1988–9), 338–40, 344.

[22] Kevin Whelan, 'Clio agus Caitlín Ní Uallacháin', in *Oghma* 2 (Dublin, 1990), 14 (my translation).

tion whether alternative interpretations should be described as 'unionist'.[23]

Writing history in the middle of a civil war is a tricky business! It was not my intention to impugn the validity of nationalist history. Traditional nationalist approaches will, it seems to me, continue to offer the most obvious perspective on the process of interaction and assimilation between *Gaedhil* and *Gaill* within Ireland (although not the wider dimensions of this process extending to Scotland). Clearly, they will also remain a most appropriate standpoint from which to assess long-term developments which led to the formation of an Irish nation and the establishment of an Irish nation-state. By characterizing traditional views on Ireland as 'nationalist' or 'hibernocentric', what I had in mind was the approach to Irish history which takes as its premiss Ireland as a separate unit of study rather than as one island in an archipelago. The use of these terms does not suggest any uniformity of approach, nor imply anything about the political outlook of its practitioners. I remain sceptical, however, about the usefulness of assessing Tudor policy for Ireland from this perspective. The polity of which early-Tudor Ireland formed part was clearly multinational in its composition and loyalist or 'unionist' in its political aspirations. The ideas of national consciousness enunciated by the political community of the early-Tudor lordship were recognizably English, not Irish, as was the language of most of the surviving sources (along with some Latin and Norman-French).[24] It can be accepted that the thought-patterns and customs of the natives— and indeed how they viewed their English neighbours—are less easily approached through the language of the conqueror than through their own language; but the fact that the descendants of the medieval Englishry generally regarded themselves as Irish and adopted the Gaelic language as their own is surely irrelevant in this context. Finally, it seems to me, traditional nationalist arguments about the growth of an 'Anglo-Irish' community, as contrasted with the English of England, are methodologically flawed, since they do not compare like with like in terms of the evidence. What is needed, in fact, is an exact comparison of the lordship, its

[23] Art Cosgrove, 'The writing of Irish medieval history', in *IHS* 27 (1990–1), 98–9.
[24] These points are developed in my 'Representations of the past in Ireland: whose past and whose present?', in *IHS* 27 (1990–1), 289–308.

political community, and the operation of English law and government there, as analysed from primary sources, with a similar analysis of another region of the English state. We may quibble about regional differences between Cumberland and Kildare, but the validity of the perspective developed here cannot be disproved by invoking modern surveys of England written from a traditional standpoint, nor by surveying the historical evidence for lordship or kingdom in isolation from the other, offering in effect half a comparison.

The positive challenge posed by these findings, however, is to establish a broader context from which to assess the lordship's significance and changing role within the Tudor state. Specifically, how representative or otherwise were developments in Ireland? In large measure, it was doubts about the evidential basis of traditional comparisons (or rather, purported contrasts) between England and Ireland which prompted me to undertake this comparative study. By the same token, however, my findings concerning the lordship's continuing influence on the wider development of the Tudor state led me to question the validity of viewing English history quite so narrowly, or 'anglocentrically', in terms of events in the region which now constitutes England—and predominantly in the southern half of it. There seemed rather too neat a contrast, for instance, between the stress laid by English historians on the peaceful extension of metropolitan values to the provinces and on progress by centralization and uniformity, and the tendency in Irish historiography to view the processes of government in terms of tension and confrontation between crown and community. These considerations prompted me to research change and continuity in another region of the Tudor state. And my initial explorations suggested that there were indeed more comparisons to be drawn than the traditional historiographies might suggest.

The choice of the early-Tudor north, and specifically the west marches towards Scotland, was dictated by a number of considerations. It was a region with which I was already comparatively familiar and which, superficially at least, seemed to possess features comparable with those previously identified as characteristic of the early-Tudor lordship—a pronounced regional identity, a varied geographical terrain, distance from the centre, an extended land frontier, and a marcher society. By comparing politics and society in English Ireland with those in another borderland of the Tudor state, it was hoped to isolate the specific from the general in marcher society. In an Irish context this would, for instance, allow a reconsideration of interaction and assimilation between English and Gaelic communities in Ireland so as to determine what aspects of this process reflected specific borrowings from Gaelic society and what features could be explained by reference to the influence of a march on English society. Yet, for the Irish sections of the book, I have concentrated on topics on which I felt I had new evidence or new insights to offer, rather than reworking themes already developed elsewhere.

Finally, what of the wider implications of this study for the development of the Tudor state and of British history in the early modern period? Proceeding from the assumption that conditions in lowland England were the norm, the outlying parts of the Tudor state—Ireland, Wales, the north, even Calais—have long been seen as posing special problems for Tudor government. These problems allegedly had nothing to do with any structural weaknesses in Tudor government itself. Rather they are held to derive from individual peculiarities of the regions themselves—geographical isolation, problems of defence, or the survival there of indigenous Celtic cultures, all of which fostered 'overmighty subjects' and the phenomenon known as 'bastard feudalism'. Thus each of these territories appears as a particular exception to the normal pattern of Tudor development. No doubt there is much truth in this characterization of Tudor history. Yet marches and marcher society were actually quite a common feature of the English dominions in early-Tudor times. In this context, the society and economy of the early-Tudor north and Ireland were perhaps in many ways more typical of the British Isles in 1500 than was the south-east which forms the traditional focus of Tudor historical attention. And before the political unification of 1603, their frontier character was certainly even less exceptional in a British than in a Tudor context. In some respects, moreover, my researches suggested that the underlying cause of the government's difficulties was the rigidly centralized character of the English system of government. This worked much less smoothly in the sparsely populated upland regions which were more typical of the Tudor state as a whole than the densely settled and relatively peaceful south-east. And the strategies devised by the government to cope with these problems arguably had a continuing influence on policy formation in the emerging British state following the political unification of the British Isles after 1603. The ways in which the core region, lowland England, dominated and controlled the borderlands was of central importance in shaping the government's response to the problems of union and also to the development of a strategy of expansion which later created the first British Empire. Thus this study pursues a more holistic approach to the problems of state formation. For Tudor specialists this may involve a major shift in their historical agenda, but it builds on good practice by the medievalists.[25] A comparative study of the two Tudor borderlands would likewise seem to offer fresh perspectives on early modern British history.

[25] Cf. Davies, *Domination and conquest*; Frame, *Political development of the British Isles*.

I

The origins of the early-Tudor problem

FRONTIERS were a natural product of the process of state formation in Europe. Their defence and policing were a constant source
of friction in international relations. In the modern age, international boundaries are very often marked with barbed wire, look-
out and customs posts, and can be depicted as a thin line on a map.
In the past, however, the frontier was typically a march, a whole
borderland with its own peculiar characteristics which marked it
off from other territories away from the exposed periphery.
Moreover, the characteristics of particular frontiers have frequently changed over time, so that comparisons between them
may only be appropriate to particular periods and aspects of their
history. This is certainly true of the two frontiers which form the
subject of the present study. The thirteenth-century Anglo-Gaelic
frontier has often been compared with the Anglo-Welsh frontier
before the completion of the English conquest of Wales.[1] In both
regions English settlements were often interspersed with native
areas, so creating multiple, localized frontiers which were fragmented and fluid, rather than consolidated blocs. Both were zones
of interaction and assimilation between peoples of very different
cultures, rather like the region east of the Elbe which then formed
the frontier between Slavs and Germans. And as with German
expansion in the Elbe–Oder region, these English frontiers were
open and expanding ones.

In Ireland, however, the division between English and Gaelic
parts was not just an issue of political control, as by 1300 it had
largely become in the mixed society of the east German frontier
region; it was also one of different societies. For reasons of ideol-

---

[1] See esp. the work of A. J. Otway-Ruthven (summarized in her *Med. Ire.*) and
R. R. Davies (in particular, his 'Frontier arrangements in fragmented societies:
Ireland and Wales', in Bartlett and MacKay (eds.), *Medieval frontier societies*,
77–100). The comparisons with Spanish and German frontiers offered here and in
the next paragraph are suggested by the essays in *Medieval frontier societies*.

ogy too, the Anglo-Gaelic frontier was seen as impermanent, not unlike that between Castile and Granada separating Christians and Muslims. Pope Adrian IV had granted the lordship of Ireland to the king of England when the native Irish were seen as a savage and primitive people whose occupation of the land was illegitimate and so with whom no permanent peace could be countenanced.[2] By contrast, cultural interaction was a much less prominent feature of the Anglo-Scottish border region. The frontier there was more like that established between France and Spain in 1659–60—continuous, delineated, and mutually accepted.[3] It was also predominantly one of exclusion, save for the relatively short period from 1296 when the conquest of Scotland was attempted. Yet as English expansion in Ireland was followed after 1300 by a period of Gaelic recovery, so the character of the frontier there changed. It too became closed and, in the east at least, more closely marked. In certain respects too, the process of acculturation there became reactive as well as conformative: thus while the Burkes in Connaught may have become almost completely Gaelic, outlying cities like Waterford consciously stressed their English identity.[4]

Both the far north of England and the English lordship of Ireland were late additions to the medieval English polity. Yet topographically they were very different, and their respective frontiers were created in rather different circumstances. The lordship was annexed out of Gaelic Ireland by a process of English colonization in the century or so after 1169. By and large, its borders reflected the limits of colonial penetration. Settlement had been extensive in the low-lying and more fertile parts of Leinster and Munster, and these areas constituted the heart of the medieval lordship and contained most of the towns and cities. Yet even here there was little colonization above the 120-metre contour line, or in boggy lowlands, so that independent Gaelic enclaves survived in the Wicklow mountains and the midlands. In Ulster and Connaught, however, settlement was much sparser, and the power of the Anglo-Norman magnates and of English government rarely amounted to more than a loose overlordship. During the Gaelic

[2] *New hist. Ire.*, ii, esp. chs. 2, 9.
[3] Peter Sahlins, *Boundaries: the making of France and Spain in the Pyrenees* (Berkeley, Calif., 1989).
[4] See, for instance, *New hist. Ire.*, ii. 534–5, 569, 580, 613–14, 625–6, 643, 649; iii. 8, 13–15.

revival between the late thirteenth and mid-fifteenth centuries, English control collapsed over the more lightly settled regions. The lordship was reduced to two main blocks of territory, the coastal plain between Dublin and Dundalk in the east—the English Pale of the Tudor period—and the area dominated by the great river valleys of the south, plus a few coastal strips controlled from outlying seaports.[5]

By contrast, the English far north was poor and barren. It was a land of mountain and forest, high pasture and moorland waste, and it was split by the Pennines and Cheviots which inhibited east–west communications. In 1563 Cumberland had about 46,000 inhabitants, or about thirty per square mile, the lowest level of population of any shire in England. The western highlands of Northumberland may have had a population density of only about seventeen per square mile in 1542. Arable farming was largely confined to the two coastal strips and the Eden and Tyne valleys. Undoubtedly, these obstacles made the north intrinsically more difficult to control. The Pale was easily governed as a natural unit. The rich arable land of this coastal plain was bounded by the Wicklow mountains to the south, the bogs of Leix and Offaly to the west, and less fertile upland to the north. Yet the English north was marginally closer to London and part of the same land mass. Couriers could usually reach Berwick or Carlisle within a week, although in severe winters the Pennine roads were impassable. By sea, contrary winds frequently delayed ships, but sea passage to Ireland was generally quicker than the voyage north which might take almost two months.[6]

The north had originally formed part of the independent kingdoms of Northumbria and Cumbria which were later absorbed into England and Scotland. In effect the border on the present line stretching from the course of the River Tweed in the east to the Solway Firth in the west was created by the political partition of

---

[5] The most detailed account of the fluctuating fortunes of the English lordship in Ireland is now Otway-Ruthven, *Med. Ire.*, ii.

[6] Robin Frame, *English lordship in Ireland, 1318–1361* (Oxford, 1982), 116–19; C. S. L. Davies, 'Provisions for armies, 1509–50; a study in the effectiveness of early Tudor government', in *Economic History Review*, 2nd ser. 17 (1964), 236; James, *Family, lineage and civil society*, 1–3; S. J. Watts, *From border to middle shire: Northumberland 1586–1625* (Leicester, 1975), 40–1; C. M. L. Bouch and G. P. Jones, *A short economic and social history of the Lake Counties 1500–1830* (Manchester, 1961), 16–18.

those kingdoms. In the east, about 973 the English accepted Scottish claims to overlordship of Lothian—that part of Northumbria between the Tweed and the Forth—but generally held on to the area south to the Tees over which Scottish claims were finally relinquished in 1157. In the west, William Rufus captured Carlisle in 1092 and annexed to England the region south of Solway as far as Stainmore (the future Cumberland and Westmorland) which had hitherto been under Scottish overlordship. Northumberland and Carlisle briefly reverted to Scottish overlordship in 1136, but the restoration of English rule there in 1157 was to prove permanent.[7]

The political partition of the Anglo-Scottish border region was initially much less disruptive than was the case in Ireland. The region's status as a march was nothing new in the eleventh century. Hadrian's Wall from the Tyne to the Solway had long formed the boundary between Roman Britain and the independent tribes to the north. And in the two centuries or so to c.850 the far north formed a moving frontier between Anglo-Saxon Northumbria and British Cumbria. Subsequently southern Northumbria was colonized by the Danes, and in the north-west a mixed Norwegian and Gaelic population from Ireland and the Western Isles colonized a region whose upland districts with their British population had been virtually untouched by the Anglo-Saxons. The Norman conquest also saw the establishment of a new aristocracy in the region rather than immigration on a large scale, but the Normans also settled (by invitation) in Scotland, so that their substantial influence was felt equally on both sides of the border.[8] Overall, therefore, the population and culture of the far north was already very mixed by the Norman period, and its new political frontier was in effect a restoration of the *status quo ante bellum*.

By contrast, Ireland had experienced much less foreign immigration since early Christian times, the only significant exception being the Norse settlements of Dublin, Wexford, Waterford, Cork, and Limerick. The broad outline of Anglo-Norman expansion there imposed some very different political divisions on the

[7] G. W. S. Barrow, *Feudal Britain* (London, 1956), chs. 8–9; id., 'The Anglo-Scottish border', in *Northern History*, 1 (1966), 21–42; *VCH Cumberland*, i. 305–6, 310, ii. 242; P. H. Blair, *An introduction to Anglo-Saxon England* (Cambridge, 1956), 90, 103.
[8] H. R. Loyn, *Anglo-Saxon England and the Norman conquest* (London, 1962), ch. 1; Barrow, *Feudal Britain*, chs. 8–9.

Irish countryside, especially in the east. Broadly, in Leinster and Munster political, cultural, and geographical frontiers came to coincide much more closely than they did in the north of England. Politically, the border divided the region of English lordship and administration from the independent Gaelic chieftaincies; geographically, it represented the area of transition from rich arable lowlands to less fertile bog or upland; and culturally, it divided the area of English, or Anglo-Norman, speech, customs, and peoples from those of the indigenous Gaelic communities. Almost exactly the same contrasts between native and settler could be found in thirteenth-century Wales. There were of course significant exceptions to this pattern, because in many parts of the Englishry the Gaelic population was retained to work the land, and elsewhere the natives soon adopted particular Anglo-Norman practices. Yet the broad outline of these differences between English and Gaelic Ireland still held good in early-Tudor times, with the result that the English lordship seemed to retain more of its character as a conquest state.[9]

Even so, the contrast should not be pushed too far. The upland parts of the north were, as in Ireland, relatively unaffected by the successive waves of settlement. When William Rufus took possession of Carlisle in 1092, the combination of a non-English population and a Scottish aristocracy with which he was confronted prompted him to adopt measures which were more characteristic of Norman expansion in Ireland a century later. His new castle of Carlisle reflected the standard Norman strategy of defence, and paralleled the New Castle upon Tyne built by his father in the east in 1080. Yet he also brought into the district Norman knights to garrison the castle and, quite exceptionally, English peasants to work the surrounding countryside. The upland region to the east (now the barony of Gilsland) remained an independent enclave in Norman territory, and its last chief, Gille son of Boet (after whom the district was named), survived there until 1157.[10] Two centuries

---

[9] Robin Frame, *Colonial Ireland, 1169–1369* (Dublin, 1981) is a good short survey of the medieval lordship. For Wales, see R. R. Davies, *The age of conquest: Wales, 1063–1415* (Oxford, 1991); and for the wider European context, see now Robert Bartlett, *The making of Europe: conquest, colonization and cultural change* (London, 1993).

[10] Barrow, 'Anglo-Scottish border', 25–30; A. J. L. Winchester, *Landscape and society in medieval Cumbria* (Edinburgh, 1987), 16–18; Loyn, *Anglo-Saxon England*, 63, 331; *VCH Cumberland*, i. 305–11, ii. 242–4.

later, when the English captured Berwick in 1296, it was rebuilt in effect as a bastide and its population replaced by English burgesses. Roxburgh also saw an influx of English burgesses.[11] Thus official measures were sometimes instrumental in colonizing strategic outposts, but extensive military colonization such as occurred in Ireland or south Wales was really only feasible in those situations where favourable demographic trends—rising population and associated land hunger—coincided with the availability of new land suitable for Anglo-Norman methods of mixed farming. Initially, the Norman invasion of Ireland created some striking contrasts between English and Gaelic districts which imparted a very different character to the Anglo-Gaelic frontier from that of the far north, but in many ways the very persistence of the border gradually created a situation in which a common way of life distinguished the borderers on both sides, English and Scottish or Irish, from those of the same nation elsewhere.

The actual line of the border was more clearly defined and stable in the north than in Ireland. The lordship, as Professor Robin Frame has pointed out, was a land of many marches.[12] Yet in the more densely settled east and south-east of Ireland the broad outlines of the boundaries between English and Gaelic parts did not alter all that much between the thirteenth and sixteenth centuries. In the English Pale—itself a product of the process—the stabilization of political boundaries was substantially assisted by the proximity of the central administration based in Dublin. Its description as a Pale (à la Calais Pale) dates from 1495, but the four shires which it comprised—Dublin, Kildare, Louth, and Meath—already existed as a separate administrative unit long before this, and by the late fifteenth century the region was increasingly delineated and divided into 'maghery' (Gaelic *machaire* = a plain), march, and waste or 'fasagh' (Gaelic *fasach* = waste) land adjoining the Irishry. The boundary between the marches, which lay open to Gaelic raids, and the more secure maghery is known with some precision, since it is noted in statutes of 1477 and 1488. Much of it followed the course of the Boyne, Blackwater, and Liffey rivers and their tributaries, but in so far as it departed from

---

[11] Michael Prestwich, 'Colonial Scotland: the English in Scotland under Edward I', in R. A. Mason (ed.), *Scotland and England 1286–1815* (Edinburgh, 1987), 12–13.
[12] 'Power and society in the lordship of Ireland, 1272–1377', in *Past and Present*, 76 (Aug. 1977), 3–33, esp. 7, 32.

these rivers it was marked physically by the digging of dry dikes to inhibit cattle rustling.[13] The boundary between the marches and the uninhabited wastelands is not now precisely known; but there are indications that its course was familiar in early-Tudor times. A statute of 1495 required each tenant of marchland as defined by the 1477 statute to make a double ditch 'at thende, syde or parte of the said lande that he doth so occupie that juneth next unto Irishemen' and further ditches 'in the wastes or fasaghe landes withoute the saide marcheis'.[14] Yet, quite clearly these boundaries would fluctuate in accordance with the particular military balance in each march. In peacetime, the nominal landlords might sometimes scratch a meagre income in rents from wastes like the Fasagh Bantry in Wexford or the Fasagh Reban in Kildare, but in wartime these tracts were immediately overrun by the Kavanaghs and O'Mores respectively.[15] Some marches could also be made more secure: the statute of 1488 placed the town of Dalkey and the manor of Thorncastle, Co. Dublin, in the maghery, whereas a few years earlier they had been described as lying in the march, and in the case of Thorncastle, 'in frontura marchie'.[16]

The English marches towards Scotland were from the later fourteenth century normally divided into two. The west march comprised Cumberland north of the River Derwent and the barony of Westmorland,[17] that is, those parts of Cumberland and Westmorland which William Rufus had conquered from the Scots. The east march comprised Northumberland; but increasingly from 1470 all but the most northerly part was administered separately as the middle march, while the east march comprised the rest of Northumberland. The precise boundary between east and

---

[13] Ellis, *Reform and revival*, 50–2; *Alen's reg.*, 250–1. See also the map depicting the maghery of the Pale (misleadingly described there) in Art Cosgrove, *Late medieval Ireland, 1370–1541* (Dublin, 1981), 70. Lord Chancellor Alen stated in 1546 that the term English Pale was sometimes used to mean all those parts of Ireland inhabited by 'Englishmen', i.e. Ireland *inter Anglicos*, but that it commonly meant 'the four obedient shires', which in turn were divided into march and maghery: PRO, SP 60/11, fos. 146–52 (*L. & P. Hen. VIII*, xxi (i), no. 915).

[14] PRO, E 30/1548, fo. 18 (printed in Conway, *Henry VII's relations*, 215–16).

[15] N. B. White (ed.), *Extents of Irish monastic possessions 1540–41* (Dublin, 1943), 23, 195–7, 360–1; Hore and Graves, *Southern & eastern cos.*, 22.

[16] *Alen's reg.*, 247, 251; D. B. Quinn (ed.), 'Guide to English financial records for Irish history, 1461–1558', in *Anal. Hib.*, 10 (1941), 24.

[17] R. L. Storey, *The end of the house of Lancaster* (2nd edn., Gloucester, 1986), 109.

middle marches is unclear. The border with Scotland followed
various streams such as the Tweed, Sark, Esk, and Liddel Water
for about half its course, but for almost sixty miles in the upland
area it followed the respective watersheds of the region or was
marked by a dry dike.[18] Substantially the present line had been
mentioned in the Treaty of York in 1237, but this boundary only
survived because subsequent attempts to alter it unilaterally—
notably the establishment of an English Pale in southern Scotland
during the fourteenth century—were in general unsuccessful.[19]

The physical delineation of territory between two polities or
states, however, did not necessarily create a frontier problem.
During the thirteenth century, Anglo-Scottish relations were generally good. What led to the problem of the far north as it existed
during the Tudor period were the Scottish wars of independence,
the long period of warfare and strained relations between the two
countries during and after the unsuccessful English attempt to
conquer Scotland. The Anglo-Scottish wars from 1296 onwards
forced lords to declare their allegiance and broke up cross-border
landholdings with estates held of both English and Scottish kings.
Instead, the border magnates acquired or retained English titles to
lands in Scotland which could only be vindicated by conquest and
expropriation. The Percies, for instance, held on to Jedburgh in
the Scottish middle march until 1404, and subsequently feuded
with the Douglases, the Scottish claimants, who had ejected
them.[20]

A similar situation occurred in Ireland where relations between
native and settler had deteriorated rather earlier and where conflicting English and Gaelic titles to borderlands fuelled rivalry
between local Gaelic chiefs and Anglo-Norman barons. In south
Leinster, for example, the ancestral Butler castles of Arklow and
Tullow were lost during the fifteenth century, but were recovered
from the MacMurroughs in the early Tudor period. In Ireland,
however, the Gaelic clans who expanded their holdings at

[18] D. L. W. Tough, *The last years of a frontier: a history of the borders during the reign of Elizabeth* (Oxford, 1928), 1–17; R. L. Storey, 'The wardens of the marches of England towards Scotland, 1377–1485', in *EHR* 72 (1957), 593–615.
[19] Barrow, 'Anglo-Scottish border', 21–4.
[20] J. A. Tuck, 'Northumbrian society in the fourteenth century', in *Northern History*, 6 (1971), 22–39; id., 'Richard II and the border magnates', ibid. 3 (1968), 32–9; J. M. W. Bean, 'The Percies and their estates in Scotland', in *Archaeologia Aeliana*, 4th ser. 35 (1957), 91–9; Goodman, 'Anglo-Scottish marches', 20–4.

the settlers' expense during the Gaelic Revival were frequently not the original occupants. They were occupying as new conquerors, which made their claims all the shakier.[21] Underlying this conflict of title was a conflict of lordship. Just as kings of England periodically attempted to reassert their long-standing claims to overlordship over Scotland, they also claimed that their lordship of Ireland extended over the Gaelic parts too.

An important difference between the two regions was the relative fragmentation of power in Gaelic Ireland. The Dublin government was forced to negotiate a series of individual treaties with particular Gaelic chiefs, whereas Anglo-Scottish negotiations could take place at national level. The political situation was also more fluid in Ireland, and concerted military pressure might lead over a period to piecemeal alterations in the border.[22] In the Anglo-Scottish marches the earlier stabilization of the frontier at a mutually accepted line (in the period between 1157 and 1296) had led to the emergence of rather different concepts of a geographical kingdom and national territory. Whereas Northumbria as far as the Forth had in Anglo-Saxon times been regarded as lying in England, during the English occupation of southern Scotland after 1296 the territory under English rule (including Teviotdale, and the castles of Roxburgh, Jedburgh, and Lochmaben) was still regarded in England as part of Scotland.[23] Thus the treaty line of 1237 retained a jurisdictional significance even when the establishment of an English Pale in southern Scotland deprived it of a political one. Disputes about what was actually part of England or Scotland were confined to relatively small parcels of debatable land. A Dacre feodary of 1502, for instance, claimed that

dominus habet in Scocia propinqua baronie de Gillesland vallem de Liddale cum castris de Armetage que sunt predicti domini & que Edvardus tertius Rex Anglie dedit per cartam suam Hugoni de Dacre avo domini nunc sibi et heredibus suis in perpetuum.

---

[21] Ellis, *Reform and revival*, 59–61; *New hist. Ire.*, ii. 243–4, 635–6, 680; Simms, *From Kings to Warlords*, 16–19. For a discussion of the problem of land titles, see Brendan Bradshaw, *The Irish constitutional revolution of the sixteenth century* (Cambridge, 1979), 11–12.

[22] BL, Harleian MS 3,756; *Red bk. Kildare*; NLI, Ormond deeds (*Ormond deeds, 1413–1509* and *1509–47*).

[23] *Cal. pat. rolls, 1374–7*, 441, 457, *1396–9*, 430, *1399–1401*, 351, *1405–8*, 73; Goodman, 'Anglo-Scottish marches', 20–5.

[The lord has in Scotland near the barony of Gillesland the vale of Liddale with the castle of Armetage which belong to the said lord and which Edward III king of England by his charter gave to Hugh de Dacre grandfather of the present lord to him and his heirs in perpetuity.]

In the case of Nether Crailing which was actually in Roxburghshire, however, the feodary asserted that

dominus habet in Tindall quandam villam vocatam Cralin qua Anthonius de Beke episcopus Dunelmensis et patriarcha de Ierusalem excquisiuit de domino de Morrauia per cartam suam antecessore domini.[24]

[The lord has in Tindall a certain town called Cralin which Anthony de Beke bishop of Durham and patriarch of Jerusalem purchased from the lord of Morrauia the lord's ancestor by his charter.]

By contrast, although royal officials in Ireland might postulate a division of the country into Irishry and Englishry, jurors there could only assert that particular castles or lands lay 'in finibus patrie anglicane in Hibernia super limites patrie de Offalye', or that they 'touch the extreme parts of the English Pale, and lie near the O'Tooles on the south'.[25] Ultimately, attempts to alter the Anglo-Scottish border only succeeded at two points. In the east, Berwick-on-Tweed, which had once been Scotland's chief town and seaport, was finally retaken by the English in 1482.[26] In the west, the parish of Kirkandrews, comprising the southern portion of 'the Debateable Land' between the two kingdoms, became part of England when the Land was finally partitioned in 1552.[27] Yet the Debateable Land, measuring some ten to fifteen miles by four miles—its boundaries were also debatable!—was only the largest of a number of such parcels of ground.[28] The border surveys of 1542

[24] Durham University, Department of Palaeography and Diplomatic, Howard of Naworth MS C/201/4A (another copy in Castle Howard Archives, MS F1/5/5, fos. 25ᵛ, 26).

[25] PRO, SP 65/3/2 (*L. & P. Hen. VIII*, xvi , no. 398); *Calendar of ancient deeds and muniments preserved in the Pembroke Estate Office, Dublin* (Dublin, 1891), no. 222.

[26] It was not, however, immediately incorporated into England, and Tudor statutes which were intended to apply to Berwick specified the town by name.

[27] W. MacKay MacKenzie, 'The Debateable Land' in *SHR* 30 (1951), 109–25; T. H. B. Graham, 'The Debateable Land', in *C. & W.*, NS 12 (1912), 33–58; 14 (1914), 132–57.

[28] *L. & P. Hen. VIII*, iv, nos. 4020, 4134. A Tudor description of the bounds of the Debateable Land is printed in J. Nicolson and R. Burn, *The history and antiquities of the counties of Westmorland and Cumberland*, 2 vols. (London, 1777), i, p. xvi.

and 1550 mention five more small areas, as well as particular
Scottish encroachments on the border.[29]

Disputes about possession of small parcels of territory were
none the less an important source of trouble in the borderlands.
Occasionally they provoked a war. The Anglo-Scottish war of
1532–3 began as a dispute about the Debateable Land and was
prolonged by Henry VIII's refusal to surrender the Cawmills, a
peel half a mile north of Berwick captured during the war.[30] At
other times they were a constant irritant to good relations. The
English warden, for instance, refused redress for outrages committed by Englishmen on Scots in the Debateable Land, because to do
so was tantamount to admitting Scottish claims to the territory.[31]
Even in peacetime a high level of co-operation between magnates
and officials on both sides of the border was necessary to curb
disorders by the borderers, but in practice this was almost unat-
tainable. The result was that, like the fasagh land in Ireland,
the Anglo-Scottish border included great strips of permanent
wasteland, abandoned townships, and lands 'unplenyshed ever
sythence before the remembraunce of any man now lyvynge'. The
border surveys of 1542 and 1550 note a good many of them, even
though the mid-sixteenth century was a period of rapidly rising
population and severe pressure on the land. For instance, Kidland
lordship which was almost on the borderline was described as
uninhabited since the fourteenth century 'when the countrye of
[Teviotdale] nowe beinge parcell of Scotland . . . was Englyshe'.
Other tracts in which English and Scot enjoyed common
pasturage were totally waste during 'warre or a troublous peace';
and some districts were 'so subject to theves' that 'true poor men
that gett their lyvinge eyther by labour in husbandrye or by
pasturinge of their cattall dare not aventure theyre lyves, bodies
& goodes' to live there.[32] Conversely, at the prospect of peace
the borders became well inhabited as the commons took farms of
land.

---

[29] Sir Robert Bowes's survey of the border, 1550; and the survey of the east and
middle marches by Bowes and Sir Ralph Ellerker, 1542, are printed in John
Hodgson, *A history of Northumberland*, 3 pts. in 7 vols. (Newcastle, 1820–5), III. ii.
171–248. See also, *L. & P. Hen. VIII*, iii, no. 3286; iv, no. 968.

[30] *L. & P. Hen. VIII*, v, nos. 595, 1254, 1460, 1635. On this war, see now R. W.
Hoyle, 'The Anglo-Scottish war of 1532–3', in *Camden Miscellany*, 31 (1992), 23–9.

[31] *L. & P. Hen. VIII*, v, nos. 465, 535, 537, 763.

[32] Hodgson, *Northumberland*, III. ii. (Bowes's survey, 1550), quotations at 184,
222, 225, 229.

The descriptions in the surveys are strikingly reminiscent of those in the 1541 surveys of crown lands in Ireland, in which large tracts of land in the Pale marches were described as 'waste and in common pasture', 'waste because no-one will farm them for fear of the Irish nearby', waste 'through the invasion of Occhonnour and other Irish', or 'uncultivated and for a long time lying waste through the daily spoils and extortions of the aforesaid wild Irish'.[33] Not surprisingly, the clerks writing the inquisitions employed the same time-honoured phrases to describe the results of border warfare. With monotonous regularity march lands were recorded as waste—'per multos annos elapsa penitus iacuerunt vasta & inculta tam pro defectu tenencium quam pro destruccione per Scotos', 'eo quod deuastabatur per Scotos inimicos domini regis', 'propter inuasionem Scotorum', 'per longum tempus elapsum iacuerunt et adhuc iacent inculte ob defectu tenencium et occupatorum pre [sic] timore hibernicorum', 'pro eo quod adiacent confinibus terre Hibernicorum', 'per invasionem Ochonnour et aliorum Hibernicorum'.[34] In both regions these difficulties were exacerbated when lords failed to reside on their border estates. In the far north, the 1542 survey complained that the lords abandoned their castles in the marches and 'for their more easye quyetness & savynge of expences did withdrawe themselfes in fermes or other smaller houses . . . further distante from the sayd borders, to the great decaye of the same'. Likewise, in the Pale they kept 'little ordinary houses as [if] they were in a land of peace'.[35] Under the early Tudors neither border suffered more than usually from absentee neglect. Many of the lands of Thomas Manners, Lord Ros and earl of Rutland (1513–43), were waste or in decay, and the lordship of Redesdale was so neglected by its lords, the Tailboys, that its value apparently shrank from 100 marks per annum in 1462 to 20 marks a year in 1494.[36] In Ireland the principal absentees were

---

[33] PRO, SC 11/934, SP 65/3/2 (*L. & P. Hen. VIII*, xvi, no. 378).

[34] The northern examples are taken from PRO, E 150/112 (inquisition post mortem into the lands of Humphrey, Lord Dacre, in Cumberland, 1486; *Inq. p.m. Hen. VII*, i, no. 157), C 142/19, no. 39 (inquisition post mortem into the lands of William Musgrave, 1505; *Inq. p.m. Hen. VII*, iii, no. 69). The Irish examples are from the inquisitions into the lands of traitors in crown hands, 1541: PRO, SP 65/3/2 (*L. & P. Hen. VIII*, xvi, no. 378).

[35] Hodgson, *Northumberland*, III. ii. 193 (Bowes and Ellerker's survey, 1542); *L. & P. Hen. VIII*, iv (ii), no. 2405 (quotation).

[36] Hodgson, *Northumberland*, III. ii. 183, 185, 186, 187, 191 (Bowes and Ellerker's survey, 1542); *Cal. pat. rolls, 1461–7*, 113–14; PRO, C 142/10, no. 6 (*Inq. p.m. Hen. VII*, i. no. 971).

the Howard dukes of Norfolk, George Talbot, 7th earl of Shrewsbury (1473–1538), and the earls of Ormond whose Irish estates were
split after 1515 between the Butlers of Polestown and the Boleyns.[37]
In both districts, however, the greatest absentee was the king
himself. In the 1530s, when the crown acquired major landholdings
there—the Percy and Fitzgerald inheritances and ecclesiastical estates—its inadequate provision for defence and good government
further exacerbated the problems of the borders.[38]

The endemic insecurity of the marches meant that the border
lords and gentry still lived in fortified dwellings, although Englishmen elsewhere were increasingly building country houses. Indeed
the condition of the castles and towers with which the two regions
were studded was a major cause of concern to government officials and figured prominently in their surveys of the borders:
'a lytle toure newlye buylded', 'a great tower . . . fallen in extreme
ruyne & decaye', 'an old fortresse or castell rased & caste downe
by the kinge of Scotts', a castle 'in decay and very ruin-
ous . . . necessary . . . for the defence of the country because it lies
on the borders of the Irish'.[39] The great age of castle building was
over in lowland England by the late fourteenth century, but in the
borderlands it was followed by an age of towerhouses, beginning
in the north in the late fourteenth century and in Ireland a generation or so later. In the coastal plains of Northumberland and
Cumberland towerhouses (free-standing stone keeps, usually three
or four stories in height and with battlements) were built in great
numbers by the lowland gentry in the late middle ages, with
smaller numbers in the sixteenth century, again mainly in the
lowlands. The same was largely true of the Scottish borders, but
tenurial differences apparently explain a significant difference in
their distribution on the two sides of the border. In the poorer
uplands of England, the leaders of local society—the headsmen
and lairds—lived in strong wooden houses with turf roofs, which
in the century or so to 1650 were replaced by pelehouses—small,
roughly built, barn-like stone houses without crenellation.
Pelehouses were especially numerous in Bewcastledale, Tynedale,

[37] See below, Ch. 4.   [38] Below, Chs. 7–8.
[39] Hodgson, *Northumberland*, III. ii. 191, 209–10, 211; PRO, SP 65/3/2 (*L. & P. Hen. VIII*, xvi, no. 378); Robert Newton, 'The decay of the borders', in C. W. Chalklin and M. A. Havindon (eds.), *Rural change and urban growth 1500–1800* (London, 1974), 21.

and Redesdale. In the Scottish borders, however, towerhouses were numerous and pelehouses rare even in upland districts, seemingly because the lairds there were not manorial tenants but landlords, with tenants of their own, who could afford the more expensive type of fortified dwelling.[40] If tenurial differences do in fact explain the distinction between types of fortified dwellings in the English and Scottish uplands, it would be useful to know whether similar tenurial differences between English and Gaelic Ireland were likewise reflected in Irish military architecture. In the present state of the evidence, however, this must remain a matter for speculation.

Irish towerhouses have a slightly different appearance, partly owing to a different style of crenellation. Yet they are like their northern counterparts in having the entrance on the ground floor, whereas in Scottish towerhouses, and a few in Northumberland, access was by ladder or staircase to the first floor.[41] Irish towerhouses also conformed to the English pattern in that they were located in the more fertile lowlands of Leinster, Munster, and much of Connaught, with very few in Ulster or in areas of mountain, moorland, or bog. The great majority were built in the century from 1450 onwards.[42] Many were located along the coastline, especially in the southern half of Ireland from Carlingford round to Galway, presumably against the threat of piracy. There was an astonishing proliferation in east Limerick, east Clare, and south Galway. In the lordship, large numbers were built in a great sweep running through Cos. Limerick, Tipperary, Kilkenny, and south Wexford, plus a cluster in Lecale, but relatively few in many parts of the English Pale. Towerhouses within the Pale were concentrated mainly in the marches, especially in a semi-circle around the Wicklow mountains in south Dublin and east Kildare. Another band ran north-west along the Kildare border with Gaelic Leix and Offaly into Westmeath, where there was another large cluster,

---

[40] Philip Dixon, 'Towerhouses, pelehouses and border society', in *Archaeological Journal*, 136 (1979), 240–52; Watts, *Border to middle shire*, 22–3. And see in general, M. W. Thompson, *The decline of the castle* (Cambridge, 1987), esp. the map of towerhouses (p. 23) which shows that they were largely confined to Ireland, Scotland, and the far north (with a few in the Welsh marches).

[41] Bouch and Jones, *The Lake Counties*, 34–8; H. G. Leask, *Irish castles and castellated houses* (Dundalk, 1951), chs. 9–11.

[42] Caomhín Ó Danachair, 'Irish tower houses and their regional distribution' in *Béaloideas*, 45–7 (1979), 158–63, includes a useful map amidst some controversial speculations.

and there were more in the Louth marches with Gaelic Ulster.
Provisionally, therefore, the pattern of distribution of towerhouses
in the English districts seems to reflect the relative insecurity of the
Pale marches and elsewhere, and peace and stability in the Pale
maghery where, as we have seen, the gentry built houses as in most
parts of England.

Military incursions were not the only threat to border security.
The infiltration and settlement of poor Scots into the north and of
native Irish into the Pale created problems of a different kind. In
the east march, with a population of about 18,000 under Elizabeth,
the warden estimated in 1569 that there were 2,500 alien Scots
there, while throughout Northumberland in 1586 every third man
within ten miles of the border was reputedly a Scot. They were
employed as servants and given tenancies, paid higher rents than
Englishmen could afford, illegally intermarried with the English,
and forewarned their friends at home of impending raids.[43] Lord
Dacre described the difficulties of the keeper of the remote outpost
of Bewcastledale in 1524 in keeping order among a mixed population of Scotsmen by birth and Englishmen married to Scots, so

that it shall pas his powier to reull & governe the same in due forme, but
being many of the same inhabitantes to be fugitives & owtlawes to lie in
woddes, wch woddes are in some partes eight miles broad and oder partes
tenn miles or more wherby they may lie seaven yeres in the same woddes
or any of them shall fortune to be taken.[44]

The proportion of Gaelic Irish in the Pale marches may well
have been of the same order. In Meath in the mid-1460s, 10 per
cent of plaintiffs in the central courts in Dublin, 8 per cent of
defendants, and a much higher proportion of the jurors had recognizably Gaelic names and were clearly substantial peasants,
husbandmen, and yeomen, who could afford the costs of
denization and litigation and were also sufficiently anglicized to
use the king's courts.[45] On individual manors in the maghery of
Dublin and Meath a few years later, the proportion of customary
tenants with Gaelic names was between a quarter and a half; but in
Kildare, particularly in the marches, it rose to almost two-thirds.[46]
Some of the problems which the denization of Irishmen caused are

[43] Tough, *Last years of a frontier*, 26–7, 179–80; Watt, *Border to middle shire*,
139–40.
[44] Castle Howard MS F1/5/5, fo. 30.   [45] PROI, EX 3/1.
[46] Ellis, *Reform and revival*, 6.

exemplified in a parliamentary statute of 1479 which quashed an indictment of the tenants in the Kildare marches of Roland FitzEustace, Lord Portlester, for combining with Irish enemies and English rebels in an attack on the Co. Dublin enclave of Ballymore Eustace. Many of the tenants came from Galmorestown, a formerly waste vill 'en lez frontures del Marche del dit Counte', which two years earlier had been rebuilt by Portlester. The statute asserted that the tenants were in fact 'les foialx homes & subiectes le Roy . . . de bone gouuernaunce & porte' to the king and his liege people, but that because of war with MacMurrough, O'Connor, O'More, and other Irish enemies, they dared not stand trial. Yet some of the tenants actually shared the surname of those Irish enemies.[47]

From the outset, the problems of defending these remote borderlands had an important impact on the administrative institutions established for their government. In Ireland, at a time when English kings had expectations of conquering the whole island, they had built up a separate central administration for the lordship, based on Dublin and modelled on Westminster. This was presided over by a justiciar, who discharged those tasks carried out by the king in England, and the Dublin administration gradually evolved as a replica in miniature of the central government for England. In the north of England, medieval kings relied more heavily on what came to seem like an alternative method of delegating royal authority. Centred on the castles constructed for the military defence and control of the region, numerous liberties and franchises had evolved as a means of reconciling the judicial and administrative claims of royal government with the military realities of a march. Yet castles and liberties were also an important instrument of control in the lordship, and by early Tudor times the institutional differences of government in the two regions were in many ways more apparent than real. Since 1296 the military defence of the northern border had been delegated to special wardens of the march who also exercised judicial powers over the marchers in their warden courts. The outbreak of war also saw the appointment of a special lieutenant to co-ordinate military operations. And when in 1483, the king's lieutenant, Richard, duke of Glouces-

---

[47] Parliament rolls, 16 & 17 Edward IV c. 24, 19 & 20 Edward IV c. 9 (*Stat. Ire., Edw. IV*, ii. 492–4, 702–10).

ter, succeeded his brother as king, his baronial council developed as a separate royal council for the government of the region, with authority in criminal and civil causes.[48] The council was in abeyance between 1509 and 1525, and thereafter its powers did not always extend to the wardens and their wardenries, but in essence the powers of the king's council and of the earl of Surrey as lieutenant there under Henry VII were similar to those enjoyed by his son, with the Irish council, as lieutenant in Ireland under Henry VIII. The Dublin administration had in any case never been omnicompetent; and the lordship's later medieval decline—more marked in the lightly settled and geographically remote north and west of Ireland—had reduced its area of authority to precisely those eastern and southern parts which were in closer contact with England.[49] Perhaps the major difference, therefore, was that in the lordship administrative, judicial, and military authority were concentrated in the hands of one man, whereas the greater resources of government in the north were normally divided among several officials.

By 1500, moreover, some of the traditional administrative institutions were perceived more as a hindrance than an aid to government. In an age in which the political community increasingly looked to the crown for 'good governance' and 'indifferent justice', the liberties were widely regarded as an anachronism and an obstacle to law and order. They were more extensive and comprehensive in the far north, where the king's writ did not run in almost half the region. The whole of Durham was administered by the bishop as a county palatine, and there were also three detached members, collectively known as North Durham, which lay geographically in Northumberland, and two more in Yorkshire. The most extensive of these, Norhamshire, was sandwiched between Northumberland and Berwick-on-Tweed, the chief garrison town of the region, which in law lay outside the realm of England and therefore received specific mention in parliamentary legislation of the period. Some distance to the south-west of Norhamshire, but still bordering the kingdom of Scotland, lay the liberties of Tynedale and

---

[48] R. R. Reid, *The king's council in the north* (London, 1921), pt. I; id., 'The office of warden of the marches: its origin and early history', in *EHR* 32 (1917), 479–96; Storey, 'Wardens of the marches', 593–615; Ellis, *Reform and revival, passim.*

[49] Ellis, *Reform and revival, passim*; Frame, 'Power and society', 3–33; R. L. Storey, *The reign of Henry VII* (London, 1968), 147–9.

Redesdale. Tynedale had once belonged to the king of Scots, while the Tailboys lords of Redesdale held the liberty by the service of guarding the valley from wolves and robbers.[50] South of Tynedale was the archbishop of York's regality of Hexham, while the prior of Tynemouth had a small liberty east of Newcastle. In each of these liberties the lord enjoyed quasi-royal power. West of the Pennines, the territorial lords enjoyed less extensive liberties, but the Cliffords were hereditary sheriffs of Westmorland, and the sheriff of Cumberland was excluded from the Percy honour of Cockermouth. This fragmentation of authority greatly complicated the administration of justice and the maintenance of order. The liberties provided a sanctuary for criminals fleeing from the sheriffs of surrounding counties.[51]

On the pretext of these disorders, Henry VII had the liberty of Tynedale incorporated by statute into the shire of Northumberland in 1495.[52] Yet Tynedale was conveniently in crown hands. In Redesdale, where the reputed insanity of Sir George Tailboys offered some excuse to suppress the liberty on the death of the 3rd lord in 1494, the king contented himself with exploiting the situation financially; and eventually in 1509 Sir George was licensed to exercise the lord's traditional liberties.[53] Not until the 1540s, when Henry VIII acquired Redesdale from the Tailboys heiress, was that lordship incorporated into Northumberland. The liberty of Hexham was only united to Northumberland in 1572, but by then the privileges of all the northern liberties had been greatly reduced by the major statute of 1536. Even so, Sir Robert Bowes reported in 1550 that, notwithstanding the 1495 statute, the keepers of Tynedale and Redesdale had execution of precepts and warrants there, and that the sheriff of Northumberland rarely intervened.[54]

---

[50] Hodgson, *Northumberland*, II. i. 62 (reproducing a court case in the exchequer in 1438).

[51] Isabel Thornley, 'The destruction of sanctuary', in R. W. Seton-Watson (ed.), *Tudor studies* (London, 1924), 182–207; Reid, *King's council in the north*, 7–15; Tough, *Last years of a frontier*, 82; Storey, *End of the house of Lancaster*, 106; Watts, *Border to middle shire*, 24–5, and maps.

[52] Statute roll, 11 Henry VII c. 9 (*Statutes of the realm*, ii. 575–6).

[53] PRO, C 142/10, no. 6 (*Inq. p.m. Hen. VII*, i. no. 971); *Cal. pat. rolls, 1494–1509*, 176, 611; *L. & P. Hen. VIII*, i (2nd edn.), no. 131, ii, no. 2979; James, *Society, politics and culture*, 227, 234–6; Hodgson, *Northumberland*, II. i. 6–7.

[54] Hodgson, *Northumberland*, I. i. 371; II. i. 6–7; III. ii. 222–4 (Bowes's survey, 1550).

Liberties presented less of a problem in the Pale, particularly after the suppression of the Meath palatinate following the crown's acquisition of the Mortimer inheritance in 1461. Juridically, they were less autonomous, since four pleas were always reserved to the crown. There was only one of palatine status—the archbishop of Dublin's liberty of St Sepulchre, which comprised eight manors scattered through Co. Dublin and survived into the eighteenth century. The only other franchise of note, the earl of Kildare's liberty of Kildare, which was briefly re-established *c.*1514–34, was arguably an aid rather than a hindrance to government.[55] Co. Kildare was difficult to defend: it was vulnerable to raids by both the Leinster and midland Irish, and the Dublin administration lacked the resources to maintain standing garrisons in the marches. Moreover, Edward IV's grant to his brother in 1483 suggests that in the north, too, the liberties might still prove useful. The grant comprised a palatinate of royal lands and rights in Cumberland and Westmorland, and in districts of south-west Scotland con-quered or to be conquered by the duke, and also included the wardenship of the west marches.[56] Where royal justice and protec-tion were inadequate, noble leadership and self-sufficiency were a good deal better than nothing.

Overall, however, the liberties were, at worst, a complication. Their abolition in the north and retention in Ireland made little difference to the fundamental nature of the problem in either region. Rather, the heart of the problem was the proximity of a turbulent border and the special arrangements needed for defence. In some respects there seemed to be a significant difference be-tween the north and the Pale in the scale of the problem. Although much less powerful than the Tudor kings, the king of Scots was a considerably more formidable adversary than any Gaelic chief. The 'auld alliance' between France and Scotland, moreover, gave the Scottish king a position in European diplomacy which Irish chiefs never enjoyed. In addition, he could normally count on the support of the Scottish nobility against the 'auld inemie', whereas coalitions of Gaelic chiefs in Ireland were exceptional and short-lived. Thus the attempted invasions with perhaps 20,000 men

---

[55] S. G. Ellis, 'The destruction of the liberties: some further evidence', in *IHR Bull.*, 54 (1981), 150–61; *Court book of the liberty of St. Sepulchre*, ed. Herbert Wood (Dublin, 1930), pp. vii–xiii.

[56] Storey, 'Wardens of the marches', 608.

mounted by James IV in 1513 and by James V in 1542 threatened to overrun the entire region. The Pale, however, suffered no worse indignity than constant border raiding and the occasional deeper penetration.[57]

Nevertheless, actual or seriously threatened invasions of the English north were few and far between in early-Tudor times— 1496, 1513, 1522, 1542. In an emergency heavy reinforcements could be drafted in, but since such situations were exceptional and short-lived, they probably had little lasting influence on border society. More normally, the scale of the problem was very similar to that in the Pale. Between 1333 and 1502 there was no formal peace between the two kingdoms, only periodic truces and temporary cessations of war.[58] For much of the period, therefore, the respective governments were actively encouraging private raiding and warfare, even when no major expeditions were in prospect; and, before long, private warfare and petty raiding had acquired its own momentum which continued regardless of the government's wishes as expressed through truce and peace.[59]

During periods of truce and peace, the wardens of the English marches were expected to co-operate with their Scottish counterparts in maintaining order. Essentially, this co-operation took the form of arbitration in accordance with march law, an amalgam of local customary law, amended and codified in successive treaties between English and Scottish kings since 1237.[60] March law may be divided into two categories. The first dealt with offences such as reiving and robbery, arson and murder, for which wronged English or Scots could seek redress from wardenry officials of the opposite march. The second laid down procedures to be used at international days of truce and at the trial of alleged offenders

[57] Scarisbrick, *Henry VIII*, 37, 435–6; Elton, *Reform and Reformation*, 39–40, 306. For the Pale, see the nature of the complaints about insecurity there during the period of exceptionally weak government in 1527–8: *L. & P. Hen. VIII*, iv (ii), nos. 3698–700, 4094, 4264, 4302, 4933 (*r.* 1527, placed in 1528 by the calendar); *SP Hen. VIII*, ii. 126–36.

[58] S. B. Chrimes, *Henry VII* (London, 1972), 90–1.

[59] See esp. J. A. Tuck, 'War and society in the medieval north' in *Northern History*, 21 (1985), 33–52; id., 'Richard II and the border magnates', 27–52; T. I. Rae, *The administration of the Scottish frontier, 1513–1603* (Edinburgh, 1966), *passim*; Frame, *English lordship in Ireland*, ch. 3; id., 'War and peace in the medieval lordship of Ireland', in J. F. Lydon (ed.), *The English in medieval Ireland* (Dublin, 1984), 118–41.

[60] See *Leges marchiarum*, ed. William Nicolson (London, 1747); Nicolson and Burn, *Westmorland and Cumberland*, i. pp. xxiii–xxx.

against march law. In addition, wardens held courts of wardenry which had criminal jurisdiction over breaches of the customary domestic law of the marches. Such crimes, known as march treasons, included the betraying of Englishmen's goods or persons to Scots, allowing thieves or raiders to escape into Scotland, and the unlicensed sale of arms to Scots.[61] This law code, and the various administrative procedures evolved to implement it, was elaborate and is known in some detail. Yet an insuperable difficulty concerned its enforcement: march law depended for its effectiveness on the state of Anglo-Scottish relations, which were usually bad in this period, and also on the personal relations between the respective English and Scottish wardens. Thus, although Anglo-Scottish march law was clearly far more developed than its counterpart in Ireland, it was probably no more effective in practice.

In Ireland, contacts with individual Gaelic chiefs were more transparently *ad hoc*, with parleys and concordats arranged according to circumstances. Very little is known about the procedures for securing compensation or the restoration of goods, other than what is contained in the treaties between the two parties. These treaties survive in some number for the 1530s.[62] They clearly reflect long-established arrangements for redress which presumably followed the frequently mentioned, but quite obscure, march law.[63] We may suspect, however, that these arrangements were heavily influenced by procedures developed within Gaelic Ireland to regulate relations between the numerous separate lordships there. Significantly, no system of criminal law as such evolved within the decentralized Gaelic world, perhaps because so much of the litigation concerned disputes between parties from different lordships. Instead matters which would by English common law have been regarded as capital offences were resolved by payment of compensation in a way which must have suggested itself as a model for relations between English and Gaelic Ireland. In other respects, however, Anglo-Irish march law, a mixture of two very different legal systems, must have differed considerably from its

---

[61] Tough, *Last years of a frontier*, chs. 6–10.

[62] See e.g. *Cal. Carew MSS, 1515–74*, nos. 54, 56, 71–2, 76–7, 79–80, 82, 90, 109–10, 116–17, 122, 124, 128, 136, 139–40.

[63] Cf. Robin Frame, 'English officials and Irish chiefs in the fourteenth century', in *EHR* 90 (1975), 748–77. For march law, see especially Gearóid Mac Niocaill, 'The interaction of laws', in J. F. Lydon (ed.), *The English in medieval Ireland* (Dublin, 1984), 105–17.

Anglo-Scottish counterpart, for which the constituent parts were essentially similar. In the lordship, the counterpart of march treason was, significantly, enshrined in statute law passed by the separate parliament there, and in both regions local legislation was clearly much more important than in most of England.[64] Thus, while cultural differences and the relative strengths, weaknesses, and stability of the respective powers may have helped to shape the form and content of arbitration in the two borderlands, the system of parleys and march law was necessarily similar because the point of departure was the same—the need for machinery to regulate relations between two independent powers.

The foundations of Anglo-Scottish enmity and the problem of the north in the later middle ages were laid by Edward I's Scottish war of 1296, which inaugurated a period of strenuous English efforts to conquer Scotland. The border became, once again, a defended line. In Ireland, the tensions between English and Irish went back a century earlier to the Norman conquest, although it was only in the thirteenth century, with the denial of English law to the natives, that attitudes hardened. In both regions, the attempt to expand the area of English allegiance, and subsequently to retain control of disputed territory, involved the English crown in considerable military expenditure from the time of Edward I to the reign of Henry VI. The defence of the borders commonly took the form of an elaborate chain of garrisons which aimed to insulate the interior from all but the most powerful Scottish or Irish incursions.[65] Among the tenantry of the borders the needs of defence prompted the development of special forms of tenure. Smallholders of the north generally held their lands by a form of tenure known as tenant right. This usually involved the obligation to undertake border service when required by the warden. And for this purpose the tenant had to maintain weapon, horse, and harness, as appropriate, on pain of forfeiture of his holding. The corollary, however, was that money rents charged on these tenancies were much lower: and when, in the later sixteenth century, better relations with Scotland led to more stable condi-

[64] See *Stat. Ire., John–Hen. V*; *Hen. VI*; *Edw. IV*, i and ii; *Stat. Ire.*, i. 51; cf. C. A. Empey and K. Simms, 'The ordinances of the White Earl and the problem of coign in the later middle ages', in *RIA Proc.*, 75 (1975), sect. C, 163.

[65] Frame, 'English officials and Irish chiefs', 748–77; id., *Colonial Ireland*, ch. 6; Tuck, 'War and society in the medieval north', 33–52; Michael Prestwich, *Edward I* (London, 1988), ch. 18; Goodman, 'Anglo-Scottish marches', 18–33.

tions, and landlords began to charge economic rents, the musters
exhibited a steep decline in the numbers of properly equipped
horsemen.[66]

By contrast, in the Pale, this obligation to maintain specified
military equipment was not normally an incident of customary
tenure or leasehold—as Robert Cowley remarked in 1536 when
comparing measures for the defence of the Englishry with those of
the Anglo-Scottish marches.[67] Rather, landlords were required to
maintain a mounted longbowman for every twenty librates of land,
in addition to the traditional obligation on all subjects to keep the
weapons specified as appropriate to their status and degree. In
practice, there were frequent complaints that landlords neglected
to maintain the appropriate retinues, and that by letting their lands
to beggarly Irish tenants for higher rents, they undermined the
defence of the marches.[68] Scottish tenants occasioned similar complaints in the north, but the problem there was not on the same
scale.[69] As we shall see,[70] there was in fact a close connection
between patterns of settlement, forms of tenure, and arrangements
for defence in the border districts.

Overall, therefore, by *c.*1500 the arrangements for the good rule
of these outlying parts were posing an intractable problem to the
early Tudors. The difficulties of defending remote frontiers
obliged the crown to delegate authority in a manner which was
rarely necessary in lowland England. Except in an emergency, it
could not afford to maintain a standing army and an elaborate paid
bureaucracy to control these regions. Its response, therefore, was
to develop a range of special administrative devices of a quasi-
military nature in which the traditional concerns of government
were subordinated to the overriding needs of defence. Although
they were a good deal better than nothing, none of these devices
was very effective. The endemic insecurity of the borders meant
that they degenerated into war zones, leading to an insidious trans-

[66] Newton, 'Decay of the borders', *passim*; R. W. Hoyle, 'An ancient and laud-
able custom: the definition and development of tenant right in north-western
England in the sixteenth century', in *Past and Present*, 116 (Aug. 1987), 24–55; id.,
'Lords, tenants and tenant right in the sixteenth century: four studies', in *Northern
History*, 20 (1984), 39; Watts, *Border to middle shire*, *passim*.

[67] *SP Hen. VIII*, ii. 329. Cf. *L. & P. Hen. VIII*, iii, no. 670ii.

[68] Ellis, *Reform and revival*, 55–6.

[69] Newton, 'Decay of the borders', 13, 18; Tough, *Last years of a frontier*, 179–82;
Goodman, 'Anglo-Scottish marches', 23–4.

[70] Below, chs. 3–4.

formation in the structures of society and the emergence of more militarized forms. In turn, however, the growth of a marcher society habituated to war exacerbated the government's difficulties in keeping control and maintaining law and order.

Early-Tudor policy towards the marches highlighted particular aspects of these problems, and these are discussed more fully in the next chapter. Other weaknesses, however, were accentuated by the crown's traditional response. This amounted to a sweeping delegation of power to the regional magnates, who thereby consolidated their position as marcher lords. The phenomenon is perhaps best exemplified by the Percy earls of Northumberland who, though distrusted by the Tudors, remained available for border service for much of the early-Tudor period. Their long tenure of the wardenships during the fifteenth century reflected their wealth and extensive possessions in the region. They were the leading landowners in Cumberland and Northumberland, and on the death of the 4th earl in 1489 the Percy estates there were worth almost £1,600 a year gross out of a total landed income of just over £4,000 per annum. They were also concentrated in feudal baronies, like Alnwick in Northumberland, from which many knights' fees were held, and the honour of Cockermouth in Cumberland, from which the king's sheriff was excluded. Their Yorkshire estates added a further £1,200 annually. Within the marches, the earl had 5,000 tenants available for border service, plus a further 6,200 in Yorkshire.[71] Northumberland's salary as warden of the east and middle marches was traditionally £2,500 per annum, and double in wartime, which enabled him to strengthen his political connexion: in 1489 he was retaining 84 lords, knights, and esquires, at a cost of over £1,700 per annum.[72] Evidently, money for its own sake was not a priority with the earl, although mounting indebtedness was to be the ruin of the family in the 1530s. Rather, Percy estate-management policies were apparently geared to border defence. This is suggested, for instance, by the contrast between the low entry-fines exacted from tenants on the northern estates and the earls' willingness to push up entry-fines to much higher levels in

[71] J. M. W. Bean, *The estates of the Percy family 1416–1537* (Oxford, 1958), 45–7, 129; Storey, *End of the house of Lancaster*, 106; James, *Society, politics and culture*, 60, 68–9, 76.

[72] Storey, 'Wardens of the marches', 604; A. J. Pollard, *North-eastern England during the Wars of the Roses* (Oxford, 1990), 125.

the West Country in Henry VIII's reign.[73] The Percy estates in the far north were all vulnerable to a Scottish invasion and needed a resident lord to defend them. Some were indeed destroyed by Scottish raids, although losses directly attributable to the Scots were no doubt small. More importantly, however, proximity to the border must have created an atmosphere of insecurity which hampered the lord in his financial exploitation of these estates. It is noticeable, for instance, that in the far north the Percy possessions included an unusually large number of manors which were of comparatively little value.[74] Two of the earl's manors in Northumberland were still waste in 1505, after three years of peace with Scotland.[75]

Thus in the case of a great regional magnate like Northumberland, there was in some ways a tension between the earl's ambition to play a leading role on the national stage and his need to supervise the defence of his border estates. Only a little lower down the social scale, a border baron like Robert, 4th Lord Ogle, whose landed inheritance, worth less than £200 a year, consisted of eighteen war-torn manors in Northumberland and a few tenements in Cumberland, never attended parliament or state occasions.[76]

A similar pattern of lordship can be detected in Ireland. Indeed the financial and military resources of the Dublin administration were even scantier, so that the residence or absence of the great marcher lords was even more crucial to defence and good government there.[77] One of the more successful magnates was James Butler, 4th earl of Ormond, who was five times governor of Ireland (1407–52). The earl had lands scattered over southern England, but his political influence rested chiefly on extensive possessions in southern Ireland, especially in Tipperary, which he held as a liberty palatine, and Co. Kilkenny. In financial terms, his income from his Irish estates was comparatively small, and the cost of defending them against the Irish was considerable. The *manraed* conferred by these possessions, however, was crucial to the gov-

[73] Bean, *Estates of the Percy family*, 51–68, 135–57.

[74] Ibid. 14–15, 23, 30–5, 45–6.

[75] *Cal. inq. p.m., Hen. VII*, iii. no. 7.

[76] PRO, C 142/27, no. 126; C 142/75, no. 16; *Cal. inq. p.m., Hen. VII*, i. no. 157, iii. no. 14; below, p. 92 n. 56; Helen Miller, *Henry VIII and the English nobility* (Oxford, 1986), 10, 44, 99, 126, 159.

[77] Frame, *English lordship in Ireland*, pt. 1.

ernment of the region.[78] Over the next fifty years or so, earls of Ormond resided chiefly in England, and without a resident lord to defend them the value of their Irish estates declined significantly. The early Tudors attempted to build up the Butlers as a counterweight to the earls of Kildare, and in the 1520s they twice served as governor of Ireland, although with very mixed results.[79]

In many ways too, some of the marcher lords of Wales seemed to fit this pattern of lordship, notably William Herbert of Raglan. Herbert became the main support of Edward IV's government in south Wales, was advanced to the peerage in 1461, and appointed chief justice and chamberlain of south Wales. Between 1465 and 1468 his landed income averaged £2,400 per annum.[80] Compact holdings and extensive feudal franchises gave the magnates there similar opportunities to dominate the government of the region. The fragmentation of authority in the march of Wales, the uninhibited character of seigneurial power there, and the division of society into separate Welshries and Englishries with different customs and laws—all these fostered the persistence there of a more turbulent marcher society. Thus the tradition of resident marcher lordship was perpetuated in early-Tudor Wales by Sir Rhys ap Thomas (d. 1525), head of the native house of Dinefwr, and by Henry Somerset, 2nd earl of Worcester (1526–49), who had acquired many of the Herbert estates.[81] Yet in Wales the military *raison d'être* of the march had been extinguished by the Edwardian conquest. This meant both that the need for a resident lord was not so compelling and also that the crown was much less reliant on noble power there for military purposes than in Ireland or the far north. Thus, although Herbert's career illustrates the possibilities open to a marcher lord prepared to reside and supervise the administration of his possessions, in practice most marcher lordships

[78] Ibid. 14, 26–7, 206–9, 335; *New hist. Ire.*, ii, chs. 17–20; C. A. Empey, 'The Butler lordship', in *Butler Society Journal*, 1 (1970–1), 174–87; id. and Simms, 'Ordinances of the White Earl', 161–87.

[79] C. A. Empey, 'From rags to riches: Piers Butler, earl of Ormond, 1515–39', in *Butler Society Journal*, 2: 3 (1984), 299–314; Ellis, *Tudor Ireland*, chs. 3–5.

[80] T. B. Pugh (ed.), *Glamorgan County History*, iii. *The Middle Ages* (Cardiff, 1971), 259–61.

[81] See esp. W. R. B. Robinson, 'Patronage and hospitality in early Tudor Wales: the role of Henry earl of Worcester', in *IHR Bull.*, 51 (1978), 20–36.

were held during this period by absentees whose main estates and political ambitions lay elsewhere.[82] In the 1530s, as we shall see,[83] a different kind of solution to the problem of the marches in Wales was successfully pursued by the Tudors.

Overall, however, the crown's traditional response to the problem of the marches, the delegation of power to the great border magnates, helped to mitigate the weaknesses of royal government there. The drawbacks of this policy became painfully apparent during the Wars of the Roses, however, when the ambitions and rivalry of these magnates led them into rebellion. In Ireland and Wales, the consequences were best illustrated by the career of Richard, duke of York. York was earl of Ulster and lord of Meath and Connaught in Ireland, and as the king's lieutenant (1447–60) he enjoyed a salary of £2,000 a year plus the king's entire Irish revenues; in Wales he was the greatest marcher lord, with an income there of £3,430 per annum. Control of these borderlands eventually gave York the men, money, and military might with which to topple the Lancastrian king.[84] In the north, the career of York's ally, Richard Neville, earl of Salisbury, who was warden of the west marches (1420–35, 1443–60), exhibited very similar characteristics.[85]

Royal policy towards the borderlands in the late fifteenth century therefore marked something of a reaction to the events of the Wars of the Roses. In particular, Henry VII had much more urgent priorities than the resumption of war with Scotland and the conquest of Gaelic Ireland, and the military effort was scaled down considerably. Following precedents established by the Yorkists, he sought to counter the risks to his own security by reducing the salaries and status of the leading border officials and ensuring a wider diffusion of power. Yet, as we shall see, this in turn greatly reduced the potential of government in the two regions, and in part it also altered the nature of the problem. The effects were less serious in the Pale, where the established pattern from 1361 of sporadic military expeditions from England had in some ways been

---

[82] See, for instance, T. B. Pugh, *The marcher lordships of south Wales, 1415–1536* (Cardiff, 1963).

[83] Below, Conclusion.

[84] Otway-Ruthven, *Med. Ire.*, ch. 12; Glanmor Williams, *Recovery, reorientation and Reformation: Wales c. 1415–1642* (Oxford, 1987), 178–89.

[85] Storey, *End of the house of Lancaster*, esp. chs. 4, 7, 14.

more disruptive than supportive of royal authority, and where the residual power of government had traditionally been much weaker. In the north, however, where power was now diffused more widely, where the reduction in resources was sharper, and where problems of defence and government were of much greater urgency, the early-Tudor period witnessed some major readjustments to changed circumstances. The result was that the similarities between the two regions which have been outlined in this chapter were reinforced, and this in turn altered official perceptions of the nature of the problem.

2

Early-Tudor policy and perceptions

THE administrative structures through which the original areas of the English kingdom were governed were, by the standards of other European states, unusually centralized and uniform. England was divided up into counties, for each of which the king appointed the same combination of local officials, headed by sheriffs, justices of the peace, escheators, and coroners. Throughout the realm, the king's subjects were governed by a uniform code of law, the common law, which depended for its enforcement on the empanelling of grand and petty juries drawn from the locality. Twice a year the king's justices visited each shire to hold assizes at which major crimes and civil suits were determined, and four times a year other crimes were tried before the local justices of the peace at their quarter sessions. The assizes offered the central government an opportunity to inform the county community of its policies and to secure their co-operation, while the system of grand juries allowed the community to bring local grievances to the attention of the centre. These links between crown and community were strengthened both by the institution of parliament and by the work of special royal commissions. Parliament, to which each shire and corporate borough sent elected representatives, was essential for law-making and grants of national taxation, and special commissioners were appointed to carry out other work, often of an important or difficult nature.[1]

In theory, the king could appoint whom he liked as his officials. In practice, however, office in local government was unpaid, and from the thirteenth century the crown relied on the leading gentry, nobles, and wealthy burgesses to supervise affairs and to discharge the most important duties themselves. The execution of policy and

---

[1] For this and the following two paragraphs, see esp. G. R. Elton, *The Tudor constitution* (2nd edn., Cambridge, 1982), chs. 5, 10; Williams, *Tudor regime*, ch. 12; Griffiths, 'English realm and dominions', 83–105; Ellis, 'Crown, community and government', 187–204.

the enforcement of law and order were liable to depend more on the hierarchies of local society than on bureaucratic channels of command. Thus political consensus between crown and the local aristocracy was fundamental to the smooth operation of the system. It depended on the establishment of effective lines of communication between the centre and the provinces, so that the views and grievances of the locality could be represented to the centre, and vice versa. Equally important was the existence of an ordered society, with the well-established, hierarchical structures which were a characteristic feature of English manorialism. Where these conditions existed, in the heavily populated regions of lowland England, with numerous towns and nucleated villages, small parishes and manors, this system of government generally worked quite effectively.

Historians have traditionally stressed the extent to which this ordered, relatively peaceful society, governed through centralized administrative structures, had already emerged in England by the thirteenth century. Surveys of Tudor government and society likewise focus on the operation of these supposedly standard administrative structures in lowland England. In over half the early-Tudor state, however, society and patterns of settlement diverged quite sharply from the norms of lowland England, links with the centre were attenuated, and the standard administrative structures operated only partially or not at all. Neither Wales (until 1542) nor Ireland were represented in the English parliament, and the north, with large counties and few towns, was greatly underrepresented. The full system of English common law operated only in parts of the north and Ireland. There it was supplemented by different systems of march law, which also operated in Wales. Many areas were not shired but were administered as feudal liberties from which royal officials were excluded. And in all three borderlands, society was more militarized, with significant cultural and legal differences between the king's English subjects and the Welsh, the Irish, or the Scots respectively. The result was that royal government was much less effective in the borderlands and the structures of power there developed rather differently. In the English lowlands, the extension of royal government in the thirteenth century had established a new, direct political relationship between the crown and the lesser landowners who administered this system, thus, potentially at least, threatening the regional influence of the magnates. The Tudor achievement was 'to make a reality of that direct relationship' between crown and subject 'which the earlier growth of royal authority had made latent'.[2] In the borderlands, however, royal government was less well developed. More importantly, the defence of the marches was most conveniently organized by a resident lord through his tenantry and political affinity. This in turn heightened the importance of the lord's *manraed* and seigneurial power over tenants, while cutting across royal authority over the subject. Thus changed circumstances created countervailing pressures which actually strengthened noble power and influence *vis-à-vis* the crown.

These contrasts within the English state between lowland England and the marcher societies to the north and west were to remain a feature of British history at least until the political unification of the British Isles in 1603. They were not new in 1500 but had existed since the thirteenth century. Yet in many ways, the military exertions of the two centuries or so from Edward I's imperialistic ventures, through the Hundred Years War with France, to the dynastic strife of the Wars of the Roses distracted attention from these differences. The borderlands formed a major asset of military manpower as successive English kings concentrated on the acquisition of continental territories and the extension of their sovereignty over other parts of the British Isles. In the period of comparative peace and internal reconstruction which followed this phase, however, the borderlands came to be singled out as a particular liability for Tudor government.

In both Ireland and the far north, the underlying problem was a dual one. By delegating authority, the king hoped to create an effective mechanism for the rule and defence of regions which, by reason of their remoteness from London, could not be administered effectively in the normal manner. At the same time, however, he needed to ensure that the men in charge of this machinery were unable to exploit it in ways which ran contrary to his interests. Initially, it was the threat to royal security from disaffected magnates in command of border troops and strongholds which exercised the Yorkist and early-Tudor kings. In the north, Richard III, and Henry VII after him, responded by retaining the warden-

---

[2] P. R. Coss, 'Bastard feudalism revised', in *Past and Present*, 125 (Nov. 1989), 27–64 (quotation, p. 62) is a useful reappraisal of research on this topic.

ships of the marches in their own hands, and instead appointing, during pleasure, lieutenants from among the lesser peerage and gentry to keep the marches. Responsibility for the east and middle marches was now regularly divided, and custody of the castles of Carlisle and Berwick-on-Tweed was also separated from the respective wardenships.[3] Concurrently, the ordinary costs of border defence were greatly reduced. The salaries of Henry VII's lieutenants—£153. 6s. 8d. a year for the west marches, and £114. 13s. 4d. for each of the east and middle marches—were only a fraction of the traditional warden salaries of £2,500 per annum for the east and middle marches, £1,250 for the west, and double those sums in wartime.[4]

Similar changes occurred in Ireland, where the status of the governorship was also diminished. The more honourable lieutenancy was reserved for absentee princes of the blood, who discharged the office by deputy recruited from among the local nobility. The salary of the deputy lieutenant was greatly reduced and was made payable from the Irish revenues; his powers—particularly the nomination of the chief ministers of the Dublin administration—were curtailed; and the office was now normally held during the king's pleasure instead of for term of years. Under the early Tudors, the Irish revenues commonly yielded about IR£1,600 per annum. This was slightly more than had been available from this source under Henry VI, but it hardly covered more than the most basic costs of government. And after 1478 the Yorkists and Henry VII discontinued the practice followed by previous kings since 1361 of shoring up royal authority in Ireland by regular financial and military subventions from England.[5]

In their primary aim of promoting acceptance of the new dynasty and ensuring that the borderlands could not be used by disaffected nobles and pretenders to mount a challenge to the throne, these changes were entirely successful. By 1500 the leading border posts were all in reliable hands. Moreover, the curbing of 'overmighty subjects', increased reliance on lesser men, and the pruning of administrative costs were all characteristic features of

---

[3] PRO, SP 1/12, fo. 49 (*L. & P. Hen. VIII*, ii, no. 1365); Storey, 'Wardens of the marches', 608–9.

[4] PRO, E 403/2558, fos. 53, 56ᵛ, 62, 69, 101, 108ᵛ, 113, 116, 127ᵛ, 142, 144, 149; SP 1/12, fo. 49 (*L. & P. Hen. VIII*, ii, no. 1365); Storey, 'Wardens of the marches', 604–9.

[5] Ellis, *Reform and revival*, chs. 1, 3.

the wider revival in the power and prestige of the monarchy under the Yorkists and early Tudors. The government of the borders was made more self-sufficient, and the special arrangements for the military defence of the region were in some respects reduced, so that in this way too the borderlands were treated more like other parts of the realm. Yet the diffusion of power and the sharp reduction in royal expenditure on the two regions created other problems.

In Ireland, the new strategy of reliance on a local noble with extensive lands and tenantry in the Pale did at least provide a degree of stability and continuity which had previously been lacking. Moreover, the military threat presented by the fragmented Gaelic lordships was much less severe. In terms of local government, the system as it actually operated in the early-Tudor lordship had evolved gradually since *c.*1300 in response to the acute shortage of resources available to the Dublin administration. In essence, it was a smaller copy of that in England, and within the four counties of the English Pale administration and justice were quite intensive and closely controlled from Dublin. Major crimes and civil suits were normally tried in the four central courts based in Dublin, although powers were frequently delegated by commissions of oyer and terminer and of gaol delivery. Commissions of the peace were small and aristocratic: except in the towns, the commissioners were keepers of the peace, rather than justices. They were chiefly concerned with local defence and lacked judicial powers to determine indictments. Normally there were no quarter sessions. The sheriff remained the normal link between central and local government, and had important military and judicial functions, besides his administrative duties. Militarily, he had charge of the county under the governor, being assisted by the keepers and, sometimes, by special county captains or wardens of the marches. Judicially, he held tourns twice a year in each barony of the county to determine minor crimes. Sheriffs in the four shires of the Pale were appointed annually, and regularly accounted at the Dublin exchequer for the profits of their shrievalties.

Outside the Pale, however, exchequer control was much more intermittent, and the office of sheriff was dominated by the great landed families who alone had the resources to organize the defence of the shire. There were no hereditary sheriffs in Ireland, but in practice the government's choice was severely limited in many counties because land and power were concentrated in relatively few hands. In these outlying parts, defence and good government depended chiefly on the magnates and towns, and the supervision exercised by the Dublin administration was much slighter. Royal officials found it very difficult to execute process among the turbulent people of the marches, and the distances and danger from the wild Irish to travellers on the king's highway discouraged litigation in the central courts at Dublin. Successive royal charters extended the self-government of the major towns and cities, and the earls of Desmond, Ormond, and Shrewsbury governed the liberties of Kerry, Tipperary, and Wexford respectively as palatinates. The government's chief means of control were the annual general commissions, on which were included a mixture of senior officials and judges and local dignitaries, and which could review all aspects of administration. Very often, however, the visits of the commissioners were hasty affairs which occurred in connection with military expeditions, usually headed by the governor. They were frequently cancelled or curtailed. In some shires, too, resident justices might be appointed. Overall, however, the lordship coped quite well with the ending of intermittent military and financial subventions from England. Royal government as it actually operated in early-Tudor Ireland now more closely reflected the realities of power in a politically fragmented land. What emerged was a system whereby the government of the outlying counties was entrusted to the local magnate, rather as in Scotland. The Dublin administration's sporadic attempts at a closer supervision which had done little more than to antagonize local interests were largely abandoned.[6]

In the English far north, however, the reduction in the resources available for the rule of the borders was much sharper, although the military threat presented by the Scots remained far more formidable. During the 1490s, for instance, the king had spent considerable sums on the defence of the castle and city of Carlisle, in the face of the military threat posed by Perkin Warbeck. In 1495 Sir Richard Salkeld had been appointed captain there with a salary of £200 a year—a larger salary than the warden's—out of which he

---

[6] This and the preceding two paragraphs are based on my analyses of English government in Ireland in *Reform and revival*, and *Tudor Ireland*, ch. 6. For the comparison with Scotland, see, for instance, Ranald Nicholson, *Scotland: the later middle ages* (Edinburgh, 1974), *passim*.

had to maintain twenty horsemen. Yet in 1501 the king accepted Lord Dacre's offer of £200, with surety of 8,000 marks, 'so he may haue the kepyng of Carlyll', 'and to repayre the towne walles and the castell at his charge'.[7] Thus the captaincy of Carlisle was merged again with the wardenship, royal expenditure on the defence of the west march was further reduced, and Carlisle castle gradually fell into disrepair.[8] Similarly, as captain of Bewcastle, Sir John Musgrave had originally been paid £100 a year. Yet when the office was regranted to him and his son Thomas in survivorship in 1493 the salary was reduced to £40. By 1517 it had been increased to £70, but even this, as Dacre complained in 1524, was quite inadequate for Musgrave to maintain good rule there.[9]

This pattern of financial retrenchment and scaling down the resources of government also affected the civil administration of the north. Even where the traditional structures of English government were in place, their operation was erratic and central control was intermittent. Few law suits came before the central courts, because the far north was so distant from the capital. Richard III's establishment of a special regional council for the north was in effect an admission of the difficulties: it intruded a bureaucratic institution to balance the traditional power of the northern nobility. Yet Henry VII allowed the council to lapse: even though it was temporarily reconstituted towards the end of his reign, its jurisdiction did not extend beyond Yorkshire.[10] Itinerant justices of assize and gaol delivery visited the north only once a year, usually during the summer, and held assizes at Newcastle, Carlisle, and Appleby. Their business did not detain them in the region beyond a week, even when the assizes were not curtailed because of war. Henry VII issued only five commissions of the peace for Cumberland and Westmorland during the whole of his reign, as opposed to six for Cumberland and nine for Westmorland during

---

[7] PRO, E 101/415/3, fo. 292, E 404/80, no. 267; Conway, *Henry VII's relations*, 237 n. 1. See now Summerson, *Carlisle*, 472–3.

[8] Summerson, *Carlisle*, 473, 477–8.

[9] PRO, E 36/125, fo. 275; *Cal. pat. rolls, 1485–94*, 56, 73, 101, 335, 429; *L. & P. Hen. VIII*, i (2nd edn.), no. 2684(86), ii (i), no. 1084, iii, no. 3383, iv (ii), no. 3747(6); Castle Howard MS F1/5/5, fos. 29ᵛ–30.

[10] Reid, *King's council in the north*, 61–90; Rosemary Horrox, *Richard III: a study in service* (Cambridge, 1989), 214–18; Storey, *Henry VII*, 147–9; id., *End of the house of Lancaster*, 118; Margaret Condon, 'Ruling élites in the reign of Henry VII', in Charles Ross (ed.), *Patronage pedigree and power in later medieval England* (Gloucester, 1979), 117–18, 137–8.

Edward IV's reign.[11] The peace commissions for these counties were also noticeably smaller than for other English counties, with often less than a dozen JPs, many of whom were non-resident. This was because, as in the case of Ireland and Wales, the economic base of the northern marches was much poorer than the south. Most of the marcher gentry were very poor, with lands worth less than £10 a year—the income of a southern yeoman—so that they could not be included on the commissions of the peace. They were also quarrelsome individuals, and few of them had much legal knowledge. Thus the work of the peace commissions was hampered by the shortage of substantial gentry.[12]

It was claimed in 1526 that there were so few justices in Northumberland, particularly of the quorum, that quarter sessions had not been kept there for a long time. And when Sir Christopher Dacre was appointed sheriff of Cumberland the same year, he warned Wolsey that

ther is no iustice of peas w'in this shire of Cumbreland but oonly my self (who cannot sitt) and oon Geffrey Lancastre, who is iustice of the quorum both in Westmorland and Cumberland and *custos rotulorum* w'in Cumbreland and noon in the quorum but he.[13]

The work of the sheriffs suffered for different reasons. The nomination of the sheriffs of Durham and Westmorland was not in the king's hands anyway, and Henry VII appointed the earl of Derby's son as sheriff of Lancashire for life. Elsewhere, he resorted to the ancient practice of farming the counties. Between 1497 and 1505 at least, Lord Dacre paid 40 marks a year for the profits of the sheriffwick of Cumberland, while Yorkshire was farmed for £100 a year about the same time. And from 1506 North-

[11] *Cal. pat. rolls, 1461–7*, 561, 575, *1467–77*, 610, 634, *1477–85*, 556, 576, *1485–94*, 484, 504, *1494–1509*, 634, 664; Storey, *End of the house of Lancaster*, 118; J. S. Cockburn, *A history of English assizes 1558–1714* (Cambridge, 1972), 19, 25, 45; C. J. Neville, 'Gaol delivery in the border counties, 1439–1459: some preliminary observations', in *Northern History*, 19 (1983), 45–60.

[12] *Cal. pat. rolls, 1494–1509*, appendix; *L. & P. Hen. VIII*, i (2nd edn.), no. 257(97), iv (i), no. 297; PRO, SP 1/45, fos. 104–7 (*L. & P. Hen. VIII*, iv, no. 3629(4); list of 55 Northumberland gentry, with their incomes and other qualities); Pollard, *North-eastern England during the Wars of the Roses*, 162–4. Cf. President Rowland Lee's scathing opinion of the wealth and discretion of the Welsh gentry: quoted in Glanmor Williams, *Wales and the Act of Union* (Bangor, 1992), 20.

[13] PRO, SP 1/37, fos. 250–1 (*L. & P. Hen. VIII*, iv (i), no. 2052); *L. & P. Hen. VIII*, iv (i), nos. 1610(11), 2435.

umberland was being farmed for 100 marks, later £100, a year by
one of the more lawless border gentry, Nicholas Ridley of
Willimoteswick.[14]

After Henry VIII's accession, the practice of farming was abandoned and the northern sheriffs were again appointed in the normal way. In the marches, however, the office was of considerable
interest to the warden because of its military importance. When
Lord Dacre took charge as warden of the east and middle marches
he immediately requested the nomination of the sheriff there. He
argued that his lieutenant should be sheriff on the grounds that
'the prouffittes of the shiriefwike were assigned during the kingges
pleasure to the payment of the fees of the lieutenauntes of the
middill marchies'. He also noted 'that noo shirief made any
accomptes in the kingges exchequier by the space of L yeres by
passed'.[15] For the next few years, he was allowed to nominate his
own sheriff, although this hardly improved the general administration of the region. In 1518 Wolsey warned Dacre on the king's
behalf to permit the 'execution of process according to his laws for
the lawful finding of his title and interesse' 'in these parties under
your governance', because the king was

credibly informed by the officers of all his courts, such remiss dealing and
colorable inventions be used, that neither his titles can be found, his
process served for recovering of his duties, ne yet justice administered
according to his laws.[16]

Subsequently, Dacre's right of nomination was withdrawn but,
despite reminders, the county was then left without a sheriff for
over a year from Michaelmas 1520. This, the warden claimed, 'has
caused theves and misguided men to be of evill demeanour because
ther was no punesshment'.[17] In 1527, the new warden, the earl of
Northumberland, also requested the office, and eventually in 1532
he was allowed to farm the shrievalty for life for £40 a year without

[14] PRO, E 36/214, 397, 403, E 101/413/2/3, 63, 133, 163, 221, E 101/414/16, fo. 120ᵛ, E
101/415/3, fo. 243ᵛ; *Cal. close rolls, 1500–09*, nos. 602, 657; *L. & P. Hen. VIII*, iii, no.
102(26); Storey, *Henry VII*, 139–44. Cf. James, *Society, politics and culture*, 143.
[15] PRO, SP 1/11, fos. 4–6 (*L. & P. Hen. VIII*, ii, no. 596). Cf. *L. & P. Hen. VIII*,
iii, no. 3286.
[16] *L. & P. Hen. VIII*, ii, no. 4547. See also below, p. 151.
[17] BL, Caligula B. II, fo. 346ᵛ (*L. & P. Hen. VIII*, iii, no. 1883), Caligula B. II,
fo. 262 (*L. & P. Hen. VIII*, iii, no. 1225).

account.[18] Cumberland was also without a sheriff in 1521, 'wherby the kinges prosses and oder mennes cannot be serued nor sessions kepit as they shuld be'; and it had had no *custos rotulorum* since the death of the last *custos* twelve months earlier. In 1526, Sir Christopher Dacre alleged that he was the first sheriff of Cumberland in twenty years to make his proffer and account in the exchequer.[19]

Once in office, sheriffs often encountered considerable difficulties in discharging their duties. Two former sheriffs of Northumberland alleged in 1536 that they had been at great costs in defending the county and executing process

agaynst the wylde and unruely persones dwelling and abiding nygh unto the said borders of Scotland, which process can not be served upon any of the said unruely persones without a grete nomber of people assisting and ayding the said shiref for the tyme being.[20]

The plight of John Skelton, sheriff of Cumberland, offers a vivid illustration of the kind of problems a sheriff might face. In 1512 he was driven to petition the king in parliament against his indictment for murder by a coroner's jury. He had been ordered to arrest three of the Taylor surname who lived with 'other yll disposed and mysgoverned persons, divers of theym beyng Scottes' in Solport, 'a strayte and perilous countrey' in Liddel barony 'in the ferthest partie of your said countie toward Scotland'. Accordingly, Skelton assembled a posse for their arrest—a common enough precaution in the marches—but after one of the thieves had been killed in the ensuing mêlée, the coroner had allegedly empanelled a jury consisting of kinsmen and allies of the Taylors, 'one of theym indited of murder and iiij of theym Scottes borne and mysgoverned persons'. It required a private act of parliament to quash the indictment.[21] In 1536, when the exchequer finally issued process against a long list of sheriffs and escheators of Northumberland going back to 1515, it was alleged that in view of their

---

[18] PRO, SP 1/45, fos. 101–2 (*L. & P. Hen. VIII*, iv, no. 3629(2))); *L. & P. Hen. VIII*, v, no. 1008.

[19] BL, Caligula B. II, fo. 262 (*L. & P. Hen. VIII*, iii, no. 1225); PRO, SP 1/37, fos. 250–1 (*L. & P. Hen. VIII*, iv (i), no. 2052). Dacre's proffer was in the unusually large sum of £100: PRO, E 375/35/2.

[20] Hodgson, *Northumberland*, I. i. 365–6 (reproducing a petition).

[21] Statute roll, 4 Henry VIII c. 20 (*Statutes of the realm*, iii. 90–1).

great expenses, sheriffs there were allowed £120 a year out of the profits 'and makyth therof noe profer nor other payment or accompte', so that no sheriff or escheator had accounted at the exchequer since 1461.[22]

Overall, these changes led to a sharp reduction in the effectiveness of government in the far north. And the resulting 'lack of governance' helped to foster strong ties of kinship, to reinforce feudal ties between lord and tenant and, in general, to perpetuate social structures and political groupings of a kind which had long been typical of marcher society in Ireland.[23] Early-Tudor policy towards the borderlands thus reveals something of a paradox. In most parts of the Tudor state, the revival of monarchical power and the long period of comparative peace which followed the Hundred Years War and the Wars of the Roses saw the regional connexions and lineage society of an earlier age gradually give way to gentry-dominated, court–country politics and the civil society of Elizabethan and Stuart England.[24] Yet the application of what were essentially the same policies to the frontier regions prompted developments in their economies and social structures which accentuated the differences of the borderlands, particularly in the eyes of officials and other outsiders, from 'normal' society in lowland England. A growing chasm developed between the peaceful, 'civil' society of lowland England and the more turbulent marcher societies of the highland zone. These differences eventually prompted Tudor officials to view the problem of the marches in a very different light.

Of course, none of the ingredients in the border problem under the early Tudors was entirely new. The basic difficulty remained the inadequacy of the normal machinery for ensuring the defence and good government of two turbulent frontiers. Yet the reduction in the level of financial and military subventions by the crown in the late fifteenth century, and the relative neglect of the borders in the period of internal reconstruction which followed, undoubtedly exacerbated the difficulties of supervising government there. They also encouraged an increased reliance on alternative methods of

[22] Hodgson, *Northumberland*, I. i. 363–6 (reproducing an entry from a pipe roll).

[23] See the illuminating analysis of politics and society in the 14th-cent. lordship in Frame, 'Power and society in the lordship of Ireland', 3–33; id., *English lordship in Ireland*, pt. I.

[24] A convenient summary of the extensive literature about this is Williams, *Tudor regime*, esp. ch. 13.

maintaining order. This was of longer standing in Ireland where the Dublin administration's inability to address the problem in conventional terms was reflected in its oft-reiterated injunction that magnates should not 'in anywyse maike in seuerall bandes seuerall warre ne seuerall peax with Englisshe or Irisshmen'.[25] During the fifteenth century, the stability of the march was frequently strengthened by marriage alliances contracted between the leading English and Gaelic families there. Seemingly, relations between English and Scottish nobles and gentry were less close. The Northumberland gentry, for instance, did not normally take Scottish wives, even though as in Ireland licences could be obtained to marry aliens.[26] Lower down the social scale intermarriage was quite common, but even quite distant ties counted for something. Responding to a request by Lord Maxwell to 'borrow', 'aftre the vse and custome of the bordours', John Steile the Kemp, a Scot recently taken prisoner, Lord Dacre informed 'my lorde and cousin' that he was unwilling to allow this for 'common robbours & misdoers' like 'Steile or any oder being of such evill demanour and mysguyding', but only for honourable persons 'takin by chaunce of warr'. Nevertheless, Dacre continued, 'seing that your lordship and I be kynnesmen', he had in this instance 'put hym out of my daingier and deliuered hym again to his taker', rather than execute the law against him. The relationship stemmed from a mid-fourteenth-century marriage between the two families.[27]

In other respects, too, the procedures developed to regulate relations between separate kingdoms also tended to colour the internal administrative practices in each kingdom. For instance, the systems of arbitration and redress, known as march law, which developed in the English borderlands—and in essentials on other international frontiers like that between Castile and Granada—had decided advantages over procedure by English common law, particularly when visits by royal justices were at best once a year. Thus in settling internal disputes in the marches, many families had recourse to private arbitration, relying on the patronage of

---

[25] Award between the earls of Kildare and Ormond, 23 Nov. 1523: NLI, D.2096 (*Ormond deeds, 1509–47*, no. 93). Cf. Frame, 'Power and society', *passim*.

[26] J. F. Lydon, *Ireland in the later middle ages* (Dublin, 1972), 155–6; Ellis, *Tudor Ireland*, 92–8; *New hist. Ire.*, ii. 552, 554, 563, 635; Watts, *Border to middle shire*, 67.

[27] BL, Add. MS 24,965, fo. 282 (*L. & P. Hen. VIII*, iv, no. 434); Goodman, 'Anglo-Scottish marches', 20–1.

more powerful men to secure justice, rather than resorting to law which might prove both fruitless and expensive.[28] In both the Pale and the north, disputes about land were commonly referred to private arbitrators, either local gentlemen or royal officials, with the parties agreeing to be bound over to accept the resultant award.[29] Murders and other felonies might well give rise to feuds in the marches; and in Ireland, too, such matters could be settled by Gaelic law by payment of a fine to the party aggrieved or his lord. Thus there was a strong incentive to ignore the provisions of the common law with its inflexible stipulation of the death penalty for even comparatively minor offences. Marcher lords in Ireland frequently kept *brehons* (Gaelic: judges), whose verdicts amounted to an arbitration between the parties; and in many cases it was possible to regularize the matter subsequently by purchasing a royal pardon from the king's deputy.[30] Even so, there were complaints that those 'indytede of felonies and treison, yf they be pore wrachys not havyng landes ne goodes ne frendes, then shall they have the extremetyss of justice', whereas rich men got their pardons, 'so as there ys noun ensample yeven of amendment by the execution of anye grete man'.[31]

In the far north, compositions for murder were likewise not uncommon. In 1499 Sir Thomas Curwen of Workington and others agreed to pay Elizabeth Dykes £80 for the murder of her husband and to pay a priest fourteen marks to sing for his soul for two years.[32] In another arbitration, Lord Dacre decreed that Clement Blennerhasset of Carlisle should pay an annuity of 33s. 4d. for life. In this case, Dacre may well have been involved as Blennerhasset's lord. Other references to mediation by Dacre, however, suggest that Lord Thomas commonly intervened in his

[28] This topic is now ably explored in Henry Summerson, 'The early development of the laws of the Anglo-Scottish marches, 1249–1448', in W. M. Gordon (ed.), *Legal history in the making* (London, 1991), 29–42. See also Storey, *End of the house of Lancaster*, 121–2, 125; Ellis, *Reform and revival*, 156. For a Spanish example, see José Enrique López de Coca Castañer, 'Institutions on the Castilian–Granadan frontier', in Robert Bartlett and Angus MacKay (eds.), *Medieval frontier societies* (Oxford, 1989), 127–50.

[29] e.g. *Dowdall deeds*, ed. Charles McNeill and A. J. Otway-Ruthven (Dublin, 1960), nos. 525, 536; *Christ Church deeds*, nos. 405, 1055, 1130; F. W. Ragg, 'Helton Flechan, Askham and Sandford of Askham', in *C. & W.*, NS 21 (1921), 185–6.

[30] Ellis, *Tudor Ireland*, 47–8; id., *Reform and revival*, 123, 194.

[31] *SP Hen. VIII*, ii. 192. Cf. ibid., ii. 116.

[32] J. F. Curwen, 'Isel Hall', in *C. & W.*, NS 11 (1911), 123. See also Summerson, 'Laws of the Anglo-Scottish marches', 33.

capacity as warden because of the danger that feuds between the border gentry might otherwise undermine the defence of the marches. A surviving receipt for 40s. by a Carlisle woman in 1504, for instance, arose from Dacre's award after the killing of her husband.[33] And in 1523 on his departure from the north, Lord Lieutenant Surrey left Lord Ogle and Sir Ralph Fenwick to arbitrate between some Northumberland borderers concerning two murders: the king's pardon was obtained, but then Surrey's deputy, Lord Dacre, had to write for instructions when one party refused to abide by the award.[34]

Most of our more detailed evidence about the state of the borders, and particularly Tudor opinion about the problem, comes from official correspondence, surveys, and reports. In terms of their diagnosis of the difficulties and the suggested remedies, these are essentially similar to the state paper material emanating from Ireland. It would be a mistake to take them at face value. As with the Irish material, the reports and surveys were, in the main, compiled by two groups of officials whose outlook and motives were rather different. Broadly, reports by the borderers themselves called for increased resources to police and defend the region. Other analyses of conditions, particularly by officials drafted in from more 'civil' parts, were more likely to blame the borderers themselves for the violence and disorders there. As the Tudors became more concerned about the apparent 'decay' of the borders, particularly from the 1530s onwards, it was this second kind of report which had the greater impact on government thinking, notably the report of Sir Robert Bowes and Sir Ralph Ellerker compiled in 1542 and Bowes's further report of 1550. Bowes and Ellerker, members of the northern council from Durham and Yorkshire respectively, were commissioned in 1542 to inquire into the decay of the east and middle marches. They compiled one of the few detailed descriptions of the borders, and in particular of the activities of the border surnames, but neither had much sympathy with the surnames or the ambitions of the great magnates.[35] They reflected the attitude of 'civil' society, and increas-

---

[33] Cumbria Record Office, Carlisle, MS D/Lons/L LO.117 (I am grateful to Dr Henry Summerson for bringing this deed to my attention); Castle Howard MS A1/182. Cf. Storey, *Henry VII*, 149. Blennerhasset held the manor of Great Stainton of Dacre's barony of Gilsland.

[34] *L. & P. Hen. VIII*, iii, no. 3670, iv (i), no. 25.

[35] Reid, *King's council in the north*, 96, 104, 109, 113, 127, 150, 252; James, *Family,*

ingly of the government, for whom the most striking feature of
marcher society—and the root cause of all the mischief—were the
highland surnames.

The clans, kindreds, and surnames were seemingly peculiar to
the border regions of the English polity, although they were of
course indigenous to Gaelic and Welsh society. By Tudor times,
English ideas had become fairly fixed about how to recognize and
deal with such peoples. From the twelfth century onwards, as
Latin Christendom had encountered a growing variety of strange
peoples and customs, ethnographical writings had become increasingly numerous and specific. Particular marks of civility had been
identified as serving to distinguish between civil and primitive
man; and of the various groups of European 'primitives' which had
been the subject of scholarly attention, English officials had long
experience in dealing with two of them, the Welsh and the Irish.[36]
Beginning with Gerald of Wales in the late twelfth century, a
stereotyped vocabulary had been developed to describe them. The
Welsh, he thought, were an untamed and undisciplined people
living like animals in a strange land, but he was harsher still
in his comments about the Irish.[37] Subsequently, the Edwardian
conquest had subjected the Welsh to more sustained anglicizing
pressures, whereas the native Irish still languished on the lower
links in the great chain of being among the various species of
Untermenschen between man and beast. Polydore Vergil in his
Anglica Historia, for instance, described the Gaelic Irish in conventional terms as 'savage, rude and uncouth', known as ' "wild
men of the woods" ' because of their primitive habits.[38] Thus by
early Tudor times, the Gaelic Irish represented for Englishmen
the outer limits of human behaviour.

In modern English usage, 'Irish' now invariably denotes the
land, culture, and peoples of Ireland, although the variant 'Erse'

lineage and civil society, 30–1, 36, 42, 45–6. The two reports are printed in Hodgson,
Northumberland, III. ii. 171–248.

[36] Felipe Fernandez-Armesto, *Before Columbus: exploration and colonisation from
the Mediterranean to the Atlantic* (London, 1987), 224–6, 240–1. For the wider
context, see now Bartlett, *Making of Europe*, 21–3. The implications for Ireland of
these attitudes have been ably explored in J. Th. Leerssen, *Mere Irish & fíor-
Ghael: studies in the idea of Irish nationality, its development and literary expression
prior to the nineteenth century* (Amsterdam, 1986).

[37] Davies, *Age of conquest*, 112–13, 139–41, 150–2, 161–2; *New hist. Ire.*, ii. 60–1,
242.

[38] *Anglica Historia*, ed. D. Hay (London, 1950), 79.

still refers to the Gaelic language as spoken in Scotland. To the Tudors, however, 'the Irish' were a savage people who inhabited parts of Ireland and Scotland. Englishmen were of course more familiar with the Irish-based clans along the western frontier of the Tudor state, but when 'the Scottyshe Irysshe' appeared on the Anglo-Scottish borders Tudor officials had no difficulty in identifying them. In the lead-up to Solway Moss, for instance, English spies decried the military capability of the Scottish army because 'the moste parte was Ershemen, whiche be veray slaves and noo men of good ordre': 'the Scottis were more aferde of the said Yrishe men than of thEnglishe army', because they destroyed 'corne and other goodes, withoute paynge any thynge therefore'.[39] Thus as the government wrestled with the problems of marcher society in the far north, it seemed natural to compare the customs of the borderers with these wild 'Irish'.

In the north the 'surnames' emerged in response to the endemic insecurity of the Anglo-Scottish marches from 1296 onwards. Yet it may well be significant that the first reference to surnames does not occur until 1498[40]—after the administrative changes of the late fifteenth century had accentuated the problems of border rule. It was then used of some English border families. The Scottish government usually referred to such families as clans—'the clannis, surnamys, induellaris and inhabitantis [in] the boundis and landis of Liddisdale', for instance—no doubt because of the resemblance to the Gaelic clans of the Western Isles. Almost from the outset, however, the Gaelic term was used as an alternative by English officials.[41] The surnames inhabited parts of the actual frontier districts, particularly the poorer west and middle marches. In the west march, the leading English border lineages were the

---

[39] Joseph Bain (ed.), *The Hamilton papers: letters and papers illustrating the political relations of England and Scotland in the XVI century*, i (Edinburgh, 1890), app; pp. lxxi–lxxii; *L. & P. Hen. VIII*, xix (ii), no. 795. Cf. Ellis, *Tudor Ireland*, 241.

[40] *Cal. doc. Scotland*, iv, no. 1649. Cf. Tuck, 'War and society', 52; Rae, *Administration of the Scottish frontier*, 5–7. For the English surnames, see now Ralph Robson, *The rise and fall of the English highland clans: Tudor responses to a mediaeval problem* (Edinburgh, 1989).

[41] R. K. Hannay (ed.), *Acts of the Lords of the Council in Public Affairs, 1501–1554* (Edinburgh, 1932), 124, 341, 410 (quotation); *A descriptive catalogue of ancient deeds in the Public Record Office*, iii (London, 1900), 497–8 (bond of four Nichsons for their 'surnames, clannes', or any other dwelling under them, 15 Oct. 1506); Nicolson and Burn, *Westmorland and Cumberland*, i, pp. xix, cx. Cf. Rae, *Administration of the Scottish frontier*, 6.

Routledges and Nixons of Bewcastle; with Storeys and Forsters in
Eskdale. In the middle march, the Charltons, Dodds, Robsons,
Halls, and Hedleys predominated.[42] Each surname was divided
into branches called 'graynes' and led by one or more headsmen,
captains, lairds, or chiefs (as they were called), who protected their
followers and dependants, and negotiated with the wardenry officials. At a warden court in 1527, for instance, 'there was oon
persone executid called Colingwod, a notable offendour in marche
treason, whiche was taken and brought in by Robert Colingwod,
chieff of his name'. Across the border there were similar surnames,
notably the Armstrongs and Elliots of Liddesdale, and the
Grahams from around Gretna.[43] The clansmen had in turn supporters among the less law-abiding border gentry, who were reputed to harbour thieves, and even understandings with magnates
like Lord Dacre.[44]

A survey of Tynedale and Redesdale in 1528 listed 403 adult
males in Tynedale and 445 in Redesdale. Tynedale was divided
into north and south valleys, of which north Tynedale was, according to Bowes, 'more plenished with wild and misdemeaned
people'.[45] In Tynedale the leading surnames were the Charltons
(54 members), Robsons (62), Dodds (53), and Milburns (30), but 30
more families were each represented by between 1 and 16 members. The inhabitants there

nothinge regard[ed] eyther the lawes of God or of the kinges majesties for
any love or other lawful consideracion, but onely for the drede and feare
of instante correccion.[46]

[42] *L. & P. Hen. VIII*, iv (ii), no. 4336(2); Hodgson, *Northumberland*, III. ii. 229–
30, 243–4 (Bowes's survey, 1550); R. T. Spence, 'The pacification of the
Cumberland borders, 1593–1628', in *Northern History*, 13 (1977), 60–1. Although
the surnames are described as kinship groups, it may be that others in the district
dominated by a particular surname assumed that name for the purposes of protec-
tion. In the lordships of Gaelic Ireland, of course, unrelated dependent clans lived
alongside the ruling clan.

[43] PRO, SP 1/45, fos. 87–8 (*L. & P. Hen. VIII*, iv (ii), no. 3610); Rae, *Administration of the Scottish frontier*, 5–7; Spence, 'Pacification of the Cumberland borders', 60–1.

[44] *L. & P. Hen. VIII*, iv (i), nos. 133, 220, 405, 1223, (ii), nos. 4420–1; BL,
Lansdowne MS I, fo. 43. See also Hodgson, *Northumberland*, III. i. 32 (answer of
Lord Dacre to complaints of misgovernment, 1525); James, *Society, politics and
culture*, 95–100, 142–3.

[45] *L. & P. Hen. VIII*, iv (ii), no. 4336(2); Hodgson, *Northumberland*, III. ii. 228
(Bowes's survey).

[46] *L. & P. Hen. VIII*, iv (ii), no. 4336(2); Hodgson, *Northumberland*, III. ii. 234
(Bowes and Ellerker's survey, 1542).

'The Riddesdall men be even of like nature and qualities as the Tyndall men, save that they be not soe trusty of their wordes and promise.'[47] There, the Halls (70 members) predominated, with Hedleys (64), Redes (39), Potts (29), and Forsters (28) influential, and 33 other families represented by between 2 and 20 individuals. By 1550, Bowes thought that north Tynedale could raise about 600 horsemen and foot, and Redesdale rather less.[48]

The government relied heavily on the surnames' services in wartime, but it found their activities much less acceptable at other times. The indigenous English surnames intermarried with Scottish clans, so that in the early sixteenth century there were English branches of the Armstrongs and Grahams established in Bewcastledale and Eskdale respectively. Indeed, the English Grahams, originating with William Graham and his eight sons, who squatted along the English bank of the Esk after banishment from Scotland *c*.1516, gradually spread over both sides of the Esk, the Debateable Land, and Nichol Forest until, under Elizabeth, they were the leading surname of the English west march. By 1603, when the government ordered their transplantation to Connaught, they probably had over 200 clansmen, as well as almost 300 subtenants.[49] Culturally, the English and Scottish surnames were virtually indistinguishable, and among them national allegiances never counted for much. The respective central governments might classify them as English or Scots depending on which side of a notional border line they resided, but this did not make them act any differently. Instead, they pursued their own interests in collaboration with other clans, English or Scottish.[50] At the battle of Flodden in 1513 the English surnames waited until the two armies dismounted to fight, and then plundered both sides indiscriminately and made off with the English horses and baggage.[51] The surname collectively answered for the conduct of individual mem-

[47] *L. & P. Hen. VIII*, iv (ii), no. 4336(2); Hodgson, *Northumberland*, III. ii. 244 (Bowes's survey, 1550).

[48] *L. & P. Hen. VIII*, iv (ii), no. 4336(2); Hodgson, *Northumberland*, III. ii. 208–9, 243 (Bowes's survey, 1550). Cf. 'A description of the power of Irishmen', in L. Price, 'Armed forces of the Irish chiefs in the early sixteenth century' in *RSAI Jn.*, 62 (1932), 202–7.

[49] Spence, 'Pacification of the Cumberland borders', 60–1, 99–122; MacKenzie, 'Debateable land', 117–20.

[50] See, for instance, *SP Hen. VIII*, iv. 370–1, 383–4; Rae, *Administration of the Scottish frontier*, 10, 11.

[51] *L. & P. Hen. VIII*, i (2nd edn.), nos. 2246, 2283.

bers, and collectively sought vengeance against outsiders who in-
jured them. Their chief livelihood was the raising of cattle, sheep,
and horses on the commons, marshes, and mosses of the marches,
supplemented by crops, chiefly oats, where the soil and political
climate allowed.[52]

Under the early Tudors, however, changes in demography and
in Anglo-Scottish relations accentuated the problems of the borderers. The scaling down of military activity—from open war to
cold war—reduced their opportunities for profit and plunder, and
population growth increased the pressure on the land. Although
population density in the region was comparatively low, the far
north was in fact severely overpopulated for its natural resources.[53]
In 1528, the earl of Northumberland proposed taking order 'for the
advoiding' of population from Tynedale and Redesdale if there
were found to be 'a gretter nombre . . . then truly may be
susteigned in the same'.[54] Bowes and Ellerker asserted in 1542 that
Tynedale was 'overcharged wth so greatt a number of people, mo
then suche proffytes as may be gotten & wonne out of the grounde
wthin the said countrey are able to susteyne & kepe'.[55] In consequence, like the Irish of the Leinster mountains, the surnames
were constrained to supplement their income by reiving and robbery. The lowland communities of the western middle marches
were obliged to keep strict watch against 'the incourses of theftes &
spoylles contynually & nyghtly attempted & enterprysed in thos
parties by the Tyndalles, Ryddesdales & other Scottes theves'
allied with them.[56]

In response, the crown appointed special keepers of Tynedale
and Redesdale, and took pledges for good behaviour in a bid to
maintain a semblance of order;[57] but no amount of persuasion or
threats could curb their activities for very long. In 1526, the earl of
Cumberland thought that the only way of reducing the Scottish
Armstrongs was by confiscating or destroying their possessions

---

[52] Hodgson, *Northumberland*, III. ii. 230–4 (Bowes's survey, 1550), 233 (Bowes
and Ellerker's survey, 1542); *L. & P. Hen. VIII*, iv (i), no. 346; Spence, 'Pacification
of the Cumberland borders', 63.

[53] Newton, 'Decay of the borders', 8–9; Bouch and Jones, *History of the Lake
Counties*, 16–18; Watts, *Border to middle shire*, 40–1; S. M. Harrison, *The Pilgrimage
of Grace in the Lake Counties, 1536–7* (London, 1981), 5.

[54] PRO, SP 1/46, fo. 130^{v} (*L. & P. Hen. VIII*, iv, no. 3816(2)).

[55] Hodgson, *Northumberland*, III. ii. 233.

[56] Ibid., III. ii. 227–8.

[57] Robson, *English highland clans*, 230. See also below, Ch. 5.

and transporting the clan into permanent exile in Ireland.[58] The earl of Northumberland actually threatened the Tynedale and Redesdale surnames with this in 1528, warning that if they did not submit, he would 'invaide theym and hange theyme vppon bowes . . . destroy their goodis, catailles and howses, and taike theire wiffes and children and shippe theyme into other straunge regions'.[59] In 1524–5 the raids were apparently masterminded from Scotland by one William Ridley, 'cheif capeteyn of all our theues and rebelles' and kinsman of a local gentleman, Sir Nicholas Ridley of Willimoteswick. He was eventually killed in Liddesdale.[60] Cardinal Wolsey's servants reported that they had urged the Tynedale men 'to obey the kinges highnes as trew subiectes, and soo haue contynewed to nowe amyable speches with theym'. Nevertheless, the thieves 'abide in their rebellious and obstinate opynionez', answering that if

their pledges nowe in prison be deliuered at large sure of their lyfez . . . and their own lyfez saved, thei be then contented to obey the kinges highnes and to make to there powers amendis for their offences to the parties greved.[61]

Yet promise of amends was worthless, because it was poverty which drove the thieves to robbery in the first place. Thus the lowlanders frequently preferred to negotiate a token composition for a theft through the surname's 'true men', who were not directly involved in reiving, rather than to risk the 'deadly feud' which would follow if the thief were subsequently tried and executed for felony.[62] Similar intermediaries could be found in Ireland and pre-conquest Wales.[63]

Another variation on the theme was blackmail, the north country equivalent of the Irish blackrent. It was eventually prohibited by statute in 1601.[64] The Northumberland gentry complained in

---

[58] *VCH Cumberland*, ii. 270; Spence, 'Pacification of the Cumberland borders', 82.

[59] PRO, SP 1/46, fo. 128 (*L. & P. Hen. VIII*, iv, no. 3816(1)).

[60] BL, Caligula B. I, fo. 47 (*L. & P. Hen. VIII*, iv (i), no. 1289); *L. & P. Hen. VIII*, iv (i), nos. 346, 405, 1223, 2110.

[61] BL, Caligula B. I, fo. 46[v] (*L. & P. Hen. VIII*, iv (i), no. 1289).

[62] Hodgson, *Northumberland*, III. ii. 230–4 (Bowes's survey, 1550), 233 (Bowes and Ellerker's survey, 1542).

[63] *New hist. Ire.*, ii. 261; Davies, 'Frontier arrangements in fragmented societies', 84.

[64] Statute 43 & 44 Elizabeth I c. 13 (*Statutes of the realm*, IV. ii. 980). See

1525 that the thieves of Bewcastledale, Tynedale, and Redesdale were so out of control

that the kinges true subiectes of Northumbreland ther by them be put in such daunger and feer that such townes as wulde leve in pease and vnrobbed and vndispoyled be enforced to pay yerly vnto the said theves and their adherentes tributes and soo to leve vnder their proteccion.[65]

The mounting of a military campaign against the surnames, as in 1525, was something of a last resort; but even this was not the threat it seemed. The chances were, in fact, that it would be no more effective than campaigns against the Leinster Irish, and for the same reasons. In north Tynedale in 1542 the only towerhouse there, at Hesleyside, belonged to the senior Charlton headsman. Other headsmen lived in wooden houses of 'greatt sware oke trees strongly bounde', with roofs of 'turves & earthe', all well hidden and difficult to break or burn. Their followers lived in clusters of flimsy clay or timber huts, with thatched roofs, which were easily burned but which could be re-erected, it was said, within three or four hours.[66] Moreover, the country was 'soe stronge, full of woodes, marresses and streat passages' half-blocked by trees, that strangers could barely enter it, particularly on horseback. And if forewarned, the thieves would 'flye and keepe themselves either in woodes or mountaynes, and rather than they will be apprehended, flye into Scotland and become outlawes and rebells'.[67] In 1525 Wolsey's servants predicted that

when so euer we begynne our werre wᵗ Tynedale, the theves shall avoide and fflee the countre, and more then to dispoyle the countre and brenne their houses we can nott doo. And they shall not feyll immediatly after our departing to invayde the good countres and doo all evylles by swarde and fyre they may.

In consequence, two hundred mounted archers would also have to be laid in 'garrysons vpon ther bordure aswell to defend their

Hodgson, *Northumberland*, I. i. 372; Watts, *Border to middle shire*, 26–7; Spence, 'Pacification of the Cumberland borders', 63, 68.

[65] Hodgson, *Northumberland*, III. i. 33 (articles of complaint against Lord Dacre, 1525). Cf. ibid., III. i. 73.

[66] Hodgson, *Northumberland*, III. ii. 204, 231–3 (Bowes and Ellerker's survey, 1542); Spence, 'Pacification of the Cumberland borders', 62.

[67] Hodgson, *Northumberland*, III. ii. 222, 235, 238–9 (Bowes's survey, 1550), 232–5 (Bowes and Ellerker's survey, 1542); BL, Caligula B. I, fos. 45–8 (*L. & P. Hen. VIII*, iv (i), no. 1289); *L. & P. Hen. VIII*, xiii (ii), no. 355; *SP Hen. VIII*, iv. 407–8, 414–15.

malice and excursez as dayly to anoye them'.[68] Overall, therefore, a military campaign was likely to be troublesome and costly and, without the active co-operation of the Scottish government in guarding the passes and controlling their own surnames, unlikely to yield many tangible benefits.

Not only were the border surnames not amenable to law, but in other obvious ways they differed from the normal habits and life-style of Tudor Englishmen. They inhabited upland or wooded areas, and their dependence on pastoralism was not simply a result of the quality of the land. It was also an insurance against border raids. Much of their land was held in common. In the barony of Gilsland in northern Cumberland, 44 per cent of the land was still held in common in 1603.[69] And in many parts of the borders and elsewhere, transhumance was practised. Beginning in April, the inhabitants would take their

cattell and goo w^t them up unto suche highe landes & waste groundes toward ye border of Scotlande and theire builde theme lodges and sheales & remayne still with there saide cattell in such hoopes and valyes wheare they can finde any pasture for theme untill the monethe of Auguste that they will repayre home agayne for gettynge y[n] there corne.[70]

Some of the shiels were occasional sites, such as one at Lowsburn Holmes—'astrong ground of woid and marres'—used by English rebels; but many were reoccupied each summer, and ownership of them was commonly vested collectively in the members of the surname to which it belonged.[71]

A further feature of border life which constituted a departure from English norms and also militated against more intensive methods of farming was the custom of partible inheritance, which applied in some parts of the north and led to subdivision of hold-ings. The custom of the manor of Harbottle, in the liberty of Redesdale, was described as gavelkind, with partible inheritance among the tenant's sons and non-forfeiture of the estate for treason or felony. The Graham surname also practised partible inherit-

[68] BL, Caligula B. I, fo. 47^v (*L. & P. Hen. VIII*, iv (i), no. 1289).

[69] Bouch and Jones, *History of the Lake Counties*, p. 89.

[70] Hodgson, *Northumberland*, III. ii. 221 (Bowes and Ellerker's survey, 1542). Cf. BL, Caligula B. I, fos. 141–1^v (*L. & P. Hen. VIII*, xv, no. 570); Joan Thirsk (ed.), *The agrarian history of England and Wales*, iv. *1500–1640* (Cambridge, 1967), 22–3.

[71] BL, Caligula B. I, fos. 141–1^v (*L. & P. Hen. VIII*, xv, no. 570); Newton, 'Decay of the borders', 10; Watts, *Border to middle shire*, 42.

ance, but in their case their only title to the land on which they
squatted was *de facto* occupation and the 'rule of the sword'.[72]
Around Kendal in Westmorland or Halifax in Yorkshire, profits
from spinning and weaving helped to supplement incomes from
subdivided holdings, but along the border 'the yonge and actyve
people for lacke of lyvynge be constrayned to steall or spoyle
contynually in England or Scotland'.[73] Many highlanders survived
by preying on their richer neighbours. 'True countreys be very
lothe to have any of Tyndall or Riddesdall inhabitinge amonge
them' because their peoples were so 'wild and misdemeaned', and
attracted 'other light persons' active in reiving and robbery.[74] Certain Newcastle guilds refused to accept them as apprentices.[75]

In sum, therefore, contemporary descriptions of the border surnames leave little doubt that royal officials regarded them as a
species of *homo silvestres*, a primitive pastoral people living in mud
huts in woods or mountains. And once attention became focused
on the problems of the Anglo-Scottish border, it was natural that
the problem should be conceived in terms of civility and savagery.
It is significant in this context, for instance, that the characteristics
of the border surnames which evoked most comment from contemporaries—clans, captains, joint responsibility, partible inheritance, cattle-rustling—were precisely those features which English
observers had long accounted peculiarities of Gaelic society. By
1560, indeed, Irishness and savagery were so closely identified in
the official mind that Archbishop Parker could warn Secretary
Cecil that if bishops were not quickly appointed to the sees in
northern England, the region would become 'too much Irish and
savage'.[76] Yet unlike the Gaelic Irish, the border surnames were at
least nominally Englishmen, to whom the benefits of English civility had long been extended. And this in turn prompted the question of why they had degenerated from their earlier civility to their

[72] Spence, 'Pacification of the Cumberland borders', 63, 102; S. J. Watts, 'Tenant-right in early 17th-century Northumberland', in *Northern History*, 6 (1971),
esp. 68–70; Thirsk (ed.), *Agrarian history of England and Wales*, iv. 9–10, 23–4;
Harrison, *Pilgrimage of Grace*, 7–11; James, *Family, lineage and civil society*, 25.
[73] Hodgson, *Northumberland*, III. ii. 233 (Bowes and Ellerker's survey, 1542);
Thirsk (ed.), *Agrarian history of England and Wales*, iv. 10–13, 20–1.
[74] Hodgson, *Northumberland*, III. ii. 228, 243 (Bowes's survey, 1550).
[75] Watts, *Border to middle shire*, 23–4.
[76] *Correspondence of Matthew Parker, D.D. Archbishop of Canterbury*, ed. John
Bruce and T. T Perowne, Parker Society (Cambridge, 1853), 123. I am grateful to
Dr Alan Ford for this reference.

present savagery. Thus instead of treating the far north as a defended border or war zone, Tudor officials increasingly identified the problem in terms of moral decline and a defect of justice.

In practice, of course, this revised appreciation of the nature of the problem mistook symptom for cause. This is most apparent from the reports of the royal commissioners, Bowes and Ellerker, in 1542 and 1550.[77] Far from calling for additional men and money for external defence, they identified the central problem as the failure both of the borderers to do their duties as the king's subjects and of the landlords there to maintain their castles or to reside on their estates in the marches. 'The whole countrey' of Northumberland, declared Bowes, 'is much given to wildnes', and also 'much given to riotte, specially the younge gentlemen, headsmen, and dyvers of them alsoe to theftes and other greater offences'.[78] Likewise, the Northumberland gentry in 1525 thought that throughout the marches

for lak of doing iustice...a grete number of thinhabitantes...ar becommen common robbours and theves and ar likly to growe and encreace in shorte tyme to suche a nomber that the gentilmen and trew inhabitauntes... shall not be able to subdue or withstonde theim.

Already, they had 'so robbed, dispoiled and impouerished the true inhabitauntes... that diuers townes ther ar become almost desolate and barayne of inhabitauntes'. There were fewer and fewer true men that 'hadd a good horse or be able to serue the king in his warres', whereby the 'countrey is like shortely to be most enhabited with thives Englisshe & Scottishe, and the kinges true subiectes ther either to be expelled or els to become subiectes to the said thives'.[79] By 1543, according to the author of another report, the county was in such misorder and justice was so seldom administered that misdoers 'have goten the over hande of the good men (if there be any)' and everywhere men practised to

be at kyndnes wth the thevis and ill doers as well Scottes as Engleshemen, and thole countrey is sore robbed and spoyled, specially the husbandmen, for the gentlemen for the most parte have their goodes and catalles saved and the pore mans spoiled.[80]

[77] Hodgson, Northumberland, III. ii. 171–248.
[78] Ibid., III. ii. 244 (Bowes's survey, 1550).
[79] Ibid., III. i. 35–6 (complaints of the Northumberland gentry, 1525).
[80] PRO, SP 1/179, fo. 157 (L. & P. Hen. VIII, xviii, no. 800).

Predictably, the state of Tynedale, Redesdale, Bewcastledale, and Gilsland was seen as lying at the heart of the problem. By 1550, Bowes asserted, there was a great conspiracy between 'the wyld people' of Tynedale and Redesdale and the Scots of Liddesdale 'to over rynne & spoyle the true poore people'. The inhabitants there continually 'commytted more heynous & detestable offences, declyninge ever from evell unto wourse'.[81] And in default of justice, 'the common sorte of people' living nearest to the thieves were 'so weake & tymorous of harte & courage & so evell prepared of horse, harnes, & other necessaries for defence', that they were 'not lyke to be recovered of themselfes' without speedy assistance.[82] Kidland lordship, for instance, was now uninhabited, not just because it lay open towards Scotland, but also because Redesdale was now 'ungoverned', whereas formerly 'thinhabytantes therof dyd not spoyle & steale their neyghbours goodes & cattalles as they now doo'.[83] Thus, the commissioners argued,

excepte those wylde countries may be stablyshed in better order then they have bene, the said wastes & dyssolate countries be lyke to encrease & waxe greatter in those parties.[84]

The remedy for this decay of the English borders, the commissioners urged, was to execute sharp justice on malefactors, to require landlords to repair their castles and either to live there or to maintain a suitable deputy, and to provide for the repopulation of deserted villages. They noted that in many parts

the said waste townes lye in suche wylde & dessolate places so farre from any strength or ayde of Englyshmen & so nere the plenyshed grounde of Scotland that the wysest borderers in those parties doo thinke yt a greatt joperdye for suche as should inhabyte in them

unless fortresses were built or repaired there as a refuge.[85] In particular, the keeper of Tynedale should be allowed a garrison of fifty horsemen 'to correcte, chastyce & kepe in due obeysaunce the prowde obstynate & rebellyous hartes of the said Tyndale'; and there should be a similar garrison of thirty for Redesdale.[86] Likewise, two fortresses lying between the valleys of the north and south Tyne should be 'inhabyted & plenyshed with some trewe &

[81] Hodgson, *Northumberland*, III. ii. 237–8 (Bowes and Ellerker's survey, 1542).
[82] Ibid., III. ii. 229.
[83] Ibid., III. ii. 222–3.
[84] Ibid., III. ii. 229.
[85] Ibid., III. ii. 206–7.
[86] Ibid., III. ii. 235, 237.

honest defenceble men', because they 'stande in suche a goole, passage & common entery of all theves' coming and going between Liddesdale, Tynedale, Gilsland and Bewcastledale.[87]

Overall, therefore, contemporary descriptions of the borders dwelt as much on the wildness and negligence of the English borderers as on the threat of Scottish invasion. The curiously unrealistic attitude of the central government to the problem occasioned little or no comment. Yet, as we shall see, it was precisely the failure of royal policy to address the basic problem of defence which accounted for the decay of the borders under the early Tudors. Later, William Camden was to depict the borderers as nomads.[88] In 1586, however, it was reported of Tynedale and Redesdale, that through the teaching of the famous Elizabethan preacher, Bernard Gilpin,

their former savage behaviour is very much abated, and their barbarous wildness and fierceness so much qualified, that there is hope left of their reduction unto civility and better sort of behaviour.[89]

As Tudor officials began to view the problem of the north chiefly as a struggle for the defence of English civility against the wild men of the marches, so officials became increasingly conscious of the similarities between northern society and Tudor Ireland, where society was likewise divided between wild Irishmen and civil Englishmen. Not all kinship groups of the Pale marches and beyond were Gaelic Irish, however. In the southern and western marches lived lineages of English descent—the Harolds, Archbolds, and Walshes of Dublin, and the Dillons, Daltons, and Delamares of Westmeath. To my knowledge, there are no contemporary descriptions of them like those of Gaelic clans or northern surnames, nor do we find for the early Tudor period the same wealth of references to their activities as in the fourteenth-century court rolls and chronicles examined by Professor Frame.[90] In part, this is because the early-Tudor government in Ireland had even less resources available than 150 years before to deal directly with these lineages. It relied more extensively on magnates like the earl

---

[87] Ibid., III. ii. 229.

[88] William Camden, *Britannia, a chorographical description* (trans. Philemon Holland, 1610), 806.

[89] Hodgson, *Northumberland*, II. i. 75. Cf. Watts, *Border to middle shire*, 87.

[90] *English lordship in Ireland*, 27–46.

of Ormond to control them as part of their connexion. Officials tended to dismiss them as English rebels—cultural degenerates who, although English subjects by birth, were otherwise indistinguishable from Irish enemies.

Nevertheless, occasional references to their activities and environment are revealing. They lived in upland or wooded areas sustaining a pastoral economy, enjoying an ambiguous relationship with the government and the more settled communities. Some of the Walshmen, for instance, lived in the townland of Kilternan, Co. Dublin, which 'touch[ed] the extreme parts of the English Pale . . . near the O'Toles on the south'. Much of it was 'stony mountain, where for the most part nothing grows but small furze and heath'; other land was covered in 'sedge and hazel and such like'.[91] The Westmeath lineages apparently practised partible inheritance on their estates.[92] Moreover, a statute of 1447 complained that there was no difference in apparel between English marchers and Irish enemies, so that the latter could travel about robbing and pillaging the English districts with impunity: it ordered that anyone who would be accounted an Englishman should shave his upper lip.[93]

Both the Dublin and Westmeath lineages figure prominently in the statutes ordering long lists of individuals to surrender at Dublin castle to answer charges of robbery, raiding, and taking pledges from the king's lieges.[94] Archbishop Alen of Dublin (1529–34) complained that between them the Archbolds, Harolds, Walshes, O'Byrnes, and O'Tooles had destroyed his estates in the Dublin marches.[95] As with Gaelic border chieftaincies and the northern surnames, such activities were probably a substantial source of income to them. In 1461, the Harolds were recorded as 'undyr wode' (presumably they had taken to the woods to avoid justice), and a Dublin city by-law prohibited citizens from contact with them and from selling corn to marchers or Irishmen.[96] Soon after,

---

[91] *Calendar of ancient deeds . . . in the Pembroke Estate Office, Dublin* (Dublin, 1891), no. 222. Cf. ibid., nos. 223–4, 227–8.

[92] K. W. Nicholls, *Gaelic and gaelicised Ireland in the middle ages* (Dublin, 1972), 64.

[93] Parliament roll, 25 Henry VI c. 20 (*Stat. Ire., Hen. VI*, 88). Cf. *L. & P. Hen. VIII*, iii, no. 2405.

[94] e.g. *Stat. Ire., Edw. IV*, i and ii, *passim*.

[95] *Alen's reg.*, 172, 242.

[96] J. T. Gilbert (ed.), *Calendar of ancient records of Dublin*, i (Dublin, 1889), 309.

Archbishop Tregury of Dublin (1450–71) was captured and imprisoned by Geoffrey Harold, 'captain of his perverse nation'; while in 1470 Harold's country was again in rebellion, so that 'no man dares to go there . . . for fear of their lives or of being made prisoners and delivered to the Irishmen'.[97] Even so, the Dublin administration attempted to exercise some control over these lineages. It supervised the election of their captains and made them responsible for the conduct of their clansmen. At times it found it expedient to use their services, as during the Warbeck crisis of 1494–6, when small holdings of marcher horse or foot were organized through Theobald Walsh and substantial rewards were paid to O'Byrne and Edmund Harold. In 1537, it even went so far as to depose the Harold captain and to appoint one of the local gentry as captain and governor of Harold's country, with custody of the castles and forts there.[98]

Traditional nationalist histories of Ireland have interpreted the emergence of kinship groups among the medieval Englishry as the product of cultural borrowings from Gaelic society, 'the gaelicization of the Anglo-Irish'.[99] There is no doubt that this form of cultural assimilation did occur. Yet equally the example of the northern surnames suggests that geography and the frontier also exercised a formative influence on English marcher society in Ireland. The fact is that in the far north of England, the political partition of what had been a culturally homogeneous region, combined with the endemic insecurity caused by constant border warfare, was alone sufficient to create very similar problems to those which characterized the marches in Ireland, even though English and lowland Scottish culture were not sharply differentiated. And, as with the English uplands of the Anglo-Scottish marches, the influences of physical geography and a political frontier combined to create in the Dublin–Wicklow area a semi-autonomous marcher region which straddled the cultural divide between English lowlanders and Gaelic highlanders.

For Tudor officials, however, speculation about the underlying forces behind the process of acculturation was quite academic. The

[97] *Alen's reg.*, 242; Parliament roll, 10 Edward IV c. 12 (*Stat. Ire., Edw. IV*, i. 666–8).

[98] *Cal. pat. rolls Ire., Hen. VIII–Eliz.*, 26; BL, Royal MS 18C, XIV, fos. 35, 45ᵛ, 46, 47, 56, 56ᵛ, 97ᵛ, 99ᵛ, 100ᵛ, 101ᵛ, 102, 130ᵛ.

[99] A recent reassertion of this perspective is Bradshaw, 'Nationalism and historical scholarship in modern Ireland'.

plain fact of the matter was that in both regions individual groups of the king's subjects had grown wild and degenerate. In both regions, therefore, the essential problem was how to promote the spread of English civility. To the Tudors, the existence among the Scots and Irish of a separate language and customs was of little account: Gaelic culture was simply a particular form of barbarism. Indeed the tensions between the border surnames and the lowland communities of the Anglo-Scottish marches seemed so closely to resemble those between the wild Irishmen of the Leinster mountains and the civil Englishmen of the Pale that it would perhaps be more useful to explore the differences than to labour the similarities. Perhaps the most basic difference concerned the relationship between culture and nationality. In the Pale marches, differences between upland and lowland were largely subsumed in the wider *Kulturkampf* between English and Gaelic. English culture was perceived as a lowland culture, and any departures from English norms were construed as cultural degeneracy. The civil Englishman was readily distinguishable from the wild Irishman by his appearance, dress, language, manners, and customs.[100]

The tripartite division into English rebels, Scottish enemies, and true subjects also parallels the traditional division of Ireland between English rebels, Irish enemies, and English subjects. Yet contemporary descriptions do not dwell on the particular attributes of Anglo-Scottish barbarity. This may be because the gap between civility and savagery was less wide than in Ireland; but more probably it was because primary cultural differences were not directly related to the political frontier. Scottish Armstrongs and English Charltons spoke the same language, practised the same customs, and followed the same pursuits—in despite of the border—and the lords and lairds of southern Scotland and the nobles and gentry of northern England were also to a large extent culturally homogeneous, despite the emergence of separate English and Scottish senses of national identity.[101] In Ireland, by contrast, race and culture were in practice primary determinants of nationality.

---

[100] Ellis, *Tudor Ireland*, ch. 2. See also the perceptive remarks in Frame, 'Power and society', esp. p. 33.

[101] See e.g. Tough, *Last years of a frontier*, pt. ii; Rae, *Administration of the Scottish frontier*, ch. 1; Jenny Wormald, *Court, kirk, and community: Scotland 1470–1625* (London, 1981), chs. 2–3.

As Professor Ralph Griffiths has shown, nationality in the English dominions was normally determined by birth and allegiance. A man was an Englishman who was born in the dominions of the English king and in his allegiance.[102] In the Anglo-Scottish border region, and given the fluctuating loyalties of the border surnames, this meant place of birth. In the later middle ages, the fluctuating political frontier had occasionally created doubts about the punishment appropriate to offences committed by criminals born in areas of English allegiance in Scotland and whose status as either English rebels or Scottish enemies was therefore unclear,[103] but race was apparently no determinant of nationality. In many parts of Ireland, however, there were no stable frontiers, and the primary determinants of nationality came to be race supported by culture. An O'Toole or O'Byrne would normally be accounted an Irishman, unless he had been granted a charter of denization. The position was less clear if he had been born within the English Pale or was long resident there. An Irish statute of 1477 prohibited Irishmen resident in the Englishry from demanding a *saute* (or monetary composition), in accordance with Brehon Law, for the death of an Irish enemy of the same nation caught and slain there. It enacted instead that if an Irish enemy committed any offence, any of the king's subjects might arrest for redress an Irishman of the same nation and using the Irish habit who was answerable, but not amenable, to common law. Similarly, a well-known act of 1465 required Irishmen living among Englishmen in the Pale to dress like Englishmen, be sworn the king's liege men, and take an English-style surname. The two statutes suggest that formal charters of English liberty might not always have been necessary.[104] Yet there was apparently no Irish parallel to a clan like the Armstrongs with English and Scottish branches, nor any northern parallel to the repeated statutes requiring Englishmen and Irishmen resident in the Englishry to dress in an English fashion.[105]

---

[102] 'The English realm and dominions and the king's subjects in the later middle ages', 83–105.

[103] e.g. Henry Summerson, 'Crime and society in medieval Cumberland', in *C. & W.*, 2nd ser. 82 (1982), 114–15.

[104] Parliament rolls, 5 Edward IV c. 16, 16 & 17 Edward IV c. 10 (*Stat. Ire., Edw. IV*, i. 290, ii. 528–32).

[105] e.g. Parliament rolls, 25 Henry VI c. 20, 5 Edward IV cc. 12–17 (*Stat. Ire., Hen. VI*, 88, *Edw. IV*, i. 288–92).

It should be emphasized that this comparison between the far
north and the Pale is not intended to suggest that the cultures of
the Gaelic clans and northern surnames were almost identical.
Clearly, there were important differences, not least in terms of
language and dress. Overall, however, there was a growing aware-
ness in official circles during the early-Tudor period of certain
close resemblances between the northern upland lineages and the
wild Irish. And from the 1520s, at least, official perceptions of the
differences between civility and savagery came to exercise a more
general influence on the government's strategy in dealing with the
problem of the borders, with unfortunate consequences. As we
have seen, because of its centralized and uniform character, early-
Tudor government faced very similar problems in the far north
and the Pale; and among royal officials and lowland gentry the
upland cultures of the marches induced similar feelings of revulsion. Yet official perceptions of the northern surnames and
marcher lineages as a rude, uncivilized people also helped to dis-
tract the government from addressing the basic problem, the crisis
of lordship, or the failure to provide adequate resources for the rule
and defence of an exposed periphery.

As we shall see in the next two chapters, this crisis of lordship
heightened the differences in power structures between the borderlands and lowland England. The crown's delegation of responsibility for the rule and defence of the marches was a major
reason for the apparently excessive power of the marcher lords and
the importance of their bastard feudal connexions in these regions.
The needs of defence impelled the gentry to seek the protection
of the great lords. Conversely, the irregular operation of royal
government there reduced the importance of the kind of direct
links between crown and gentry which were fostered by the Tudors in lowland England.

Under the first Tudor, the crisis of lordship was of little concern
to the crown, since Henry VII's policy for the borderlands was a
minimalist one of maintaining just enough control to safeguard his
own security. Indeed in Ireland this had in effect been established
policy since the 1460s, and Tudor attitudes to Ireland altered only
slowly from the 1520s. When, however, Henry VIII eventually
responded to the inevitable complaints of 'lack of governance' in
the borderlands, it was the activities of the border lineages rather
than the reduced provision for the defence of these regions which

attracted the king's attention. If the highland men had become 'wild' through 'lack of governance', the obvious solution was to execute sharp justice among them.

Thus, in retrospect, the years from Henry Tudor's accession to the onset of the Reformation crisis appear as a distinct period in border administration. They witnessed the drastic curtailment of financial and military subventions by the central government and a comparative neglect of good rule, initially in favour of dynastic security. And when the resultant 'lack of governance' prompted a more interventionist approach in the 1530s, the attention of officials was focused on the problem of degeneracy and the activities of the border lineages rather than the crisis of lordship. This then was the political environment in which border magnates like Dacre and Kildare were expected to operate. The next part of the study investigates how they responded to this challenge.

PART II

Noble power and border rule

3

The estates and connexion of Lord Dacre of the North

SOCIETY in the west march at Henry Tudor's accession had long been dominated by a few great families. Foremost were the Percies who held the honour of Cockermouth and half the barony of Egremont in west Cumberland. The estates of their erstwhile rivals, the Nevilles of Middleham, which included the lordship of Penrith and Castle Sowerby in the south, had recently been forfeited to the crown, which also had title to Liddel Strength and Bewcastle in the wasteland abutting the border line. Apart from Lord Dacre, the only other prominent Cumberland tenant-in-chief was Lord Greystoke, with estates around Greystoke castle, while to the south the barony of Westmorland was held by the Cliffords. In 1429, according to an inquisition taken into knights' fees, there were only two other crown tenants in Cumberland who held as much as half a knight's fee. The properties of other tenants were small indeed.[1] Thus the large numbers of wealthy county gentry who were so influential in local politics further south were effectively absent from the west marches.

A Dacre first became sheriff of Cumberland in 1248, and with the acquisition of Gilsland in 1317 the nucleus of the Dacre estates as they existed in 1485 had already been assembled. Under Richard II Lord Dacre was one of three or four nobles regularly included on commissions of wardenry for the west march, but thereafter the Dacres were overshadowed by the Nevilles and then Richard of Gloucester.[2] Their status as border barons stemmed chiefly from their possession of two of the most northerly of the great feudal baronies created in twelfth-century Cumbria to keep out the Scots.

---

[1] *Inquisitions and assessments relating to Feudal Aids . . . 1284–1431*, 4 vols. (London, 1899–1906), i. 244–5; Storey, *End of the house of Lancaster*, 106–7.
[2] Storey, 'Wardens of the marches', 609–11; id., *End of the house of Lancaster*, 124; Harrison, *Pilgrimage of Grace in the Lake Counties*, 26–7.

In north-east Cumberland they held the barony of Gilsland, a compact block of fifteen manors with a perimeter of over 80 miles which extended from the Northumberland county boundary to within a few miles of Carlisle.[3] The small baronies of Liddel and Levington, north of Carlisle, controlled the central portion of the marches, while to the west lay the Dacre barony of Burgh-by-Sands, which protected the region from Scottish raids across the Solway Firth.[4] Thus Dacre played a key role in the defence of the west marches. Yet the exposed location of his estates also meant that they were regularly destroyed by Scottish raids and provided an uncertain source of income.[5] Elsewhere, his only considerable possessions were the barony of Barton, and the manors of Hoffe and Orton, held of the Clifford family, in Westmorland, and three manors in Lancashire.[6] Not surprisingly, therefore, the Dacres fared poorly in those tables of landed income by which historians appear to determine the relative importance of individual members of the English nobility. For the income tax of 1436, Dacre was rated as among the poorest of the baronage, worth only £320 per annum.[7] Throughout this period, in fact, the family just struggled along: successive lords avoided the worst accidents of inheritance and high politics, but failed to add significantly to the Dacre possessions. The fourteenth-century English expansion into southern Scotland and a Maxwell marriage brought the Dacres a paper rental of 400 marks for Liddesdale and Hermitage castle, and they added to this by purchasing the manor of Nether Crailing in Roxburghshire, worth a nominal £40; but with the collapse of the English Pale there the Dacres were left with worthless titles.[8]

The dynastic strife of the mid-fifteenth century brought both new opportunities and new dangers. When the 6th Baron Dacre

---

[3] Vicary Gibbs *et al.* (eds.), *The Complete Peerage by G.E.C.*, 13 vols. (London, 1910–59), iv. 1–2; Winchester, *Landscape and society in medieval Cumbria*, 16; T. H. B. Graham, 'The border manors', in *C. & W.*, NS 11 (1911), 41, 46–7; Bouch and Jones, *Lake Counties*, 88.

[4] Graham, 'Border manors', 1–7 Ric. II, no. 972; *Cal. inq. p.m., Hen. VII*, i, no. 157.

[5] *Cal. inq. p.m., 1–7 Ric. II*, no. 972; *Cal. inq. p.m., Hen. VII*, i, no. 157.

[6] *Cal. inq. p.m., Ric. II*, nos. 971, 973; *Cal. inq. p.m., Hen. VII*, i, no. 10.

[7] H. L. Gray, 'Incomes from land in England in 1436', in *EHR* 49 (1934), 617–18. T. B. Pugh and C. D. Ross, 'The English baronage and the income tax of 1436', in *IHR Bull.*, 26 (1953), 1–28, demonstrate that the assessments were generally too low.

[8] Durham, H. of N. MS C/201/4A; Castle Howard, MS F1/5/5, fos. 25v–6; Goodman, 'Anglo-Scottish marches', 20–4.

died in 1458, his heir-general was his granddaughter, whose husband then received the family title and was later known as Lord
Dacre of the South. In the event, the Dacre family lost only three
manors in Lancashire and Lincolnshire by this, because most of
the estates were entailed and passed to the lord's second son,
Randolph, as heir-male. He was created 1st Lord Dacre of
Gilsland (his successors were also described as Lord Dacre of the
North), but was killed fighting for Henry VI at Towton, and
attainted.[9] A younger brother, Humphrey, claimed the title and
held out for Henry VI in the Dacre stronghold of Naworth until
July 1462, when he surrendered to Lord Montagu.[10] Initially, this
allowed the heirs-general to take possession of the Dacre estates,
but Dacre was gradually rehabilitated and in 1472 the attainder was
reversed by parliament. Finally, by award of King Edward IV in
April 1473, Humphrey, Lord Dacre, recovered possession of the
ancestral estates in Cumberland and Westmorland and also, somewhat surprisingly, the manor of Halton in the duchy of Lancaster.[11] Subsequently, Dacre served as deputy to the king's brother
and lieutenant, Richard, duke of Gloucester, and was appointed to
the king's council. And after Richard had seized the throne, he
kept the wardenship of the west march in his own hands and
appointed Dacre as his lieutenant.[12] Dacre's salary as lieutenant,
£200 per annum, and the annuity of 100 marks which the king also
granted him, thus meant that the 2nd lord died a comparatively
wealthy and influential man, even though many of his estates
had been devastated by the Scots following renewed war with
Scotland.[13] Moreover, in view of Dacre's close identification
with Richard III, his death in May 1485 on the eve of Bosworth
perhaps also made it easier for the family to avoid a repeat of the
débâcle of 1461.[14]

[9] Gibbs *et al.* (eds.), *Complete peerage*, iv. 8–22.
[10] Charles Ross, *Edward IV* (London, 1974), 48, 50; John Gillingham, *The Wars
of the Roses* (London, 1981), 138, 140–1.
[11] Gibbs *et al.* (eds.), *Complete peerage*, iv. 1, 7, 18–19; Ross, *Edward IV*, 69 n.;
Cal. pat. rolls, 1461–7, 140, *1467–77*, 26, 90, 96, 183.
[12] Charles Ross, *Richard III* (London, 1981), 160; *Cal. pat. rolls, 1476–85*, 485–6;
Horrox, *Richard III*, 65, 217, 259; *British Library Harleian Manuscript 433*, ed. R.
Horrox and P. W. Hammond, 4 vols., Richard III society (London, 1979–83), i. 136;
J. R. Lander, *Crown and nobility 1450–1509* (London, 1976), 318–19.
[13] *Cal. pat. rolls, 1476–85*, 388, 485–6; *Harleian MS 433*, ii. 136; *Cal. inq. p.m.*,
Hen. VII, i, no. 157.
[14] Horrox, *Richard III*, 65, 217, 259.

Despite the 2nd lord's career, the transformation of the Dacres from impoverished border barons into great regional magnates stemmed in large measure from the marriage of Thomas, 3rd Lord Dacre, to Elizabeth Greystoke, heiress of a much wealthier baronial family. The marriage occurred shortly after the death of her grandfather, Ralph, Lord Greystoke, in June 1487, when Dacre abducted her from the Clifford castle of Brougham.[15] Yet there is more to the marriage than meets the eye. To abduct the king's ward was a serious offence—Henry VII later fined Dacre's mother 1,000 marks (wrongfully, it was alleged) for ravishing a royal ward.[16] Yet to marry a wealthy heiress such as Lady Greystoke in a conventional aristocratic marriage of the period would have been far beyond the means of a poor border baron. And even after the marriage, it was only through the king's favour and the untimely deaths, in turn, of her uncle, Sir John Greystoke, and his son, that Dacre had secured, by the end of the reign, the whole Greystoke inheritance.[17] Much later, in 1523, Dacre himself threw some light on the circumstances, when writing to his son-in-law, Lord Scrope, about a projected marriage between Scrope's grandson and the daughter of Lady Parr. Dacre urged that if Scrope were

disposed to marie hym before or [*sic*] he com to full age, when he may haue some saing hym self, I cannot see, w'out that ye wold mary hym to one heir of land, which wolbe right costly, that ye can mary hym to so good a stok as my Lady Parr.

Dacre then remarked that Parr's daughter 'has but one child betwene her & viij[c] marc. land', which he thought to mention 'because of the possibilitie that fell vnto my self by my marriage'.[18]

If we assume that the Greystoke marriage had been contracted when the couple were very young—he was almost 21 and she

---

[15] *Selections from the household books of the Lord William Howard of Naworth castle*, ed. George Ornsby, Surtees Society, lxviii (Durham, 1877), 391; Gibbs *et al.* (eds.), *Complete peerage*, vi. 197–201; R. S. Ferguson, *History of Cumberland* (London, 1890), 164–6.

[16] Lander, *Crown and nobility*, 292 n.

[17] Gibbs *et al.* (eds.), *Complete peerage*, vi. 197–202. Cf. Barbara J. Harris, *Edward Stafford, 3rd duke of Buckingham* (Stanford, Calif., 1986), 51–7, for a useful discussion of aristocratic marriages under the early Tudors.

[18] BL, Add. MS 24,965, fos. 200ᵛ–1 (*L. & P. Hen. VIII*, iii, no. 3649). This projected marriage is discussed in a different context in Barbara J. Harris, 'Women and politics in early Tudor England', in *Hist. Jn.*, 33 (1990), 262.

was just 16 when it was celebrated—then this would broadly ac-
cord with the contingencies which had occurred in Dacre's case.
Elizabeth Greystoke's father, Lord Greystoke's son and heir apparent, had died in 1483, leaving no other children, although he
had a younger brother, Sir John Greystoke, who now stood to
inherit the feudal barony of Greystoke and those lands which had
been entailed to the heirs male.[19] In the circumstances, Lord
Greystoke apparently decided to divide his estates between his
granddaughter and younger son. By common recoveries, some of
his lands in Yorkshire, Northumberland, Cumberland, and
Westmorland were held to the use of Sir John in tail male; and
between 1484 and 1486, by another set of recoveries affecting other
lands, the earlier entail was cut off so that the lands descended in
fee.[20] Despite this, when Lord Greystoke finally died in 1487, there
ensued a long, complicated dispute over the Greystoke inheritance
between his male heir and his heir-general.

Initially, Lord Dacre seems to have profited very little by his
marriage. Inquisitions *post mortem* concerning the Greystoke lands
in six counties (Bedfordshire, Cumberland, Leicestershire, Shropshire, Suffolk, and Westmorland) all returned that Elizabeth
Greystoke was the heiress and aged 13 or more; although, as Dacre
later proved, she was in fact within forty days of her sixteenth
birthday.[21] Even so, in December 1487 the king granted the ward-
ship and marriage of Elizabeth and the keeping of all the lands
of her grandfather and father during her minority to the earl of
Oxford.[22] As the male heir, Sir John Greystoke took the title of
Lord Greystoke and claimed the barony of Greystoke and other
estates, briefly occupying Greystoke castle in 1489.[23] Thus the
king was for long able to use the dispute over the Greystoke
inheritance as a kind of bond for Dacre's good behaviour as
lieutenant of the west marches. Lord Greystoke was allowed
possession of the family's four manors in the palatinate of
Durham, although in 1490 he had to assign one of them as dower

---

[19] Gibbs *et al.* (eds.), *Complete peerage*, vi. 197–202.

[20] *L. & P. Hen. VIII*, i (2nd edn.), no. 381(15); *Household books of the Lord William Howard*, 375–7.

[21] *Cal. inq. p.m., Hen. VII*, i, nos. 231, 243, 245, 304, 307, 432; Gibbs *et al.* (eds.), *Complete peerage*, vi. 198–9. Elizabeth Greystoke was also returned as heiress of one acre of land in Northumberland: *Cal. inq. p.m., Hen. VII*, iii, no. 1010.

[22] *Cal. pat. rolls, 1485–94*, 178, 197.

[23] Ibid. 285–6; Gibbs *et al.* (eds.), *Complete peerage*, vi. 201–2.

for his father's widow.[24] He apparently also got possession of the
Greystoke lands in Yorkshire,[25] and also of the lands in the barony
in Westmorland, chiefly the manor of Dufton. In 1499, however,
when the death of the rector of Dufton presented Lord Dacre with
an excuse to seize possession of the manor and to intrude his
brother as rector of the parish, the king responded by taking the
manor into his own hands.[26] Dacre was required to enter into a
recognizance in £500 'for keping of the peax anempst the Lord
Graystoke', and for his appearance in Star Chamber.[27] And then in
July, the king cynically regranted the Greystoke lands in
Westmorland to Lord Greystoke, to be held by him during the
minority of Elizabeth Greystoke.[28] Finally, Lord Greystoke's
claim to the barony of Greystoke was eventually also admitted,
although probably not until after his death in 1501 allowed the
king to keep possession as guardian of his son and heir, John, then
aged 14.[29]

In fact, Lord Greystoke's death seems to have broken the im-
passe, and over the next nine years Lord Dacre gradually secured
possession of the whole Greystoke inheritance. In 1502 Dacre paid
the king 250 marks 'for lyuerey of his lands', and agreed to pay a
further £100 a year; and in 1505 he owed another 400 marks 'for the
lyverey of his landes and his wyffes landes'.[30] Yet many of the more
important Greystoke lands were still in the king's hands in 1505,
and in order to secure them Dacre was obliged to allow the king
effective control of many of his own estates in Cumberland and
Westmorland. In 1506 he allowed several recoveries of his lands for

---

[24] Ibid.; *Cal. inq. p.m., Hen. VII*, ii, no. 560. See also S. E. Thorne (ed.),
Prerogative regis (New Haven, Conn., 1949), 87, which shows that some time before
1495 Robert Constable, who had married Ralph, Lord Greystoke's widow, claimed
his wife's dower from Lord Dacre. (I am grateful to Dr Henry Summerson for this
reference.) Subsequently, a new inquisition for the manor of Wybolston, Beds.,
found that the late Lord Greystoke's wife was in possession, but that the heir to the
estate was unknown: *Cal. inq. p.m., Hen. VII*, iii, no. 885.
[25] *Cal. inq. p.m., Hen. VII*, i, no. 363, ii, nos. 38, 90, 105, iii, no. 275.
[26] PRO, STAC 2/18/268, STAC 2/34/51.
[27] PRO, SP 1/1, fo. 71ᵛ (*L. & P. Hen. VIII*, i (2nd edn.), no. 131).
[28] *Cal. pat. rolls, 1494–1509*, 177.
[29] Gibbs *et al.* (eds.), *Complete peerage*, vi. 201–2; *Cal. pat. rolls, 1494–1509*, 452,
554, 564, 587.
[30] PRO, E 36/214, 430, 498; E 101/413/2/3, 20. In Apr. 1504 Dacre was given
special livery, without proof of age, of the lands of his father, with a pardon of
intrusions and a grant of the profits, without account, since his death: Castle
Howard, MS A1/187 (*Cal. pat. rolls, 1494–1509*, 333).

payment of a debt of £1,333. 6s. 8d. at the rate of £100 a year, and in 1509 after the death of his mother, the instalments were increased to £240 a year by virtue of several more recoveries.[31] Only in 1507 were Dacre and his wife given special livery, without proof of age, of all the lands of Ralph, Lord Greystoke, but still without prejudice to the king or John, baron of Greystoke, concerning any manors which should descend to the latter.[32] These apparently still excluded the barony of Greystoke, and the Greystoke lands in the palatinate of Durham, which only came into Lord Dacre's hands following the sudden death of the young John Greystoke from sweating sickness in August 1508.[33] And the fact that, despite the special livery, Elizabeth Dacre had to submit to a proof of age in Northumberland in June 1509, even though she was then almost 38 years old, suggests that she did not secure possession of her estates in that county until then.[34]

The barons of Greystoke had been a considerably wealthier family than the Dacres. In 1436, Lord Greystoke's lands had been rated as worth £650 per annum for the income tax, or just over twice the value of Dacre's inheritance: and even this was a considerable underassessment, for a valor of the Greystoke estates in 1426 indicated a clear value of £847. 10s. 4¾d.[35] Moreover, the Greystoke inheritance was scattered throughout the north, with most of it well away from the border, so that Dacre now had a dependable source of income even when his own ancestral possessions were swept by Scottish raids. Strategically the most important of these new estates was the barony of Greystoke, with Greystoke castle. This lay on the southern side of Inglewood Forest and the king's lordship of Penrith—the farm of which was

---

[31] PRO, E 101/413/2/3, 20; Castle Howard, MSS A1/188, A1/191, A1/192, A1/220. The indenture and recoveries by which this transaction was arranged are summarized (rather inaccurately) in *Household books of the Lord William Howard*, ed. Ornsby, 384–5.

[32] PRO, C 66/601, m. 3 (26) (*Cal. pat. rolls, 1494–1509*, 506). The original deed is Castle Howard, MS A1/189. Cf. Gibbs *et al.* (eds.), *Complete peerage*, vi. 200.

[33] Gibbs *et al.* (eds.), *Complete peerage*, vi. 200–2; *Cal. pat. rolls, 1494–1509*, 554, 564, 587. Dacre and his wife received special livery of the Greystoke lands in Durham in Nov. 1508: Castle Howard, MS A1/190.

[34] PRO, C 142/24, no. 78. I am grateful to Dr Henry Summerson for this reference.

[35] Castle Howard, MS F1/5/2; Gray, 'Incomes from land in England', 617–18. This excluded the barony of Wemme and the manor of Hinstock in Shropshire, which were valued at £161. 6s. 8d. in 1487: *Cal. inq. p.m., Hen. VII*, i, no. 231.

normally granted to the warden—and formed a useful staging post
between the Dacre baronies in northern Cumberland and his
Westmorland estates. The acquisition of the feudal overlordship of
the ancestral manor of Dacre, with Soulby and Newbiggin, formerly held of Lord Greystoke, also marked the final stage in the
family's transformation from mesne tenants of the baronies of
Multon and Greystoke into the crown's principal tenant-in-chief
in Cumberland.[36] The barony of Greystoke itself was worth £200 a
year or more, but still more valuable was the Greystoke lordship
of Henderskelf (now Castle Howard) in the East Riding of Yorkshire, worth £270 per annum, while the barony of Morpeth in
Northumberland (worth c.£180 per annum) provided Dacre with a
useful base in the middle marches. Dacre's acquisitions also included substantial estates in Shropshire (the barony of Wemme
and manor of Hinstock, worth c.£130 per annum) and in the
palatinate of Durham (the manors of High and Low Coniscliffe,
Neasham, and Brierton, worth c.£100 a year). Finally, there were
isolated manors in Westmorland (Dufton, worth c.£20 a year, held
of the Cliffords), Leicestershire (Northborough, c.£20), Bedfordshire (Wyboston, c.£10), and Suffolk (Willisham, c.£8).[37] In practice, the inquisitions *post mortem* on the Greystoke lands valued
some of the estates at rather less than these figures, notably the
barony of Greystoke at only £128. 10s. 7d. which may have been
affected by the Scottish wars. Even so, the combined value of the
Dacre and Greystoke estates must have ensured Thomas, Lord
Dacre, an income of at least £1,250 a year.[38] From a poor border
baron, Dacre had become a leading northern magnate.

[36] *Cal. inq. p.m., Hen. VII*, i, nos. 157, 245; Ferguson, *History of Cumberland*,
160–6; Susan Cott, 'The wardenship of Thomas Lord Dacre 1485–1525', MA
thesis, University of Manchester, 1971, 7–8.

[37] Calculated from Castle Howard, MSS F1/5/1, F1/5/2; Durham, H. of N. MSS
C/201/2, C/201/3; PRO, C 54/394, m. 7; *Cal. inq. p.m., Hen. VII*, i, nos. 231, 243, 245,
304, 307, 432, ii, no. 560.

[38] *Cal. inq. p.m., Hen. VII*, i, nos. 10, 157, 231, 243, 245, 304, 307, 432, ii, nos. 560,
809, 819, iii, nos. 885, 1010. The surviving records concerning the administration of
the Dacre estates under the early Tudors are unfortunately quite scanty. After the
death of George, 6th Lord Dacre, in 1569, and the rebellion of his brother, Leonard,
most of the estates eventually passed to Lord William Howard, ancestor of the earls
of Carlisle: Gibbs *et al.* (eds.), *Complete peerage*, iv. 23–6. The Dacre muniments
were later divided and passed to Durham University and Castle Howard respectively, with a few items ending up in the Cumbria Record Office, Carlisle. For the
purposes of this study, the most important are those in the Department of Palaeography and Diplomatic at Durham, which include a set of receivers' accounts for

Like other Tudor magnates, the Dacres organized the administration of their estates with the aim of maximizing their power and influence in those areas which they regarded as coming under their rule. In particular, they attempted to secure additional lands in these areas, either by purchase, lease, or gift from the crown, or sometimes by exchanging with other landowners possessions in less favoured locations for more desirable properties. In Dacre's case, however, considerations of border defence imparted an added urgency and a particular character to his estate management policies. The key to the defence of the English west march was the most northerly barony of Liddel, with its castle known as Liddel Strength built on a clay cliff commanding the crossing of the river Liddel 160 feet below.[39] An inquisition of 1282 valued the barony at over £295 per annum;[40] but, with the outbreak of hostilities along the Anglo-Scottish border in 1296, the barony was reduced to a war zone.[41] The castle was captured and destroyed by the Scots in 1346, and in 1351 the barony was granted to Edward III by the earls of Kent and remained in crown hands, later as part of the duchy of Lancaster, until 1603.[42] In the circumstances, much of the burden of defence fell on the mesne lords of the small barony of Levington immediately to the south, and on the lords of the manors held of the adjoining baronies of Burgh and Gilsland. Levington was divided between six heiresses in 1281, and in the fourteenth century none of the four lords who acquired sixths and thirds was resident there. Subsequently, many of these mesne lordships were further divided, so that the defence of the march was thoroughly undermined by partition and absenteeism. By the late fifteenth

21–2 Henry VIII (1529–30), together with the receiver-general's summary book of receipts for the years 1530 to 1551, and some rentals and a feodary, mainly of Gilsland: Durham, H. of N. MSS C/201/2–9. The Castle Howard Archives include a collection of Dacre and Greystoke deeds, a miscellaneous volume misleadingly entitled 'Description of the boundary of Gilsland', and two early Greystoke valors: Castle Howard, MSS A1, F1/5/1–2, 5. Finally, the Howard of Greystoke archive in the Cumbria Record Office, Carlisle, includes an account of a general fine (gressum) on the barony of Greystoke, 1472, and a survey of the barony c.1520: Carlisle, MSS D/HG/16, 18. All three archives include more estate material relating to the mid-Tudor period and later.

[39] J. F. Curwen, 'Liddel Mote', in *C. & W.*, NS 10 (1910), 93–7.
[40] T. H. B. Graham, 'The annals of Liddel', ibid., NS 13 (1913), 45–50.
[41] Winchester, *Landscape and society in medieval Cumbria*, 44.
[42] T. H. B. Graham, 'Six extinct Cumberland castles', in *C. & W.*, NS 9 (1909), 212–14.

century much of the region was waste and uninhabited and had been for many years.[43]

These developments highlighted Dacre's key position in the defence of the west marches. Over half of the lord's patrimony lay in northern Cumberland, and the barony of Greystoke swelled the value of Dacre's Cumberland estates to around £650 a year, over £100 more than the Percy possessions there, which in any case were in the strategically less important west of the county.[44] To a large extent the very concentration of his holdings in this region shaped the nature of Dacre's political ambitions. His estates in northern Cumberland lay open even to minor Scottish incursions, and needed a resident lord to defend them. The inquisitions *post mortem*, taken in winter 1485–6 after the death of the 2nd lord, returned that many of the lord's manors there were destroyed by the Scots, totally wasted by the Scottish war, or worth nothing in time of war. For example, the whole barony of Gilsland, which had once been worth £116. 17s. $8\frac{3}{4}d$. per annum, was valued at a mere £17. 12s. $4\frac{2}{3}d$. annually. And large tracts were waste because no one would farm them for fear of the Scots.[45]

The response of successive Lords Dacre to this situation evidently mirrored that of marcher lords elsewhere in the British Isles, including the Fitzgeralds in Ireland as we shall see. They tried to strengthen the Cumberland marches by buying up titles to land, building peles and castles, and attracting in new tenants for their defence. Already in Henry VI's reign, Thomas, 6th Baron Dacre (1399–1458), had bought out the mesne lords who held the manors of Aikton and Blackhall of his barony of Burgh, and a moiety of the manor of Castle Carrock and the manor of Brackenthwayte held of his barony of Gilsland.[46] And this policy of purchasing freeholds from minor gentry who were feudal tenants of the Dacre baronies continued under Humphrey, 2nd Lord Dacre of Gilsland, who purchased two-thirds of the mesne manor

[43] *Cal. inq. p.m., Hen. VII*, i, no. 157, ii, no. 292, iii, no. 68. For the feudal descent of these lordships, see esp., Graham, 'Border manors', 38–51.

[44] Durham, H. of N. MSS C/201/2–3; Bean, *Estates of the Percy family*, 46.

[45] PRO, E 150/112 (*Cal. inq. p.m., Hen. VII*, i, no. 157).

[46] 'An accompt of the most considerable estates and families in the county of Cumberland. By John Denton', ed. R. S. Ferguson, in *C. & W. Tract Series*, 2 (1887), 72, 104, 137; Henry Barnes, 'Aikton church', in *C. & W.*, NS 13 (1913), 267–8; T. H. B. Graham, 'The manor of Blakhale', ibid., NS 18 (1918), 129; id., 'The eastern fells', ibid. 19 (1919), 103.

of Cumrew (Gilsland barony), and Thomas, 3rd Lord.[47] John Denton in his *Accompt* alleged that in this way the Dacres gradually wrung out all the freeholders of Irthington and Brampton within Gilsland, except the manor of Corby.[48] No doubt these marchlands could be purchased very cheaply because many of them were largely waste, and remained so in 1486. The manors of Brackenthwayte and half of Castle Carrock, for instance, were then worth just 7s. and 5s. a year respectively; and the lord's two-thirds of the manor of Cumrew was valued at a mere 6s. 8d.[49]

Under Thomas, the 3rd lord, this policy of land acquisition accelerated, no doubt reflecting the family's enhanced position in the region. Among his more valuable purchases were freeholds in Bowness, Etterby, Rockcliffe, Brimstath-on-Esk, Thursby, and Aikton—all held of the barony of Burgh—the manor of Little Croglin, parcel of the Dacre manor of Kirkoswald, and lands in Tryermain near Bewcastle in the barony of Gilsland.[50] He also exchanged the manor of Warnell in Sebergham parish, south of Carlisle, with his cousin, John Denton, for the manor of Nether Denton in Gilsland.[51] Lord Thomas took a particular interest in the strategically important border manors lying between, and north of, Burgh and Gilsland. Within Levington barony, the family had already acquired the chief or cornage rents of the Kirkbride inheritance in two of the barony's four manors (Kirkandrews-on-Eden, and Orton), and in 1505 Lord Thomas laid claim, unsuccessfully, to the Kirkbride third of the manor of Kirklinton. Yet by 1530 the Dacres had purchased most, if not all, the freehold of Kirkandrews and enjoyed a rental there of almost £11.[52] On the north bank of the Eden, the manor of Westlinton, and twelve miles

[47] *Cal. inq. p.m., Hen. VII*, i, no. 157; Graham, 'Eastern fells', 103–6.
[48] *Accompt*, ed. Ferguson, 140. See also Castle Howard, MS A1/180: deed of 1493 by which Clement Blennerhasset of Carlisle sold his lands in Fenton in Gilsland to Dacre for 100s. Cf. T. H. B. Graham, 'The annals of Hayton', in *C. & W.*, NS 25 (1925), 313–14.
[49] *Cal. inq. p.m., Hen. VII*, i, no. 157.
[50] Durham, H. of N. MS C/201/2, mm 7–8d, 11d; *Cal. inq. p.m., Hen. VII*, i, no. 157; Graham, 'Eastern fells. Part II', 35–8.
[51] T. H. B. Graham, 'The family of Denton', in *C. & W.*, NS 16 (1916), 49; Durham, H. of N. MS C/201/2, m. 10; James, *Society, politics and culture*, 142.
[52] Durham, H. of N. MS C/201/2, mm 7, 8; *Cal. inq. p.m., Hen. VII*, i, no. 157; C. R. Huddleston, 'Cumberland and Westmorland feet of fines in the reign of Henry VII', in *C. & W.*, NS 66 (1966), 164 (Dacre quitclaimed his right to Kirklinton in return for 100 marks). Cf. Graham, 'Border manors', 43–5.

away in the extreme north-east of the county, the manor of
Bewcastle, were actually held of the barony of Burgh. Lord
Thomas purchased Westlinton, apparently in 1490; and in
Bewcastledale, where in 1486 Dacre had held just one waste ten-
ement, he also gradually bought up freehold tenements.[53] Finally,
just before his death he also bought the Stapleton inheritance,
including a moiety of the manor of Stapleton, held of his barony of
Gilsland.[54]

Altogether, Lord Thomas's land purchases alone were yielding
an income of £104. 18s. 0½d. a year by 1530, and this did not
include his lands in Bewcastledale.[55] Very significantly, however,
almost all these lands were located in the one area. Apart from a
few minor purchases around Netherton and Morpeth in Northumberland and on his Shrewsbury estates,[56] Lord Thomas concentrated his efforts on northern Cumberland. He was normally
resident in the area, and even when in his later years he was
required, as warden-general, to reside at Harbottle or Morpeth in
the middle marches, his brother, Sir Christopher, or his son, Lord
William, was on hand to oversee the defence of the region. Revealingly, the life grant which Sir Christopher received of certain
Dacre possessions consisted chiefly of marchlands (Westlevington,
Brimstath, and Blackhall, worth £61 a year); while Dacre's other
brother, Sir Philip, who normally resided in Northumberland was
given a similar life grant of Dacre lands in that county.[57] Thus
there seems little doubt that the chief motive for the purchase of so
much marchland was military, although no doubt the additional

---

[53] PRO, SP 1/36, fos. 238–45 (*L. & P. Hen. VIII*, iv (i), no. 1855), SP 1/141, fos.
248–51 (*L. & P. Hen. VIII*, xiii (ii), app. no. 36); STAC 2/19/127; Durham, H. of
N. MS C/201/2, mm 7, 8; *Cal. inq. p.m., Hen. VII*, i, no. 157, iii, no. 68; T. H. B.
Graham, 'The de Levingtons of Kirklinton', in *C. & W.*, NS 12 (1912), 68; id.,
'Border manors', 43.

[54] Durham, H. of N. MS C/201/2, mm 10, 11d; PRO, SP 1/36, fos. 238–45 (*L. &
P. Hen. VIII*, iv (i), no. 1855).

[55] The value of Lord Thomas's land purchases is calculated from Durham, H. of
N. MS C/201/2, where they are so marked. For the lands in Bewcastledale, which
in 1530 were the subject of a dispute with Sir William Musgrave, see PRO, STAC
2/19/127 (the document is dated by *L. & P. Hen. VIII*, xiv (i), no. 750), and below,
pp. 95–7, 199–205.

[56] Durham, H. of N. MS C/201/2, mm 22, 23d, 24, 28d. The most significant of
these were the lands around Netherton acquired from Robert, Lord Ogle, in 1521
and worth around £3 per annum: Castle Howard, MS A1/198; Durham, H. of N.
MS C/201/2, m. 24.

[57] Durham, H. of N. MS C/201/2, mm 8d, 24; PRO, C 54/394, m. 7.

income was also welcome. By contrast, William, the 4th lord, could afford to buy lands elsewhere. Although Dacre expansion in northern Cumberland continued under Lord William— already by 1530 his purchases there were worth an additional £8. 1s. 3d. per annum—his principal project of this period was the attempted purchase in 1531 of the substantial inheritance of Sir James Strangeways who had large estates in Yorkshire and Northumberland.[58]

Fortunately, a little further light is thrown on the circumstances of Dacre expansion in northern Cumberland by a few other scraps of evidence, many of which were generated by litigation between Lord William and Sir William Musgrave in the 1530s. Sir John Stapleton told one of his tenants that he was selling his Cumberland possessions to Dacre 'because he dwelt at London so farre from his land & that his tenauntes coud haue no socoure of hym'; and after he had received the final payment he commented 'that he wold by asmoche land nerer hand to hym for asmoche money as he had of my said lorde for his land'.[59] Yet because Dacre was resident in the district and now had the resources to defend and develop these borderlands, some of them showed an astonishing increase in value. The manor of Westlinton, for instance, was worth £21. 6s. 8d. a year by 1530, which was considerably more than its value (£10) in 1303, shortly after the start of the Anglo-Scottish wars;[60] while the manor of Blackhall, valued at a mere £3. 3s. $1\frac{1}{2}d$. net in 1486, when it was largely waste, yielded the much more considerable sum of £27. 6s. 2d. in 1530.[61] Similarly, the Dacre moiety of the manor of Castle Carrock had increased in value from 5s. a year in 1486 to £12. 13s. $7\frac{1}{2}d$. in 1530.[62]

These improvements are attributable to changes in three main areas. First and foremost, the Dacres embarked on a very necess-

---

[58] Durham, H. of N. MS C/201/2; *Household books of the Lord William Howard*, ed. Ornsby, 386–8; *L. & P. Hen. VIII*, xix (i), no. 25. Strangeways married Ann, sister of Thomas, Lord Dacre. On his death in 1541 the common-law heirs disputed the Dacre title, and this led to an award by the king's council which was subsequently confirmed by act of parliament. By this, Dacre was granted nine manors, mainly in Yorkshire, and the reversion of a further £80-worth of land, but the dispute dragged on into the 1560s.

[59] PRO, SP 1/36, fos. 242, 243ᵛ.

[60] Durham, H. of N. MS C/201/2, mm 7, 8; Graham, 'De Levingtons of Kirklinton', 68.

[61] *Cal. inq. p.m., Hen. VII*, i, no. 157; Durham, H. of N. MS C/201/2, m. 8d.

[62] *Cal. inq. p.m., Hen. VII*, i, no. 157; Durham, H. of N. MS C/201/2, m. 11d.

ary policy of castle-building, a policy which must have appeared curiously anachronistic, if not sinister, to those in lowland England who were unacquainted with the realities of life on the border. Kirkoswald castle and Dacre tower were both described as newly built in the inquisitions taken in 1486 after the death of Lord Humphrey, but Lord Thomas strengthened Kirkoswald with a large ditch. He also substantially rebuilt Naworth castle, repairing the upper part of the Dacre tower there, rebuilding the other tower, and adding a hall, houses, and offices to form an outer bailey.[63] Closer to the border, Lord Thomas also built three new castles, at Askerton, Rockcliffe, and Drumburgh. Askerton was the largest of these, built two miles from the royal outpost of Bewcastle, which was then in decay, to guard against Scottish inroads from Liddesdale through Bewcastledale. It was the normal residence of the steward of Gilsland, in whom lay 'all the safety of that Barony, without either help of warden or other; for that it lyeth somewhat farre of'.[64] The small castle of Rockcliffe which Dacre built to command the crossing of the Eden was capable of lodging a hundred horsemen. Its design was so successful that it was later suggested as a model for fortifying a town near Wark on the opposite march with 'a stronge tower with stables beneath and lodgings above after the fashion of Roclyf my Lord Dacres howse uppon the west borders able to contayne many men and horses'.[65] And at Drumburgh Dacre built out of materials from Hadrian's Wall 'a pretty pile for defence of the country' against incursions across the Solway.[66]

Undefended borderlands were almost worthless to their lords. All along the border, 'every apparence of a troublous worlde' led to the abandonment of any township where 'there ys nether towre barmekyn nor other fortresse yn yt whereyn the tenents may be releved in tyme of war'. 'And then yt is a greatt tyme after or it can

[63] *Cal. inq. p.m., Hen. VII*, i, no. 157; M. W. Taylor, 'Kirkoswald castle', in *C. & W.*, 2 (1876), 3, 8; R. S. Ferguson, 'The barony of Gilsland and its owners to the end of the sixteenth century', ibid. 4 (1880), 478; C. J. Ferguson, 'Naworth castle', ibid. 4 (1880), 487–91; Thompson, *Decline of the castle*, 24–5.

[64] R. S. Ferguson, 'Two border fortresses: Tryermain and Askerton castles', in *C. & W.*, 3 (1878), 179 (quoting a tract of 1591 in the BL).

[65] Hodgson, *Northumberland*, III. ii. 203 (Bowes's survey, 1550); *L. & P. Hen. VIII*, xx (ii), no. 700.

[66] Ferguson, 'Barony of Gilsland', 477–8; T. H. B. Graham, 'Extinct Cumberland castles. Part III', in *C. & W.*, NS 11 (1911), 242–3 (quoting Leland).

be replenyshed againe.' Thus a major cause of the decay of the
borders was that the 'people was not so well cheryshed by their
lordes, maysters and offycers as yt were convenynte they should
have bene in suche a troublous quarter'. Conversely, as hopes of a
truce or abstinence rose, poor people were drawn towards the
border. Moreover, 'towneshippes dwellinge inwarde towarde the
sea syde & forther from the frounter' 'payed greatter rentes to their
lordes for their fermeholdes then the other said uttermost townes
do'.[67] On Dacre's estates, this process of 'replenishing' wastelands
can be followed in some detail in respect of the lord's possessions
in Bewcastledale. Bewcastle had become a crown possession in
1421-2 when it had 'lapsed' into the king's hands as lord para-
mount. Yet Dacre had a particular interest in the manor. Apart
from his recently acquired lands there, the feudal overlordship of
Bewcastle pertained to Dacre's barony of Burgh, even though it
was geographically separated from Burgh by the baronies of
Liddel and Levington. Strategically, it lay between the Dacre
barony of Gilsland and the border; and militarily the crown keeper
of Bewcastledale was under the supervision of Dacre as warden of
the west marches.[68] After its acquisition by the crown, however,
the manor had long lain waste until 'the Liddesdale men came into
England' about 1485, when Cuthbert and John Routledge, Robert
Elwald and Gerard Nixon 'were sworne to King Richard at
Carlile' before Sir Richard Ratcliffe and other royal commissioners.[69] This practice of recruiting Scottish tenants, who were then
'sworn English' by tendering the oath of allegiance to them, was
evidently very common in the marches, but it is unusual to find the
process specifically documented. In this case, the predominance of
military over economic considerations in the lease is illustrated by
the fact that, apart from the castle demesne, the whole manor was
let rent-free to the four tenants, who 'had it holye to theire owne
vses to thentente to mayntaine the kinges [   ] warres & to kepe

[67] See, in particular, Hodgson, *Northumberland*, III. ii. 182–3, 225, 229, 241–2
(quotations, Bowes and Ellerker's survey, 1542); *L. & P. Hen. VIII*, iii, no. 2612.
[68] For the feudal history of Bewcastle, see T. H. B. Graham, 'The lords of
Bewcastle', in *C. & W.*, NS 29 (1929), 57–68; for the Dacre–Musgrave dispute, see
below, pp. 200–5.
[69] PRO, SP 1/141, fo. 248 (*L. & P. Hen. VIII*, xiii (ii), app. no. 36). The mention
of Ratcliffe, who briefly held the office of king's deputy on the west marches after
the death of Humphrey, Lord Dacre, in May, would seem to date the incident to
summer 1485. For Ratcliffe's appointment as deputy, see Horrox, *Richard III*, 259.

the bo[r]ders there & to m[aintain] the captaine vndir the king of
the same castell'.[70]

The appointment of a separate captain or keeper of Bewcastle in
1485 was apparently also a new departure, and the castle must also
have been repaired at this time. Initially, Nicholas Ridley was
appointed captain, but Sir John Musgrave, later knight for
the king's body, was associated with the office from soon after the
accession of Henry VII. He and his son Thomas retained the
keepership for almost forty years by virtue of a grant in
survivorship of the office in 1493.[71] As captain, Musgrave had the
leading of Dacre's tenants in Bewcastledale. Yet since the
Musgraves were Dacre followers, and since Dacre had overall
charge of the west marches, the conflicting demands of the situation were reconciled by having all the inhabitants of
Bewcastledale under their captain do suit at Dacre's court of
Askerton in Gilsland, and by giving Dacre the rule of the
Bewcastlemen under their captain.[72] Following the completion of
Askerton close by, Bewcastle was almost superfluous in strict military terms, and in 1517 the king seriously considered a proposal by
Dacre for 'the removeing ande rebuylding of the said castell, to be
set w[t]in the kinges lordship of Arthurheth'.[73] Arthuret was one of
the three manors in the barony of Liddel, and Dacre presumably
hoped to strengthen the marches west of Bewcastle by rebuilding
Liddel Strength. Even so, the English presence in this remote
outpost was eventually sufficiently secure to allow Dacre to impose
rents on his tenants there. By the 1530s these rents were worth an
estimated £26. 3s. 4d. a year.[74] Yet, as Dacre observed in 1524, the
maintenance of good order there among thieves, malefactors, fugitives, and outlaws was always difficult, 'by reason þ[t] thinhabitants
of the same dale dwell in a corner in thextreme partes of the

---

    [70] PRO, SP 1/141, fos. 248–51 (*L. & P. Hen. VIII*, xiii (ii), app. no. 36).
    [71] Ibid.; *Cal. pat. rolls, 1485–94*, 56, 73, 101, 335, 429; *L. & P. Hen. VIII*, i (2nd
edn.), no. 2684 (86), ii (i), no. 1084. See also below, pp. 199–205.
    [72] PRO, SP 1/36, fos. 238–45 (*L. & P. Hen. VIII*, iv (i), no. 1855); SP 1/141, fos.
248–51 (*L. & P. Hen. VIII*, xiii (ii), app. no. 36); STAC 2/18/269, fos. 1, 2; Durham,
H. of N. MS C/201/2, m. 7; *L. & P. Hen. VIII*, iv (i), no. 1289. Thomas Musgrave
was also described as the king's servant in 1524: Castle Howard, MS F1/5/5, fo. 29[v].
For the links between the Musgraves and Lord Dacre, see below, pp. 203–5.
    [73] BL, Caligula B. II, fos. 347–7[v] (*L. & P. Hen. VIII*, ii, no. 3383).
    [74] PRO, STAC 2/19/127. A rental of Feb. 1537 valued the lord's possessions in
Bewcastledale at £27. 3s. 4d. gross, or £21. 18s. 6d. net: Durham, H. of N. MS C/
201/7, fo. 48[v].

borders, and þᵗ allso parte of them are Scotts men borne, & those þᵗ be Inglishmen born maries wᵗʰ Scotts'.[75]

Lord Thomas's building activities, the 'replenishing' of Bewcastledale, and other purchases of march land were but the most visible aspects of a wider policy of estate management in which the accent was on the development of a loyal tenantry, inured to march warfare, as part of an effective system of border defences. As part of this process, Dacre certainly took the opportunity to raise rents on marchland and to impose them where none had existed, but not to the same extent as nobles in lowland England. Rents on Dacre's border estates remained comparatively low: in Gilsland in the 1530s rents for arable and meadow land were commonly only 12*d.* per acre.[76] And the Dacre tenantry also had considerable obligations in connection with border service which would not have been required of tenants in the south. The arrangements for border service must originally have been devised and promulgated by Lord Thomas at the time of his military reorganization of his north Cumberland estates, although the form in which they have come down to us relates to their reimposition in Gilsland in September 1584 and their subsequent 'reconfirmation and agreinge' for the lordship in October 1595.[77] They laid down 'that euerie tenande provide him selfe steelecappe, jacke, sworde and dagger, with a bowe, spere or gunne', and that such of the lord's tenants as were obliged 'by tenure of theire fermeholdes' to keep a horse or a nag should have ready at six hours' warning 'a goode and a sufficiente horse . . . hable to do seruice where any horsemanne ys to be charged', or a nag 'hable sufficientlye to beare a manne xxᵗⁱᵉ myles wᵗʰin Scotlande and backe agayne wᵗʰout a bate'. 'And what tenande as by wretchedness ys founde in faulte that for sparinge doth not feede and keape his horse or nagge so' should forfeit 12*d.* per week.[78] Each tenant was also obliged to answer the bailiff's summons 'for the Queenes seruice or for the common wealthe of the lordshippe'; to 'keape his nighte watche as he shalbe appoincted by the balif' after Michaelmas between 10 p.m. and cock crow, with day watches after Candlemas; to 'rise and go readilye to fraye and folowinge', setting forward with the bail-

[75] Castle Howard, MS F1/5/5, fo. 30.
[76] Durham, H. of N. MS C/201/6, 7.
[77] Ibid., MS C/201/9, fos. 1–5.
[78] Ibid. (quotations at fo. 2).

iff's deputy 'with horse, armoure, and weapon as he ys appoincted to haue', 'and to holde on forwarde with the deputie till the deputie turne backe'.[79]

Similar articles for the enforcement of these regulations bound both the landsergeant of Gilsland and the bailiffs and their deputies in each of the sixteen bailiwicks into which the lordship was divided. The articles were to be inquired of and the fines arising answered at the weekly court in the moothall of Brampton every Tuesday, and the monies used to buy weapons and replace losses. Moreover, in view of Lord Dacre's many building projects in the region, it may well be significant that on many of his estates in Cumberland—in Gilsland, and around Kirkoswald and Greystoke in the south—the lord still demanded token labour services of some of his tenants-at-will. In Gilsland in 1537, for instance, the lord was entitled to a total of over 200 days' work a year. In Kirkoswald and Staffull, where 66 services were owed in 1529, they were mostly employed in reaping the lord's corn; but in Lazonby the 69 services due were held over to the following year and employed 'in carriagium le plaister usque ecclesiam de Carlaton'. In addition the tenants of Irthington were also required to maintain the lord's mill at their own costs.[80]

The form of land tenure described in these arrangements is generally known as tenant right. Its chief characteristic was the obligation to do military service and to maintain weapon, horse, and harness for that purpose, on pain of forfeiture of the holding. In addition to the rent, an entry fine or gressum, at a level determined by the lord, was payable at each change of lord or tenant. A further characteristic, however, was the right of a son to succeed to his father's holding on payment of this fine, so that what had earlier been a life tenancy now became virtually hereditary. Although in practice tenements would tend to descend from father to son over several generations, on most northern estates this 'tenant right' had still not been admitted by the lord at the time of the Pilgrimage of Grace, when the peasantry demanded that their tenures should be converted into tenant right and that entry fines should be restricted to one or two years'

[79] Durham, H. of N. MS C/201/9, fos. 1–5 (quotations at fos. 1, 2ᵛ, 3).
[80] Ibid., MSS C/201/2, mm 4d, 5, C/201/5, fos. 12ᵛ–13, C/201/7; CRO, Carlisle, MS D/HG/18, fo. [14].

rent.[81] Yet although rentals of Dacre's Cumberland estates at this time indicate that most tenants held their lands at the lord's will, a commission given by Lord William to his estate officials in the year immediately preceding the rising for a survey of his lands in the west marches suggests that in practice Dacre had already admitted his tenants' demand for tenant right. The commission also offers a more general insight into the lord's estate management policies and is therefore worth more extended consideration here.

Since Dacre was, exceptionally, in pressing need of money at this time to pay the heavy fine imposed on him in 1534, it is not surprising that the lord's profit was a major consideration in many of the articles of the commission. Arrangements were made for a general fine at the rate of three years' rent, payable over three years; provision was made for the sale of woods; parks were to be viewed 'to thintente theye may be rented for my mooste prouffyt'; any decays of rent were to be investigated and the lands 'to be sell and inhanced again to the full rentes and myne old precedentes and rentalles'; copyholders were to be asked for their copies to ensure 'that thei occupie noo landes of myne but that they haue right vnto' and that tenants-at-will had not illicitly converted their lands into copyhold; and finally new feodaries, 'bownders', and rentals of all the lordships were to be made to 'be ingrossed vp in parchiemente to the beste that they now paye or the beste precedent that they haue payed'. Even so, Lord William was careful to ensure that his need for money did not undermine the traditional Dacre *manraed* or arrangements for border defence. His commissioners were not to 'cesse any ffyne or gryssome of all suche personnes that haith contented and agreed with me sence I entred vnto my laundes, excepte they may be lovingly enduced theruntoo'; they should not let his tenements to any parson or vicar, nor 'to any owtwarde personnes dwelling in any oder towne or lordeshippe, excepte the same personne do dwele vpoun the same tenemente hymself'. Yet if 'a tenaunt cometh to a tenement as a straunger, having no title therunto, my said commissioners to take vpon him asmuche as the same fermeholde wolde geve'; and most revealingly, if any tenement were void, 'none oder personne having tenaunt righte

[81] Fletcher, *Tudor rebellions*, 29, 108, 111; Bean, *Estates of the Percy family*, 57, 65; Hoyle, 'Lords, tenants and tenant right in the sixteenth century', 39 and the references there cited; id., 'An ancient and laudable custom', 24–55.

TABLE I. *Income from entry fines on Dacre estates, 1530–1531*

Barony	Total entry fines			Total receipts		
	£	s.	d.	£	s.	d.
Burgh	9	9	2	165	16	11
Gilsland	10	16	4			
(charged in previous account)	17	17	2	164	3	$6\frac{1}{2}$
Greystoke	26	8	4			
(paid directly)	11	6	8	277	19	$11\frac{7}{8}$
Morpeth	7	13	4	161	18	$11\frac{1}{4}$
Westmorland estates	8	14	2			
(arrears levied)	2	12	$10\frac{1}{2}$	186	15	$10\frac{1}{4}$

therunto', they were to 'lett the same to a personne being a good archer and able for the seruing of the kinges highnes, and rather to him for lesse gryssome then to ane oder being none archer'.[82]

In most respects these instructions were apparently a restatement of the lord's traditional policies. They also indicate a marked preference for tenant right as the normal form of land tenure on the Dacre estates in the west marches. Yet the demand for a general fine at the rate of three years' rent payable over three years seems to have been a new departure, and was presumably forced on Dacre by his need for money. Although the evidence is generally scanty, in 1530–1 the gressums levied on Dacre's tenants in Cumberland, Westmorland, and Northumberland yielded £77. 0s. $10\frac{1}{2}d$. It is not possible to determine precisely what rate was charged for entry fines, but if we compare the amounts levied in entry fines on these estates with the total receipts it is clear that the level of fines must have been no higher than on the Percy estates in the region, where the rate was between one and one-and-a-half years' rent at this time (see Table 1).[83] Even this was probably an increase on the levels of the later fifteenth century, for a general fine levied on the barony of Greystoke in 1472 yielded only £101. 14s., which was probably about half the annual rental of the barony

[82] Durham, H. of N. MS C/201/5, fos. 4–6.
[83] Calculated from ibid., MSS C/201/2, 3. Cf. Bean, *Estates of the Percy family*, 51–68.

at the time.[84] Thus the general fine of 1535–6 represented a very considerable increase on previous levels. Moreover, the gressums of 1530–1 had usually been payable over four years, although occasionally a longer period was allowed, or a respite given.

Nevertheless, the major consequence of this military reorganization under Lord Thomas was that in Gilsland alone Dacre had available under the leading of the landsergeant no less than 434 horsemen and nagmen, and 196 footmen, 'besydes in Lannercoste and Walton balifwickes about 100'.[85] Bearing in mind that only 1,974 of the 6,502 able-bodied men listed on the Cumberland muster roll of October 1534 had any kind of horse,[86] the Dacre tenantry would appear to have comprised a relatively high proportion of the most valuable troops on the west marches. Lord Thomas's estate management policies explain why he could, as the earl of Surrey remarked in 1523, bring over 4,000 men on a raid into Scotland, 'and may at all tymes with litle charge have 4 or 5,000 men off his owne' to resist invasion, 'and so can noone other man doo'.[87]

The evidence concerning the management of Dacre's possessions further south is unfortunately much less detailed. Even so, the southern estates do seem to have been managed on rather different lines, in ways which were perhaps more typical of nobles in lowland England. The impression gained from a comparison of the individual receivers' accounts for 1529–30 is that rents per acre were often much higher on the more southerly estates, labour services were much less in evidence, and copyhold and freehold tenures were much more common.[88] Many of these differences no doubt reflect the normal contrasts between upland and lowland regions. Yet there appear to be some more significant contrasts in Dacre's handling of his estate officials. The management of Dacre's northern estates was concentrated in the hands of about a dozen key officials, including no less than four members of the Threlkeld family of Melmerby. They were drawn mostly from the

[84] CRO, Carlisle, MS D/HG/16, fos. 1–4.
[85] Durham, H. of N. MS C/201/9, fo. 6.
[86] PRO, E 101/549/13. The roll may be missing a few membranes, but the numbers seem about the same as musters taken later in the century. Cf. Nicolson and Burn, *Westmorland and Cumberland*, i, p. xci.
[87] *SP Hen. VIII*, iv. 12, 29, 51, 54; Ellis (ed.), *Original letters*, 1st ser., i. 214–18; Miller, *Henry VIII and the English nobility*, 147–9.
[88] Durham, H. of N. MS C/201/2. See also the extant steward's account rolls for the early 1540s: Castle Howard MSS F1/2/1–3.

lower ranks of the Cumberland squirearchy and were modestly rewarded.[89] The three receivers of Dacre's lordships in Cumberland and Westmorland were each paid 53s. 4d. a year, but the fee of John Myre as receiver of his Shrewsbury lands was £4. The lord's steward there was his father-in-law, George, earl of Shrewsbury, whose deputy received 40s. a year, as did John Dodd, bailiff of Hinstock, and Dacre even retained Richard Salter as his legal counsel there.[90] The bailiffs of some of his Yorkshire estates were also unusually well paid: Thomas Haltclyf received £3. 0s. 8d. as bailiff of Fangfoss, as did William Jackson, bailiff and forester of Hilderskelf, while William Anlaby was paid 40s. as bailiff of Thorpbasset.[91] Similarly, Dacre's bailiff of his lands in Suffolk was Andrew, Lord Windsor.[92] By contrast, most of the bailiffs and reeves of Dacre's Cumberland manors were humble men who received only a few shillings.

A similar contrast may be discerned in respect of Dacre's attitude to arrears of rents on his estates. In Cumberland and Westmorland arrears were rarely allowed to accumulate, whereas William Farnham as bailiff of Northborough in Leicestershire ran up enormous debts of £91. 19s. 11¼d. before he was dismissed and Sir Richard Sacheverell brought in as Dacre's steward to investigate. Similarly, Robert Boston, Dacre's bailiff of Wyboston, was paid 40s. a year and by 1530 had accumulated arrears of £53. 17s. 2d., or about four times the net annual value of the manor.[93] Overall, these differences suggest that outside the traditional areas of Dacre influence in the west march, Lord Dacre tended to look upon his southern possessions more as a means of purchasing the political support of influential men. In this, his attitude evidently reflected the contemporary practice of using leading offices, especially stewardships, to strengthen political ties rather than to maximize income or improve the management of his estates.[94] It probably also reflects a conventional distinction between home and distant estates, since Dacre could hardly employ another peer at

---

[89] The following remarks are based on Durham, H. of N. MS C/201/2. See also, ibid., MS C/201/3. Cf. James, *Society, politics and culture*, 142–3.

[90] Durham, H. of N. MS C/201/2, m. 28d.

[91] Ibid., mm 26–7.

[92] Ibid., C/201/3. Cf. Miller, *Henry VIII and the English nobility*, 23.

[93] Durham, H. of N. MS C/201/2, m. 29d.

[94] Cf. Harris, *Buckingham*, 105; K. B. McFarlane, *The nobility of late medieval England* (Oxford, 1973), 107.

his home base. Even so, in Dacre's case the contrast does seem particularly sharp and his management of his border estates unusually tight and personal.

This impression is reinforced by evidence about the Dacre connexion in the far north. Mervyn James has remarked with regard to the families who followed the Dacres that the 'dominant impression is one of weakness, since none of these families (perhaps with the exception of the Leighs [of Isel]) belonged to the leadership of the county'.[95] This observation seems, however, to be an oversimplification of the position. It is certainly true that, unlike the Percies, Dacre did not fee the leading gentry of the region. His officers and household men were mostly of humbler status. In 1526 the gentlemen of his household included Edward Aglionby, Henry Wallace, George Skelton, and Peter Moresby, while in 1529–30 the only member of Dacre's household who enjoyed anything approaching a national standing was, ironically, Sir William Musgrave.[96] Otherwise, the only persons identified in Lord William's accounts as in receipt of annuities were his uncles, Sir Christopher and Sir Philip, and other close relatives.[97] Nevertheless, Dacre's failure to retain the leading gentry families did not reflect a reluctance on the part of the wealthy squires to accept Dacre's leadership. Indeed nearly all of the Cumberland gentry who served on the commissions of the peace or as sheriff there in the first quarter of the sixteenth century can be shown to have been closely associated with Lord Thomas. Some, like John Skelton of Armathwayte, Edward Musgrave of Edenhall, and Henry Denton of Cardew, gave bonds to the king for Dacre or vice versa;[98] or like John Lowther and John Radcliffe witnessed charters in Dacre's favour.[99] Thomas Beverley was Dacre's servant,[100] and both Dacre's kinsman, Thomas Curwen, and Humphrey Coningsby sought his good lordship.[101] Dacre also had the ward-

[95] James, *Society, politics and culture*, 142.

[96] Durham, H. of N. MSS C/201/2, C/201/3; *L. & P. Hen. VIII*, iv, no. 2374.

[97] Ibid., C/201/2, mm 8d, 11d, 18, 24. Earlier, however, Lord Thomas had granted an annuity of £7 to Sir Henry Wyatt, treasurer of the king's chamber: PRO, C 54/394, m. 7.

[98] *Cal. close rolls, 1500–09*, no. 582; *L. & P. Hen. VIII*, i (2nd edn.), no. 132 (50). Cf. Castle Howard, MS A1/201; PRO, E 36/214, 391; E 101/72, file 3/1062.

[99] Castle Howard, MSS A1/180, 201. Cf. *L. & P. Hen. VIII*, i (2nd edn.), no. 2443.

[100] *L. & P. Hen. VIII*, i (2nd edn.), nos. 1297, 3170, ii, no. 63.

[101] *L. & P. Hen. VIII*, ii, nos. 3395, 3429, 3473–4, iv (i), no. 190.

ship of Christopher Pickering's daughter and heiress,[102] and at one stage contemplated marrying Lady Pickering.[103] In 1521 he recommended that Skelton or Curwen's son, Christopher, be appointed sheriff of Cumberland, and in 1526 his brother asked that Lowther, Radcliffe, and Beverley be included on the peace commission.[104]

That Dacre's links with men like Lowther and Radcliffe were not more formal may well reflect Wolsey's own feeing of the leading gentry. As Dacre explained to Lord Clifford in 1523 when the latter summoned 'my cousin Sir John Lowther' to do border service under him, Lowther had accustomably 'attended vpon me in the kinges seruice' because he 'is reteigned as houshold seruaunte of my Lord Legates grace, of whom I haue auctoritie wᵗ the guyding, ordering & leding of all and euery his seruauntes reteined & tenauntes wᵗin the countties of Cumbreland Westmorland & Northumbreland'.[105]

Dacre's influence in Westmorland was less pervasive, but it was far from being restricted to his steward there, Lancelot Lancaster of Sockbridge.[106] Walter Strickland and Thomas Parr were both closely associated with Dacre in Henry VII's last years. Like Lowther, Strickland later became Wolsey's retainer, while Dacre's continuing good relations with the Parrs of Kendal are attested by the family's acceptance of his mediation in negotiations for the projected marriage between Lady Parr's daughter and Lord Scrope's grandson.[107] Some of Dacre's Cumberland allies also had substantial possessions in Westmorland—the Musgraves, Lowthers, Humphrey Coningsby—while after Sir Christopher Moresby's death, Dacre had the leading of his tenants. Finally, another prominent Westmorland JP, Geoffrey Lancaster, was retained as counsel by Dacre.[108]

In Northumberland, as Mervyn James has noted, Dacre's fol-

[102] *L. & P. Hen. VIII*, iii, nos. 3395–6, 3473–4, iv (i), no. 190.

[103] *L. & P. Hen. VIII*, ii, no. 4541.

[104] *L. & P. Hen. VIII*, iii, no. 1225, iv, no. 2052.

[105] BL, Add. MS 24,965, fos. 186–6ᵛ (*L. & P. Hen. VIII*, iii, no. 3427). Cf. *SP Hen. VIII*, iv. 457.

[106] Durham, H. of N. MS C/201/2, m. 2d; *L. & P. Hen. VIII*, i (2nd edn.), no. 132 (50), iv (ii), no. 4421. Cf. James, *Society, politics and culture*, 143.

[107] PRO, E 36/214, 430, 498, E 101/415/3, fo. 189; *Cal. close rolls, 1500–09*, no. 315; BL, Add. MS 24,965, fos. 23–4 (*L. & P. Hen. VIII*, iii, no. 3178), fos. 200ᵛ–1 (*L. & P. Hen. VIII*, iii, no. 3649); *L. & P. Hen. VIII*, iv (i), nos. 162, 189.

[108] *L. & P. Hen. VIII*, iii, nos. 3395–6, 3474; Durham, H. of N. MS C/201/2, m. 2d.

lowing was much weaker, and was largely confined to the border gentry of the middle marches. His lieutenants there, Edward Radcliffe and Roger Fenwick and later his son, Ralph, were in reality the king's men.[109] Yet Nicholas Ridley was a Dacre follower. More surprisingly, William Heron of Ford, a Percy retainer, eventually also took Dacre's fee and became captain of Redesdale in 1523.[110] Dacre also had some following among the lesser borderers, but when the king allowed him a say in the nomination of the sheriff of Northumberland, Dacre could find no more substantial candidates for the office than his brothers, Sir Christopher and Sir Philip, or gentlemen of his household like William Threlkeld and his sons, Richard and Christopher, Christopher Leigh, George Skelton, and Henry Wallace.[111]

Overall, therefore, the Dacre affinity was apparently well geared to the lord's political ambitions in the region—chiefly the rule and defence of the west marches. Old-style feudal lordship in the strategically more important parts of the marches meant that Dacre's need to augment the military service available to him through retaining and the system of bastard feudalism was probably less pronounced than in the case of other marcher lords such as the earl of Northumberland. Accordingly, Dacre's outlay on the paid part of his affinity was probably much closer to the norms of lowland England than Percy's, as indeed was his preference for the humbler squires with purely local territorial interests. The contrast here is perhaps between a magnate who dominated his chosen region with the king's support and a nobleman whose ambitions were wider but more contested. For although Dacre ruled the east and middle marches for much of Henry VIII's reign, he did so with reluctance, in default of a more acceptable candidate; and it is significant that he made little attempt to build up a following there.[112]

[109] *L. & P. Hen. VIII*, i (2nd edn.), nos. 984, 2443, 2840, 2863 (5), 2913.

[110] *L. & P. Hen. VIII*, i (2nd edn.), no. 2443, iii, nos. 1225, 3218–19, 3381, iv (i), nos. 133, 346, 405, 427; James, *Society, politics and culture*, 78–80. Dacre described Heron as his cousin and had in 1504 stood surety to the king for him: *Cal. close rolls, 1500–09*, no. 315; *L. & P. Hen. VIII*, iii, no. 3219.

[111] *L. & P. Hen. VIII*, ii, nos. 2460, 2533, 3783, 4547, 4562, iii, nos. 500, 1042, 1225; Hodgson, *Northumberland*, I. i. 363–4; James, *Society, politics and culture*, 142–3.

[112] For the comparison with other lords, see esp. T. B. Pugh, 'The magnates, knights and gentry', in S. B. Chrimes, C. D. Ross, and R. A. Griffiths (eds.), *Fifteenth-century England 1399–1509* (Manchester, 1972), 101–9; Christine Carpenter, 'The Beauchamp affinity: a study of bastard feudalism at work', in *EHR* 95 (1980), 514–32; Bean, *Estates of the Percy family*, 85–98, 128–43.

On his death in 1525, the landed possessions of Thomas, Lord Dacre, were worth over £1,500 net per annum, making him the eighth most wealthy peer in the realm. In addition, the annual salary of £433. 6s. 8d. which he long enjoyed as warden-general was nominally higher than that of any other of the king's ministers at the time except the lord chancellor.[113] Thus even if we accept traditional arguments that there was a close correlation between a lord's income and his power, Dacre was one of the most important men in the early-Tudor state. Yet the exposed location, in a marcher society, of most of the lord's estates, together with the heavy military responsibilities of his office (discussed in Chapter 5), were evidently the formative influence on Dacre estate-management policies. The acquisition of the Greystoke inheritance was of course the primary reason for Dacre's transformation into a great provincial magnate, and his policies also led to some spectacular increases in the value of his ancestral estates. Despite the recent war with Scotland, his barony of Gilsland was valued at £138. 19s. 3½d. on his death, and the barony of Burgh which had also been badly wasted by war with the Scots in 1485 was worth no less than £206. 11s. 0½d.[114] Judged by the policies of magnates in lowland England, Dacre's estate-management policies were no doubt old-fashioned, not to say eccentric. At a time when nobles elsewhere were taking advantage of the growing peace and political stability to build comfortable country houses, and were raising their rents, in response to the first signs of the price inflation, to pay for them, Dacre failed to charge economic rents and spent what money he had in building and repairing old-fashioned castles. In the context of marcher society, however, his policies made perfect sense. This point may be established by analysing the policies of another English border magnate, the earl of Kildare, whose estates were strategically located along the western frontier of the Tudor state, and whose traditional office as governor of Ireland conferred on him very similar responsibilities to those of Lord Dacre.

---

[113] PRO, C 54/394, m. 7 (which omits the Dacre estates in the palatinate of Durham, worth *c*.£100 a year); Durham, H. of N. MS C/201/3. Cf. Helen Miller, 'Subsidy assessments of the peerage in the sixteenth century', in *IHR Bull.*, 28 (1955), 15–34; id., *Henry VIII and the English nobility*, ch. 6; J. C. K. Cornwall, *Wealth and society in early sixteenth century England* (London, 1988), 143–4.
[114] PRO, C 54/394, m. 7, E 150/112 (*Cal. inq. p.m., Hen. VII*, i, no. 157).

4

The estates and connexion of the earl of Kildare

THE prominence of Dacre and Kildare in early-Tudor provincial administration was something of a novelty. Neither lord had ranked among the great regional magnates of the later middle ages. In the north the most powerful families were the Nevilles and the Percies who had dominated the wardenships of the marches during the fifteenth century. The earls of Westmorland and Northumberland remained the most prominent northern nobles until the ill-fated Northern Rising of 1569. In Ireland the crown was traditionally less reliant on local nobles to undertake the office of governor. The highest and most honourable of titles conferred on the Irish viceroy was that of king's lieutenant; and in the later middle ages the three families with extensive Irish possessions whose heads occupied this office were the Mortimers, the Talbots, and the Butlers. The Mortimers (earls of Ulster and lords of Connaught and Meath in Ireland (1369–1425); earls of March in England (1328–30, 1354–1425)), and their successor, Richard Plantagenet, duke of York (1425–60), were the only really great feudatory of the crown in Ireland at that time, and much the most powerful of the three. Yet neither Mortimer nor Talbot was normally resident there. The famous English military commander, Sir John Talbot of Hallamshire, inherited the lordship of Wexford and lands in western Meath, and was created earl of Shrewsbury in England in 1442 and earl of Waterford in Ireland in 1446. He was twice appointed lieutenant of Ireland and also served as justiciar there, but none of the later earls of Shrewsbury spent any time in Ireland. The Butlers were the most prominent of the four families of second rank in Ireland to be advanced to an earldom there between 1316 and 1329, and the only one of them with extensive possessions outside Ireland. The 4th earl (1411–52) was three times lieutenant of Ireland, and his son, later the 5th earl (1452–61), was in 1449 created earl of Wiltshire in England.[1]

The middle years of the fifteenth century thus saw the lordship at the centre of national politics, with representatives of the three leading families there both active in Ireland and influential at court. Not for another two hundred years was this situation to recur. And after 1460, for one reason or another, political power in the lordship passed into other hands. York's estates were vested in the crown following the accession of his son as King Edward IV in 1461. The Talbots were also absentees; as was the senior line of the Butlers after the reversal in 1475 of the Lancastrian 5th earl's attainder and forfeiture in 1461. Thus, in view of the crown's growing reluctance to undertake the expense of appointing an outsider as governor of Ireland, the heads of the two surviving Irish-based comital houses, the Fitzgeralds of Desmond and the Fitzgeralds of Kildare, were the obvious candidates for the post. The 8th earl of Desmond served as deputy lieutenant for four years in the mid-1460s.[2] Yet the estrangement of the family from the crown following Desmond's attainder and execution for treason in 1468, and the more convenient location of Kildare's estates near the lordship's centre of power in Dublin, made Kildare the regular choice as governor from the 1470s onwards.

The careers of successive earls of Kildare in the later middle ages gave scant indication of the political ascendancy which the house was to enjoy in early-Tudor Ireland. The Kildares were, it is true, the senior comital family in Ireland, the earldom having been created in 1316, but this was because greater feudatories, like the lords of Meath, Carlow, and Wexford, had no Irish title. In the thirteenth century, the Geraldine lords of Offaly had been subtenants of the Kildare fifth of the old liberty of Leinster, which had passed to the absentee de Vescy family, who in 1297 surrendered it to the crown.[3] Even after the creation of the earldom of Kildare, however, Fitzgerald remained primarily a local figure, although

---

[1] This and the following paragraph are based on the tables in *Handbook Brit. chron.*, 160–7, 447–97. On the status and possessions of the leading families in Ireland, see Frame, *English lordship in Ireland*, chs. 1–2; Otway-Ruthven, *Med. Ire.*, esp. 348, 377.

[2] Art Cosgrove, 'The execution of the earl of Desmond, 1468', in *Kerry Archaeological Society Journal*, 8 (1975), 11–27.

[3] Frame, 'Power and society', 17; A. J. Otway-Ruthven, 'The medieval county of Kildare', in *IHS* 11 (1959), 195–6.

during the next century earls of Kildare occasionally acted as a stopgap governor of Ireland for a few months.[4]

Viewed from London, the turbulent marcher societies of the lordship and the far north and the defence of two remote frontiers might seem to present the same problem of government. In essentials, this was true, but a closer comparison between them also discloses significant differences. This went beyond the obvious contrast between the pronounced cultural rivalry between English and Gaelic in Ireland and the much more muted cultural differences of the Anglo-Scottish frontier. The Norman conquest and settlement of Ireland had been a piecemeal, haphazard, and incomplete affair, with much dependent on physical geography, the private initiative and resources of particular lords, and the capacity of individual Gaelic chiefs to resist. The result was that, unlike the north, there was no continuous border line capable of being depicted on a map, only innumerable balances of power in particular marches. The marches in fact were more fluid and shifting along this western frontier, government was on a smaller scale, and power was more decentralized. In these circumstances even the most powerful of the lordship's magnates was driven in the fifteenth century to negotiate marriage alliances with Gaelic chiefs as a means of stabilizing the marches.[5]

In part this was because their landed holdings, and so their financial and military resources, were comparatively small. For instance, when the earldom of Ormond was regranted to Piers Butler in 1537, his lands scattered over eight counties were valued at only IR£388. 17s. 7¼d., while the most powerful of the ecclesiastical magnates, the archbishop of Dublin and the prior of Kilmainham, were not all that much wealthier. The archbishop of Dublin was then worth IR£534. 15s. 2½d. and the landed endowment of Kilmainham priory was valued at IR£744. 4s. 11d.[6] At the other end of the scale, the principal endowment of Nicholas St Lawrence, Lord Howth, was the manor of Howth, with other messuages and farms in Co. Dublin, worth no more than IR£100

---

[4] Frame, 'Power and society', 17; *Handbook of Brit. chron.*, 162–6.

[5] Cf. Frame, *English lordship in Ireland*, 50; *New hist. Ire.*, ii. 551–5; below, pp. 135–6.

[6] PRO, SP 60/2, fos. 46–7 (*L. & P. Hen. VIII*, xii (ii), no. 964iii); *Cal. Carew MSS, 1515–74*, nos. 107–8; *Valor Beneficiorum Ecclesiasticorum in Hibernia* (Dublin, 1741), 9; White (ed.), *Extents of Irish monastic possessions, 1540–41*, 117.

annually; and the bishopric of Kildare, worth IR£69. 11s. 4d. a
year, was so poor that Walter Wellesley, prior of Connall, a peer
who enjoyed an income of IR£136. 2s. 4d. a year from his priory,
was licensed to hold Kildare *in commendam*.[7] No doubt the relative
poverty of a minor peer like Howth explains why he was also
prepared to serve as a clerk in the exchequer.[8] Yet, as in the far
north, the *manraed* which these border holdings conferred was at
least as important to the lord as the comparatively low rents at
which the lands could be leased.

The landed endowments which had accompanied the creation of
the four new earldoms of early fourteenth-century Ireland were, as
Professor Robin Frame has recently observed, also quite small.
They fell far short of the 1,000 marcates of land regarded as a
suitable comital endowment in England.[9] Extents and inquisitions
taken following the deaths of the 2nd and 3rd earls of Kildare in
1328 and 1331 suggest that their estates were then worth about £430
a year, which was certainly less than their value in the late thirteenth century. More than half of this total accrued from the four
large manors of Maynooth, Rathmore, Rathangan, and Lea in Co.
Kildare, and together with the neighbouring manor of Geashill
which had by then been reclaimed by the Gaelic Irish, these had
been among the earliest estates belonging to the family. More
recently, the family had acquired the manor of Kildare and the
smaller manors of Rathbride and Kilcork, and the whole shire had
been granted to them as a palatinate in 1317.[10] Elsewhere, they held
another cluster of manors in Co. Limerick, notably Croom and
Adare, which were still worth about £100 annually even though
many of the lands were waste, and a few isolated possessions in Co.
Carlow or Leix (particularly the manors of Morett and Timogue,
largely occupied by the Irish), Co. Kilkenny (the manor of
Glashare) and Co. Cork.[11]

Inquisitions after the death of the 5th earl in 1432 suggest that
the extent of the Kildare inheritance had altered very little over the

---

[7] *Cal. inq. Co. Dublin*, 12, 16–18, 123–5, 168–70, 298–9, 302; PRO, SP 60/1, fo. 117
(*L. & P. Hen. VIII*, iv, no. 4277); *Valor Beneficiorum*, 10; White (ed.), *Extents*, 163.

[8] Ellis, *Reform and revival*, 223–4.

[9] Frame, *English lordship in Ireland*, 14.

[10] *Red bk. Kildare*, nos. 1, 126–35, 162; Otway-Ruthven, 'Medieval county of
Kildare', 181–99.

[11] *Red bk. Kildare*, nos. 1, 35, 80–2, 127–8, 132–5, 162; Otway-Ruthven, *Med. Ire.*,
252–3.

previous century. The earl's daughter and heiress received possession of all the ancestral estates, except the manor of Kildare which had originally been granted in tail male; the liberty of Kildare which had been suppressed in 1345; and in addition three small border manors held of her husband, the earl of Ormond's manor of Nenagh, which must have been worth very little.[12] As other nobles discovered, however, the continued decline of the English lordship meant that the 5th earl's rental must have been worth much less than that of his uncle the 3rd earl, particularly receipts from his estates outside Co. Kildare. Yet worse was to follow. Following the 5th earl's death, James Butler, 4th earl of Ormond, secured possession of the Kildare estates in right of his wife, despite an entail made in 1397 by which the 5th earl had restricted the succession to heirs male. And without a resident earl to guard them, the value of the Kildare estates fell sharply and the defence of the Carlow and Kildare marches virtually collapsed. In the south, Tullow castle was lost some time after 1435 and Castledermot was destroyed *c*.1443 as the Irish exploited the abeyance in the earldom to push into south Kildare. Of Co. Carlow there remained only Carlow castle itself and Baltinglass abbey.[13] To the north-west, O'Dempsey captured Lea castle and the O'Connors reoccupied the manor of Rathangan. On the Meath–Kildare border the Berminghams of Carbury had long been uncontrollable, and by 1453–4 a dispute between the earl of Wiltshire (Ormond in Ireland), who succeeded to the Butler estates on the death of his father in 1452, and Thomas FitzMaurice, grandnephew of the 5th earl of Kildare, concerning possession of the manors of Maynooth and Rathmore was causing terror and destruction among the English of Meath and Kildare. After approaching the deputy lieutenant unsuccessfully, the leading men of Kildare wrote directly to the duke of York, then lord protector, alleging that the dispute had

caused more destruccioune in the said counte of Kildare and liberty of Mith within shorte tyme now late passed, and dayly doth, then was done by Irish ennemys and English rebelles of long tyme befor, and is likly to

---

[12] *Ormond deeds, 1413–1509*, no. 101; *Red bk. Kildare*, no. 142; Otway-Ruthven, *Med. Ire.*, 263, 271, 273–4, 386.

[13] *Ormond deeds, 1413–1509*, no. 320 (3); *Red bk. Kildare*, no. 158; Otway-Ruthven, *Med. Ire.*, 369; M. C. Griffith, 'The Talbot–Ormond struggle for control of the Anglo-Irish government', in *IHS* 2 (1940–1), 396.

be the fynall destruccioune of the said county of Kildare and liberty of Mith.[14]

Thus by the mid-1450s, the community of Kildare was experiencing a crisis of lordship, which was the more severe because it was replicated both on a regional and a national level. The deaths of the 4th earl of Ormond in Ireland in 1452 and of John Talbot, 1st earl of Shrewsbury, in France in 1453 had removed two of the three magnates who had dominated politics in the lordship over the past forty years, and neither of their successors ever visited their Irish estates. Richard, duke of York, the third major landowner, had resided in Ireland for over fourteen months in 1449–50, as king's lieutenant, but was now, like Wiltshire, increasingly distracted by developments at court. And when the ensuing civil war led to the death of York, the accession of his son as King Edward IV, the attainder of Wiltshire, and the forfeiture of the Butler inheritance, the structure of power in the lordship was fundamentally and permanently changed. It was in these years, when the fortunes of the English of Ireland were at their lowest ebb, that Thomas FitzMaurice, grand-nephew of the 5th earl, was recognized as 7th earl of Kildare and laid the foundations for the Kildare ascendancy and the English recovery which characterized early-Tudor Ireland.[15]

Almost nothing is known of the circumstances or the precise date of the earl's accession. After the death of York's deputy, Edward FitzEustace, on 25 October 1454, Kildare was elected justiciar by the king's council, and was later appointed by York as his deputy. The previously quoted appeal to York of 22 January 1454 names him only as 'Thomas fitz Morice of the Geraldynes', but he was certainly styled earl of Kildare the following 6 November in a patent of the Irish chancery, so it may be that he was only recognized as earl during the course of 1454. He apparently remained deputy lieutenant until York's second visit in December 1459, and was periodically reappointed as governor, acting in 1460–2, 1464, 1470–5, and from 1477 until his death on 25 March 1478.[16]

---

[14] Ellis (ed.), *Original letters*, 2nd ser., i. 117–22; *Stat. Ire., Hen. VI*, 293, 336–8; Otway-Ruthven, *Med. Ire.*, 296 n. 43, 297, 354, 363, 380, 385–6; *New hist. Ire*, ii. 633; Nicholls, *Gaelic and gaelicised Ireland*, 174–5.

[15] *Handbook Brit. chron.*, 163–4, 482, 489, 494, 496; *New hist. Ire.*, ii. 562–3.

[16] *Handbook Brit. chron.*, 164, 166–7, 494; *Stat. Ire., Hen. VI*, 456–8, 606–8; Ellis (ed.), *Original letters*, 2nd ser., i. 117–22.

As with Lord Dacre in the west marches, Kildare's long occupancy of the governorship must have assisted the earl considerably in reorganizing the administration and defence of his wasted inheritance. Quite how devastated his estates were on his accession can only be conjectured, although income from his principal manor of Maynooth appears to have held up well under Butler rule. Ormond's receiver there accounted for rents amounting to £133. 9s. 2¼d. a year in 1450–1, although the manor had been valued at £112. 15s. 7½d. in 1329 and rents of £137. 17s. 10¼d. were levied in the year 1537–8 shortly after the rebellion.[17] Maynooth, however, was situated in one of the more secure parts of the English Pale. Since in 1329 none of the other Kildare manors was valued at more than £51 a year, and since the manors of Rathangan and Lea (together then worth £73. 6s. 7½d.) had recently been reconquered by the Irish, it is difficult to believe that Kildare's ancestral estates were worth more than £250 a year on his accession. In addition, however, he managed in the confusion of these years to hang on to some estates belonging to the attainted earl of Ormond. Initially, these included the manors of Oughterany, Oughterard, Castlewarden, and Clintonscourt in Co. Kildare. Nominally these were forfeited to the king in 1468, but in practice the earls of Kildare still detained them in 1486. And in the case of the manors of Lucan, Co. Dublin, and Kildrought (Celbridge), Donadea, and the two Cartons in Co. Kildare, the earls eventually established a good title to them.[18] Although the first group were worth no more than IR£30, the 8th and 9th earls were eventually able to extract a rental exceeding IR£100 from Lucan, Celbridge, and Carton.[19]

Whatever the financial value of the Kildare estates, however, they were of major strategic importance because of their proximity to the king's highway south through Cos. Kildare and Carlow down the Barrow valley. This was the only overland route con-

---

[17] PRO, SC 6/1238, nos. 17–18; *Red bk. Kildare*, no. 126; *Cal. Carew MSS, 1515–74*, no. 111. There is also extant a rental relating to Maynooth, made on 20 May 1451, which lists tenants and rents worth £77. 17s. 8½d. per annum. If, as seems likely, this rental corresponds with the section in the receiver's account which comprised the rents of the English tenants, it shows a small reduction (from £78. 11s. 11¾d.) in rents by comparison with the previous year. See BL, Add. Ch. 62,243. I am grateful to Professor Gearóid Mac Niocaill for drawing the 1451 rental to my attention and for providing me with a transcript.

[18] *Stat. Ire., Edw. IV*, i. 586, ii. 270–4; *Ormond deeds, 1413–1509*, nos. 213, 242, 1509–47, app. i, nos. 1, 93.

[19] BL, Royal MS 18C, XIV, fo. 216; *Cal. Carew MSS, 1515–74*, nos. 108, 111.

necting the two major areas of English lordship in the Pale and the
south. The subsequent English recovery in Co. Kildare can only
be traced in outline from the surviving evidence. Kildare's prede-
cessor as deputy lieutenant, Sir Edward FitzEustace, had already
begun the military reorganization of the shire by promoting statutes for the building of castles there, and organizing the taking up
of labourers and workmen to make trenches and build fortresses in
the marches.[20] He also ordered the repair of the key border castle of
Ballymore Eustace, and in 1468 the hereditary constable, Sir
Robert Eustace, was ordered to keep a sufficient company of
Englishmen there for the defence of the manor against the
O'Tooles and O'Byrnes.[21] FitzEustace's estates lay in the east of
the county, and after his death Kildare co-operated closely with his
son Roland, whose daughter later married his son and heir. For
instance, a statute of Kildare's parliament of 1456 granted
FitzEustace £10 for building a tower in the town of Kilcullen
which then lay 'en lez frontures del marches del dit counte pres
adioynaunt as irrois enemies du roy', the Mores and the Dempsies.
This was followed in 1468 by the building of a castle at Kilcullen
bridge, again supervised by FitzEustace, to protect the crossing of
the Liffey; and finally the town itself, along with Calverstown
nearby, was walled in 1478. By the late fifteenth century Kilcullen
bridge was securely within the Pale, and marked the boundary
between march and maghery in that part of Kildare.[22] Elsewhere,
in the more exposed southern parts of the shire, towers were built
at Narragh and Ballynagappagh in 1465, near the Windgates in
1472, at Galmorestown in 1477, at Bolablught in 1480, and at
Lackagh in 1484.[23]

During the period of the 7th earl, attention seems to have focused on the Gaelic encroachments in north-west Kildare. In 1459
Earl Thomas's defeat and capture of Conn, chief of the O'Connors
of Offaly, was a notable success, and the probable occasion of the
earl's recovery of the manor of Rathangan. Throughout the 1460s,
however, the O'Connors continued to exert strong military press-

[20] *Stat. Ire., Hen. VI*, 299.

[21] *Stat. Ire., Hen. VI*, 299, *Edw. IV*, i. 582–4.

[22] *Stat. Ire., Hen. VI*, 456, *Edw. IV*, i. 608–10, ii. 614; Conway, *Henry VII's relations*, 215–16.

[23] *Stat. Ire., Edw. IV*, i. 368, 396, ii. 48, 492–4, 710; Parliament roll, 1 Richard III cc 4, 18 (PROI RC 13/8).

ure on the borders of Meath and Kildare. In 1466 Kildare was in turn captured by the chief and subsequently rescued by Teague O'Connor, the chief's brother who had married his sister.[24] Gradually, the O'Connors were contained however. At the ford of Kinnegad, O'Connor's most convenient entry into Meath, a substantial pele was constructed by labourers who, significantly, included the inhabitants of the barony of Carbury; a small tower was built at Kilmahuke in Allon by one of the Geraldines there; and in 1468 arrangements were made for the sure keeping of the castles of Cloncurry, Ataghtyn, Coransford, Ballivor, and Ballycor against O'Connor, and another small tower was being built at the ford of Agane.[25] By 1468 even the county town of Naas was being walled.[26]

There are occasional indications under the 7th earl of the family's future greatness. In 1465 Edmund Butler, the newly restored lord of Dunboyne, granted Kildare an annuity of 10 marks out of the manor 'pro supportacione & defensione tam mei quam omnium tenencium meorum manerij siue dominij predicti'. And on the earl's own restoration in 1468, a clause required him 'defaire les Irrois hommes de Leynstre de estre al peix solonque son power'.[27] Yet throughout his career, Earl Thomas seems to have been somewhat overshadowed by his son-in-law, Roland FitzEustace, whose support for Richard, duke of York, was lavishly rewarded by Edward IV in 1462 by a grant of the border manor of Portlester, near the O'Connors and Berminghams, and his elevation to the peerage as Lord Portlester.[28] Portlester served briefly as deputy lieutenant in 1462–3, and also as lord chancellor on two or three occasions, but for most of the reign he was lord treasurer.[29] It may be no more than coincidence, but some of the earliest evidence concerning the process, continuing throughout this period, of resettling Co. Kildare marchlands relates to Portlester. A statute of 1477 noted that he had recently built anew a town with a castle in Galmorestown, 'la quele gise en lez frontures del marche' near Baltinglass, where he kept a household and intended to dwell. Galmorestown contained 120 acres of arable land which had lain waste for many years but were now cultivated by two ploughs of his. Twelve of these tenants were

---

[24] *New hist. Ire.*, ii. 633–4.   [25] *Stat. Ire., Edw. IV*, i. 22–4, 146, 608–10.
[26] Ibid., i. 606–8.   [27] Ibid., i. 302–4, 586.
[28] *Cal. pat. rolls, 1461–7*, 117, 178.   [29] Ellis, *Tudor Ireland*, 326, 331–2.

named in a statute of 1480 which annulled a malicious indictment of 111 of Portlester's tenants and servants in the region for
going to Ballymore Eustace in 1478 and burning the corn of Sir
Robert Eustace. And interestingly, although they were all described as 'les foialx homes & subiectes le roy', half of them
had Gaelic surnames.[30] As in the Anglo-Scottish marches, many
of the tenants who colonized these borderlands were originally
aliens who later took the oath of allegiance and became English
subjects.

The circumstances in which the 8th earl succeeded to his inheritance were clearly much more propitious than those obtaining
in the 1450s. We cannot quantify the improvements in his landed
income, but the Kildare marches had by then been significantly
strengthened, and this process continued over the next decade.
Equally importantly, after the death of Earl Thomas, there was,
unlike 1453–4, no succession dispute or even a quasi-interregnum
which the Gaelic borderers could exploit: by statute of 1470 the
future 8th earl was empowered to enter his estates without suing
his livery by common law.[31] Earl Gerald's shrewd interventions in
the marriage market also added significantly to his reputation
and landed inheritance. His first marriage to Alison Eustace consolidated his alliance with Portlester. His wife's dowry may not
have been large, but it apparently included the manor of
Moynalvy, Co. Meath, worth about 20 marks per annum (which
the earl soon improved by the erection of a tower there),[32] and the
reversion to the manor of Portlester. Despite Lord Rowland's
efforts to resettle the manor, Portlester was valued at no more than
IR£34 per annum in 1495, when it was temporarily in the king's
hands through Poynings's act of resumption; but it was worth 80
marks annually within a few years of its acquisition by Kildare
after the death of his father-in-law in 1496.[33]

After the death of his first wife in 1495, he married Elizabeth St
John, a relative of the king, whose dowry was much more valuable

[30] *Stat. Ire., Edw. IV*, i. 492–4, 702–10.

[31] Ibid., i. 660–2. Cf. ibid., ii. 278.

[32] Gearóid Mac Niocaill (ed.), *Crown surveys of lands 1540–41* (Dublin, 1992),
115; *L. & P. Hen. VIII*, Add. i, no. 297; *Stat. Ire., Hen. VI*, 370–2, *Edw. IV*, ii. 724;
Cal. Carew MSS, 1515–74, no. 111.

[33] *Stat. Ire., Edw. IV*, ii. 220, 274, 454; BL, Royal MS 18C, XIV, fos. 106, 112; Sir
James Ware, *The histories and antiquities of Ireland*, ed. R. Ware (Dublin, 1704), 34;
Cal. close rolls, 1500–09, no. 243; *Stat. Ire., Hen. VII & VIII*, 129–31.

but perhaps less important strategically. It comprised IR£600 in cash, and lands which were reputedly worth IR£200 a year in England and Ireland. The English lands were worth about £60 (sterling) a year. They lay in Warwickshire and Gloucestershire and had formerly belonged to Sir Simon Mountford, one of the largest landowners in Warwickshire until his attainder for treason. In Ireland, the couple were granted the manors of Leixlip, Co. Kildare, Ratoath, Co. Meath, and Cowley, Co. Louth. In fact, the grant was not quite as generous as it seemed: the Irish lands yielded no more than about IR£70 per annum altogether, and the earl had previously received a life grant of Cowley from Edward IV and of Leixlip from Richard III which had recently been resumed into the king's hands by a statute of Poynings's parliament. As his part of the agreement, Earl Gerald settled on his wife in jointure lands in the Pale and Co. Limerick worth 380 marks per annum.[34] The settlement, though very generous, proved to be something of a mixed blessing to the earl in terms of family cohesion. The estate was entailed to the male heirs of Gerald and Elizabeth, who bore him seven sons, whereas the earldom descended to his only son by his first wife. The effect was therefore to establish a powerful cadet branch of the family which the 9th earl found rather more difficult to control than the other numerous, but comparatively poor, junior branches of the family.

Other royal grants also helped to swell the earl's patrimony. Edward IV had granted him the manor of Moylagh, Co. Meath, worth IR£40 a year, and had made him a grant for life of the manors of Ardmullan and Belgard, Co. Meath, worth IR£44 per annum.[35] These manors too had initially been taken into the king's hands by virtue of Poynings's act of resumption, but Moylagh must have been quickly restored, for it formed part of Lady Kildare's jointure in 1496–7.[36] Perhaps because the original grant of Leixlip, Ratoath, and Cowley failed to realize as much as had been expected, the earl and his countess received an additional grant in 1506 of the manors of Carlingford, Greencastle, and Mourne in Ulster, plus the customs of Carlingford. By 1534 these

---

[34] BL, Royal MS 18C, XIV, fos. 106, 112, 216; Conway, *Henry VII's relations*, 94; Bryan, *Great earl*, 196–7; *Cal. pat. rolls, 1494–1509*, 84–5, 109, 308, 443; *Cal. inq. p.m., Hen. VII*, iii, nos. 760, 943, 1169; PRO, E 101/248, no. 17.

[35] *Cal. pat. rolls, 1477–85*, 341; PRO, E 101/248, no. 17.

[36] BL, Royal MS 18C, XIV, fos. 106, 112, 216.

were worth IR£40 a year.[37] Finally, Gerald Fitzgerald, the future
9th earl, received a number of grants from the time of his marriage
in 1503 to Elizabeth Zouche, also a relative of Henry VII. The earl
settled the manors of Moylagh (again!), Rathangan, Portlester, and
Moynalvy, worth 200 marks, on the couple in jointure, while the
king agreed to grant them lands in England worth £40. This took
the form of a grant of the manor of Cawston in Norfolk, worth 50
marks (sterling) a year.[38] In 1515 Gerald, now the 9th earl, received
a grant in tail male of the manor of Ardmullan, which he had held
since 1510 at the king's pleasure, the port of Strangford, and
the seawreck of Ardglass.[39] His second marriage in 1522 to Lady
Elizabeth Grey, daughter of the marquis of Dorset, was aimed at
strengthening his ties with the Tudor court. His countess brought
him a dowry, probably £250, but apparently no lands, and in
return he granted her an annuity for life of 300 marks (Irish) from
the manors of Portlester, Moylagh, Moynalvy, Ardmullan, Lucan,
and Rathmore.[40] Thus, altogether, royal grants and marriage
settlements by the 8th and 9th earls may have increased the
family's landed rental by IR£350 a year.

Nevertheless, in the marcher conditions obtaining in large parts
of the lordship, the acquisition of title to land, and the extraction of
rents and services from the land were by no means the same thing.
Although these acquisitions were no doubt a welcome addition to
the family's income, the key to the earl's success was his ability to
concentrate sufficient power and armed might to establish and
maintain possession of border estates and to defend his tenants
there from external aggressors. Only the broad outlines of this
process can be described, although the crown surveys and accounts
of forfeited land taken after the 9th earl's attainder provide a much
more detailed picture of the eventual outcome. Overall, the evidence suggests that the main period of Kildare expansion occurred
under the 8th earl (1478–1513), in the 1480s and again after 1496;
but much of the work of developing these borderlands fell to the
9th earl (1513–34). This difference seems to be captured in contem-

---

[37] PRO, SP 65/1, no. 2; *L. & P. Hen. VIII*, v, no. 676; *Cal. pat. rolls, 1494–1509*,
443.
[38] *Cal. close rolls, 1500–09*, no. 243; *L. & P. Hen. VIII*, i (2nd edn.), no. 2055
(95iii); *Cal. inq. p.m., Hen. VII*, iii, no. 790.
[39] *L. & P. Hen. VIII*, i (2nd edn.), no. 632 (24), ii, no. 999.
[40] *L. & P. Hen. VIII*, iii, no. 2703; *SP Hen. VIII*, ii, 101; *Stat. Ire., Hen. VII &
VIII*, 129–31.

porary assessments of the two earls: the 9th earl was known as 'the
gretest improver of his landis in this land',[41] whereas the obituary
of his father, composed by Philip Flattisbury, compiler of the 9th
earl's Red Book, stated that he excelled all previous governors of
Ireland in defeating the Irish enemies and reducing them to the
king's peace, and also

plures villas in diversis partibus Hibernice longe tempore devastatas cum
colonis et aliis edificiis reedificandis, ac diversa castra et pontes et alia
fortilagia manuforti in frontiera Hibernicorum construxit & edificavit ad
magnam vtilitatem et defensionem Anglicorum.[42]

[Many towns in different parts which had long been laid waste by the Irish
and needed replenishing with colonists and other buildings, and also
many castles and bridges and other fortresses, he forcibly constructed and
built on the borders of the Irish to the great utility and defence of the
English.]

In practice, much of this expansion involved the expropriation
of Gaelic landowners and their replacement by tenants of the earl
(who might occasionally be the same persons). In legal terms,
however, the earls frequently bought up the common-law titles to
these estates, and in many cases their title stemmed from a clause
in the successive commissions to the earls as the king's deputy
from 1496 onwards. These commissions granted them any crown
lands which they could recover from the Gaelic Irish.[43]
    Under the 8th earl, the process of fortifying key river crossings
and highways in Co. Kildare continued, with the building of a
tower at Lackagh and the strengthening of Kildare castle in 1484.[44]
In the south, Leighlin castle was recovered in 1480, and a substantial castle at Castledermot, under construction in 1485, promised
'la vray readepcion de toutz lez terrez gastez del counte de
Cathirlagh'.[45] An important legal prop to Kildare power in south
Kildare and Carlow was a statute of 1483 passed in a parliament at
Limerick which, on the grounds that Kildare had recovered them
from the Irish, vested in the earl all waste lands between
Calverstown and Leighlinbridge, unless their owners reoccupied
them within six years. By the time the statute was repealed in 1531,

[41] *SP Hen. VIII*, ii. 300.   [42] BL, Add. MS 4787, fo. 252ᵛ.
[43] *New hist. Ire.*, ii. 646.
[44] Parliament roll, 1 Richard III cc 4, 18 (PROI, RC 13/8).
[45] Parliament roll, 2–3 Richard III c. 15 (PROI, PRO 7/1).

the Geraldines had penetrated down the east bank of the Slaney to build up a large rental in Carlow, worth over IR£105 a year in 1537, chiefly from the manors of Rathvilly and Clonmore, while the tower and manor of Clonogan formed a Geraldine military outpost there.[46] Further south still, along the northern marches of Co. Wexford, the 8th and 9th earls were buying up mesne tenures within the duke of Norfolk's estates. Between 1508 and 1526 they purchased large tracts of land in the manors of Fassaghbantry, Deeps, and Old Ross, replacing the Gaelic occupants with their own tenants. For instance, one of the local gentry, Fulke Den, gave the 9th earl the townland of Reddina, containing 120 acres, in return 'for the twicone and defence of the residue of his landes'. The earl received 10s. a year rent for it, but by 1540 it lay waste 'causa guerre per le Caveners'.[47]

The chronology of Kildare expansion in the west is more obscure, but probably in the late fifteenth century the earls recovered the ancestral manors and castles of Lea and Morett from the midland Irish. Their value was strategic rather than financial. Lea castle was the earl's chief military base in the region, and was redesigned to perform a similar role in the Anglo-Gaelic marches to Rockcliffe's in the Anglo-Scottish marches. A jury reported in 1540 that it was

valde tutum et necessarium receptaculum pro ceteris hominibus domini regis ad arma illuc missis pro defencione anglicane partis terre Hibernie adversus insultus ferocium Hibernicorum predictorum eandem partem invadere conancium ad opprimandum maliciam eorundem adeo quod extra limites suas evadere non auderent.[48]

[A very secure and necessary shelter for the rest of the king's men-at-arms sent there for the defence of the English parts of the land of Ireland against the inroads of the said wild Irish trying to attack that region, to suppress their malice so that they do not dare to go beyond their own boundaries.]

The earls also renewed their claims to the manors of Geashill and Timogue, but apparently this process had not progressed far

[46] *Alen's reg.*, 276; PRONI, D.3078/1/18/9; *New hist. Ire.*, ii. 635; *Stat. Ire., Hen. VII & VIII*, 132–4; *Cal. Carew MSS, 1515–74*, nos. 108, 111; PRO, SP 65/1, no. 2; *Crown surveys of lands 1540–41*, ed. Gearóid Mac Niocaill (Dublin, 1992), 175–7.
[47] PRONI, D.3078/1/18/9–22; BL, Harleian MS 3756, fos. 85ᵛ–86 (*Crown surveys*, ed. Mac Niocaill, 307–8); *New hist. Ire.*, iii. 7. For Reddina: PRONI, D.3078/1/18/24, fos. 1ᵛ-2; *Crown surveys*, ed. Mac Niocaill, 12, 307.
[48] *Crown surveys*, ed. Mac Niocaill, 160–1, 171–3 (quotation, p. 161).

beyond the exaction of tributes from the existing Gaelic occupants.[49] Further north, the independent enclave established by the
Berminghams of Carbury was progressively reduced. The 8th earl
was buying up titles to land there as early as 1483, and by 1519 the
9th earl's justices were holding sessions at Carbury castle.[50] The
activity of the earl's justices arose out of the restoration to the earl
by Henry VIII about 1514 of the liberty of Kildare which had been
suppressed in 1345. Although the restored liberty did not amount
to a palatinate, since pleas of the crown were reserved to the king,
it was none the less a recognition of the earls' success since the
1450s in defending a region which was of vital strategic importance
and in strengthening English control of the marches there.[51]

The early-Tudor period also witnessed significant expansion by
the Fitzgeralds in three other districts. Militarily, the defence of
the Dublin and Meath marches adjoining Kildare was inseparable
from the defence of Kildare: hence the earls' interests in these
regions. In the south-west marches of Co. Dublin, the 8th earl
purchased from the Polestown Butlers the mesne tenures of abandoned townships in the manors of Ballymore Eustace and
Castlekevin and the barony of Coillache, which they held in freehold from the archbishop of Dublin. He then recovered these lands
from the O'Tooles and O'Byrnes. He also seized parts of Fassaroe
and Fercullen from them, and by 1500 he had built Powerscourt
castle to control the region. After the earl's death, the archbishop
as chief lord commenced litigation against the 9th earl and Sir
Thomas Fitzgerald of Leixlip, securing favourable judgments in
respect of some of these archiepiscopal lands in 1514 and 1521.
Other townships, however, were still in the 9th earl's hands on his
attainder.[52] During the ensuing revolt, the O'Tooles razed
Powerscourt castle. It was rebuilt in 1536–7, but the manor was
eventually returned to the O'Tooles by Lord Deputy St Leger as
part of the 'surrender and regrant' strategy.[53]

[49] BL, Harleian MS 3756, fos. 8, 26, 33, 45–6 (*Crown surveys*, ed. Mac Niocaill,
235, 258, 267–8, 277–8, 287).
[50] PRONI, D.3078/1/16/44; TCD MS 1731, 60; BL, Harleian MS 3756, fo. 57ᵛ
(*Crown surveys*, ed. Mac Niocaill, 290).
[51] Ellis, 'Destruction of the liberties', 150–61.
[52] *Alen's reg.*, 190–3, 262, 266, 291–2; PROI, RC 8/43, 201; James Murray, 'Archbishop Alen, Tudor reform and the Kildare rebellion', in *RIA Proc.*, 89 (1989), sect.
C, 12–14; Lord Walter Fitzgerald, 'The manor and castle of Powerscourt . . . in the
sixteenth century', in *Kildare Archaeological Society Journal*, 6 (1909–11), 127–39.
[53] Fitzgerald, 'Manor and castle of Powerscourt'; Bradshaw, *Irish constitutional
revolution*, 202.

In Meath, the earls attained their principal military objectives through the acquisition of the manor of Portlester and the reduction of Carbury. In Carbury, the 9th earl's receiver-general, Sir Walter Delahide, gradually built up an estate worth IR£39 per annum around the manors of Castlecarbury and Ballina.[54] Further west, a number of Gaelic and English marcher lineages had earlier erected independent lordships on the ruins of the feudal settlement of the region, notably the manors of Loughsewdy and Kilkenny West. By the 1520s the earls had consolidated their hold over the territories of the Tyrrells of Fertullagh and the MacGeoghegans of Kineleagh, and had built up a substantial rental there. The 9th earl also began to buy up disputed marchland which was held in pledge by the Dillons and Daltons.[55] One entry in the 9th earl's Rental vividly epitomizes the conflict between common-law tenure and actual possession which eventually brought firm title by Gaelic law to 'swordland':

Kyllinnower [Killenner] was in pledg with Geralde fitz Edmond Dyllon is sonnys for £20 money, 37 incalf kyne and 3 melsh kyne which were all paid by th'ands of Patrike Fay, and besyde that the said land was purchased of Morice Mape, rightfull heyre of the same.[56]

By 1534 the earl's lands in Kineleagh were worth IR£41. 18s. 8d. and his possessions in Fertullagh—'ubi tamen breve domini regis non currit'—were valued at IR£19. 3s. 4d.[57]

Finally, a late and rather unlikely extension of the family's landed interests occurred in the earldom of Ulster. The main phase of this activity probably dated from 1496, following the grant to the earl of the manor of Cowley and of any lands he might recover from the Gaelic Irish. In the years following, the earls gradually secured control of the waste manors and ports of the Ulster coast as far north as Strangford. These included the manors of Dundrum and Ardglass, as well as the formal grant by the king of the manors of Carlingford, Greencastle, and Mourne, the port of Strangford, and the seawreck of Ardglass. By 1534, the 9th earl

---

[54] *Crown surveys*, ed. Mac Niocaill, 183–7; PRO, SP 65/1, no. 2.

[55] BL, Harleian MS 3756, fos. 18, 18ᵛ, 22, 22ᵛ, 23ᵛ, 24, 26, 27, 36ᵛ–7ᵛ, 65ᵛ–8ᵛ (*Crown surveys*, ed. Mac Niocaill, 240, 242, 247–8, 249, 251, 254, 258–9, 261–2, 270–3, 297–301).

[56] BL, Harleian MS 3756, fo. 68 (*Crown surveys*, ed. Mac Niocaill, 300).

[57] PRO, SP 60/5, fos. 148–9 (*L. & P. Hen. VIII*, xii (ii), no. 1317); *Crown surveys*, ed. Mac Niocaill, 126–9 (quotation, p. 126).

had built up a rental of over IR£150 a year in Lecale in the old earldom of Ulster.[58]

The absence of receiver's accounts for the Kildare estates is a major handicap in assessing the value to the earls of their landed possessions. Nevertheless, it is possible to construct a rough estimate of their overall value on the eve of the 1534–5 rebellion based on various surveys and accounts. These include Undertreasurer Brabazon's accounts of receipts (1534–7) from Kildare estates after their forfeiture; the crown surveys of lands 1540–1; the 9th earl's Rental, begun in 1518 and subsequently updated; and two Elizabethan copies of, respectively, receipts from the Kildare estates in 1537–8, and a valuation of Kildare possessions granted to the earl of Ormond in October 1537.[59] In particular, the crown surveys and undertreasurer's accounts frequently include details of the 9th earl's receipts from individual estates, in addition to receipts and valuations (often much reduced) after their seizure by the crown. Many of the earl's possessions were included in the crown surveys as part of the crown's ancient demesne rather than as forfeited lands. Although this was technically correct, these crown lands had usually been waste until the earls had recovered them from the Gaelic Irish, and they have therefore been included in the following estimates. In other instances, the crown surveys include an estimate of what particular lands might be worth if tenants could be found for them; but these lands, it is clear, were waste even under the 9th earl and have therefore been excluded from the estimate. Lastly, it should be stressed that the estimate reflects the optimum values of the earl's possessions (but net of the usual fees, allowances, and other deductions), in periods of comparative peace, and when the earl was deputy. The values would have been significantly less in wartime or when Kildare was detained at court.

---

[58] *Crown surveys*, ed. Mac Niocaill, 75–82; BL, Harleian MS 3756, fo. 24ᵛ (*Crown surveys*, ed. Mac Niocaill, 254); PRO, SP 65/1, no. 2; D. B. Quinn, 'Anglo-Irish Ulster in the early sixteenth century', in *Proceedings and reports of the Belfast Natural History and Philosophical Society*, 1933/4 (1935), 56–78.

[59] PRO, SP 65/1, no. 2; SC 11/934–5; SP 65/3, no. 2 (printed in *Crown surveys*, ed. Mac Niocaill, 1–229); BL, Harleian MS 3756 (printed in *Crown surveys*, ed. Mac Niocaill, 231–357); SP 60/5, fos. 148–9 (*L. & P. Hen. VIII*, xii (ii), no. 1317; another copy in Lambeth MS 611, fo. 157 (*Cal. Carew MSS, 1515–74*, no. 111)); SP 60/2, fos. 46–7 (*L. & P. Hen. VIII*, xii (ii), no. 964iii; another copy in Lambeth MS 611, fo. 12 (*Cal. Carew MSS, 1515–74*, no. 108)).

By the 1530s the earl's ancestral manors in Co. Kildare were still his most valuable possessions, worth IR£709 a year from twenty manors and other scattered lands. By comparison with the early fourteenth century, however, the balance of Fitzgerald landed influence in the county had shifted further east and south. The earls had recovered possession of at least parts of the manors of Lea, Morett, and Geashill in the west, but their value was now chiefly military. Maynooth, valued at IR£237 a year, was worth more than double its value in 1329. The value of Kildare, now estimated at IR£140 a year net (IR£39 was allowed for the wages of thirteen horsemen for defence) had increased similarly. In south Kildare, the earls had since acquired another cluster of manors (Kilkea, Castledermot, Woodstock, and Athy), of which Kilkea (valued at IR£112) was their third most valuable possession.

In the south-west of Ireland by contrast, the second cluster of ancestral manors around Croom and Adare was generally worth much less than it had been two centuries earlier. Although the 7th earl had founded the monastery of Adare together with his countess, Joan Fitzgerald, daughter of the earl of Desmond, who was buried there, the 8th and 9th earls showed little interest in these estates. They were all leased to the earl of Desmond for £100 sterling (of which the manor of Tobernea yielded £72 sterling), except for Carrickittle which had been granted outright to Desmond. And after 1534, the Munster Geraldines simply refused to surrender them.[60] The other ancestral possessions in Carlow, Kilkenny, and Cork were of very little value.

In their place, however, the earls had built up, almost out of nothing, an imposing rental of IR£460 a year in Co. Meath. The rents of the manors which Kildare had acquired by marriage or specific royal grant, such as Portlester (now valued at IR£69) and Moylagh (IR£95), had increased substantially, but further west in Fertullagh, Kineleagh, and Annaly in the erstwhile manors of Loughsewdy, Kilkenny West, and Granard, the earls had built up a rental of about IR£150 among the Gaelic and English marcher lineages of Westmeath. Elsewhere, the 9th earl possessed four manors in Co. Tipperary, but only Knockgraffon (worth 32 marks) was of any considerable value. The manor of Lucan in Co. Dublin was worth IR£31 a year, and Kildare had a few scattered pos-

---

[60] *Crown surveys*, ed. Mac Niocaill, 177–83; PRO, SP 65/1, no. 2.

sessions elsewhere in Co. Dublin (valued at IR£2 a year), and in Cos. Louth (IR£11), Carlow (IR£4), Cork (IR£16), and Wexford (10 marks). Altogether, therefore, the 9th earl's Irish estates were worth IR£1,585 a year. In addition, other members of his immediate family also held substantial estates in their own right, which are discussed below.

Many of the 9th earl's other sources of income are listed in his Rental. Landlords in England might have thought the earl's listing of the scutage (or royal service, as it was usually called in Ireland) due from his military tenants an antiquarian exercise. In Ireland, however, scutage ran eight times between 1450 and 1531 (the last proclamation), and Kildare's Rental shows that he was entitled to IR£145 from each proclamation. Most of this was due from Co. Kildare, for which he could collect IR£102 from nine and a half baronies, but he was also entitled to IR£43 from subtenants in the manors of Rathmore, Kilkea, and Knockgraffon, Co. Tipperary. A more consistent source of income, however, would have been the wardships, fines, and liveries due from the earl's military tenants, especially in Kildare. Significantly, the earl entered in his Rental the procedure for doing homage and fealty, and in some cases he noted which freeholders owed suit of court.[61] Overall, these arrangements must have helped to promote the cohesion of the Kildare lordship and the earl's influence over his military tenants. A more familiar aspect of the earl's standing was the list of fees included in the Rental. Altogether, there were forty-five entries of annuities, mainly in money but some in kind, which were worth IR£112 a year, and most were granted for the life of the earl or of the grantor. Over half the grantors were beneficed clergy, mainly with livings in Meath and Kildare, but including the bishop of Waterford, the vicar of Clonmel, and the prior of Llanthony. Other grantors included John de Courcy, lord of Kinsale, Sir Christopher Plunket of Dunsoghly, and a number of lesser gentry of the Pale. And occasionally, it is specifically stated that the fees were granted to the earl in return for 'his just favours in his rightfull causes', 'for his lafull diffence against the Irish men', or 'for helpe & favors'.[62]

---

[61] BL, Harleian MS 3756, *passim* (*Crown surveys*, ed. Mac Niocaill, 232–357); S. G. Ellis, 'Taxation and defence in late medieval Ireland: the survival of scutage', in *RSAI Jn.*, 107 (1977), 5–28.

[62] BL, Harleian MS 3756, fos. 18–27ᵛ (quotations, fos. 26, 27; *Crown surveys*, ed. Mac Niocaill, 238–63).

Nearly all these fees were granted by members of the Englishry or those who would probably have been denizened as Englishmen. A separate section of the Rental listed 'Th'erll of Kyldaris duties upon Irishmen'. These annual tributes were levied on almost all the Gaelic chieftaincies bordering the Pale, ostensibly in return for the earl's defending them. With the revival of Kildare fortunes and of the English lordship, the earls could bring unprecedented pressure to bear on the comparatively weak and divided border chieftaincies. The tributes listed in the Rental reflected agreements with the 9th earl, but in most cases they probably renewed arrangements made with his father. Altogether twenty-four chieftaincies are listed, and they include every significant chief and a host of weaker ones in a wide arc around the Pale, plus a few more remote chieftaincies, such as MacDermot and O'Rourke in north-east Connaught, and O'Dwyre in north Tipperary. Particularly in Gaelic Leinster, these tributes took the form of a levy of 4d. on every cow in the lordship. Their value cannot now be calculated, but other renders in money and kind were worth IR£138 a year.[63] In some lordships, such as those of MacGeoghegan and O'Farrell in the midlands, the exaction of tribute was turning into the establishment of lordship, as the earl bought up lands held in pledge. A similar process had no doubt occurred rather earlier in those parts of Leinster which the earls had recovered from the Irish. The tributes were of course the reverse of the annual blackrents which some English counties had traditionally paid to Gaelic chiefs for 'defence' (freedom from raids). They were won and maintained by the continuous campaigning which characterized the Kildare ascendancy, and were therefore a less certain source of income than landed rents. Militarily, however, they were closely linked with the increased rents which the earls extracted from border manors.

Two other sections of the Rental list property which the earl had taken to farm and also farms set. The value of farms set, ranging from money to renders in kind such as cattle and eels, and mill and tithe corn (2,350 pecks of wheat and malt, worth perhaps IR£135, depending on the state of the harvest) may have amounted to IR£700 a year in the 1520s. Since these rents accrued from lands and rights belonging to the earl, they were simply an aspect of his landed possessions, included in the crown surveys of his estates,

---

[63] BL, Harleian MS 3756, fos. 30–42 (*Crown surveys*, ed. Mac Niocaill, 264–77).

rather than an independent source of income. In the case of 'Such tethes & fermes as the said erle hath to ferme', however, Kildare no doubt made a profit on the IR£200 or so which he laid out annually on these leases, but how much is uncertain. Most of the twenty-two transactions listed related to tithes, usually for seven years or longer, and to border areas for which the earl could presumably expect a larger profit for his services.[64] The advowsons of the forty benefices in the dioceses of Dublin, Kildare, Limerick, Cork, and Meath which belonged to the earl were presumably also a significant source of income.

Finally, there were the profits accruing from the earl's long tenure of the deputyship. After 1496, the king's deputy normally received the balance of the revenues without account in return for defending the land at his own costs. In theory, after payment of ministers' fees and other expenses, between IR£800 and IR£900 per annum was apparently available to the deputy to meet the costs of defence. Yet this balance reflected more the traditional accounting procedures of the Irish exchequer than the income actually realizable from the deputyship. As deputy, Kildare was better placed than most governors to profit from these arrangements because he could deploy for this purpose the system of defences which he had built up for the protection of his own estates. Moreover, certain perquisites and fines accruing to the deputy did not normally appear in exchequer accounts, and under the 8th and 9th earls other sources of revenue were also withdrawn from exchequer control. For instance, when arranging for the marriage of his daughter, Elizabeth Barnewall, to Christopher Eustace of Ballycutland in 1525, Lord Trimblestone paid the earl of Kildare as the king's deputy IR£20 for a special livery of Eustace's lands, IR£5 for a pardon of outlawry and 2 marks for sealing it, IR£2 and 15s. for two debts to third parties, and IR£12 for a dispensation for the marriage.[65]

Overall, there are many aspects of Kildare's finances which remain obscure—the complete absence of receiver-general's accounts is particularly unfortunate—but on the evidence available, the 9th earl probably enjoyed an income well in excess of IR£2,000 a year. This would have placed him among the top ten of the

---

[64] Ibid., fos. 18–24ᵛ (*Crown surveys*, ed. Mac Niocaill, 238–56).

[65] *Cal. inq. Co. Dublin*, 50–1. See, in general, Ellis, *Reform and revival*, ch. 3, for this paragraph.

Tudor nobility in financial terms; and of course it meant that Kildare towered head and shoulders above all the other nobles in the lordship. Equally importantly, the earl built up, with his acquisition of so much marchland, a key position in the defence of the lordship, and command of a private army of battle-hardened tenants.

Considering the extent of his possessions, Kildare held surprisingly little land in the Pale maghery where his tenants, and therefore his rents, would have been fairly secure from the constant cattle raiding and endemic unrest of the marches. On his estates close to Dublin, at Maynooth and Lucan, the earl could let his demesne land for 2*s.* or even 3*s.* an acre a year. Similarly, in the more sheltered parts of Co. Meath, around Moylagh and Moynalvy, the 9th earl was increasing rents in the 1520s. Yet in the Pale marches, even arable land commonly yielded no more than 12*d.* per acre, and lands in exposed areas close to the Irishry might be worth as little as 2*d.* or even 1*d.* an acre. The demesnes of Kildare's manor of Moynalvy, consisting of 120 acres of arable land, 4 acres of meadow, and 8 acres of pasture, were worth IR£10 a year, 'pro eo quod libere sunt de le hostyngis', but this was quite exceptional. The earl's tenants were normally expected to attend hostings when summoned. Thomas Fitzgerald of Dollardstown, for instance, undertook to appear 'at euerie royall seruice whe[n] the kinges bannour shalbee displayed and alsoo [he] shall trwe and faithfully serue the said Ge[rald] and his heires when it shalbee required'.[66]

In addition, the earls made arrangements for a standing defence force to discourage casual raiders. From *c.*1500 the 8th earl had maintained a retinue of 120 galloglass and 120 kerne for the defence of his estates and of the country. At need they could be quartered on the tenants for defence, but some of the tributes which Kildare exacted from the Gaelic Irish included the right to quarter his troops on them for specific periods. MacMahon, for instance, agreed to bear 160 galloglass for three months each year. The 9th earl was credited with shifting most of the cost of the maintenance of his troops on to Irishmen.[67] In Cos. Kildare and Meath,

    [66] PRONI, D.3078/1/1/3, 18. See also *Crown surveys*, ed. Mac Niocaill, 115, 171, 293–5, and *passim*.
    [67] BL, Harleian MS 3756, fo. 40ᵛ (*Crown surveys*, ed. Mac Niocaill, 276); *SP Hen. VIII*, ii. 503.

too, the rents on particular lands were reduced or remitted in return for bearing coign and livery or other military impositions. In the vill of Rathangan, for instance, the tenants held 260 acres of pasture, 3 acres of wood, and a turbary and common pasture rent-free

quia onerati sunt cum viis et vadiis quorundam hominum equestrium et pedestrium anglice vocatorum horsemen, galoglasse et keren' retentorum ad vices pro defensione patrie.

[Because they are charged with journeys and the wages of certain horse and foot men called in English horsemen, galoglasse and keren. retained at times for the defence of the country.]

And there were similar arrangements on lands in Moylagh and Kilkea.[68] Elsewhere, in Rathangan and in the manors of Kildare and Kilkea, at least twenty rent-free holdings of around sixty acres each were created for the maintenance of horsemen. This suggests that a distinction was made between the traditional obligation of the earl's tenants, and indeed all the king's subjects, to do military service in defence of their country, particularly at hostings, and a special obligation attaching to individual holdings and tenants for the defence of particular marches. These tenants were required to maintain horse and harness, and the earl commonly distributed among his horsemen between sixty and a hundred horses a year from his stud farms.[69]

Some details concerning these military holdings emerge in the case of Meyler Fay, the 9th earl's confidential servant. On his death in 1550, Fay was seised of the castle of Ballinure, a messuage, and 150 acres of land in Rathangan, which he had by grant of the 9th earl in 1517. He held these lands by knight service in tail male, with reversion to the grantor. He was required to reside on the property, not to alienate his holding, and to pay 4d. per annum for every horse and cow pasturing on the lands.[70] The 9th earl's Rental also noted that he owed royal service (scutage) for the holding; and the crown survey of 1540 stated that he held 60 acres of land rent-free 'pro defensione patrie ibidem', but that elsewhere another 40 acres were waste adjoining

---

[68] BL, Harleian MS 3756, fo. 60ᵛ (*Crown surveys*, ed. Mac Niocaill, 157–8, 162).
[69] *SP Hen. VIII*, iii. 379.
[70] *Cal. inq. Co. Dublin*, 128; *Crown surveys*, ed. Mac Niocaill, 152, 157, 159, 160, 162, 168.

olim quoddam castrum in tutissimo loco vocato Bellanure in extrema
parte anglicane patrie super costeras Offalye scituatum nuper prohibens O
Cconour et aliis ferocibus Hibernicis patriam illam depredare conantibus
quod circa 20 annos elapsos per predictos Hibernicos laceratum ac
disruptum fuit et sic modo iacet vastatum.[71]

[A certain former castle sited in a very secure place called Bellanure in the
outermost part of the English country on the borders of Offalye recently
restraining O Cconour and other wild Irish trying to plunder that country
which around 20 years ago was razed and broken by the said Irish and so
lies just waste.]

Not all these new military tenures can be identified, because
Kildare's Rental and title deeds were withheld from the government after the 1534 rebellion, and some of his tenants evidently
seized their opportunity. Some of the holdings seem to stand out,
however, because, like Lord Dacre's Cumberland estates, the vast
majority of tenants on the Kildare estates held their lands at the
lord's will. What tenure-at-will amounted to in practice is very
difficult to say. The 8th and 9th earls were seemingly very reluctant
to grant long leases, life tenures, or freeholds, except in the case of
close relatives or leading estate officials.[72] Exceptionally, in the case
of the manor of Maynooth, a little more is known about the customary tenants. Names of cottiers or crofters for the vill of
Maynooth are listed in the rental of 1451, the Rental of 1518, and
the crown survey of 1540. Only 10 out of 59 of the customary
tenants listed in 1518 had the same surnames (mostly very common
ones) as the 62 'firmarii' listed in 1451; and none of those 10 was
among the 11 noted in the 1540 survey. This may indicate a rapid
turnover of tenants in the later fifteenth century. On the other
hand, in the case of 5 of the 11 tenants noted in 1540, tenants of the
same name and surname are listed in 1518 (including some unusual
surnames), and one more had the same (unusual) surname. If a
custom of tenant right analagous to that in the far north were
beginning to develop in early-Tudor Maynooth, we might expect
this level of continuity, as political conditions stabilized and population increased. Moreover, this demographic increase was largely
brought about, to judge from the evidence concerning Maynooth,
by an influx of Gaelic tenants: the proportion of tenants with

---

[71] BL, Harleian MS 3756, fo. 56; *Crown surveys*, ed. Mac Niocaill, 159, 290.

[72] For instances of more secure tenures created by the earls, see *Cal. inq. Co.
Dublin*, 43, 128; PRONI, D.3078/1/1/3, 118, D.3078/1/19/1.

Gaelic surnames rose from 37 per cent to 54 per cent between 1451 and 1518.[73]

In other respects, too, conditions of tenure on the Kildare estates seem quite similar to those on Dacre estates in the far north. Like Lord Dacre, the earl continued to exact labour services on many of his manors. Tenants of the manor of Moynalvy, for instance, were obliged to do '1 turffdaye, 1 wedyngdaye et 2 hokdayes in autumpno', and in Corbally in Kilkea manor the tenants did three days' ploughing for the sowing of wheat and three more for oats in the spring, and three days' carting grain and three days' carting turf (peat) in the autumn: but six or seven days' work annually was more usual. Many tenants were also obliged to give a hen at Christmas. In view of Kildare's policy of land improvement and the needs of defence, these labour services, though light, must be seen as an integral part of customary tenures rather than a feudal anachronism. David Sutton, the earl's receiver, deposed in 1537 that if any of his manors lacked 'eny house of office, as hall, kitchyn, barne or stable', the earl's tenants were bound to 'make it upon their owne charges and to bringe the stuf to hande', Kildare providing the masons and carpenters. Every 'plough' or three cottagers was also obliged to supply a labourer for up to a week each year 'to cast diches and fastnes upon the borders', 'to cutte passages upon the borders of Irishmen', and 'to cary stones to the castels on the borders'.[74] The exploitation of these services was co-ordinated through four castles to which, depending on their location, the earl's tenants were assigned. In north-west Kildare, tenants of the baronies of Clane, Connell, and Carbury were assigned to Rathangan. Kildare supervised services owed from Salt, Ikeathy, and Oughterany in the north-east, Offaly in the west, and also the king's lands which the earl controlled as deputy. In the south, Athy was the centre for Narragh, Naas, Reban, the earl's half of Kilcullen barony, and also the 'quarters' of Kilkea, Carlow, and Rathvilly in Co. Carlow. And in Co. Meath the baronies of Moyfenrath, Moylagh, Moygar, and Lune owed suit to Portlester.[75] Strategically, these arrangements faced west and south-west against a military threat from the Gaelic midlands. In

---

[73] Calculated from BL, Add. Ch. 62,243; Harleian MS 3756, fos. 48–9; *Crown surveys*, ed. Mac Niocaill, 133–4, 280–1.

[74] Hore and Graves, *Southern & eastern cos.*, 161–2.

[75] BL, Harleian MS 3756, fo. 46 (*Crown surveys*, ed. Mac Niocaill, 278).

particular, the choice of Athy rather than Kilkea for the southern
base, and the allocation to it of Naas barony in the east, must reflect
the earl's confidence in his ability to control the Irish of the
Leinster mountains. And this, plus the choice of Portlester in the
north-west and the arrangements for Carlow and Rathvilly, suggest that the scheme was relatively new in 1518. The manor of
Carlow had actually belonged to the duke of Norfolk, but the earls
occupied it, claiming title by the statute of 1483, and they subsequently leased it from the duke. In 1540, the inhabitants of four
vills there claimed with regard to services that 'nulla opera
huiusmodi nec consuetudines ante 40 annos proxime elapsos facere
consueverunt sed modo faciunt per cohercionem nuper comitis
Kildare'.[76]

In the defence and administration of their enlarged possessions,
the 8th and 9th earls were singularly fortunate in the large numbers
of close relations on whom they could rely—in marked contrast
with the 3rd and 4th Lords Dacre. The 7th earl had at least four
sons and two daughters; the 8th earl one son and six daughters by
his first wife, and seven sons by his second wife; the 9th earl had
one son and four daughters by his first wife, and two sons and three
daughters by his second wife.[77] Not all of these relations lived long
enough to exercise a major influence on family politics, and the
very size of Kildare's extended family eventually created its own
problems, by the period of the 9th earl at least, but Kildare's male
kinsmen provided him with an abundant and trusty supply of
military captains and deputies. In 1519–20 the 9th earl's uncle,
Maurice Fitzgerald of Lackagh, deputized for him as governor
after Kildare had been summoned to court. He was killed by the
O'Mores in Leix soon after. Kildare's brother, Thomas of Leixlip,
in 1526–7, and his son, Thomas, Lord Offaly, in 1534, also acted
as his deputies.[78] The 8th earl settled many of the Leinster
marchlands he recovered from the Irish on his younger brothers.
Oliver received lands in Westmeath and Annaly which were eventually worth IR£38 a year. In the south Dublin marches, Richard

[76] BL, Harleian MS 3756, fo. 84ᵛ; *Crown surveys*, ed. Mac Niocaill, 7, 307; *Ormond deeds, 1509–47*, no. 140; PRO, SP 60/1, fo. 127 (*L. & P. Hen. VIII*, iv, no. 4302).
[77] Marquis of Kildare, *The earls of Kildare and their ancestors* (3rd edn., Dublin, 1858), 42, 71–9, 122–9.
[78] *Handbook Brit. chron.*, 164, 192; TCD, MS 543, s.a. 1520.

had a grant of the manors of Powerscourt, Fassaghroe, and Crevaghe, with other lands in Fercullen, recovered from the O'Tooles, with the stipulation that, if he should die without a male heir, his brother Walter, who held other lands nearby in the Dublin–Kildare marches, might have these manors in exchange for his own lands.[79] It would appear that James was originally granted the manors of Hollywood and Threecastles with other lands in the same region worth IR£45 a year, with remainder to Oliver.[80] Presumably there was also some provision for John.

By far the richest of these endowments, however, was the Leixlip inheritance, which had been specifically entailed to the 8th earl's sons by his second wife. This estate passed successively to Henry (who died *c.*1519), Thomas (who died in 1530), and James (who was attainted in 1536).[81] It included the possessions of the 8th earl in England, valued at £60 annually; the manors of Cowley, Carlingford and Omeath, Greencastle and Mourne, in Louth and Ulster, worth IR£64 per annum by the 1530s; the manor of Ratoath in Co. Meath (IR£21); the manor of Leixlip, Co. Kildare, worth IR£46; and probably also the manors of Rathvilly and Clonmore, Co. Carlow, which were eventually worth IR£75 and IR£27 a year respectively.[82] Sir Thomas of Leixlip was reputed in official circles to be able to 'despende 400 markis by yere or above', and on these figures his estates alone were worth well over IR£300, which was more than many Irish peers. He married Margaret Stafford, the duke of Buckingham's illegitimate daughter, and in 1529 received licence to alienate his estates in England to her use.[83] On his death the following year, the northern estates and Ratoath reverted to the crown, and a dispute occurred between his widow and his brother and heir, Sir James, over possession of the remain-

[79] PRO, SP 65/1, no. 2; *Cal. inq. Co. Dublin*, 66, 68, 401.

[80] *Cal. inq. Co. Dublin*, 106; BL, Harleian MS 3756, fo. 23; *Crown surveys*, ed. Mac Niocaill, 203–11, 250; PRO, SP 65/1, no. 2.

[81] *L. & P. Hen. VIII*, iii, nos. 497, 1070, 1285, 2145, iv, no. 6135 (26), x, no. 323.

[82] *Crown surveys*, ed. Mac Niocaill, 203–11; PRO, SP 65/1, no. 2; SP 60/2, fos. 46–7 (*L. & P. Hen. VIII*, xii (ii), no. 964iii); SP 1/102, fo. 53 (*L. & P. Hen. VIII*, x, no. 323); PRONI, D.3078/1/25/2; *Cal. inq. Co. Dublin*, 17, 18, 52; *Inq. p.m., Hen. VII*, iii, nos. 760, 943, 1169; PROI, Statute roll, 28–9 Henry VIII c. 11. The crown may have recovered the northern estates and Ratoath from Sir Thomas by act of resumption in 1521–2, but they were regranted for life only, within five years: PROI, MS 1A 49 149, 108; *Stat. Ire., Hen. VII & VIII*, 121–2 (it is not certain that the transmitted resumption bill was enacted); *SP Hen. VIII*, ii. 169.

[83] *SP Hen. VIII*, ii. 175; *L. & P. Hen. VIII*, iii, no. 1070, iv, no. 6135 (26).

der. Dame Margaret was awarded the English estates for life, plus IR£20 a year out of the manor of Leixlip; but before his attainder in 1536 Sir James had secured possession of the lands in Cos. Kildare, Carlow, and England.[84]

Among the 9th earl's cousins and more distant kinsmen were others who played a key role in the defence of the lordship under Kildare. And many of their estates lay in districts which had been marchlands before the English recovery in the later fifteenth century. Thomas FitzMaurice Fitzgerald, the earl's cousin, held 1,700 acres of land in Co. Kildare, mainly in the manors of Kildare and Kilkea, as well as lands valued at IR£15 per annum in Co. Meath: he must have been worth over IR£100 a year. In 1526 the earl conferred the captainship of Old Ross and the governance of his Wexford estates on FitzMaurice; and he also granted him custody of the duke of Norfolk's possessions in the region.[85] Similarly, James Fitzgerald of Osbertstown received a lease of the manor of Morett 'for 10 rudders yerly besides mete and drinke', i.e. about 5 marks; and in the aftermath of the 1534–5 rebellion he was given custody of Lea and Morett rent-free in return for the defence of the country.[86] Another influential Geraldine was Sir Gerald Shanesson, who held the manor of Cloncurry, near Bermingham's country, of the earl of Ormond, and other lands worth 200 marks a year. Sir Gerald was one of the earl's principal advisers, and if 'Kyldare be in Inglande, dureng his absentie he wilbe as strange as any Irishman in Irelande; and if he be ther he wilbe as familiare in Dublin, and elliswher, as others and yit shall he not obey the lawe'.[87]

Thus the earl's kinsmen were formidable marchers in their own right, and needed someone of Kildare's stature and influence to control them. Even so, the Leinster Geraldines exhibited a remarkable degree of cohesion for so extended a lineage. After Kildare was dismissed as governor for maladministration in 1520

---

[84] PRONI, D.3078/1/10/1–3; PRO, SP 1/102 fo. 53 (*L. & P. Hen. VIII*, x, no. 323); SP 65/1, no. 2; PROI, Statute roll, 28–9 Henry VIII c. 11.

[85] PRONI, D.3078/1/18/22; PRO, SP 60/1, fo. 127 (*L. & P. Hen. VIII*, iv, no. 4302); *Cal. inq. Co. Dublin*, 61–2, 224–7.

[86] BL, Harleian MS 3756, fo. 54 (*Crown surveys*, ed. Mac Niocaill, 289); PRO, SP 65/1, no. 2. In 1540 Fitzgerald had a lease of lands in the manor of Kildare, paying IR£21 yearly: *Crown surveys*, ed. Mac Niocaill, 150–1.

[87] *SP Hen. VIII*, ii. 174–5; PRO, SP 60/1, fos. 110, 139 (*L. & P. Hen. VIII*, iv, nos. 4248, 5392); *Ormond deeds, 1509–47*, no. 93.

and replaced by the earl of Surrey, his kinsmen were almost un-controllable during the earl's subsequent detention at court, and no subsidy could be levied in Co. Kildare. And in 1522, after the earl of Ormond had succeeded Surrey as governor, he reported that Kildare's kin would do nothing for the king's service nor even defend their own country, and he asked for the earl's return to arrange their disputes and defend his lands.[88] Kildare's brothers, James and Thomas, stirred up serious trouble for the Dublin administration later in the decade, but by a combination of patron-age and blackmail Wolsey eventually managed to detach the two from their uncritical support of the earl's policies: in the early 1530s the crown could sometimes secure the support of the Leixlip branch against the earl.[89]

The practice whereby the early-Tudor earls married the daugh-ters of courtiers and the royal family reflected the family's en-hanced standing among the Tudor nobility, and helped to forge firmer ties with the court. The earl's brothers mostly married into the lordship's other leading families. More significantly, many of his sisters and daughters were married into leading Gaelic families, in what was clearly an attempt by the earl to strengthen his influ-ence in Gaelic Ireland and the defence of the marches. The 7th earl had married his daughter, Eleanor, to Con More O'Neill, son to the chief of Tyrone; and this alliance was strengthened in the next generation when the 8th earl's daughter, Alice, married her cousin, Con Bacagh O'Neill. Most unusually, Con More was denizened as an Englishman: he later succeeded his father as O'Neill (1483–93). Subsequently, Donnell (1498–1509), Art Oge (1513–19), and Con Bacagh (1519–59, the 9th earl's nephew, later created 1st earl of Tyrone) all relied on Kildare support for their election as O'Neill. And in return Con Bacagh was 'the scourge that the said erle had uppon the bordores of Mith and Uriell [Co. Louth] when the said erle wolde procure him to styrre'.[90] The 8th earl similarly matched three more of his daughters: Eleanor, with Donnell MacCarthy Reagh, Eustacia, with Ulick MacWilliam Burke, and Joan, with

[88] PRO, SP 1/30, fo. 93 (*L. & P. Hen. VIII*, iv, no. 81 (2)); E 101/248, no. 21; Ellis, *Tudor Ireland*, 108–16.

[89] PRO, SP 1/55, fo. 5 (*L. & P. Hen. VIII*, iv, no. 5795), SP 1/67, fos. 33–6 (*L. & P. Hen. VIII*, v, no. 398); *SP Hen. VIII*, ii. 179–80; *Ormond deeds, 1509–47*, no. 144. See also below, pp. 180–97.

[90] *Stat. Ire., Edw. IV*, ii. 786–7; *SP Hen. VIII*, iii. 32; Bryan, *Great earl*, 92; Nicholls, *Gaelic and gaelicised Ireland*, 131–2; *New hist. Ire.*, ii. 623–4.

Maelruana O'Carroll of Ely; and the 9th earl also married two of
his daughters to Gaelic chiefs, Mary to Brian O'Connor Faly, and
Cecily to Fergananym O'Carroll of Ely.[91]

This preference for Gaelic sons-in-law rather than daughters-
in-law probably reflects the lower status of women in Gaelic
society—although at least one of the 8th earl's sons, Oliver of
Killeigh, married the daughter of a chief, O'Connor Faly.[92] Yet the
Fitzgerald women were no mere ciphers in the male-dominated
world of Anglo-Gaelic politics. In a recent article on the role of
women in early-Tudor politics, Professor Harris has drawn attention to the influence both of the 9th earl's countess and also of Lady
Dacre in marcher politics.[93] They were not unusual. The 8th earl's
daughter, Margaret, who married Piers Butler, 8th earl of
Ormond, was by all accounts a formidable woman and the making
of her husband. Stanyhurst wrote of her that she was

so politeque that nothing was thought substantially debated without her
advice; man-like, tall of stature, very rich and bountiful, a bitter enemy,
the only meane at thos dayes whereby hir husband's country was
reclaymed from the sluttish and unclean Irish custome to English habits,
bedding, house-keeping, and civilitie.[94]

Her sister, Eleanor, was instrumental in keeping her nephew,
Gerald, the future 11th earl, out of the king's grasp after the
attainder and execution of her brothers in 1536–7.[95] In some circumstances, too, it was possible for one of the earl's daughters to
undertake a mission which would have been much more problematic for his male relatives or servants. On past experience, the 9th
earl knew, on going up to London in 1526, that the government
would bind him over not to depart from court or to send messages
into Ireland without permission. Thus, he agreed a secret signal
with his chief advisers, that if his daughter Alice returned home
before him they should know that he had been denied permission
to leave. Upon arrival, she rode straight to O'Connor, her brother-
in-law, and together with the earl's receiver-general and his wife,
was commonly reputed to be the instigator of O'Connor's Wars
which followed. In 1529 she received the king's pardon for all

[91] *SP Hen. VIII*, iii. 32; Bryan, *Great earl*, 92; Kildare, *Earls of Kildare*, 42, 71,
74, 77–9, 122–9.
[92] Bryan, *Great earl*, 92; Kildare, *Earls of Kildare*, 79.
[93] Harris, 'Women and politics in early Tudor England', 270, 272, 273, 281.
[94] Holinshed, *Chronicles*, vi. 280.   [95] *New hist. Ire.*, iii. 43–5.

treasons and conspiracies with Irish rebels.[96] As Harris notes,[97] the preoccupation of political historians with those bureaucratic institutions which excluded women marginalizes the role of aristocratic women in the less formal aspects of the political process—and this study would argue that that 'bureaucratic' perspective is seriously inadequate in other respects too.

With regard to Kildare's political connexion, the best indication of its extent are the chief horses, hackneys, and harness given by the 9th earl each year and listed in his Rental. These lists covered the years from 4 September 1513 (the day after his father's death) to 3 September 1518, from 16 January 1523 (about the time of his return from England after his absence since 1519) to 21 February 1527, and from 1 August 1530 to 31 July 1532.[98] On average, the earl gave away around 65 chief horses a year from his stud farms in Maynooth, Fercullen, Annally, Fassaghbantry, and in Ulster, which in 1534 contained an estimated 1,000 horses and mares.[99] In addition, he made gifts of around 33 hackneys a year (apparently the Irish equivalent of the northern 'nags'), and about a dozen sets of harness.[100] In some cases, the value of these gifts is noted, or money was given instead to buy a horse: they varied considerably, from IR£6 in money given to an O'Reilly in 1526 to 50 marks for 'a don' [= brown] horse given to Richard Fitzgerald, the earl's brother, the previous year. Nevertheless, even allowing only IR£10 per chief horse, and 5 marks for a hackney or set of harness, it is apparent that Kildare's outlay on these gifts was very considerable, around IR£800 a year.

It is not clear how these gifts should be interpreted. Proportionately, just over half the recipients were from the local Englishry, a little over 40 per cent had Gaelic names—although some were the earl's servants—and about 5 per cent were courtiers or other important figures in England. Evidently, in many cases the gifts had a military purpose. They represented part of the earl's fee to his

---

[96] PRO, SP 60/1, fo. 139 (*L. & P. Hen. VIII*, iv, no. 5392); *L. & P. Hen. VIII*, iii, no. 2693, iv, no. 5748 (2); *SP Hen. VIII*, ii. 145–7. See also below, pp. 182–5.

[97] Harris, 'Women and politics in early Tudor England', 259, 281.

[98] BL, Harleian MS 3756, fos. 177ᵛ–85ᵛ (*Crown surveys*, ed. Mac Niocaill, 319–20).

[99] *L. & P. Hen. VIII*, vii, no. 1382; *SP Hen. VIII*, iii. 379. The totals range from 127 in 1513–14, the 9th earl's first year, to 38 in 1531–2, which is presumably incomplete.

[100] No lists of harness appear for the years 1514–18, and 1525–6.

retainers or household servants, especially his horsemen. Chief horses and harness were needed for English-style cavalry, as opposed to the small ponies used by Irish horsemen. Some recipients were members of his immediate family; and other gifts were made to independent figures whose goodwill and support the earl wished to cultivate. Some servants could expect a horse almost every year, such as Edmund and Oliver Seis, Piers Boy, and Edmund Eustace; and Sir Walter Delahide, the earl's receiver-general, Meyler Fay, his confidential servant, Hubert Fitzgerald of the Grange, and important border chiefs like O'Connor and O'Carroll received a horse about every second year. Altogether, around twenty individuals received gifts of horses in at least four of the ten years recorded between 1514 and 1532. If we look more closely at three particular years in the period (1516–17, 1525–6, 1530–1), it appears that in each year the recipients included a number of the lordship's chief landowners, some leading gentry of Co. Kildare, and important men in England. In 1516–17 those in the first group included Sir John Fitzgerald of Dromana, Gerald Fitzwilliam of Co. Limerick, and William Power of Kilmedan; in 1525–6 Patrick Betagh of Moynalty, Richard Nevill, and Sir John again; and in 1530–1 Edward Nugent, the Red Barry, and Richard Vale. Kildare gentry who were so favoured included Sir William Wogan and Thomas Eustace of Harristown in 1516–17; William Bermingham and Gerald Aylmer in 1525–6; and Edward Wellesley, John FitzMaurice of Blackhall, and in all three years Tibbot Creff. Referring to this practice, David Sutton, the earl's receiver, observed in 1537 that Kildare 'used to give many horses to gentylmen, and to every man within the said counties [of Kildare and Carlow] that he gave eny suche horse, if the man were able to receave hym, he wold be with hym ii daies and twoo nights, to have bothe mete and drinke with hym'.[101] The courtiers in receipt of horses were Sir Thomas Boleyn and Sir Owen Perrot in 1516–17, the duke of Norfolk, the marquis of Exeter, and the king himself in 1525–6; and in 1530–1 Lord Leonard Grey (also in 1525–6) and the two captains of Cumberland spears then in Ireland, Leonard Musgrave and Edward Aglionby.

Unfortunately, very little work has yet been done for Ireland upon such questions as the emergence of a gentry, the concept of a

---

[101] Hore and Graves, *Southern & eastern cos.*, 161.

county community, and the extent of central control and supervision of local government in the late medieval lordship. Professor
Robin Frame has published lists of the membership of 218 commissions of the peace issued in the period 1302–1461;[102] but we still
lack lists of other officials such as sheriffs and escheators. In default, it is very difficult, as Professor Frame remarks, 'to calculate
the number of families available in various areas to undertake the
"self-government at the king's command" that was the hallmark of
the English tradition, and to estimate the depth (or shallowness) of
central intrusion into the local environments of a warlike gentry'.[103]
Similarly, many questions concerning the relationship between the
earls of Kildare and other leading Co. Kildare landowners are
almost impossible to answer. After the rebellion, David Sutton
implied that the earl had exercised absolute power in Co. Kildare,
rather like a Gaelic chief, except that 'he used two lawes, our
princes lawes and brehens lawes, which he thought most
beneficiall as the case did require'.[104] There is no doubt that
Kildare dominated county society, but his relations with the local
gentry seem more like those between Lord Dacre and the
Cumberland gentry than between a Gaelic chief and his clansmen.
Sutton himself observed that the 9th earl had

sent to all or the most parte of the lords and gentylmen of [Kildare and
Carlow] for to have had the defense of them, and also to spende them, as
he said in his supplicacion or writting, but at their owne pleasure,
wherunto the most parte of the forsaid gentylmen put to their hands to the
aforsaid writting, as of trothe durst not saye the contrary.

Similarly, thirty years later reference was made to 'a graunt
made by the gentry of the countie of Kyldare' permitting coign
and livery to be imposed by 'the late earl of Kyldare, but for a
certayne tyme limited in the sayde graunt towards the sustenance
of his chardges for the defens of the same countie, till farther ayde
were sent from the prince'.[105] Evidently, the earl supervised
the defence of the shire, but only in consultation with the county
gentry whose consent and support could not be taken for
granted.

[102] 'Commissions of the peace in Ireland, 1302–1461', in *Anal. Hib.*, 35 (1992),
1–43. [103] Ibid. 5.
[104] Hore and Graves, *Southern & eastern cos.*, 162–3.
[105] Ibid. 160, 168.

Who these men were can in part be determined from appointments of sheriffs and escheators. For most of Henry VIII's reign, until the rebellion, Co. Kildare was administered as a liberty whose officials were appointed by the earl, but evidence for the reigns of Richard III and Henry VII, and for the years after 1534 suggests that there were at least a dozen gentry who were of sufficient means to serve as sheriff. In addition, five more families supplied escheators, and a commission of 1496 for erecting ditches and dikes in the Kildare marches, in accordance with a recent statute, was directed to Edward [Lane], bishop of Kildare and prior of Connell, Richard Eustace [of Kilgone], Thomas Eustace, the sovereign of Naas, and the sheriff of Kildare, who was then Bartholomew Aylmer of Lyons.[106] This commission was comparable in size to the peace commissions for the county issued under the Lancastrian kings, which were normally directed to between five and eight leading gentry.[107] Overall, therefore, the earl probably had to deal with twenty or so substantial gentry families in Co. Kildare whose consent and support were worth cultivating. They included the Suttons of Tipper, three or four branches of the Eustace family, the Wogans, Aylmer of Lyons, the senior Bermingham family, and cadet branches of the Fitzgeralds—of Ballysonnan, Osbertstown, and FitzMaurice of Allon—all of whom supplied sheriffs for the county. Among those appointed escheators were the Langs, Synnagh of Oldton, Eustace of Mullaghcash, and Birt of Donavale. In nearly every case the heads of these families received occasional gifts of horses from the earl—Birt and Lang were exceptions—as did James Wellesley, baron of Norragh, and Tibbot Creff, heads of families who in earlier periods had been important enough to be appointed to the Kildare commission of the peace.[108] Thus, although the earl may not always have seen eye to eye with the leading Kildare gentry, these gifts do suggest that he actively sought their support and that, as we might expect, he was assured of a large following of county gentry. The fact that Kildare distributed horses rather than money was of

---

[106] *Rotulorum patentium et clausorum cancellariae Hiberniae calendarium*, 271, no. 27; St Peter's College, Wexford, Hore MS I, 1147; BL, Royal MS 18C, XIV, fo. 151ᵛ.

[107] Frame, 'Commissions of the peace', 14–17.

[108] BL, Harleian MS 3756, fos. 177ᵛ–85ᵛ; Frame, 'Commissions of the peace', 14–17.

course a departure from normal English practice. The reason was probably military rather than the shallowness of Ireland's monetary economy: few others in the lordship had stud farms.[109] His expenditure on these fees was also very high, but it reflected his responsibilities as the king's deputy.

Finally, some brief consideration is necessary here of one apparent difference between Dacre and Kildare. This concerns the significance of Kildare's links with the Gaelic Irish and Dacre's Scottish associations. As is related below, in both cases these cross-border connections were liable to be viewed with suspicion in London; and in 1534 they were at least in part the reason why both magnates were charged with treason. In view of the comparative weakness and political fragmentation of Gaelic Ireland and the need to negotiate with many chiefs and clansmen for the defence of each march, Kildare's dealings with Gaelic Ireland were undoubtedly more extensive than Dacre's with Scottish lords and lairds which are considered in the next two chapters. Even so, the basic differences do seem more historiographical than historical. No doubt with an eye to the future, Irish historians have traditionally been much more preoccupied with these Anglo-Gaelic links than have English or Scottish historians with Anglo-Scottish contacts. The English of Ireland are described as 'Anglo-Irish' and a 'middle nation' because of their increasing association with the Gaelic Irish and Gaelic culture, their weakening ties with England, and the growth among the medieval settlers of an Irish sense of identity—all of which are allegedly epitomized by the Kildare ascendancy. The implication is that English and Irish senses of identity were incompatible, and that Gaelic cultural ties were undermining the earl's political loyalty.[110]

The fact that arguments of this sort are still being seriously advanced does of course underline the need for a balanced history of the Tudor state of the kind explored here; but it would be

---

[109] *SP Hen. VIII*, iii. 379.

[110] For the debate on this topic, see esp. Lydon, 'The middle nation', and Alan Bliss, 'Language and literature', in J. F. Lydon (ed.), *The English in medieval Ireland* (Dublin, 1984), 1–26, 27–45; Cosgrove, 'Hiberniores ipsis Hibernis', 1–14; and my response, 'Nationalist historiography', 1–18. For Kildare's role in this, see Simms, *From Kings to Warlords*, 20; Bryan, *Great earl*, pp. x, 134, 235–41. The latest restatements of traditional perspectives are Bradshaw, 'Nationalism and historical scholarship', 330–2; Cosgrove, 'Writing of Irish medieval history', 101–11.

tedious to embark here on a lengthy refutation of them. The evidence discussed below clearly demonstrates that shifting alignments at the Tudor court and the ambitions of nobles whose estates spanned the Irish Sea remained central to the lordship. It also shows that Kildare was acutely conscious of these facts and, until 1534, moderately successful at manipulating them to his advantage. In 1525, for instance, when the earl detected a note of suspicion and displeasure in a letter from the king, he replied that he was peculiarly bound to Henry, not only by his duty of allegiance, but by service to the king at court in their youth together, by the king's grant of lands to him, by his continuing good lordship, and because both his first wife and his present wife were the king's kinswomen. He then offered a conventional Tudor declaration of loyalty, which ended with a particularly frank assessment of the realities of power:

And though there were no suche cause, yet cowd I fynde in my hart to serve your grace before all the princes in the world, aswell for the grete noblenes, valiaunt proweys, and equitie which I ever noted in your most noble personne, as also for the vertuous qwalities wherin ye excelle all other princes. And besides that, I do knowe right wele, if I did the contrary, it shulde bee the destruccion of me and my sequele for ever.[111]

Likewise, contemporary views of the national identity and political ideas of the English of Ireland are sufficiently established from such facts as that, in writs and official correspondence of the Dublin administration, they are consistently described as the king's English subjects, or as Englishmen, of English blood and nation (even though, as the same documents acknowledge, they were born in Ireland); that accounts emanating from the lordship of warfare and battles in Ireland speak of the chief division as between English and Irish there; and from the importance of the cult of St George there as the national saint. This is not to deny that the English of Ireland could also have an Irish identity: after all, British citizens nowadays might also describe themselves as English, Scottish, Irish, or Welsh. Indeed the practice of labelling the king's subjects according to their country of birth, instead of in accordance with their allegiance and culture, was sufficiently common—and viewed so seriously as a potential threat to good order!—for orders to be given on the assembly of Henry VIII's

---

[111] *SP Hen. VIII*, ii. 125.

'army royal' in 1513 that no man reproach another 'because of the countree that he is of, that is to say, be he French, English, Northern, Walshe, or Irysh'.[112] Overall, however, it was so evident that he was an Englishman who was born within the territories and under the allegiance of the king of England that the matter of the earl of Kildare's nationality and political outlook was simply a non-issue. The question of the status of the 'Old English' only arose in the mid-Tudor period, with the development of the concept of England as an elect nation, and with the establishment of a New English interest in Ireland.[113] It is simply anachronistic to look for an explanation of the crisis of 1534 in Ireland in terms of a conflict of identity or loyalties within the Kildare family.

Overall, the evidence surveyed here explains a feature of early-Tudor Ireland which has only received extended consideration in terms of its political manifestation. The earl's estate-management policies; his land purchases, expansion, and colonization; his aristocratic connexion and his relations with other major figures in English and Gaelic Ireland: all these help to explain why Kildare was so dominant a figure in early-Tudor Ireland. They laid the foundations for the political phenomenon traditionally known as 'the Kildare ascendancy', the period of English recovery in Ireland extending from the 1470s to the 1530s when English kings deliberately built up the earls of Kildare as the ruling magnate for Ireland. They did so because Kildare was an acceptable English noble and politician, not a latent Anglo-Irish separatist. And significantly, the broad thrust of the earl's land-management policies were the same as those of Lord Dacre along the northern frontier of the Tudor state. Particularly in terms of the problems and political conditions which they were aimed at addressing, they are also very familiar to historians of Ireland two centuries earlier, when the evidence first permits a sustained analysis of politics and society in the English lordship.[114] In both cases, the possession of large amounts of marchland which offered an uncertain source of income, especially in wartime, exercised a formative influence on their careers and political ambitions. The Dacres were perhaps

---

[112] *The Loseley manuscripts*, ed. A. J. Kempe (London, 1835), 114–15.

[113] This paragraph is based on Ellis, 'Crown, community and government', 195–7, 201–4; id., 'Nationalist historiography', 12–16; id., 'Representations of the past', 299–301.

[114] Cf. J. F. Lydon, *The lordship of Ireland in the middle ages* (Dublin, 1972); Frame, *English lordship in Ireland*.

more fortunate than the Fitzgeralds in their acquisition from the Greystokes of extensive possessions in lowland England which ensured them a dependable source of income even in wartime. The comparative strength of their Scottish adversary, however, and the much closer supervision exercised by the crown over Anglo-Scottish affairs meant that the Dacres had less freedom to manœuvre. Even so, the evidence for Dacre expansion in northern Cumberland is unusually detailed by Irish standards, and throws considerable light on the renewed phase of colonization under the earls of Kildare. Ultimately, however, the success of both magnates depended on the high priority they gave to military matters and the defence of their estates over other political considerations, in a society organized for war. This involved not simply the martial skills, experience and leadership qualities appropriate to a marcher society, but a willingness to reside on the borders and the energy to undertake the ceaseless campaigning which characterized the principal duties of a governor or warden.

The traditional assumptions and predilections of Irish historiography have generally been much more conducive than those of English historiography to the sympathetic portrayal of the phenomenon of magnate power, self-help, and local particularism exemplified by the Kildare ascendancy. For Irish historians, the relationship between crown and magnate usually reflected an uneasy compromise between conflicting interests: nobles defended the locality against excessive demands or the heavy-handed policies of the metropolitan government. Thus Irish historians have generally had little difficulty in highlighting the local dimensions of the political circumstances which gave rise to the Kildare ascendancy as a major theme in the unfolding pattern of Anglo-Irish relations during the medieval and early modern periods. Little was then known about Kildare estate-management policies; but by focusing on the 8th earl's alliance with Gaelic chiefs and his occasional clashes with the crown, an earlier generation of historians was able to portray Kildare, somewhat misleadingly, as the Great Earl and All-but-King of Ireland, who stood for Home Rule against English interference.[115] By contrast, magnates in England were not seen to represent local interests. English historiography

---

[115] Edmund Curtis, *A history of medieval Ireland from 1086 to 1513* (London, 1938); Bryan, *Great earl*.

has traditionally stressed the early emergence in England of a centralized monarchy, with a uniform culture and structure of government, and the peaceful extension to the provinces of metropolitan values. And since the similar career of Thomas, Lord Dacre, seemed to fly in the face of these traditions, it is perhaps not surprising that it has received far less attention at the hands of English historians. The fact remains, however, that Dacre's effective tenure of the wardenship was even longer and more continuous than Kildare's career as governor of Ireland. Accordingly, the next chapter of this study aims to assess the Dacre ascendancy in the far north in the manner of the more familiar episode of the Kildare ascendancy in Ireland, and thus to address the themes which are common currency in Irish historiography.

5

The Dacre ascendancy in the far north

THE verdict of modern historians on the early-Tudor Lords Dacre of the North is that they were a minor and disreputable peerage family, advanced by the king to keep out the Percies, and quickly discarded when circumstances changed.[1] Thomas, the 3rd lord, ruled the west marches for almost forty years until his death in 1525; and for the last fourteen years he was usually warden-general of all three marches. William, the 4th lord (1525–63), was initially excluded from even the wardenship of the west marches, but he recovered this office owing to the failure as warden of Henry Clifford, 1st earl of Cumberland. He retained the office for seven years until his well-known trial for treason in 1534. It was widely believed that he had been framed and, most exceptionally, the lords triers ventured to agree. But Dacre was none the less dismissed from office, induced to confess misprision of treason—for which he paid a swingeing fine of £10,000— and spent the rest of the reign in disgrace. Overall, therefore, the rise and fall of the Dacres looks like a classic example of the traditional crown strategy of extending royal influence and control by promoting a lesser lord at the expense of a great magnate, and then in turn switching support to someone whose position depended still more on royal favour. And in many ways the career of the Dacres does fit this pattern. In the political circumstances created by a turbulent frontier, however, this strategy was less successful than in lowland England. The strengths and weaknesses of Dacre rule in the far north (particularly when considered in conjunction with the parallel and more familiar career of the Kildares in Ireland) offer some unusual and instructive

[1] James, *Society, politics and culture*, 78, 80–1, 94–113, 142–3; M. L. Bush, 'The problem of the far north: a study of the crisis of 1537 and its consequences', in *Northern History*, 6 (1971), 42–3; Miller, *Henry VIII and the English nobility*, 187–92; Harrison, *Pilgrimage of Grace in the Lake Counties*, 26–38; Guy, *The Cardinal's Court*, 19, 122–3, 163; Reid, *King's council in the north*, 93.

insights into the limitations of royal power in the early-Tudor state.

The Dacre ascendancy reflected a particular phase in the government's attempts to grapple with the problem of the north. In the later fourteenth century, the Dacres had been one of perhaps half a dozen noble families who were regularly appointed to the commissions of wardenry. But from 1384 successive kings normally relied for wardens on the two comital families of Neville and Percy. Their eagerness to serve reflected the crown's willingness to pay the wardens inflated salaries which, together with the traditional military and administrative authority pertaining to the office, facilitated the development of strong regional connexions. The civil strife of the mid-fifteenth century exposed the dangers of this strategy for defending the north,[2] and the ensuing reaction saw a sharp reduction in the salaries of the wardens and a wider diffusion of power. In an earlier chapter, some of the implications of early-Tudor policy for the defence and good government of the borders were explored. Yet the new strategy imposed serious constraints in other directions too. Quite clearly, a greatly reduced salary, but with the traditional, very considerable military and administrative responsibilities of the warden, made the office a much less attractive proposition. At the same time, however, the gradual extension northwards (into Durham and Westmorland) of the kind of socio-political change which has been aptly described as the transformation from a lineage to a civil society[3] meant that there were less nobles about who were both willing and capable of undertaking the wardenship on the terms offered. The problem was highlighted by the experiences of the first Clifford earl of Cumberland as warden of the west march (1525–7). Despite Clifford's initial enthusiasm for the job, the king's commission was far from ensuring the local co-operation he needed to discharge his duties as warden effectively. In the circumstances, relations with the disappointed Dacres were likely to be strained, but the hostility of the leading Cumberland family was practically guaranteed when Clifford was promoted earl of Cumberland, even though he had almost no land in the county. By comital standards, moreover, Clifford's landed inheritance was meagre, and coupled with his ill-

---

[2] Storey, 'Wardens of the marches', 593–615.
[3] James, *Family, lineage, and civil society, passim*.

advised attempt to govern the marches from Skipton castle, this effectively ensured the failure of his wardenship. By contrast, in the fourteenth century, Cliffords had acted successfully on commissions of wardenry.[4]

The *reductio ad absurdum* of early-Tudor policy was the career of Thomas, Lord Dacre, as warden-general of all three marches from 1511 to 1525. As warden-general, Dacre received far greater power and responsibility than he had enjoyed under Henry VII, and Henry VIII was also laxer in his supervision of Dacre's rule of the borders. Initially, Henry VII had retained the wardenship of the west march in his own hands, appointing Lord Thomas as his lieutenant there with a salary of £100 a year, plus £20 for four commissioners to keep the march days with the Scots, from 1 May 1486.[5] Dacre's salary was raised to £133. 6s. 8d. the following year, but it was not until 1504 that he was given the more honourable title of warden, and even then his salary remained unchanged.[6] In addition, the king also took care at first to divide among several men powers which had previously been exercised by the warden. Sir Richard Salkeld was appointed captain of Carlisle, John Musgrave as captain of Bewcastle, while Sir Christopher Moresby was retained as steward of Penrith.[7] And during the crisis over Perkin Warbeck in the 1490s, the king's servant, Sir Henry Wyatt, was interposed as the leading official in the west marches;[8] and overall military command of the region was entrusted to the earl of Surrey, who had been retained as vice-warden of the marches with a salary of £1,000 a year.[9] Surrey was nominally succeeded in 1499 by Prince Henry as warden-general of the three marches with the same salary.[10] By then, however, a truce had been agreed between

[4] James, *Society, politics and culture*, ch. 4; R. W. Hoyle, 'The first earl of Cumberland: a reputation re-assessed', in *Northern History*, 22 (1986), 63–94; Storey, 'Wardens of the marches', 596–9.

[5] PRO, E 101/72, file 3/1062.

[6] Ibid.; E 403/2558, fos. 116, 144, 149, 159, E 405/183, fos. 79, 150; *Cal. pat. rolls, 1494–1509*, 379.

[7] William Campbell (ed.), *Materials for a history of the reign of Henry VII*, 2 vols. (London, 1873, 1877), i. 224, 231; PRO, E 404/80, no. 267; *Rotuli Scotiae, 1291–1516*, ii, ed. D. Macpherson, Record Commissioner (London, 1819), ii. 472, 479, 486, 498, 501, 515, 518; above, pp. 51–2, 95–6, below, pp. 203–5. On all this, see now Summerson, *Carlisle*, 472–3.

[8] Conway, *Henry VII's relations*, 8, 34, 38, 59, 86, 100, 104, 114–15; *Rotuli Scotiae*, ii. 500–1.

[9] PRO, E 403/2558, fos. 37, 41ᵛ, 42ᵛ, 51, 58, 69, 75ᵛ, 85; *Cal. pat. rolls, 1494–1509*, 32.

[10] PRO, E 403/2558, fos. 85, 101, 113; *Cal. pat. rolls, 1494–1509*, 200, 202, 213.

England and Scotland, to be followed by the treaty of Ayton in
1502 and the marriage between James IV and Margaret Tudor the
following year.[11]

Accordingly, as relations with James IV improved in Henry
VII's later years, the military effort on the borders was wound
down and Dacre was given wider responsibilities. In 1501, after
Moresby's death, Dacre became steward of Penrith,[12] and probably about the same time he also assumed responsibility for
Carlisle.[13] In 1502 he was appointed lieutenant of the middle
march, with a salary of £114. 13s. 4d. for himself, four deputies,
and four warden sergeants there; and probably at the same time he
was given custody of Redesdale and Harbottle castle on behalf of
Sir George Tailboys, the lord of the liberty.[14] The following year
he was one of the ambassadors to arrange the forthcoming Anglo-
Scottish marriage.[15] Finally, in 1504 his enhanced position in
the region was recognized by the conferral on him of the more
honourable title of warden-general of the west and middle
march, although in the event he was discharged from his responsibilities in the middle marches within two years.[16] The extension of
Dacre's authority at this time, however, reflected the king's increasing optimism about the state of Anglo-Scottish relations
rather than a new-found confidence in Dacre's ability to defend the
region in the event of war. Dacre had still not secured all of his
wife's inheritance, and he was obliged to give so many bonds
for good behaviour and the proper execution of his duties on
the border that he remained very much under royal control.
Altogether, at least twelve bonds were executed, including one of
£2,000 in 1506 which was without condition but respited at the
king's pleasure.[17]

With Henry VII's death in 1509, however, the situation soon
altered considerably. Initially, Henry VIII confirmed the existing

[11] R. G. Eaves, *Henry VIII's Scottish diplomacy 1513–1524: England's relations
with the regency government of James V* (New York, 1971), 25.

[12] PRO, E 40/14638.

[13] PRO, E 101/415/3, fo. 292.

[14] PRO, E 403/2558, fos. 101, 108ᵛ, 116, SP 1/1, fos. 71ᵛ–72 (*L. & P. Hen. VIII*,
i (2nd edn.), no. 131); *Cal. doc. Scotland*, iv, no. 1683.

[15] *Cal. doc. Scotland*, iv, nos. 1707–8, 1710, 1712; *Accounts of the Lord High
Treasurer of Scotland*, ed. Sir James Balfour ii. *1500–04* (Edinburgh, 1900), 363, 373.

[16] *Cal. doc. Scotland*, iv, nos. 1744, 1746; *Cal. pat. rolls, 1494–1509*, 379; PRO, SP
1/1, fos. 71ᵛ–72 (*L. & P. Hen. VIII*, i (2nd edn.), no. 131).

[17] PRO, SP 1/1, fos. 71ᵛ–72 (*L. & P. Hen. VIII*, i (2nd edn.), no. 131; *Cal.
close rolls, 1500–09*, no. 543; Lander, *Crown and nobility*, 292–3; above, pp. 84–7.

arrangements for the rule of the borders, and Lord Thomas was reappointed warden of the west march.[18] By then, however, Dacre was in possession of the Greystoke inheritance, and he very soon sought to be discharged from five bonds which he had given to the old king on the grounds that they had been wrongfully made or that the conditions specified had already been performed.[19] In May 1510, for reasons unknown, he was bound over in 10,000 marks to appear before the council on 3 November. He remained at court till 19 February, when he was licensed to depart, but ordered to re-appear the following November.[20] Meanwhile, however, Anglo-Scottish relations had deteriorated to the point that the king had to look to the defence of the borders.[21] In the changed circumstances, the government had some difficulty in finding a suitable warden for the east and middle marches. The obvious choice was Henry Percy, 5th earl of Northumberland, who was certainly anxious for office but who, for reasons now unclear, was distrusted by the Tudors. The newly ennobled Lord Darcy had discharged the office during the peaceful interlude following the Anglo-Scottish treaty, but he was essentially a courtier, without lands or tenants in the marches.[22] During the summer Dacre was given a commission for six weeks to keep the warden courts in the east and middle marches during the absence of Lord Darcy, who was leading a military expedition to Spain.[23] And then, on his reappearance at court in November, Dacre received a commission as warden of the east and middle marches until the following Easter and further at the king's pleasure.[24]

What apparently had happened was that with war looming, and the king of Scots 'aboutward to have stolen the town of Berwick', a resident warden had been deemed necessary and Lord Darcy had refused the office 'but vpon inreasonable sommes of money be hym desyred'. Dacre had therefore agreed to serve as a stopgap. In the middle march, he had the support of Edward Radcliffe and Roger

---

[18] *L. & P. Hen. VIII*, i (2nd edn.), nos. 94 (53, 65–9, 77), 132 (5, 38).

[19] PRO, SP 1/1, fos. 71ᵛ–72 (*L. & P. Hen VIII*, i (2nd edn.), no. 131); above, pp. 86–7.

[20] *L. & P. Hen. VIII*, i (2nd edn.), no. 1003 (15).

[21] Eaves, *Henry VIII's Scottish diplomacy*, 27–8; Scarisbrick, *Henry VIII*, ch. 2.

[22] James, *Society, politics and culture*, 74–5, 95.

[23] *L. & P. Hen. VIII*, i (2nd edn.), no. 857 (19); *Rotuli Scotiae*, ii. 575; Scarisbrick, *Henry VIII*, 28.

[24] *L. & P. Hen. VIII*, i (2nd edn.), no. 1003 (17, 23); *Rotuli Scotiae*, ii. 576–8.

Fenwick, two local gentry, who had long acted as lieutenants.[25] Yet he undertook the wardenship of the east march only with serious misgivings. He had, as he later observed, 'no strienth, ne help of men, freyndes ne tenauntes' there, and the gentry 'woll noder ryde ne goo, ne non o[f] them doo seruice for me, ne at my commaundment in the kinges name'.[26] In the middle march, he served without salary, and his indenture specified that he should have the nomination of the two lieutenants, to be paid by the king. For the east march he received the usual £114. 13s. 4d.[27] In 1514, when Roger Fenwick died and Dacre appointed his brother, Philip, as lieutenant, the king overruled him.[28] In 1515, however, when Dacre's indenture was renewed following peace with Scotland, he was able to exact slightly better terms. He asked for his brother, Sir Christopher, to be his deputy and sheriff of Northumberland, in place of the two lieutenants, and also for a force of sixty horsemen, costing £400 a year. In the event, he had to be content with a small increase of his salary as warden of the east and middle marches to £280 a year, although he was also granted the nomination of the sheriff.[29] Yet Dacre's nominations were carefully scrutinized and sometimes overruled, and the king recouped most of the additional expenditure by not paying for lieutenants and by charging 100 marks of Dacre's salary on the sheriffwick of Northumberland. Thus, although exaggerated, Dacre's claim in 1524 that he had never received a penny in wages as warden of the east and middle marches contained more than a grain of truth.[30]

[25] BL, Caligula B. II, fos. 200–0ᵛ (*L. & P. Hen. VIII*, i (2nd edn.), no. 2913); PRO, E 403/2558, fos. 101, 108ᵛ, 116; E 405/183, fos. 79, 150; SP 1/12, fo. 49 (*L. & P. Hen. VIII*, ii, no. 1365).

[26] BL, Caligula B. II, fo. 201 (*L. & P. Hen. VIII*, i (2nd edn.), no. 2913).

[27] BL, Caligula B. II, fos. 200–0ᵛ (*L. & P. Hen. VIII*, i (2nd edn.), no. 2913); PRO, E 403/2558, fos. 189, 189ᵛ, 216ᵛ, 217, 229, 253ᵛ, 264, 265, 272ᵛ, 287; *L. & P. Hen. VIII*, i (2nd edn.), nos. 857 (19), 984, 1003 (15, 17, 23); Miller, *Henry VIII and the English nobility*, 187–8.

[28] BL, Caligula B. II, fo. 202 (*L. & P. Hen. VIII*, i (2nd edn.), no. 2913; PRO, E 101/72, file 7/1166; *L. & P. Hen. VIII*, i (2nd edn.), nos. 2840, 2863 (4, 5).

[29] PRO, SP 1/11, fos. 4–6 (*L. & P. Hen. VIII*, ii (i), no. 596); E 405/2558, fos. 297, 306, 317, 331, 345, 355ᵛ, 362, 372, 379ᵛ; BL, Caligula B. II, fo. 262 (*L. & P. Hen. VIII*, iii, no. 1225). The king may also have accepted Sir Christopher Dacre as deputy warden: see PRO, SP 1/45, fos. 101–2 (*L. & P. Hen. VIII*, iv (ii), no. 3629(2)).

[30] BL, Caligula B. II, fo. 262 (*L. & P. Hen. VIII*, iii, no. 1225); *L. & P. Hen. VIII*, iv (i), no. 279. Cf. *L. & P. Hen. VIII*, ii, nos. 1120, 2533, 2736, 3783, 4547, 4562.

Moreover, by 1523 he was also defending the west march at his own
cost by deputy (his son), but with the promise of some future
award; and when open war recommenced, his only assistance there
was thirty gunners and spies paid for by the king.[31]

Despite the manifest weakness of what had clearly been a stopgap arrangement, Dacre continued to serve as warden-general,
very reluctantly and with short breaks, until 1525. In response to
an inquiry from Wolsey, Bishop Fox recalled that the last warden
who had indented for the keeping of the marches at his own cost in
time of war had been the old earl of Northumberland in 1486, for
which he had received, as Fox recalled, either 3,000 marks or
£3,000, but he had also had to keep Berwick. Fox added, however,
that if Dacre left his son and brother on the west march and
himself resided on the east march, 'for the great experyence,
acquayntance, and landes which he hath in Northumbreland', he
might possibly 'bere the burdeyn of all three marches in tyme of
werre', provided his fee covered the cost of the retinue he was
required to maintain.[32] In a crisis, Dacre received additional
financial and military support, and he was occasionally placed
under the command of a lieutenant with an army royal. Yet the
keynote of his administration, and its chief recommendation to the
crown, was its cheapness. In other respects, it exhibited serious
shortcomings, although Dacre did eventually build up a tolerable,
but distinctly *ad hoc* system of border administration.

The wardenship of the marches was an extremely arduous
office which made a number of potentially conflicting demands
on its holder. We can get a fair impression of the extent of the
difficulties which the warden faced, and the range of his duties, by
looking at how Dacre performed in the office. Dacre's rule depended very heavily on exploiting to good effect his position as a
border magnate, with all that that term implies. By English standards, this position was perhaps untypical (though shared with
other northern nobles), because Tudor England had only the one
landed political frontier; but by British standards, or in the context
of the Tudor state as a whole, it was not unusual. In Scotland
and Ireland, Dacre's position was closely paralleled by such

[31] *L. & P. Hen. VIII*, iii (ii), nos. 3106, 3626, iv (i), nos. 220, 278, 1310.
[32] Ellis (ed.), *Original letters*, 3rd ser., i. 321–3 (*L. & P. Hen. VIII*, iii, no. 2859);
Miller, *Henry VIII and the English nobility*, 187–90.

magnates as the Campbell earls of Argyll or the Butler earls of Ormond.[33]

The nature of Dacre's landholdings, together with the financial constraints under which he was expected to serve, imposed on Dacre's rule of the borders a rather different character from the rule of a Percy or a Neville. About half of Dacre's landed income accrued from the border counties of Cumberland and Northumberland, as opposed to only 38 per cent of the Percy patrimony, although Percy estates there were worth about £500 per annum more.[34] The Dacre estates around Morpeth and Coniscliffe were also subject to raids by the reiving surnames of Tynedale and Redesdale; and of course Gilsland, together with Bewcastledale, constituted the western end of the highland zone inhabited by the border surnames. Thus, even if he were not warden, Dacre could not afford long periods of absence at court. As warden-general, Dacre spent much of his time at the crown outpost of Harbottle in Coquetdale, or at Morpeth, from where all parts of the east and middle marches were readily accessible, while his brother or his son acted as his deputy at Carlisle.[35]

The key to Dacre's influence was of course his *manraed*, but this did not simply mean having large numbers of tenants and a big following of county gentry. In fact, part of the reason why Dacre's following in northern Cumberland included few gentry of substance was because there were few such in the area. It has been calculated that the earl of Northumberland was theoretically able to raise over 11,000 men from his own tenants for border service, but over 6,000 of these would have had to come from Yorkshire, and at considerable cost.[36] Yet, as the earl of Surrey remarked, Dacre had at little additional cost to himself four or five thousand

[33] For Argyle, see Jane Dawson, 'The fifth earl of Argyle, Gaelic lordship and political power in sixteenth-century Scotland', in *SHR* 67 (1988), 1–27; ead., 'Two kingdoms or three? Ireland in Anglo-Scottish relations in the middle of the sixteenth century', in R. A. Mason (ed.), *Scotland and England 1286–1815* (Edinburgh, 1987), 120–31; Jenny Wormald, *Lords and men in Scotland: bonds of manrent 1442–1603* (Edinburgh, 1985), 84–5, 108–14, 121–6. On the Butlers, see Empey, 'The Butler lordship', 174–87; id., 'From rags to riches: Piers Butler, eighth earl of Ormond', 299–314; id. and Simms, 'Ordinances of the White Earl', 161–87.

[34] Calculated from Durham, H. of N. MS C/201/3; Bean, *Estates of the Percy family*, 45–6, 139.

[35] *L. & P. Hen. VIII*, iii, nos. 1190iii, 1883, 1986, 2931, iv, nos. 220, 278, 726, 1310.

[36] James, *Society, politics and culture*, 60, 76.

men constantly available to resist invasion.[37] Of course any noble had large numbers of tenants—Cumberland's besieged him in Skipton castle during the Pilgrimage of Grace—but few were prepared (as we have seen with regard to Dacre's estate management policies)[38] so carefully to cultivate the loyalty and support of their tenants at the expense of revenue. This policy permitted Dacre to raise an army for the defence of the west march cheaply and speedily from among his own tenants, and he had the less need to cultivate a following of county gentry. Despite the comparative weakness of Dacre's affinity outside the west marches, however, his standing at court and among his peers remained high, as appears from the double marriage of Dacre's son and heir to Shrewsbury's daughter, and his daughter to Shrewsbury's heir.[39] Shrewsbury was not only a leading nobleman but a conscientious royal servant who was lord high steward and very much in favour with the king.

Thus the compactness of his landholdings, coupled with his estate-management policies, gave Dacre a secure power base in the English borders. The effective exploitation of this base encouraged Dacre to develop relations not simply with the more disreputable elements in border society but also with Scottish lords and lairds. In this respect, Dacre's response reflected the state of Anglo-Scottish relations and the particular problems of border administration during Dacre's period of rule. Cross-border connections were of course traditionally strong in the English marches, because the Anglo-Scottish border region had originally formed one society. Politically, these links had been broken by the fourteenth-century Scottish wars of independence, which consolidated a distinct border line and separate aristocracies looking to London and Edinburgh respectively.[40] Yet, paradoxically, the increasing acceptance by the English crown of Scottish independence, the

[37] *SP Hen. VIII*, iv. 12, 29, 51, 54; Ellis (ed.), *Original letters*, 1st ser., i. 214–18; Miller, *Henry VIII and the English nobility*, 147–9; Dawson, 'Two kingdoms or three?', 121.

[38] Above, pp. 90–101.

[39] G. W. Bernard, *The power of the early Tudor nobility: a study of the fourth and fifth earls of Shrewsbury* (Brighton, 1985), 11, 51, 114, 153–5. Another of Dacre's daughters married Lord Scrope of Bolton: *L. & P. Hen. VIII*, iii, no. 3210.

[40] See esp. J. A. Tuck, 'The emergence of a northern nobility, 1250–1400', in *Northern History*, 22 (1986), 1–17; id., 'Northumbrian society in the fourteenth century', 22–39; Goodman, 'Anglo-Scottish marches in the fifteenth century', 18–33.

relaxation of military pressure, and the more economical system of border defence employed by the early Tudors led in turn to a partial *rapprochement* between the two border societies. Among the border lineages—the Armstrongs of Liddesdale and the Charltons of Tynedale, for instance—national allegiances had never counted for much anyway.[41] Yet among the wealthier English borderers, the reduction in opportunities for prizes and plunder in Scotland, and the increased premium on local defence which followed the scaling down of the English military effort, encouraged a modest strengthening of cross-border ties in a bid to stabilize the frontier. There was no return to a cross-border aristocracy of course, nor did the two aristocracies intermarry, as happened in Ireland where a similar pattern of development occurred.[42] Yet successive English wardens or a border baron like Lord Dacre clearly had some influence, and even following, in Scottish politics, if only because sentiments of national interest and identity were less developed among Scottish lords and lairds. In his Scottish wars Henry VIII frequently enjoyed the support of a leading Scottish border family like the Homes or the Douglases.[43]

No doubt this was in part a reflection of the relative weakness of the Scottish borderers and the localized nature of their holdings. Whereas during the fourteenth and fifteenth centuries the Scottish wardens had normally been great territorial magnates like the earl of Douglas or the duke of Albany, in the sixteenth century even the most powerful of them—Home, Maxwell, and Ker of Cessford— were essentially border barons.[44] Their influence depended on close ties with the border surnames, frequently formalized by bonds of manrent, and on landed estates concentrated in the marches, so leaving them very vulnerable to English pressure.[45] Dacre's particular influence in Scottish politics was widely recognized in English government circles. Lord Darcy doubted in 1512 'if any Inglisshman know more of the Scottes secrettes' than Dacre.[46]

---

[41] See above, pp. 63–4. [42] Ellis, *Tudor Ireland*, ch. 4.
[43] Gwyn, *The king's cardinal*, 83, 213; Robson, *English highland clans*, 102, 184–5.
[44] Rae, *Administration of the Scottish frontier*, 24–7; Alexander Grant, *Independence and nationhood: Scotland 1306–1469* (London, 1984), 190–6.
[45] Rae, *Administration of the Scottish frontier*, 8–11, 25–6; Wormald, *Lords and men in Scotland, passim.*
[46] BL, Caligula B. VII, fos. 226–7ᵛ (*L. & P. Hen. VIII*, i (2nd edn.), no. 1329). Cf. BL, Caligula B. VI, fo. 25 (*L. & P. Hen. VIII*, iii, no. 1048).

This influence had been developed during the period of comparatively good Anglo-Scottish relations in Henry VII's final years. As early as 1498 Dacre had been granted a three-year lease of the Esk fishery by James IV, thus supplying a temporary solution to a long-standing dispute between the two kingdoms.[47] And as is attested by the rewards and gifts granted by James to Dacre's servants and kinsmen in the years following, Lord Thomas was very much in favour at the Scottish court.[48] Dacre himself visited Scotland on a number of occasions during this period. In 1502 he journeyed to Melrose; the following year he seems to have visited Linlithgow and Stirling as one of the ambassadors to arrange the marriage between Margaret Tudor and the king of Scots; and in 1504 he accompanied James on the 'raid of Eskdale' to 'justify' the thieves of Canonbie, during which the two hunted and played cards together.[49] The only other Englishman to maintain such close relations with the Scottish court at this time was the keeper of Bewcastledale, Sir John Musgrave, whose wife was one of Queen Margaret's ladies-in-waiting.[50] Dacre liked to portray himself as a poor and simple border baron, living on horseback patrolling the moors, and training the wild borderers to peace and civility. He readily acknowledged, as an essential tool of his trade, his acquaintance with the lowland Scots and their politics. Indeed in many respects the border region shared the same culture and dialect, although the young James V could neither understand nor read southern English.[51] Yet French was another matter: Dacre could sometimes muddle through letters of thanks, but inconvenient demands from the duke of Albany found his French clerk absent. Verbal instructions and secret signs and tokens, rather than formal writs and commands, were the order of the day. Yet in his correspondence with London and Edinburgh Dacre carefully had copies made and kept.[52]

---

[47] *Register of the privy seal of Scotland*, ed. M. Livingstone, i. *1488–1529* (Edinburgh, 1908), no. 192.

[48] *Accounts of the Lord High Treasurer of Scotland*, ed. Balfour ii. 49, 98, iv. 325, 334, 335, 343, 376, 408.   [49] Ibid., ii. 345, 363, 364, 373, 440, 453–5.

[50] Ibid., ii. 34, 106, 120, 134, 157, 350, 415, 454–6, iii. 104, 130, 398, iv. 63, 125, 230–1, 326, 328, 404, 410, 434.

[51] BL, Caligula B. II, fos. 200–0ᵛ (*L. & P. Hen. VIII*, i (2nd edn.), no. 2913); *L. & P. Hen. VIII*, iv (i), no. 1372.

[52] See e.g. Ellis, *Original letters*, 1st ser., i. 132; *L. & P. Hen. VIII*, ii, nos. 788, 2253, iii, nos. 1078, 2525iii–iv, iv, nos. 133, 139, 200, 219, 1223, 1429, 1517ii. BL, Add. MS 24,965 is Thomas Lord Dacre's letter book for June 1523 to Aug. 1524.

Thus when Anglo-Scottish relations deteriorated again under Henry VIII, Dacre could turn his acquaintance with the leading Scottish politicians to other uses. Just what Dacre could do emerged in the aftermath of Flodden. His main contact at this time was the lord chamberlain, Alexander, Lord Home, although he also got much intelligence from the treasurer, the abbot of Kelso, and from the bishop of Glasgow. These and other lords were personally known to him; and through them, from his own spies, and from Queen Margaret, he could provide detailed reports of Scottish intentions, even down to who said what in debates in council.[53] Dacre relied on these contacts to dismiss suggestions of imminent invasion, or to countermand reinforcements even at a time when the captain of Berwick was hourly expecting a Scottish siege.[54] Yet the king's suspicions were soon excited by reports of his warden's secret communications and familiarity with the chamberlain in wartime. Dacre was obliged to make a detailed refutation of the charges to the council, claiming that he had no familiarity with either the chamberlain or any other Scot, that he had met him only once for ransoming of prisoners, that he would spare neither him nor his lands, and that at Flodden many of the Homes had been slain by Dacre's company. In a less guarded reply to Bishop Ruthal, however, Dacre asserted that he had no intelligence with any Scot but for the advancement of the king's causes, and asked his advice on how to conduct himself in future so as to avoid misconstruction.[55] As the duke of Albany's influence in Scotland rose, Dacre offered on different occasions to conduct Queen Margaret into England from ten miles south of Stirling or from one mile outside Edinburgh.[56] Letters reached him direct from the chamberlain, and verbal messages via the laird of Fernihurst.[57] Other intelligence was brought back by Dacre's own servants, such as Tom Scot (!), Tom Rutherford who arrived from Edinburgh disguised as a Scot, and William Hetherington whose wife, abducted and married in Scotland, was Scottish.[58]

---

[53] e.g. *L. & P. Hen. VIII*, i (2nd edn.), nos. 1342, 1504, 2381, 2390; Ellis, *Original letters*, 1st ser., i. 241–5.

[54] *L. & P. Hen. VIII*, i (2nd edn.), nos. 1329, 2026, ii, nos. 819, 850–1.

[55] *L. & P. Hen. VIII*, i (2nd edn.), nos. 2381, 2390, 2443, 2913.

[56] *L. & P. Hen. VIII*, ii, nos. 62, 66, 886ii, vi.

[57] *L. & P. Hen. VIII*, i (2nd edn.), no. 3181.

[58] *L. & P. Hen. VIII*, i (2nd edn.), no. 3181, ii, no. 819xiv, iv, no. 1151.

In May 1515, Scotland was comprehended in the truce with France, and Dacre was ordered secretly to foment disorders in Scotland so as to drive out the duke and force the Scots to sue for peace.[59] Using his brother, Sir Christopher, Dacre quickly detached Lord Home, the earl of Angus, and the laird of Fernihurst.[60] Home was soon garrisoning castles against Albany, and Dacre secretly supported him with troops, and also gunpowder from Berwick. Since Home was technically still warden-general, Dacre proposed that he be encouraged to invade England with 300 men or more so as to make void the comprehension. For this purpose, Dacre's officers were reputedly scouring Carlisle for Scots to serve in a force of 300 horsemen which Sir Christopher was sent to offer.[61] The Scottish borderers of the west march were likewise stirred up in the knowledge that, if the Scottish warden were unable to make redress for the murder of three Englishmen which resulted, the comprehension would likewise be void.[62] When Albany countered by outlawing Home, Dacre suggested to Henry that Sir Christopher should be made an outlaw too, so that they could combine their powers to waste Scotland. The conspiracies culminated in a plot to capture Albany: Home seemingly offered Albany his conditional submission, and the English borderers were held ready to intercept him if the duke ventured too close in order to accept it.[63] After Queen Margaret's escape into England, Dacre reported that he was giving rewards to 400 Scottish outlaws for burning in Scotland, and that he secretly harboured the master of Glencairn, for whose surrender Albany had written to the king.[64] Eighteen months later, the Homes were still raiding the Merse from Cawmills just north of Berwick, and at his own cost Dacre supplied them with ordnance, and assisted 'the Armstrongs, and other evil-disposed persons, their adherents'. The king also sent Dacre £100 for the entertainment of Scottish gentlemen discontented with Albany.[65]

Yet, throughout all this, Albany was unable to obtain hard evi-

[59] *L. & P. Hen. VIII*, ii, nos. 596, 779, 850. For the political background, see Eaves, *Henry VIII's Scottish diplomacy*, ch. 2.
[60] *L. & P. Hen. VIII*, ii, nos. 779, 783, 788, 845–6, 850, 1044.
[61] *L. & P. Hen. VIII*, ii, nos. 783, 788, 819(iii, x, xiii), 834i–ii, 850, 1672ii.
[62] *L. & P. Hen. VIII*, ii, nos. 834i–iii, 850, 855, 863, 898i, 1672ii.
[63] *L. & P. Hen. VIII*, ii, nos. 834i–ii, 850, 885, 1044, 1098.
[64] *L. & P. Hen. VIII*, ii, nos. 2253, 2293, 2313.
[65] *L. & P. Hen. VIII*, iii, nos. 3383, 3385 (quotation).

dence of Dacre's complicity in these disorders. Taxed with failure
to make redress and maintain good rule, the duke promised action
and amendment, asked for assistance against fugitives, and wrote
regularly of his good mind for peace. He even wrote directly to
warn Henry that he was being deceived by Dacre and the borderers, and threatened Dacre with this; but on the surface all was
co-operation and peace.[66] Of course many of Dacre's activities
were technically treason, and the king was free to disown them. It
was a dangerous game, because there was more than enough evidence in Dacre's dispatches to incriminate him. And as we shall
see, Dacre could just as easily and secretly employ his influence
with the Scots and the border thieves to stir up trouble south of the
border. For the moment, however, the king chose to turn a blind
eye.

Nevertheless, underhand incitement of trouble in Scotland was
incidental to the warden's main duties. And in the east march,
where Dacre was very much an outsider, without the range of
personal contacts and loyalties essential to the office, the inadequacies of Dacre rule were very quickly exposed. In the aftermath
of Flodden, the king commanded him to make three great raids
from each of the three marches into Teviotdale and the Merse.
Dacre reluctantly agreed to attempt the raid into Teviotdale, but
he observed that the dukes of Gloucester and Norfolk and the old
earl of Northumberland had thought such a raid a great enterprise.
An additional 1,000 marks had been allocated for the raid into the
Merse, but Dacre asked that Lord Darcy should undertake it as
captain of Berwick and steward of Bamburgh and Dunstanburgh.
He pointed out the risk if he were to strip the west march for the
purpose, that it would be unwise to trust himself to strangers, and
that at Flodden the Northumberland men assigned to his company
had fled at the first shot.[67] Neither coaxing by Bishop Ruthal and
Cardinal Wolsey nor a letter of encouragement from Henry himself would make him change his mind. Moreover, his experiences
in making the warden-rode into Teviotdale were hardly reassur-
ing. Neither Lord Ogle nor the captain of Alnwick kept their
appointment, and he was forced to set out with only 1,000 men

---

[66] *L. & P. Hen. VIII*, iii, nos. 834, 855, 863, 868, 898, 1024, 1026, 1030, 1098, 1598,
1672, 2253, 2313, 2465, 2711, 3125, 3139; Hannay (ed.), *Acts of the Lords of the Council
in Public Affairs*, 57–8.
[67] *L. & P. Hen. VIII*, i (2nd edn.), nos. 2382, 2386–7, 2390.

under his two wardenry lieutenants, and his brother Philip. In consequence, he was almost intercepted by two Scottish forces, before effecting a prearranged junction with his brother Sir Christopher with Dacre tenants and retainers from the west marches who had come in via Liddesdale.[68] His reports of the raid were accompanied by complaints of the backwardness of the gentry, and a request that Lords Clifford and Northumberland order their tenants to attend the warden as usual.[69]

Not only was Dacre a stranger in the east march, but he further antagonized the gentry there by economizing on its defence. He advised the king that 'wages given to the inhabitants there were in maner waisted and lost', because the borderers were obliged to do military service anyway. They in turn blamed Dacre because the king sent down no soldiers, and complained that the marches were being destroyed.[70] Lord Darcy reported that thirty towns next to Scotland 'be patished with the Scottish warden' for want of defence, although this was formerly considered treason; and he claimed that it would ultimately cost the king more than the savings.[71] Yet, although the Great North Road running through the east march was the chief route for armies in time of war, the east march in fact comprised lowland settlements easily organized for defence and adequately protected from casual Scottish raiders by the garrison at Berwick-on-Tweed. Additional garrisons continued to be laid in wartime, but mainly recruited from 'inlandmen'. Early in 1522, for instance, when the king allowed the warden an additional 500 horsemen on the recommencement of war, Dacre was obliged to place them on the east marches which 'will follow no counsaill for the helping of them self'. The garrison was mainly drawn from Yorkshire, with the local gentry encouraged by fees and rewards to augment the garrison for raids into Scotland.[72] Dacre's influence there was also bolstered slightly through his tenure from 1521 of the constableship of Norham

[68] *L. & P. Hen. VIII*, i (2nd edn.), nos. 2387, 2390, 2394, 2423, 2443.

[69] Ellis, *Original letters*, 1st ser., i. 93–9; *L. & P. Hen. VIII*, i (2nd edn.), no. 2443; *Clifford letters of the sixteenth century*, ed. A. G. Dickens, Surtees Society, clxxii (Durham, 1962), 96–9.

[70] BL, Caligula B. II, fo. 201 (*L. & P. Hen. VIII*, i (2nd edn.), no. 2913); *L. & P. Hen. VIII*, i (2nd edn.), no. 2793.

[71] *L. & P. Hen. VIII*, i (2nd edn.), no. 2576 (quotation).

[72] BL, Caligula B. VI (II), fos. 542–3 (*L. & P. Hen. VIII*, iii, no. 1986); Caligula B. I, fos. 9–10 (*L. & P. Hen. VIII*, iii, no. 2068); *L. & P. Hen. VIII*, iii, no. 2075.

castle, an outpost of Wolsey's palatinate of Durham, and because his brother Philip had earlier acquired some land there by marriage,[73] but Dacre's control was never satisfactory.

The problems of government in the much larger middle march were somewhat different. The barrier of the Cheviots precluded the possibility of any major Scottish incursion by this march, but control of the independent reiving clans of Tynedale and Redesdale, and those just across the border in Liddesdale and Teviotdale, was a major headache. The geography of the region left Dacre at a disadvantage in this regard, because the passes ran north-west/south-east, giving the border surnames easy access into lowland Northumberland and Durham. The traditional Percy solution was to retain the leading gentry, both those of the highlands who maintained the thieves, and the lowland gentry who suffered at their hands. Dacre's Northumberland territorial base around Morpeth was inadequate for this purpose, but his estates in north-east Cumberland were actually closer to Tynedale and Redesdale than the major concentrations of Percy lands. And from 1515 Dacre was also given oversight of Wolsey's regality of Hexham in south Tynedale.[74] The Percy baronies of Alnwick, Warkworth, and Prudhoe were in the lowlands, with only the barony of Langley nearby. Thus Dacre's estates enabled him to build up an alternative system of defence by attempting to control directly both the humbler squires who kept thieves and even the thieves themselves. The advantage of this system was of course its cheapness. Tynedale and Redesdale could each raise around 500 men for military exploits, and during periods of war and 'troublous peace' Dacre unleashed them to harass the Scots.[75]

There were, however, considerable drawbacks to Dacre's patronage of the border thieves. Tynedale and Redesdale were severely overpopulated for their natural resources, so that the inhabitants were forced to supplement their income by reiving and

---

[73] *L. & P. Hen. VIII*, iii, nos. 1169–70, 2031. By his marriage to Ann Delavale, widow, Philip Dacre secured a life interest in lands worth 200 marks p.a.: *L. & P. Hen. VIII*, i (2nd edn.), no. 2913; PRO, SP 1/45, fo. 106 (*L. & P. Hen. VIII*, iv, no. 3629(4)).

[74] *L. & P. Hen. VIII*, ii, nos. 64, 158, 250, 396, 841, iv, nos. 726, 1057–8; James, *Society, politics and culture*, ch. 2.

[75] Hodgson, *Northumberland*, III. ii. 184, 208–9, 222, 225, 229, 243 (Bowes's survey, 1550); *L. & P. Hen. VIII*, iv (ii), no. 4336(2); James, *Society, politics and culture*, ch. 2.

robbery.[76] This in turn set further limits on the levels of public order attainable in the marches, despite Dacre's periodic encouragement of them to combine with the Armstrongs of Liddesdale and raid northwards. During the Anglo-Scottish war of 1522–4, for instance, the Scottish marches were so wasted by constant English raids that there were no worthwhile spoils to be had, and the border thieves perforce switched their attentions southwards.[77] In any case, some such raiding was unavoidable: Dacre did from time to time execute a few thieves in a purge, particularly when under pressure from London, but vigorous sustained action against them would have destroyed his following there.[78] Not surprisingly, therefore, there were very soon complaints from the gentry of Northumberland and Durham that Dacre failed to keep good order. These reached a climax in 1518 when the gentry had a thousand bills of complaint put in to the justices of assize, with 400 persons in attendance to justify the complaints and to exclaim against Dacre and his lieutenant, Sir Ralph Fenwick. Concurrently, mass indictments of the highlanders were organized at peace sessions in the bishopric.[79]

It is unclear how far the king and council were aware of the circumstances of Dacre rule, but this transparently organized campaign coincided with renewed suspicions by the king of the earl of Northumberland's conduct.[80] Accordingly, although Dacre was summoned to justify his proceedings, with Wolsey's support he escaped with a caution. A Dacre retainer, Christopher Threlkeld, was appointed sheriff of Northumberland, an office of enhanced importance for border administration, and countercharges of maintenance were entertained against the organizers of the complaints.[81] In 1523–4, however, another campaign against Dacre succeeded. The Northumberland gentry eventually lodged a formal complaint with the duke of Norfolk against Dacre rule, citing particularly his failure to control the surnames of Tynedale, Redesdale, Bewcastledale, and Gilsland.[82]

---

[76] Above, pp. 62–5.

[77] *L. & P. Hen. VIII*, iii, nos. 3544–5, 3574, 3598; and see below, pp. 163–8.

[78] Cf. *L. & P. Hen. VIII*, iv, no. 1482.

[79] PRO, SP 1/16, fos. 313–14ᵛ (*L. & P. Hen. VIII*, ii, no. 4258). *L. & P. Hen. VIII*, ii, no. 4452 seems to relate to 1524, where it is calendared again as *L. & P. Hen. VIII*, iv (i), no. 682.

[80] *L. & P. Hen. VIII*, iii (i), no. 1; Guy, *Cardinal's Court*, 27, 31, 34, 119, 163 n. 146.   [81] *L. & P. Hen. VIII*, ii, nos. 4547, 4562, 4676, iv, no. 157.

[82] *L. & P. Hen. VIII*, iv (i), nos. 133, 218, 220, 682, 687, 726, 893.

Dacre was by 1524 increasingly anxious to be relieved of his unprofitable duties on the east and middle marches. He alleged sickness and old age as his excuse. Yet Norfolk and Wolsey were equally reluctant to allow him to retire to the west march, and he was ordered to stay at his post until he had repressed the disorders which had allegedly arisen since Norfolk's departure.[83] Finally, in January 1525, after an Anglo-Scottish truce had been agreed, Dacre was summoned before Wolsey and the council in Star Chamber for an investigation into his conduct as warden.[84] He submitted and 'confessed the bearinge of theaves and his remysnes & negligens in ponishem[t] of them, & also his famylyer and conversiunte beinge wth them, knowinge them to have commytted felonye, & dyvers other his mysdoinges'.

He was committed to the Fleet and forfeited his recognizances.[85] After a lengthy spell of detention, he was released in September and sent north to help negotiate an extension of the truce with the Scots. He compounded in 1,500 marks for his maladministration of justice, and was dismissed from all three wardenships, and also from the commissions of the peace.[86] In addition, he entered into a series of recognizances for his future behaviour, notably one in 5,000 marks to appear before the council on twenty days' warning and not to depart without licence, to make recompense within six years to any who might have suffered by his administration of justice, and also to assert himself to bring to justice all thieves, murderers, and outlaws within the bounds of his office with whom he had been conversant.[87] By the end of October he was dead from a fall from his horse.[88]

In the interlude between the ending of the French war and the crisis of the royal divorce, the focus of historians' attention has traditionally shifted in the mid-1520s to the internal administrative reforms initiated by Cardinal Wolsey. And, in this context, surveys of Tudor England frequently include a brief discussion of the

---

[83] *L. & P. Hen. VIII*, iv (i), nos. 133, 218, 220, 279.

[84] The articles of complaint by the inhabitants of Northumberland, together with Dacre's replies to each of them, are printed in Hodgson, *Northumberland*, II. ii. 31–40.

[85] BL, Lansdowne MS I, fo. 43; *L. & P. Hen. VIII*, iv (i), nos. 988, 1058, 1117; Guy, *Cardinal's Court*, 122–3, 163 n. 146.

[86] *L. & P. Hen. VIII*, iv, nos. 1637, 1665, 1700, 1725, 1727, 1762; Guy, *Cardinal's Court*, 122–3, 163 n. 146.

[87] PRO, C 82/585 (*L. & P. Hen. VIII*, iv (ii), no. 3022).

[88] *L. & P. Hen. VIII*, iv, no. 1727.

circumstances which led to Lord Dacre's removal from the wardenship, portraying it as an example of vigorous and effective action by the central government to clamp down on disorders in outlying parts. Dacre's punishment in Star Chamber has been hailed as 'a major triumph for Wolsey's policy of [law] enforcement' which 'marked the end of the age of the medieval robber baron'.[89] In reality, the dominant influence on the government of the far north at this time was an unwonted alliance between the Dacre and Percy families. Wolsey's intervention, if it proved anything, simply underlined the powerlessness of the central government to uphold law and order without the co-operation of powerful local interests. The king's decision to dispense with the services of Lord Dacre, at a time when the rule of the borders was already weakened by the continued exclusion of the Percies from authority there, drove the two families together and led to a period of violent disorders. These began in the last year of Dacre rule, continued throughout the virtual interregnum which followed, and also ensured the failure as deputy wardens of the earls of Westmorland and Cumberland. They have been characterized by Mervyn James as a concerted attempt by the Percies to force Henry VIII to re-establish the traditional Percy ascendancy in the region by making the borders ungovernable. This view is substantially correct, but it is only half the story. Northumberland's proceedings did not precipitate a 'slow crumbling of good order which characterized [Dacre's] rule'.[90] Government, in fact, broke down quite quickly from late 1523 onwards, and with Dacre's connivance.

The background was the Anglo-Scottish war of 1522–4, in which Dacre was eventually superseded by the appointment of the earl of Shrewsbury as lieutenant-general and Lord Ros as warden of the east and middle marches. After the summer's campaigning, Shrewsbury and Ros went home and Dacre was left to hold the fort. Significantly, however, Dacre had recommended that Lord Percy, Northumberland's heir, be made warden instead.[91] In 1523 the same pattern of events recurred. This time Lord Percy was seriously considered for the wardenship, and the lieutenant-

---

[89] Guy, *Cardinal's Court*, 123.
[90] James, *Society, politics and culture*, 82.
[91] *L. & P. Hen. VIII*, iii, no. 2645; Miller, *Henry VIII and the English nobility*, 188–9.

general, Surrey, initially recommended that if Percy were not then ready, Dacre should be appointed his deputy, so as to encourage the people to support him.[92] In the event, however, the campaigning lasted well into the autumn, no truce followed, and Surrey pleaded illness in order to get home for Christmas.[93] Accordingly, it was thought that a warden-general was necessary, and that 'there is no man so mete as the Lord Dacre is, aswell for his grete wisedome and experience, as for his power redy at hand to withstande excourses to be made by the Scottes'.[94] This decision was highly unwelcome to Dacre, since he had previously agreed to defend the west march at his own cost, was troubled by gout and, for good measure, had also been appointed captain of Carlisle in response to the Scottish attempt on it the previous year. In the circumstances, however, he reluctantly agreed to serve until Easter;[95] but when Easter came, he was still not allowed to retire.

In effect, the question of governing the Anglo-Scottish borders developed into a battle of wills between the crown and the combined influence of the Percies and the Dacres. By this time the 5th earl of Northumberland had effectively abandoned his pretensions to the wardenship but, with the support of Dacre and Surrey, he was pushing the claims of his son. Accordingly, his previously obstructive attitude to Dacre as warden had given way by 1523 to moderately good relations and co-operation between them. Northumberland's brother, retainers, and tenants were now attending Dacre on border rodes,[96] and there seems to have been a tacit understanding that Dacre would retire from the east and middle marches in favour of Lord Percy.[97] Indeed, relations were so good that Northumberland was writing to 'my owne good lord and cousynne', asking Dacre for loans, and giving him 'faithful' thanks for his kindness to the earl's brother.[98] Then in 1525 Dacre was detained at court and subsequently dismissed in disgrace from all three wardenships. Percy, however, was still excluded from the

---

[92] *L. & P. Hen. VIII*, iii, nos. 3365, 3384.

[93] *L. & P. Hen. VIII*, iii, no. 3531.   [94] *SP Hen. VIII*, iv. 53–6.

[95] *L. & P. Hen. VIII*, iii, no. 3544.

[96] BL, Caligula B. VI (II), fo. 325 (*L. & P. Hen. VIII*, iii, no. 2955); Add. MS 24,965, fos. 150–1 (*L. & P. Hen. VIII*, iii, no. 3097); *L. & P. Hen. VIII*, iii, no. 3100, iv (i), no. 278.

[97] *L. & P. Hen. VIII*, iii, nos. 2645, 3365, 3384, iv (i), no. 218.

[98] BL, Add. MS 24,965, fo. 10 (*L. & P. Hen. VIII*, iii, no. 3078); *L. & P. Hen. VIII*, iii, nos. 3106, 3603.

east and middle marches by Westmorland's appointment, and in the west march the young Lord Dacre was forced to watch an upstart earl of Cumberland consolidate Clifford influence at his expense. The result was that the king's insensitive handling of the wardenry appointments precipitated an unusual alliance between Percy and Dacre, in which the two families combined to make the marches ungovernable.

The most obvious result of this alliance was the lords' unleashing of the border surnames on the English marches—in the same manner as the earl of Kildare deployed the border clans in Ireland against officials who incurred his displeasure.[99] Already in late 1523, Surrey was expecting trouble from the border surnames. The garrisons had so wasted the Scottish marches that there was almost nothing left to raid, and fodder and corn were extremely scarce on the English side.[100] The men of Tynedale were required to swear and put in pledges to assist the king's officers and to be of good bearing to all the king's subjects until February 1525, and Dacre was advised to administer strict justice to malefactors.[101] Not surprisingly, however, many of the borderers preferred reiving at the risk of hanging to going hungry. Dacre was blamed, rather unfairly, for the ensuing disorders,[102] but he took vigorous action against those responsible, notably the Charltons and Ridleys, and won the king's approval.[103] In 1525, however, following Dacre's detention and disgrace, this restraining influence on the border gentry and surnames was replaced by underhand incitement to disorder. The activities of Percy retainers like Sir William Lisle of Felton, Sir William Heron of Ford, and Sir John Heron of Chipchase in stirring up the border thieves at this time are well known.[104] Yet concurrently, Dacre followers were acting similarly, in particular the Charltons and Ridleys, and Sir William Heron had recently taken Dacre's fee. As early as March, the palatinate

[99] Cf. Ellis, *Tudor Ireland*, 73, 109–16.

[100] *L. & P. Hen. VIII*, iii, nos. 3544–5, 3570, 3574, 3615, Add., i, no. 374; *SP Hen. VIII*, iv. 54.

[101] *L. & P. Hen. VIII*, iii, nos. 3545, 3576, 3579, 3598. See also, James, *Family, lineage and civil society*, 54.

[102] *L. & P. Hen. VIII*, iv (i), nos. 133, 220, 279.

[103] *L. & P. Hen. VIII*, iv (i), nos. 328–9, 346, 405, 482, 530.

[104] James, *Society, politics and culture*, 56–62, 78–82, 98–9; R. G. Eaves, *Henry VIII and James V's regency 1524–1528: a study in Anglo-Scottish diplomacy* (Lanham, 1987), ch. 7.

was reportedly much vexed by bands of up to 400 thieves from Tynedale, Bewcastledale, and Gilsland, with banished men, both English and Scottish. In Northumberland, 400 highlanders and Scottish thieves raided to within eight miles of Newcastle. And by May the rebels had been joined by the Armstrongs of Liddesdale and thieves from Ewesdale.[105] In Durham, it was thought that the raids were incited 'upon a sinister policy' to make the king think that the country could not be quietened without the help of Lord Dacre. Allegedly, Sir Christopher Dacre could have taken the headsmen, Tom Charlton and William Ridley, if he had wished.[106] Tynedale was eventually subdued over the summer by a military campaign involving the laying of garrisons and the mounting of a series of raids by Durham levies. Even so, one or two captains still held out, and the Northumberland gentry remained uncooperative.[107] William Ridley was eventually killed in Scotland; and Hector Charlton refused to submit 'to tyme he see the seid Lord Dacre', adding that he 'did no thing sithen the departure of Lord Dacre, his master, but that it was his pleasure and commandment', and that he would 'cause the Lord Dacre laugh when he comes home'.[108]

The king's response, however, was to appoint the duke of Richmond in mid-1525 as head of a revived council in the north and also as warden-general. The earls of Westmorland and Cumberland were appointed his deputy wardens, but since they lacked military retinues, which were withdrawn following the truce with Scotland, they were quite unable to keep the borderers quiet: neither earl had much land or following there.[109] Finally, at the end of 1527, Henry VIII accepted the inevitable, and the old order was restored on the borders: the 6th earl of Northumberland was appointed warden of the east and middle marches, and William, Lord Dacre, was made warden of the west march. There was, however, one significant difference. Despite the truce with Scotland, Northumberland's salary as warden was fixed at £1,000 per annum, which was far more than Dacre had received as warden-general, and recalled the

[105] *L. & P. Hen. VIII*, iv (i), nos. 278, 1223, 1239, 1289, 1338, 1372. For Sir William Heron, see above, p. 105.
[106] *L. & P. Hen. VIII*, iv (i), nos. 1223, 1239.
[107] *L. & P. Hen. VIII*, iv (i), nos. 1289, 1429, 1469, 1482, 1517.
[108] BL, Caligula B. I, fos. 46ᵛ–7 (*L. &. P. Hen. VIII*, iv (i), no. 1289); *L. &. P. Hen. VIII*, iv (i), nos. 346, 405, 1223, 1289, 1429 (quotations), 1517, 2110.
[109] James, *Society, politics and culture*, 80–2.

inflated salaries of fifteenth-century wardens.[110] In addition, the earl was allowed an impressive following costing the king £486 a year: three officials were appointed of counsel with the warden; each march had a lieutenant and three deputies; and a large number of gentry were fee'd on the warden's recommendation—in Northumberland, Lord Ogle and 5 knights, 13 esquires, and 31 gentlemen, plus 19 gentlemen of Norhamshire, 69 in all.[111] Administratively, this arrangement prefigured the system of crown pensioners established by Henry VIII in 1537 after the Pilgrimage of Grace, when the king took the wardenships into his own hands and governed through deputies.[112] Yet, since Northumberland effectively nominated the fee'd gentry, the arrangement was really a thinly disguised reversion to the traditional bastard-feudal methods of the fifteenth century. Despite the expense of the arrangement and its dangerous potential for aristocratic autonomy, the king seems to have accepted it, in the crisis which had now developed, as the most effective method of bringing the borderers to heel, and perhaps also because the 6th earl seemed so much more subservient than his father had been. Significantly, Dacre's appointment on the west march involved only the restoration of the usual Tudor salary of £153. 6s. 8d., without any additional payments for fee'd retainers.[113]

Overall, therefore, the career of Thomas, Lord Dacre, as warden-general offers an instructive commentary on the limitations of royal power in the marches. There was a significant contrast between his firm control of the west march, and even of the Northumbrian highlands, and his weak rule of the eastern lowlands, a

---

[110] PRO, SP 1/45, fos. 101–7 (*L. &. P. Hen. VIII*, iv (ii), no 3629(2–4)). Cf. Storey, 'Wardens of the marches', 606–9. Dr Miller in *Henry VIII and the English nobility*, 188, 191, suggests that both Lord Darcy and the earl of Westmorland had received £1,000 per annum as wardens of the east and middle marches, but this seems to be an extrapolation from Northumberland's fee. Certainly, Darcy's fee as lieutenant (1502–5), and later warden (1505–11), of the east march had been the usual £114. 6s. 8d.: PRO, SP 1/12, fo. 49 (*L. &. P. Hen. VIII*, ii (i), no. 1365); E 101/72, file 7/1166; E 403/2558, fos. 116, 127ᵛ, 142, 164; E 405/183, fos. 79, 150; *L. &. P. Hen. VIII*, ii (i), no. 2736.

[111] PRO, SP 1/45, fos. 101–7 (*L. &. P. Hen. VIII*, iv (ii), no. 3629); *L. &. P. Hen. VIII*, iv (ii), nos. 3689, 5085, Add., i, nos. 618, 828.

[112] Bush, 'Problem of the far north', 45–6.

[113] James, *Society, politics and culture*, 56–62; PRO, E 101/72, file 7/1167. The evidence perhaps also supports Mr James's suggestion (ibid. 81–2) that one reason why the 5th earl of Northumberland was not appointed warden, notably in 1523, was that his terms were thought too high.

contrast which is even more apparent when Dacre's political role is considered in conjunction with the evidence discussed in Chapter 3 concerning his estate-management policies. This contrast clearly reflects the extent and antiquity of the lord's landed holdings and the size of his affinity in the two areas. In Cumberland, where he was the largest landowner and where his ancestral estates lay, the rule and defence of this the most remote shire in England presented no problems to Dacre. As we have seen, the crown's long-term reliance on Lord Thomas as warden allowed him to establish a more effective system of defences for the region as well as to build up his own estates there. In the east and middle marches, however, the king's preference for Dacre as warden-general cut across, instead of acknowledging, the traditional loyalties of the region. Dacre had recently acquired substantial possessions in Northumberland, and his influence was further strengthened by the conferring on him of stewardships and constableships of Wolsey's estates there: but he was still seen as an outsider by the more respectable Northumberland county gentry, and even with the king's commission he proved no match for the status and influence of the earl of Northumberland.

By building up his cross-border ties with Scottish lords and lairds and with the border surnames, Dacre was able to strengthen his grip on the two most disruptive influences in English marcher society. As in the case of the earl of Kildare's alliances with the Gaelic chiefs, these links helped to stabilize the defence of the east and middle marches and to mitigate the crisis of lordship created by the dismantling of the traditional arrangements for border defence. Dacre's parsimony with fees and wages, however, did not endear him to the local gentry, who grumbled about his failure to keep good rule. Indeed, there is no evidence that Dacre was ever more than a reluctant warden of the east and middle marches. His acceptance of office was a recognition of the king's right to exclude from power a Percy earl whom he mistrusted, but Dacre made no attempt to build up his affinity in Northumberland so as to challenge the earl's standing there. Thus a kind of political stalemate developed. The king's commission did not make the leading gentry follow Dacre with any enthusiasm, even after a dozen years; but Northumberland gradually accepted his exclusion from office and confined himself to occasional demonstrations of Percy influence, to which Dacre took care not to react. Gradually relations between the two magnates grew less strained. Indeed, in 1523, when the king again overlooked Lord Percy's pretensions and insisted on Dacre's reappointment, Lord Thomas eventually decided that King Henry's attitude was unreasonable, and he combined with the earl to sabotage Tudor policy. The resultant disorders underlined in no uncertain fashion the limitations on royal authority in the region as the underhand incitement of disorder by the two lords undermined Henry's attempts to intrude other nobles as alternative candidates for the wardenships. In 1527 the king grudgingly backed down, as he had earlier in Ireland. Yet he was far from reconciled to these restraints on his authority, and the growing tensions between Henry VIII and the ruling magnates eventually brought about a major crisis in 1534.

PART III

The crisis of 1534

6

The origins of the crisis

1534 is usually seen by Tudor historians as the crisis year for the acceptance of the Henrician Reformation. The king's divorce and the royal supremacy led to a need for a period of major administrative reform. Over the next three years, it is argued, Henry and his chief minister, Thomas Cromwell, sought to centralize control and to strengthen royal government in the provinces. They introduced more effective, bureaucratic structures and built up a crown interest among the gentry so as to stamp out disorders and to reduce the power and bastard feudal connexions of the great provincial magnates. In Ireland, allegedly, these measures 'passed sentence of death on bastard feudalism . . . and decreed the resuscitation of crown government' in the lordship; in the far north, they likewise announced the king's intention to rule the marches through 'mean men' instead of great nobles; and in Wales they led to the dismantling of the great marcher lordships and the effective incorporation of Wales into England. Throughout the Tudor state, it is suggested, the destruction of feudal particularism and noble power promoted the rule of law, the advance of civil society, and strong royal government in accordance with Cromwell's vision of the unitary state.[1]

This, at any rate, is how things looked from the 'centre' in lowland England, and to those elements of marcher society which shared these lowland perceptions of 'English civility'. From the borderlands, however, things looked rather different. This next section of the book aims to reconsider the genesis and conse-

[1] Elton, *Reform and Reformation*, chs. 9, 11, offers the most persuasive account of this interpretation, although Elton inclines towards Bush's interpretation ('Problem of the far north', 40–63) in the debate on the reasons for the appointment of 'mean men'. Cf. James, *Society, politics and culture*, ch. 3. For a more sweeping statement focusing on Ireland, see Brendan Bradshaw, *Irish constitutional revolution*, pt. 2; id., 'Cromwellian reform and the origins of the Kildare rebellion, 1533–4', in *TRHS*, 5th ser. 27 (1977), 69–93 (quotation, p. 85). On the significance of 1534, see Elton, *Policy and police*, 278.

quences of 'the Tudor revolution' as it applied to the periphery. The present chapter examines the origins of the administrative changes of the mid-1530s. Admittedly, the political unrest generated by the king's divorce and the royal supremacy underlined the need to ensure that control of the borderlands was in reliable hands. There seems very little evidence, however, to support the assertion that the king pursued from the outset a deliberate policy of reducing noble power and centralizing control in response to complaints of 'lack of governance'. The argument developed here is that the origins of the crisis of 1534 in the borderlands reflected more the growth of faction at court and the king's inept handling of the traditional ruling magnates there than any marked decline in their local standing or in their capacity to rule the marches. The following two chapters analyse both the difficulties which the crown faced in responding to this crisis of its own making and also the impact of the changes on the quality of government in the two regions. The most evident result, it is suggested, was pronounced political instability. Since the traditional ruling nobles were no longer available for border service, the crown was forced to develop an alternative system of government. But the more bureaucratic and centralized system which emerged was a distinctly *ad hoc* response to the crisis, which failed to address adequately many of the problems created by the absence of noble power, particularly with regard to border defence. And if, in other respects, the new arrangements improved the quality of government, this was chiefly because the crown now made available for the rule of the marches additional financial and military resources which had not been available to the old order.

At the end of April 1534, the king decided to make changes in the arrangements for the government of the borderlands. A new governor for Ireland was chosen in place of Kildare, who had been summoned to court, and a new president was to head the council in the marches of Wales. In May, at the conclusion of peace with Scotland, Lord Dacre was suddenly arrested at court. Charged, as we have seen, with treasonable dealings with the Scots in wartime, he was found not guilty at his trial—to the surprise of many—but he was heavily fined and dismissed from office, and he spent the rest of the reign in disgrace. A few weeks later, Kildare was similarly arrested for treason after his son and deputy, Lord Offaly, denounced the king's policies at a council meeting in Dublin and committed a series of outrages which gradually developed into a full-scale rebellion. In September, the traitor James ap Gruffydd ap Hywel, who had escaped from the Tower to Scotland and whose nephew had been executed for allegedly conspiring with James V of Scotland, joined the rebels in Ireland. Also that month, Lords Darcy and Hussey held treasonable communications with Eustace Chapuys, the Imperial ambassador, in which they sought a military intervention by the Emperor against the king's divorce and remarriage and the breach with Rome.[2]

These episodes have generally been seen by historians as basically unrelated incidents, arising out of Henry VIII's centralizing policies in response to the Reformation crisis. Although each of the lords nursed grievances, they were not seen to be closely allied with each other. Darcy and Hussey were primarily courtiers, whose plottings in 1534 would not have attracted attention but for their key roles in the Pilgrimage of Grace and the Lincolnshire rebellion in 1536.[3] Dacre and Kildare were both border magnates, and the circumstances which led to their fall were also quite similar. But there were no known ties between them, nor with ap Gruffydd's influential family in south-west Wales, and neither was closely connected with the Tudor court. Despite the lack of hard evidence concerning an organized conspiracy, however, circumstantial evidence suggests that the king came to believe in mid-1534 that disaffected nobles were plotting against him and that he lashed out against the two magnates he suspected might be his most dangerous opponents. In both borderlands, moreover, the fall of the two families who had dominated the Tudor borderlands since the start of the reign eventually forced the king into far more sweeping changes for the rule of these regions than had been contemplated before 1534.

As it will appear, the grievances against crown policy nursed by Dacre and Kildare which led to the breach between crown and magnates in 1534 were political and had little to do with the royal divorce and the Henrician Reformation. It is surely significant,

---

[2] *L. & P. Hen. VIII*, vii, nos. 650, 710, 1206; *Cal. SP Spain, 1534–8*, pt. i, no. 90; Williams, *Recovery, reorientation and Reformation*, 253–9. For Kildare and Dacre, see below.

[3] G. R. Elton, 'Politics and the Pilgrimage of Grace', in B. Malament (ed.), *After the Reformation* (New Haven, Conn., 1980), 25–56.

however, that once the breach occurred, Kildare's kinsmen, led by his heir, Thomas, Lord Offaly, immediately denounced the royal divorce and ecclesiastical policies, even though the earl had previously shown himself co-operative on these issues: they asserted that the rebellion was a Catholic crusade against the king's heresies. Upon news of the rising, Lord Darcy urged Chapuys to write to Charles V to send help for the rebels; and two years later, during the Pilgrimage, he remarked to Somerset Herald that if the duke of Richmond, the titular lieutenant of Ireland, had been able to secure Offaly's pardon, Lord Thomas would have surrendered to Richmond. The government was later very anxious to learn how he knew this.[4] In the case of Lord Dacre, Chapuys predictably conjectured that Dacre had been tried for treason because of his support for Queen Catherine, and he later reported a conversation in which Darcy had asserted that Dacre was one of his two most powerful allies.[5] Finally, the circumstances and procedures surrounding the arrest of Dacre and Kildare also suggest that, not least in the growing insecurity of the king's mind, their offences were connected.

Dacre's arrest and the seizure of his property were very carefully co-ordinated. At the end of April, Sir Thomas Clifford and Cromwell's servants, John ap Rhys and William Brabazon, were dispatched with instructions and a commission to the earls of Westmorland and Cumberland concerning the impending arrest. Concurrently, Dacre's uncle and deputy warden, Sir Christopher, and Bishop Tunstall of Durham, a persistent critic of the divorce and royal supremacy, were summoned to court. The commissioners gathered first at Bishop Auckland to search Tunstall's chief residence for incriminating papers, but found none.[6] Then travelling again by different routes to conceal their intentions, the party arrived at Naworth on 9 May to attach Dacre's goods and search for papers. They arrested Sir Christopher's goods at Carlisle on the 11th, followed by Dacre property elsewhere. Again, however, they expressed surprise and disappointment at finding so few letters of any consequence: 'howe that shulde happen we doo not well knowe'. They could only conclude that the Dacres had

[4] S. G. Ellis, 'The Kildare rebellion and the early Henrician Reformation', in *Hist. Jn.*, 19 (1976), 812–13, 829.

[5] *L. & P. Hen. VIII*, vii, nos. 1013, 1206.

[6] *L. & P. Hen. VIII*, v, nos. 986–7 (misplaced in 1532), vii, nos. 522, 679–80, 886.

had 'some coniecture of this busynes or euer we came to thies parties'.[7] Once in London, Bishop Tunstall was apparently told to choose between the king and the Tower: he chose the king's supremacy and subsequently departed on embassy to Scotland, while by 15 May Lord Dacre, his uncle, and his illegitimate half-brother, Thomas Dacre, were all in the Tower awaiting trial for treason.[8] Yet the association of Tunstall with Dacre in this way may suggest that the king suspected treason concerning Henry's great matter, rather than the peripheral issue of treasonable dealings with the Scots. Similarly, in Kildare's case, two of Cromwell's clients, Thomas Cusack and Thomas Finglas, were dispatched about the same time with letters to his son and deputy and to the Irish council. Lord Offaly was ordered to summon a meeting of the council at which the king's further pleasure would be declared by Cusack and Finglas. Again the intended victims got wind of what was afoot, and Kildare warned his son of the impending summons and arrest. In this case, however, Offaly reacted differently.[9]

Overall, therefore, the timing and immediate reasons for proceedings against the two magnates seem to relate chiefly to the king's distrust and suspicions arising out of the Reformation crisis rather than the ostensible charges against them. Yet, like many of the factional intrigues at the Henrician court, the manœuvres against Dacre and Kildare effectively operated at two levels. From the king's viewpoint, Dacre and Kildare were powerful independently minded provincial magnates who held two of the most important military commands in the Tudor state, with control of large numbers of troops. Moreover, their dubious activities and obstreperous conduct had attracted the king's attention on a number of occasions in the past. In 1534 the formal charges against them related to the misgovernment of the regions under their rule. Yet behind these charges the influence of faction may be detected.

The circumstances of their rule and authority dictated that neither lord was closely connected with the Tudor court, but after 1529 both looked for support to the conservative faction led by the

---

[7] PRO, SP 1/84, fo. 60 (*L. & P. Hen. VIII*, vii, no. 679); *L. & P. Hen. VIII*, vii, nos. 646, 663, 674, 676, 680, 687.

[8] *L. & P. Hen. VIII*, vii, nos. 627, 646, 663, 674, 676, 679–80; Scarisbrick, *Henry VIII*, 330–1.

[9] PRO, SP 1/238, fo. 188 (*L. & P. Hen. VIII*, Add. i, no. 889), SP 60/2, fo. 159 (*L. & P. Hen. VIII*, ix, no. 514); Lambeth MS 602, fos. 139–9ᵛ (*Cal. Carew MSS, 1515–74*, no. 84).

duke of Norfolk; whilst it was chiefly through the good offices of the king's secretary, Thomas Cromwell, that the complaints and charges of their respective opponents were entertained. The eventual outcome in the two regions was very different. Although both magnates were dismissed in disgrace from the offices they traditionally controlled, the decision of the Fitzgeralds to contest the king's pleasure, while Dacre submitted, led to the elimination of Kildare power and influence in the ensuing rebellion. By contrast, Dacre preserved his power base in the west marches by avoiding any involvement in the subsequent Pilgrimage of Grace. In consequence, the structures of power for the rule and defence of the two marches were affected in different ways, so prompting the crown to pursue rather different strategies to restore royal control.

Although Henry VIII's distrust of Dacre and Kildare in 1534 reflected in large measure the charged atmosphere at court during the Reformation crisis, the background to the breach was furnished by the developments of the 1520s when the king had experimented unsuccessfully with the appointment of other lords to the positions which Dacre and Kildare felt were rightfully theirs. As we have seen, the arrangements for the rule and defence of the borders rested chiefly on the personal influence and military might of the ruling nobles there rather than on money and men provided by the crown. Thus, both the earl of Cumberland as warden of the west marches (1525–7) and the earl of Ormond as governor of Ireland (1522–4, 1528–9) proved unable to discharge effectively the duties with which they had been entrusted because they lacked the military and financial resources to do so. Even so, they were not helped by the obstructive attitudes of Dacre and Kildare respectively. In the face of the ensuing disorders, Henry had judged it expedient to back down and restore the traditional order on the borders, but relations between the respective nobles and their followers were not so soon restored. Thus in the aftermath of these experiments, there were continuing tensions between the various parties which demanded the king's attention.

In the west marches rivalry between Dacre and Clifford after 1525 centred initially on custody of Carlisle which the old Lord Dacre and then his son, Lord William, refused to deliver to the earl without a sufficient letter of discharge.[10] Henry and Wolsey continued to use the services of Sir Christopher Dacre, who was

---

[10] *SP Hen. VIII*, iv. 420, 437; *L. & P. Hen. VIII*, iv, no. 1896.

appointed sheriff of Cumberland in 1526 in addition to offices in
the other marches; but this attempt to employ the Dacre influence
without involving Lord William led to disputes between sheriff
and warden over farms of crown land which were traditionally
associated with one or other office.[11] The evidence is very scanty,
but these disputes seem to have developed into a power struggle
between the two families concerning the perquisites of the
wardenship. By April 1527 Lord William had secured the steward-
ship of Penrith which in November 1525 Cumberland had seen as
vital to his discharge of the wardenship.[12] And after Dacre had
been reappointed warden at the end of 1527 relations between the
two lords were so bad that first the earl of Northumberland, and
then Wolsey, attempted to arbitrate between them.[13] Yet riots and
disturbances continued, particularly over Dacre's attempts to eject
Clifford tenants and followers from farms of crown land which
were traditionally at the disposal of the warden.[14] A similar source
of friction was the governorship of the city and castle of Carlisle
which had been granted to the earl of Cumberland on his appointment as warden with an ample fee and allowance for a garrison, but
which, despite the change of warden, remained in the custody of
Sir Thomas Clifford. Eventually in mid-1529 Dacre was made
governor of Carlisle, which by then was in disrepair, with a fee of
100 marks and the wages of twenty horsemen.[15] By way of compensation Clifford was appointed deputy governor of Berwick on the
opposite march.[16] Concurrently relations with Scotland were de-
teriorating over the question of the Debateable Land, where Dacre
conducted a series of raids to eject the Armstrongs, and concerning
Canonbie, which the English argued was debatable and the Scots
claimed as part of Scotland.[17] At court, Dacre continued to enjoy
the support of the duke of Norfolk, but his credit was declining,

[11] *L. & P. Hen. VIII*, iv, nos. 2052, 2483.

[12] *L. & P. Hen. VIII*, iv, nos. 1763, 3087; *SP Hen. VIII*, iv. 421.

[13] PRO, SP 1/47, fos. 20–1 (*L. & P. Hen. VIII*, iv (ii), no. 3971); *L. & P. Hen.
VIII*, iv, nos. 4020, 4132–3, 4790, 4855.

[14] PRO, SP 1/48, fos. 235–40 (*L. & P. Hen. VIII*, iv (iii), nos. 4420–1), SP 1/50,
fos. 202–8 (*L. & P. Hen. VIII*, iv (iii), nos. 4419, 4495, 4531, 4790, 4855, app. no. 184;
SP Hen. VIII, iv. 502–3).

[15] *L. & P. Hen. VIII*, iv, nos. 1431 (6), 1763, 4828, 4835, 5906 (6), 5952; *SP Hen.
VIII*, iv. 516. Dacre's own estate accounts show only one receipt of £50 in 1532–3
for the governorship of Carlisle, which suggests that most of the money must have
been spent on repairs to the castle: Durham, H. of N. MS C/201/3.

[16] *L. & P. Hen. VIII*, iv (iii), no. 5748 (22).

[17] *SP Hen. VIII*, iv. 489, 492–3; *L. & P. Hen. VIII*, iv, nos. 3972, 4020, 4134,
4323, 4531, 4709, 4925.

particularly after the fall of his chief patron, Cardinal Wolsey; and his relations with Northumberland were also cooler and deteriorated still further over their joint conduct of the Anglo-Scottish war of 1532–4.[18] Yet as Anglo-Scottish relations turned sour, Dacre's manpower and military experience became increasingly necessary to the king for the defence of the marches.[19]

In Ireland a very similar struggle between king and magnate was being played out, leading eventually to the restoration of the earl of Kildare to the deputyship in 1532. As with the Dacres, however, there was certainly a crisis of confidence between king and magnate. The earl of Ormond's failure as deputy in 1522–4 and his supersession by Kildare had earlier left a legacy of ill will between the two earls which troubled the peace of the lordship for the rest of the decade.[20] A further complication was the intrigues of Kildare's kinsman, James Fitzgerald, 10th earl of Desmond, with Francis I during the Anglo-French war of 1522–4. By late 1524 Desmond was exploiting the Kildare–Ormond feud to organize a series of raids on the Butler territories. Ormond in turn astutely represented to the king that Kildare was in treasonable communication with Desmond. And the deputy's denials seemingly carried less weight because he was unable to apprehend Desmond. He was understandably reluctant to campaign against Desmond to Ormond's benefit, and when he did lead a hosting into Munster, Desmond had ample time in which to disappear. The council could only send the king a draft bill for Desmond's attainder against a projected parliament scheduled to meet before summer 1527, but it gradually became apparent that only by getting Ormond and Kildare to work together could Desmond be brought to book, order restored, and the threat of continental intervention ended.[21]

In autumn 1526, as disturbances increased, the king summoned both earls for an extended sojourn at court. Kildare appointed his brother, Sir Thomas Fitzgerald, as vice-deputy in his absence, but

---

[18] *SP Hen. VIII*, iv. 579–80, 612, 614, 617–18; *L. & P. Hen. VIII*, iv (iii), no. 5750, 5920, v, nos. 314, 434, vi, no. 876, vii, no. 281.

[19] *SP Hen. VIII*, iv. 576–96, 608–11; *L. & P. Hen. VIII*, v, nos. 465, 535–7, 595, 609, 1078–9.

[20] S. G. Ellis, 'Tudor policy and the Kildare ascendancy in the lordship of Ireland, 1496–1534', in *IHS* 20 (1976–7), 240–5.

[21] PRO, PRO 31/18/137 (*L. & P. Hen. VIII*, iii, no. 3118); Ellis, *Tudor Ireland*, 116–17.

Fitzgerald was soon replaced, apparently on the king's orders, by the veteran border baron, Richard Nugent, Lord Delvin.[22] Yet, since Henry made no adequate provision for the lordship's government in the interim, the absence of the two earls rapidly exposed the limitations of the crown's heavy reliance on noble power for the good rule of the borders. Exploiting the weakness and dissensions of the Englishry, the border Irish conducted a series of damaging raids which the vice-deputy was unable to prevent.[23] Yet individual Gaelic chiefs did not pose the same kind of military challenge to the lordship as the Scots to the north. Thus for almost eighteen months matters were allowed to drift, although members of the Irish council spelled out quite plainly to Wolsey and Norfolk what needed to be done. Faced with the prospect of a second winter without the earls, the council warned that owing to division and lack of captains the Englishry were never weaker since the conquest; that 'these two honourable men now being with the king's grace, confirmed in amity, should never do our sovereign lord better service in this poor land than now'; and that if Kildare returned as deputy, he should find sureties to accomplish the king's command, 'for there is none of this land that can or may do for defence of the same so well as he'.[24] And of Lord Delvin they wrote that, lacking extensive possessions, he was 'nat of power to defend the Englishrie, and yet the poor people is ferr more chargid and oppressed by hym than they have been, therll of Kildair being here'.[25]

At court, Ormond was in much the weaker position because his title to the earldom as male heir to the 7th earl (d. 1515) was disputed by heirs-general—the old earl's two daughters, one of whom was the grandmother of Anne Boleyn. He was forced to submit to arbitration by Wolsey and to accept an unfavourable settlement by which he secured only two of the more profitable Ormond manors in the Pale, plus a preferential thirty-year lease for £40 sterling per annum of all the Ormond lands west of the River Barrow, except the manor of Carrick-on-Suir. He also relinquished the title of earl of Ormond and was created instead earl of

[22] *SP Hen. VIII*, ii. 120–8; *L. & P. Hen. VIII*, iv, nos. 2424, 2433, 2468, 2751.
[23] *SP Hen. VIII*, ii. 126–8; *L. & P. Hen. VIII*, iv, nos. 3698–700, 4094, 4302, 4933.
[24] PRO, SP 1/51, fos. 18–19 (spelling modernized). The date is Nov. 1527, but placed in 1528 by *L. & P. Hen. VIII*, iv, no. 4933.
[25] *SP Hen. VIII*, ii. 126–8.

Ossory.[26] As a sop, the king made him a grant in prospect of the
lordship of Dungarvan, detained by the rebel earl of Desmond,
and also lands in Ossory which he might recover from the Gaelic
Irish. And Norfolk made him a lease of all his extensive but largely
waste or Irish-occupied estates in Carlow and Wexford (except the
lordship of Carlow) which had previously been leased to Kildare.[27]
He was licensed to return to Ireland in spring 1528, and he had just
started to restore order in his own lands in Kilkenny and Tipperary when the lordship was plunged into crisis by O'Connor's
capture of the vice-deputy, Lord Delvin, at a parley on the borders
of Meath. Ossory was too far off to be of any immediate assistance
in the emergency, so because 'the strength, if any be, is by the
Garrantynes', the council elected Sir Thomas Fitzgerald captain
and again appealed for aid from England, 'for undoubted, ther is
no man here now being that can or may defend this londe, as well
for lacke of power as substance'.[28]

O'Connor Faly was the son-in-law of Kildare (still in England),
and although the reason given by him for kidnapping the vice-
deputy was that Delvin withheld his blackrent, 'O'Connor's wars'
(as they were called) were widely thought to have been instigated
by Kildare's councillors 'in the hope that he should the rather
come home'.[29] On leaving for court at the end of 1526, Kildare had
allegedly taken an oath from each member of the king's council,
unbeknown to each other, to write in his favour.[30] He had also
asked his allies and satellites among the Gaelic Irish, particularly
O'Neill, O'Brien, and O'Connor, not to cause trouble until the
king's intentions became apparent.[31] Thus, as proceedings dragged
on at court, so in Ireland the earl's supporters held their hand.
About All Hallowtide 1527, it began to look as if matters would be
settled to the earl's satisfaction, and some of his servants returned

[26] PRO, SP 1/46, fos. 265–9 (*L. & P. Hen. VIII*, iv, no. 3937); *Ormond deeds,
1509–47*, nos. 136, 139; PRO, C 66/650, m. 11 (*L. & P. Hen. VIII*, iv, no. 4241);
Handbook Brit. chron., 496.
[27] PRO, C 66/651, m. 20 (*L. & P. Hen. VIII*, iv, no. 3973); *Ormond deeds, 1509–
47*, no. 140; *L. & P. Hen. VIII*, iv, no. 4302.
[28] *SP Hen. VIII*, ii. 127–33; *L. & P. Hen. VIII*, iv, nos. 4263–5, 4283–4.
[29] *L. & P. Hen. VIII*, iv, no. 3698 (quotation); PRO, SP 60/1, fo. 139 (*L. & P.
Hen. VIII*, iv, no. 5392).
[30] PRO, SP 1/45, fos. 264–5 (*L. & P. Hen. VIII*, iv, no. 3698).
[31] PRO, SP 1/45, fos. 266–7 (*L. & P. Hen. VIII*, iv, no. 3699), SP 1/51, fos. 18–
19 (*L. & P. Hen. VIII*, iv, no. 4933), SP 60/1, fos. 111–12 (*L. & P. Hen. VIII*, iv,
no. 4094), fo. 127 (*L. & P. Hen. VIII*, iv, no. 4302).

to Ireland to tell Kildare's friends to keep the peace until St Nicholas tide (9 May) in expectation of his return.[32] By March, however, news had reached Ireland that Kildare was in disgrace, and on 12 May Lord Delvin was captured in a parley. Early in August Kildare sent back his daughter Alice as a 'prevy token' that he was 'not at his pleasour to come home'. She rode straight to O'Connor, who immediately began new hostilities.[33] And despite his election as captain, Fitzgerald permitted 'O'Connor and his adherents to invade, rob and destroy divers of the said king's subjects . . . in the English Pale', as he later admitted, 'by reason of certain intelligence had with O'Connor, contrary to his allegiance'.[34]

Clearly the renewed unrest in Ireland was a direct response by Kildare to his continued detention at court after the release of Ossory, even though Ossory had had in fact to make considerable concessions to win royal approval. Yet despite all this, and knowing how unwelcome their views would be, the chancellor and chief justice could only reiterate that the land would be ruined unless Kildare came home shortly or the king sent a 'substantial power' for defence, and they urged that good order would the sooner be restored by the firm unity of the two earls.[35] Similarly, Norfolk advised Wolsey that, short of sending back Kildare, the only remedy was to continue his brother in authority and either to wage soldiers for defence or send over money for that purpose. Yet 'iff any labour be made . . . to make therle of Ossery, or his son deputie, in no wise to condessende theronto', because 'being so fer off as they be', and owing to the war in Munster, 'it shalbe unpossible for them to deffende the 4 sherys, nor skante their owne contre'.[36] The king, however, rejected requests for financial aid, determined that either Ossory or his son, Lord James Butler, the king's servant, should be appointed governor, and remitted the details to Wolsey.[37]

[32] PRO, SP 60/1, fo. 139 (*L. & P. Hen. VIII*, iv, no. 5392); *L. & P. Hen. VIII*, iv, nos. 3698–700.

[33] PRO, SP 60/1, fo. 139 (*L. & P. Hen. VIII*, iv, no. 5392), fos. 111–12 (*L. & P. Hen. VIII*, iv, no. 4094); *SP Hen. VIII*, ii. 126–36, 143–7.

[34] *Ormond deeds, 1509–47*, no. 144.

[35] PRO, SP 60/1, fo. 127 (*L. & P. Hen. VIII*, iv, no. 4302).

[36] *SP Hen. VIII*, ii. 135–6.

[37] PRO, SP 60/1, fo. 129 (*L. & P. Hen. VIII*, iv, no. 4422); *SP Hen. VIII*, ii. 136–40.

Faced with conflicting advice and instructions, Wolsey's ingeni-
ous response was to prevaricate by drawing up a scheme for Butler
to be appointed vice-deputy to Kildare, with Kildare retaining
overall responsibility and some of the profits of the deputyship—in
the hope that the two factions would then co-operate until 'by a
substanciall debatement and consultation a bettre ordre mought
bee takene'.[38] This scheme, which seems to have originated in
a suggestion by John Rawson, prior of Kilmainham,[39] earned
Wolsey a sharp rebuke. The king, he was told, 'in no wes lykes the
instroxons' and felt that Kildare 'goeth fraudelently about to
colour that the king shuld thinke that his grace couthe not be
served there but oonly by hym'. On balance, he preferred Ossory
for the deputyship, thinking that his son, Lord Butler, was 'to yong
to take so grett a charge', and he insisted that the new deputy be
given all the profits of the office.[40] Wolsey responded by excusing
himself and deferring to the king's pleasure, but he then proceeded
to justify his proposal. He argued that it was unwise to discharge
Kildare as deputy until some substantial provision had been made
for defence and to deal with any disorders which might be stirred
up by the earl's followers; and that conversely so long as Kildare
stood charged as deputy, his followers would not attempt anything
that might be laid to his charge.[41] The king overruled him, however, and on 4 August Ossory was appointed deputy.[42]

Ossory's appointment was widely seen as merely temporary, and
this detracted from his authority as deputy. He soon complained of
the cost of maintaining two armies—one in Munster against the
rebel earl of Desmond, and the other to defend the Pale, where
Kildare's kinsmen and followers combined with O'Connor and
other Irish borderers to raid the Englishry in his absence.[43] Antici-
pating that the deputy would not be able to maintain his retinue
without taking coign and livery, Kildare's servants encouraged the
Palesmen to complain about his extortions,[44] while his supporters
on the king's council obstructed Ossory's proceedings and spread

---

[38] *SP Hen. VIII*, ii. 136–7.

[39] BL, Titus B XI (II), fos. 306–8 (*L. & P. Hen. VIII*, iv, no. 4510).

[40] Ibid., fos. 349–50 (*L. & P. Hen. VIII*, iv, no. 4562; *SP Hen. VIII*, ii. 140 n.).

[41] *SP Hen. VIII*, ii. 136–40.

[42] PRO, C 82/605 (*L. & P. Hen. VIII*, iv, no. 4609).

[43] *SP Hen. VIII*, ii. 143–7; PRO, SP 1/53, fos. 87–8 (*L. & P. Hen. VIII*, iv, no. 5349).

[44] PRO, SP 1/49, fo. 228 (*L. & P. Hen. VIII*, iv, no. 4635).

rumours of Kildare's imminent return.[45] No sooner had Ossory been installed as deputy than he and the council renewed the request for military assistance, asking for an army of 'Northumberland speres, light fote men, apte to take payn and labours, as the marchers of Scotland and the men of warr of this contre doo'.[46] Yet the only assistance received was £100 sterling sent over with John Alen, archbishop of Dublin, on his appointment as chancellor in September, for distribution among those whose support the king and Wolsey, acting on Norfolk's advice, decided to cultivate.[47] The Irish administration gradually sank deeper into debt, and was left to cope throughout the winter with successive wars raised by O'Connor, O'More, O'Neill, and the Geraldines as best it might.[48] At length, in summer 1529, the king relented and Ossory was discharged, leaving the way open for Kildare's eventual return. Although the king's honour would not allow the earl's immediate restoration as deputy, Kildare like Lord Dacre in 1526–9 had successfully imposed his will on Henry VIII.

Yet, as the events of 1533–4 were to show, in both Ireland and the north the political cost in terms of good relations and mutual trust between king and magnate was very high. In 1528 Kildare had come within an ace of being tried for treason. His brother Thomas, his daughter Alice, and a leading counsellor, Meyler Fay of Rathangan, all received pardons for treason in 1529; and Kildare himself was given a general pardon in 1530.[49] And when, after his death, Kildare was eventually attainted of treason for the rebellion of 1534–5, the act recited that in 1524–5 the earl had had treasonable communication with the earl of Desmond, then in league with the king's enemies, and that on 8 July 1528 he had through his daughter stirred up war against the king's deputy and subjects. Accordingly, the attainder took effect from 8 July 1528.[50]

In mid-1529 one of Wolsey's final initiatives before his fall involved the appointment of Henry's illegitimate infant son, the

---

[45] PRO, SP 1/53, fos. 87–8 (*L. & P. Hen. VIII*, iv, no. 5349).

[46] *SP Hen. VIII*, ii. 146.

[47] PRO, E 101/420, no. 11 (*L. & P. Hen. VIII*, v. 303–26), SP 1/67, fos. 33–3ᵛ (*L. & P. Hen. VIII*, v, no. 398).

[48] PRO, SP 1/53, fos. 87–8 (*L. & P. Hen. VIII*, iv, no. 5349), SP 1/67, fo. 43 (*L. & P. Hen. VIII*, v, no. 398).

[49] *Ormond deeds, 1509–47*, no. 144; *L. & P. Hen. VIII*, iv, nos. 5748, 5815 (8), 6363 (8).

[50] Statute roll, 28–9 Henry VIII c. 1 (PROI, CH 1/1).

duke of Richmond, as lieutenant of Ireland—in a move which resembled the experiment for the government of the north in 1525. Since Richmond remained in England, the government was committed to a 'secret council' of three ministers—Lord Chancellor Alen, the treasurer John Rawson, and Chief Justice Bermingham—while the master of the ordnance, Sir William Skeffington, was sent out as 'counseller and commissioner in Ireland' to report on the military situation.[51] By then, the problem of the rebel earl of Desmond had disappeared with the earl's death and the desire of his successor for royal recognition. Ossory was given charge of the south midlands, and Sir Thomas Fitzgerald, who had been summoned to court and given the lavish reward of 100 marks in June, was apparently entrusted with the military defence of the Pale again.[52] Yet in practice these arrangements left the administration reliant on Kildare's support within the Pale, and Skeffington quickly concluded that military assistance was essential. As a temporary measure, Norfolk arranged for the dispatch in March of one hundred horsemen from the Carlisle garrison under the conduct of Leonard Musgrave, one of the captains who had accompanied the duke to Ireland during his reconnaissance in force there in 1520–2.[53]

More importantly, the duke also persuaded the king to terminate Wolsey's empty bureaucratic experiment in favour of a substantial initiative involving both military and financial assistance, the return of Kildare (without office), and the appointment of a professional soldier, Skeffington, as deputy lieutenant. Although Skeffington and Kildare did not arrive until 24 August, the main decisions had been taken four months earlier, when Richmond's servant had been dispatched into Ireland and Skeffington wrote to Musgrave and another Carlisle officer, Edward Aglionby, warning them 'that ye shall haue letters of the kynges pleasure & my lord of Norff. and also money for the traunsportyng of shuch sodeours as be vnder you into Yrelond', asking them to arrest shipping, and advising them that 'my lord of Kyldare & I shall

---

[51] PRO, SP 1/67, fos. 33–6 (*L. & P. Hen. VIII*, v, no. 398); D. B. Quinn, 'Henry Fitzroy, duke of Richmond, and his connexion with Ireland, 1529–30', in *IHR Bull.*, 12 (1935), 175–7.

[52] *Ormond deeds, 1509–47*, nos. 149–51; PRO, E 101/420, no. 11 (*L. & P. Hen. VIII*, v. 303–26), SP 1/67, fos. 33–6; Ellis, *Tudor Ireland*, 117–18.

[53] PRO, E 101/420, no. 11; *SP Hen. VIII*, ii. 32–3, 48, 61.

make the spede we can to you'.[54] Revealingly, Kildare had 'made
faithfull promise unto the kynges highnes to employe and
endevour hym selfe, to the uttermost of his power, for the annoyance of . . . the wyld Iryshry'.[55] Skeffington also brought two
pieces of heavy siege artillery, and his retinue, augmented to two
hundred Cumberland horse and fifty gunners, was an adequate
and balanced force, enabling him to operate independently.[56]
Finally, the king agreed to pay for the deputy's salary—set at an
ample 1,000 marks per annum—and retinue, and ordered that the
troops were to be used primarily for defence, and that the country
was not to be needlessly charged with 'any hostyng or mayne
invasion upon the wyld Iryshry' without the council's full
consent.[57]

For almost a year the new arrangements worked well, and, with
co-operation restored, the military situation quickly improved. Yet
this new-found stability was in many ways superficial, because it
depended on the king's willingness to continue the financial and
military subventions which underpinned the new deputy's authority. And hitherto neither Henry VIII nor his father had been
prepared to contemplate funding the government of the lordship
on a continuing basis. Thus as soon as the immediate problems
were resolved, developments elsewhere prompted the king to reconsider the extent of his commitments in Ireland. Conduct
money, equipment, and wages for Skeffington and his retinue
cost the king £3,300 during the summer of 1530.[58] Yet even
this expenditure was considered heavy, and ominously
Skeffington's instructions included a long article about 'the
immediat conducing and attaynyng of a subsydie . . . towardes the
supportation and alleviacion of the kynges charges' upon the deputy's arrival. Rather impractically, the deputy and council were to
secure the immediate and retroactive grant of a subsidy, if poss-

[54] CRO, Carlisle, MS D/Ay/1/199; PRO, SP 1/67, fos. 33–6; BL, Add. MS 20,030,
fo. 23 (*L. & P. Hen. VIII*, v. 747–62); Ellis, *Tudor Ireland*, 119–20, 328.
[55] *SP Hen. VIII*, ii. 150.
[56] The precise numbers and proportions of horse and foot are not quite certain:
see *SP Hen. VIII*, ii. 148; PRO, E 101/420, no. 11, SP 1/57, fos. 280–1 (*L. & P. Hen.
VIII*, iv, no. 6541); S. G. Ellis, 'An indenture concerning the king's munitions in
Ireland, 1532', in *Ir. Sword*, 14 (1980–1), 100–3.
[57] *SP Hen. VIII*, ii. 148–9; PRO, E 101/420, no. 11.
[58] PRO, E 101/420, no. 11; SP 1/57, fos. 280–1 (*L. & P. Hen. VIII*, iv, no. 6541);
SP 1/67, fos. 33–6.

ible, without waiting for parliament to meet, payable for a year from Michaelmas 1529.[59] Not surprisingly, nothing further was heard of this proposal. Skeffington was licensed to convene a parliament before Candlemas 1531, but by the time the council had formally transmitted the subsidy bill and other measures in accordance with Poynings' Law, the licence had expired. A new licence, together with formal approval of the bills to be considered, was therefore issued on 16 May 1531.[60]

Without a subsidy to defray expenses, the full cost of Skeffington's salary and retinue, exceeding £3,850 per annum, had to be borne by the king. Yet Henry was desperately short of money at this time, and with Anglo-Scottish relations continuing to deteriorate, both money and men were now needed for the defence of the northern frontier.[61] Thus when Skeffington's initial advance was exhausted in February 1531, most of the northern men were sent home. The deputy's retinue was reduced to a mere hundred horsemen, and soon after Skeffington's position was further undermined when Archbishop Alen, one of his chief supporters, was crippled financially by an enormous fine of £1,466. 13s. 4d. demanded by the king for offences discussed below. In May the king sent over a further £1,550 to cover expenses until November.[62] Before then, it was anticipated, the subsidy to be granted in the parliament which eventually met in September and October 1531 would be leviable. In fact, by July Skeffington and Kildare had fallen out, the Geraldine–Butler feud had recommenced, and a 'great frey' ensued between the citizens of Dublin and Skeffington's troops. Finally, when parliament met, the subsidy bill was thrown out.[63] Thus politically, militarily, and financially, the deputy's position was, from autumn 1531 on, increasingly untenable.

Financially, Skeffington had been reduced by September to proclaiming a royal service, in order to levy a scutage worth about

[59] *SP Hen. VIII*, ii. 149–50.
[60] PRO, C 66/656, m. 5 (*L. & P. Hen. VIII*, iv, no. 6490 (22)), C 66/ 658, mm 2–3 (*L. & P. Hen. VIII*, v, no. 278 (21): printed in *Stat. Ire., Hen. VII & VIII*, 126–32).
[61] J. A. Guy, 'Henry VIII and the praemunire manoeuvres of 1530–31', in *EHR* 97 (1982), 482–503.
[62] Ibid.; Murray, 'Archbishop Alen, Tudor reform and the Kildare rebellion', 11–12; PRO, E 101/420, no. 11; Ellis, 'Indenture concerning the king's munitions', 100–3.
[63] Ellis, *Tudor Ireland*, 120.

IR£200 from the king's tenants-in-chief.[64] And in October, in the face of a growing reluctance on the part of the Palesmen to attend hostings against the Irishry, an order in council reimposed a graduated scale of fines for absence.[65] When the treasurer and chief justice, together with Kildare and Ossory's son, Lord Butler, were summoned to court in May 1532 to discuss the conduct of government, they deposed before the king's council that the deputy appropriated these fines without answering the king for them. More generally, they had nothing to say in Skeffington's favour, accusing him of partiality, faking musters, and other serious malpractices— fines for pardons, bribes, and rewards, abuses of purveyance, and licences for export. They exonerated Kildare, claiming that he had done good service until recently when provoked by Skeffington's favour for Ossory, and Butler deposed that the deputy was largely responsible for resurrecting the Kildare–Ossory feud.[66] The king therefore concluded that the lordship could be governed more effectively, and £2,000 a year saved, by appointing Kildare as deputy in place of Skeffington, and balancing this by inserting Butler into government as treasurer.[67]

Kildare owed his restoration as deputy in 1532 to the support he got at court from the duke of Norfolk and Anne Boleyn's father, Thomas, who in December 1529 had been created earl of Ormond and Wiltshire. Since the fall of Wolsey, Norfolk had been the major influence on Henry VIII's Irish policy, and he it was who had pressed the charges of misconduct against Skeffington before the king's council in May 1532.[68] The duke supported Kildare for reasons of expediency: he was no uncritical admirer of the earl's methods—of which he had had personal experience as lieutenant of Ireland in 1520–2—but given the king's unwillingness to make a long-term commitment to the government of Ireland, he felt that Kildare represented the best hope for peace and stability there. And the recent investigations had also suggested that Kildare's

---

[64] Ellis, 'Taxation and defence in late medieval Ireland', 5–28.

[65] PRO, C 113/236, box 51. I am indebted to Dr Margaret Condon for drawing this document to my attention.

[66] PRO, SP 60/1, fos. 150–1 (*L. & P. Hen. VIII*, v, no. 1061); Ellis, *Tudor Ireland*, 120.

[67] PRO, C 66/661, m. 33 (*L. & P. Hen. VIII*, v, nos. 1207 (14–16)).

[68] PRO, E 36/143 (*L. & P. Hen. VIII*, vi, no. 299); *SP Hen. VIII*, ii. 153–5; PRO, SP 1/235, fo. 286 (*L. & P. Hen. VIII*, Add. i, no. 596); *Handbook Brit. chron.*, 487, 496.

conduct under Skeffington had been reasonably satisfactory.[69] Wiltshire's main motive was probably the need to protect his interests in the Ormond inheritance against the Butlers.[70]

At this juncture, however, the supervision of Irish affairs was increasingly given over to the king's secretary, Thomas Cromwell, whose rising influence at court soon outweighed that of Norfolk.[71] So far as Kildare was concerned, this development had two main consequences. It meant that royal supervision of his deputyship was both tighter than normal and also in unsympathetic hands. At Cromwell's request, Ossory had been sending him reports about Irish affairs since late 1531; and Archbishop Alen renewed his links with Cromwell about the same time, when he enlisted the secretary's support in securing the king's pardon for praemunire.[72] The ostensible reason behind the heavy fine which Alen paid was his involvement in the exercise of Cardinal Wolsey's legatine jurisdiction: it was part of the king's campaign against the clergy which led to the breach with Rome and the royal divorce. Yet since his arrival in Ireland in 1529, Alen had been closely linked with the attempts to curb Kildare's influence in Irish affairs; and in his efforts to recover control of marchlands belonging to his see and to increase his episcopal revenues, the archbishop had also begun litigation against the earl and other influential members of his connexion. Thus, it has been plausibly suggested that Kildare's influence with the Norfolk–Wiltshire group played a part in the factional intrigue at court which resulted in Alen's fine. In any event, Kildare had his revenge because the archbishop's influence was so thoroughly undermined that the earl was able to procure his dismissal as chancellor in July 1532.[73]

In practice the shifting alignments at court meant that Kildare's success in 1532 in securing the recall of Skeffington and his own reappointment, and also the removal of Archbishop Alen from the chancellorship, was less decisive than it appeared. Once again the

---

[69] PRO, SP 60/1, fos. 150–1 (*L. & P. Hen. VIII*, v, no. 1061).

[70] *SP Hen. VIII*, ii. 153–5; PRO, SP 1/237, fo. 237 (*L. & P. Hen. VIII*, Add. i, no. 793).

[71] G. R. Elton, *The Tudor revolution in government* (Cambridge, 1953), 76–97.

[72] *SP Hen. VIII*, ii. 153–9; PRO, SP 1/68, fos. 158–9 (*L. & P. Hen. VIII*, v, no. 657); *Cal. Carew MSS, 1515–74*, nos. 36iii, 37; *L. & P. Hen. VIII*, v, no. 838 (10).

[73] On all this, see now Murray, 'Archbishop Alen, Tudor reform and the Kildare rebellion', 1–16, which convincingly revises my earlier views about Alen's role in the causation of the revolt.

king made no serious effort to secure a reconciliation between Kildare and Ossory, which was the key to stability in Ireland, so that factional rivalry continued much as before. Characteristically, Kildare began his deputyship by settling his score with Skeffington 'wher of great myscheff came'.[74] While taking a muster of Skeffington's troops before their departure, he publicly humiliated him, and the 'gunner' was then forced to dance attendance on the earl while the king's pleasure was ascertained about the ordnance and military stores which Skeffington had brought with him to Ireland.[75] In the interim, the Irish council used the opportunity to inquire into aspects of Skeffington's government. The former deputy was bound over to pay Archbishop Alen his fee as chancellor which had been in arrears before his dismissal. Goods of a merchant of the Steelyard seized for debt were found 'by diligent and great inquiry' to have been illicitly retained by Skeffington, his kinsmen, and servants—including Archbishop Alen's namesake, John Alen, the erstwhile clerk of the council. And the archbishop himself was troubled for his account of the £166. 13s. 4d. of the king's money distributed in 1529–30.[76] Eventually Skeffington handed over custody of the ordnance to the council on 20 October and retired to England to add his weight to the campaign against Kildare resumed soon after by the Butlers.[77] Within a year Kildare had been summoned before the king's council to answer a number of serious charges made by Skeffington; and at Cromwell's instance the former deputy was ready 'trewly to justify all I have sayde and wretten of hym'.[78] By mid-1534 Cromwell had amassed a distinctly one-sided collection of rolls and papers about Ireland, ranging from Skeffington's answers to particular complaints about his deputyship, to reports to the king and profits won by Skeffington, writings by Archbishop Alen, and matters against Kildare.[79]

[74] TCD, MS 543/2, *sub anno* 1532.
[75] *L. & P. Hen. VIII*, vii, no. 923xxxi, x, no. 298; Ellis, 'Indenture concerning the king's munitions', 100–3.
[76] PRO, SP 1/67, fos. 33–6 (*L. & P. Hen. VIII*, v, no. 398), fos. 45–6 (*L. & P. Hen. VIII*, v, no. 399), SP 1/79, fos. 100–1 (*L. & P. Hen. VIII*, vi, no. 1170 (2)), SP 1/235, fo. 286 (*L. & P. Hen. VIII*, Add. i, no. 596), SP 60/2, fo. 28 (*L. & P. Hen. VIII*, vi, no. 1588).
[77] Ellis, 'Indenture concerning the king's munitions', 100–3.
[78] *SP Hen. VIII*, ii. 181.
[79] PRO, E 36/143 (*L. & P. Hen. VIII*, vi, no. 299), E 36/139 (*L. & P. Hen. VIII*, vii, no. 923).

What precisely the charges were against Kildare is not known, but the earl was unwise or unfortunate in some of his associations and activities which came to Cromwell's attention and which aroused Henry's suspicions about his reliability. One such concerned John Wolfe, the merchant of the Steelyard whose goods in Ireland had been seized for debt. Upon Skeffington's recall in mid-1532, Norfolk had ordered him to deliver them to three Dublin merchants for safe keeping, but not all were. Subsequently, when Lord Keeper Audley countermanded this arrangement and ordered Wolfe to appear before the council at Candlemas, Kildare demurred, wrote instead to Norfolk, and asked for Wolfe's appearance to be postponed.[80] After a spell in the Tower, Wolfe returned to Ireland, but by September 1533 he had still not paid his debts. Thomas Houth advised the earl from London that Wolfe—by then in Kildare's service—certainly owed one Peter Rich £41. 14s. 9d., as Houth himself had ascertained, that the rumour was that Kildare was harbouring him, and that if Wolfe did not satisfy Rich he would appeal to the king and Kildare would be held responsible. Soon after, Cromwell's preparations for the next session of parliament included the drafting of a bill for Wolfe's attainder for murder.[81] Potentially more serious were the reports that Kildare's servant, Edmund Sexton, and others were importing large quantities of ordnance and gunpowder from Flanders. Two merchants examined by the Irish council in May 1533 deposed that the imports were on a very small scale, and that they knew of no links with Kildare. Yet at the end of August, after Kildare had been reprimanded for his conduct as deputy, he began transferring the king's ordnance out of Dublin castle into his own strongholds. And when, about November, he was ordered by the king in a letter delivered by John Alen to desist from this, he ignored the order.[82] These actions may have been viewed in a very different light by the king if and when he learned of the renewed intrigues by Kildare's

[80] PRO, SP 1/79, fos. 100–1 (*L. & P. Hen. VIII*, vi, no. 1170 (2)), SP 1/235, fo. 286 (*L. & P. Hen. VIII*, Add. i, no. 596); BL, Vesp. F. XIII, fo. 189 (*L. & P. Hen. VIII*, iv, no. 4958, v, no. 1560).

[81] PRO, SP 1/79, fos. 98–9 (*L. & P. Hen. VIII*, vi, no. 1170), SP 1/83, fos. 48–54 (*L. & P. Hen. VIII*, vii, no. 418 (2ii)); BL, Titus B. I, fo. 150 (*L. & P. Hen. VIII*, vi, no. 1381 (3)).

[82] *SP Hen. VIII*, ii. 181; D. B. Quinn, 'Henry VIII and Ireland, 1509–34', in *IHS* 12 (1960–1), 341 n. 97; PRO, E 36/143, fo. 29 (*L. & P. Hen. VIII*, vi, no. 1370).

kinsman, the earl of Desmond, with Charles V for an Imperial intervention in Ireland.[83]

As Kildare's credit declined at court, so too did his hold in Ireland over the patronage normally at the deputy's disposal. At first upon the earl's reappointment as deputy in mid-1532, there had also been a reshuffle of other offices to exclude Skeffington's clients and advance Kildare's. In particular, the former deputy's brother, Anthony Skeffington, keeper of the rolls, and John Alen, clerk of the council, had been dismissed; Thomas Houth replaced Walter Cowley as the king's attorney; and the earl made sure of his control of the revenue by appointing William Bath as undertreasurer to Lord James Butler, whose office as lord treasurer now became largely honorary. Altogether, in the two months after his return to Ireland in August 1532, Kildare made changes in 16 of the 28 patentee offices in the central administration for which evidence survives, another 8 being offices reserved to the king's nomination.[84] And many of those appointed in 1532 were later associated with the Fitzgeralds in the ensuing rebellion.[85] By early 1533, however, Cromwell's influence was apparent in a number of appointments which advanced officials unfavourable to Kildare. Christopher Delahide was appointed second justice of the king's bench in a reshuffle which followed the death of Chief Justice Bermingham in December 1532; and John Alen was made master of the rolls in July 1533.[86]

These were both offices reserved to the king's nomination in Kildare's appointment, but in addition Cromwell secured the appointment of Thomas Cusack as chancellor of the exchequer—at the expense of Kildare's client, Richard Delahide—and John Alen's reappointment as clerk of the council, even though these offices were normally in the deputy's gift.[87] Thus when Chief Justice Dillon died in summer 1533 the deputy moved quickly to

[83] PRO, SP 2/O, fo. 3 (*L. & P. Hen. VIII*, vi, no. 567); *L. & P. Hen. VIII*, vi, nos. 1056, 1381; *Cal. SP Spain, 1534–8*, pt. i, no. 8.

[84] *Cal. pat. rolls Ire., Hen. VIII–Eliz.*, 3–6; PRO, SP 65/1, no. 2 (*L. & P. Hen. VIII*, xii (ii), no. 1310 II 1). See Ellis, *Reform and revival*, app. 1.

[85] Ellis, 'Tudor policy and the Kildare ascendancy', 266–8.

[86] *L. & P. Hen. VIII*, vi, nos. 105 (11), 929 (26), Add. i, no. 944; Ellis, *Reform and revival*, app. 1.

[87] PRO, SP 1/83, fo. 39 (*L. & P. Hen. VIII*, vii, no. 407); SP 2/O, no. 12 (*L. & P. Hen. VIII*, vi, no. 841), SP 2/O, fo. 29 (*L. & P. Hen. VIII*, vii, no. 553); *L. & P. Hen. VIII*, vi, nos. 105 (16), 929 (26). See also, Ellis, 'Tudor policy and the Kildare ascendancy', 252–3.

rally support for an acceptable replacement. Informing Wiltshire of Dillon's death, Kildare asked the earl to stay any suit for the office 'unto suche tyme as ye shalbe furdre advertised by the counsaill here', and in case Chief Baron Finglas or Christopher Delahide asked for it 'that your lordship in anny wyse do lett thexpedicon therof', because they were both 'assured unto therle of Ossrie'. Dillon had also been chief remembrancer of the exchequer, and Kildare lost no time in appointing Thomas Houth to succeed him in that office. Yet significantly the deputy felt it necessary to inform Wiltshire of this too and to ask him to stay any labours for the office, because it was 'in my gift by my patent of deputacion'.[88] Concurrently, the king's secretary was attempting to build up a party in Ireland in other ways too. Drawing on the patronage of Archbishop Alen, who remained at odds with Kildare over the possession of lands in the Dublin–Kildare marches, Cromwell was able to secure further information about developments there by intruding two of his chaplains into livings in the archdiocese.[89] And when John Alen returned to Ireland as master of the rolls, he brought the king's letters to those of the earl's brothers thought least likely to favour Kildare, commending their service and requesting their advice about the political situation.[90] By then, Kildare's credit had sunk so low that his countess was writing to Cromwell to 'labour' the king for a lease of five manors in Meath for her son which the earl intended for his eldest son.[91]

Thus by mid-1533 Cromwell's growing influence and interventions in Irish politics had led to an alignment between factions at court and factions within the Dublin administration and the local Englishry which had disturbing implications for the government of Ireland. During Cardinal Wolsey's ascendancy Irish affairs had rarely been an issue in the struggle for influence at court. Kildare was occasionally able to use the good offices of a leading courtier like Thomas Grey, marquis of Dorset, his father-in-law

[88] PRO, SP 1/78, fo. 91 (*L. & P. Hen. VIII*, vi, no. 944).

[89] *SP Hen. VIII*, ii. 180–1; Ellis, 'Kildare rebellion and early Henrician Reformation', 811; Murray, 'Archbishop Alen, Tudor reform and the Kildare rebellion', esp. p. 13.

[90] *SP Hen. VIII*, ii. 179–80; PRO, SP 1/78, fos. 243–4 (*L. & P. Hen. VIII*, vi, no. 1057).

[91] PRO, SP 60/2, fo. 3 (*L. & P. Hen. VIII*, vi, no. 857); BL, Titus B. XI (II), fo. 382 (*L. & P. Hen. VIII*, iii, no. 3051, where the letter is placed in 1523). See also Ellis, 'Tudor policy and the Kildare ascendancy', 251–2.

from 1523, to smooth relations with the king, but Henry VIII's
Irish policy had usually been conducted independently of such
factional considerations. The fact that Cromwell was associated
with such leading opponents of Kildare as Ossory, Skeffington,
and Archbishop Alen made the earl deeply suspicious of any policy
initiatives promoted by the minister, regardless of Cromwell's
intentions.[92] Thus the final events of Kildare's deputyship took
place in an atmosphere of growing suspicion, as the earl
manœuvred to secure a more sympathetic hearing against the
charges levelled by his rivals.

In September, Kildare, Ossory, and other officials were summoned to court, and the Irish council sent over its assessment of
the situation and recommendations by John Alen. The council
urged the appointment of an English-born deputy who was familiar with the land. Kildare was no doubt kept informed by his agent,
Thomas Houth, of the speculation at court about his impending
dismissal.[93] Certainly, the Imperial ambassador, Eustace Chapuys,
who was now interesting himself in Irish affairs, reported a
rumour that the nominal lieutenant of Ireland, the duke of
Richmond, was to be sent over; and a month later, he also reported
the arrival on 3 October, in response to the king's summons, of
Kildare's countess, who excused the earl's absence on the grounds
of illness caused by an old gunshot wound sustained the previous
winter.[94] Lady Kildare was apparently accompanied by William
Bath, the undertreasurer and one of the earl's leading political
advisers.[95] By then, the question of a successor for Chief Justice
Dillon had broadened into a proposal by Cromwell 'for the
establisshement of the iudges of Irelonde and other offices there'.
It entailed the promotion of five ministers, only one of whom was
favourable to Kildare.[96] The king, moreover, refused to accept
Kildare's excuses and insisted on his appearance, notwithstanding

---

[92] I am here arguing against the view advanced by Dr Brendan Bradshaw
('Cromwellian reform', 75–7) that, despite his contacts with the Butlers, Cromwell
was in 1533 a neutral figure.
[93] *SP Hen. VIII*, ii. 162–6; PRO, SP 1/79, fos. 98–9 (*L. & P. Hen. VIII*, vi, no.
1170).
[94] PRO, PRO 31/18/2/1, fos. 953–8 (*L. & P. Hen. VIII*, vi, no. 1069), fos. 983–7ᵛ
(*L. & P. Hen. VIII*, vi, no. 1249), PRO 31/18/3/1, fos. 77–82ᵛ (*L. & P. Hen. VIII*,
vii, no. 530); *SP Hen. VIII*, ii. 161–2.
[95] PRO, 1/73, fo. 109 (*L. & P. Hen. VIII*, v, no. 1729), PRO 31/18/2/1, fos. 983–
7ᵛ (*L. & P. Hen. VIII*, vi, no. 1249); *SP Hen. VIII*, ii. 182.
[96] BL, Titus B. I, fos. 453ᵛ, 464 (*L. & P. Hen. VIII*, vi, nos. 1381–2).

his infirmities. And, before the end of the year, the earl's impending dismissal was public knowledge. John Alen carried letters both
from the king and from Sir William Skeffington announcing the
change to those Gaelic chiefs thought favourable to a new deputy.[97]

Throughout the autumn, Kildare had suffered one reverse after
another. Decisions remained to be finalized of course, and the
evidence derives chiefly from Cromwell's papers, but it looks as if
the earl's supporters were able to do no more than delay the
inevitable. Yet about a month before Christmas the king seemingly
caught wind of conspiracies afoot. The development is apparent in
one of Cromwell's remembrances 'to send som trustie persons into
Irelonde to see that domynyon established and also to draw,
combyne, and adhere towardes the king asmany of the grete
Yrysshe rebelles as is possible, and to practice to kepe peax there',
to which the secretary himself added 'and to withstand all other
practysys that might be practysyd ther with other'.[98] Presumably
the earl's disobedience regarding the king's ordnance and rumours
of Desmond's intrigues with Charles V had aroused the king's
suspicions. It is not entirely clear whether the granting of a commission to Kildare to appoint his own deputy during his absence,
'pro quo nobis respondere volueritis', was a concession by the king
to coax the earl into appearing or whether it had accompanied
the earlier summons. Yet the earl was undoubtedly reluctant to
place himself in the king's hands again and risk a third spell in
the Tower. One of the earl's servants, Robert Reyley, who accompanied Lady Kildare to London, later deposed that he was
sent back to Kildare with two letters, one from the king and the
other from Lady Kildare, and that Edmund Sexton, another servant who was 'more put in trust' by Kildare, had been dispatched
home a little before him.[99] Skeffington reported of them that they
made 'no maner of exspedicion nor hast with the same', but Reyley
caught up with Sexton at Beaumaris and deposed that on receipt of
the king's letters the earl 'prepared hymself towardes his ioarney to

[97] *Cal. Carew MSS, 1515–74*, no. 41; *SP Hen. VIII*, ii. 182; PRO, PRO 31/18/2/
1, fos. 983–7ᵛ (*L. & P. Hen. VIII*, vi, no. 1249).

[98] PRO, SP 6/3, fo. 178ᵛ (*L. & P. Hen. VIII*, vi, no. 1487 (2)), SP 1/80, fo. 172 (*L.
& P. Hen. VIII*, vi, no. 1487 (3)).

[99] Lambeth MS 602, fos. 138–40ᵛ (*Cal. Carew MSS, 1515–74*, no. 84); *Stat. Ire.*,
i, 28 Hen. VIII c. 1. The commission of 1533–4 has not survived, but cf. that of 1519:
Red bk. Kildare, 188–9.

London wyth spede'.[100] Moreover, before Lady Kildare's arrival at court, the earl's son and heir, Thomas, Lord Offaly—the Silken Thomas of nationalist tradition—must also have been dispatched home, because Reyley was interrogated as to whether Lady Kildare had sent him any message. And with hindsight, one of the Cowleys could write to Cromwell, after the revolt had broken out, that

it had been good that the said erles heyre had been styll kepte in England. I am sure your wisedome gave no advise to sende hym home, and whoo soo ever counsailid the kinges grace thertoo was farre over seen.[101]

After receipt of the king's letters, the earl 'sent for the said Thomas and for all [his] brethren . . . wyth whom he had seuerall convercacions' before he left for court. Upon his departure he summoned a meeting of the council at Drogheda, to which he was accompanied by Lord Thomas, where he 'caused thesaid Thomas ffitzgerald to be made deputie and caused hym to be sworne before the counsaill and delyuered hym the sworde. And ffrom thens he toke his iorney towardes Englande'.[102] Lord Thomas had been entrusted with the leading of a rode upon O'Reilly the previous year,[103] but he was certainly very inexperienced for the office of vice-deputy. Even so, the earl's choice must be regarded as deliberate because, although the kinsmen he had appointed to this office in 1519 and 1526 had since died, Kildare could have appointed one or other of his five remaining brothers. Very significantly, the earl also appointed a special private council to advise Offaly: each councillor was sworn to Offaly, but Offaly was forbidden to act without their consent.[104] The appointment of this council was a means of safeguarding the Kildare interest and of reducing the influence of the king's council in the earl's absence. At court, one of Kildare's opponents, learning of the earl's choice of vice-deputy, could only urge that a new deputy

[100] *SP Hen. VIII*, ii. 182; Lambeth MS 602, fos. 138–8ᵛ (*Cal. Carew MSS, 1515–74*, no. 84).

[101] *SP Hen. VIII*, ii. 198. Cf. *Cal. pat. rolls Ire., Hen. VIII–Eliz.*, 71–2.

[102] Lambeth MS 602, fo. 138ᵛ (*Cal. Carew MSS, 1515–74*, no. 84).

[103] *SP Hen. VIII*, ii. 169.

[104] Lambeth MS 602, fo. 130 (*L. & P. Hen. VIII*, ix, no. 347), fos. 138ᵛ, 139 (*Cal. Carew MSS, 1515–74*, no. 84); PRO, SP 60/2, fo. 64 (*L. & P. Hen. VIII*, viii, no. 82), fo. 159 (*L. & P. Hen. VIII*, ix, no. 514); *Stat. Ire.*, i, 28 Hen. VIII c. 1; *SP Hen. VIII*, ii. 273.

repair thethir in as short and convenient tyme as may be devysed, afffter
that your deputye aryv in this your realme of England; for as much that his
son, is governor in his absentie, is takin to be yong and wilfull, and moste
to this tyme orderyd by light counsaill.[105]

The evidence is not conclusive, but it does suggest that Kildare
was preparing for trouble in 1534, that he was dilatory in responding to the king's summons, and that his use of the king's commission to appoint his son as vice-deputy had not been anticipated.
Yet the earl can have had no illusions about what lay in store for
him, having been dismissed from office and detained in disgrace
on the last two occasions on which he had been summoned before
the council in England to answer charges about his conduct as
governor. Upon his arrival, about the end of February,[106] Kildare
was examined in council about his conduct. Proceedings dragged
on, but by late May 'manyfold enormyties' had been proven
against him and he was forbidden to return to Ireland.[107] Yet the
government soon realized that, even more so than in 1527–8, the
earl's detention at court was no guarantee of the behaviour of his
followers. Already at the start of April, Cromwell minuted for 'a
deputye to be sent into Irelande with all spede to set a stay ther'.[108]
The fact was that Kildare's health was now failing, and he was
reputedly 'not like to live long'. His death threatened to deprive
the government of its chief influence over his connexion. Accordingly, in late May, the king summoned Offaly to court, thus forcing the earl to choose between submission and resistance.[109]

As Kildare weighed his response to the king's summons, he
would have been mindful of the fate which had recently befallen
another of Norfolk's clients through the manœuvrings of Henry
VIII's chief minister. A fortnight before, Lord Dacre, who had

---

[105] *SP Hen. VIII*, ii. 183.
[106] The date of Kildare's arrival is established by Reyley's deposition (Lambeth
MS 602, fo. 138ᵛ (*Cal. Carew MSS, 1515–74*, no. 84)), and between 4 Feb. and 22
Apr. Chapuys's surviving dispatches make no mention of Ireland, probably because he thought affairs had been settled by Kildare's tardy appearance: *Cal. SP
Spain, 1529–33*, pt. ii (2), no. 1161, *1534–8*, pt. i, nos. 4, 8, 9, 45; *L. & P. Hen. VIII*,
vii, no. 121.
[107] *SP Hen. VIII*, ii. 194–5.
[108] BL, Titus B. I, fo. 467 (*L. & P. Hen. VIII*, vii, no. 420).
[109] Lambeth MS 602, fos. 138ᵛ–9ᵛ (*Cal. Carew MSS, 1515–74*, no. 84); PRO, SP
1/238, fo. 188 (*L. & P. Hen. VIII*, Add. i, no. 889); *L. & P. Hen. VIII*, vii, nos. 614,
736, ix, no. 514; *Cal. SP Spain, 1534–8*, pt. i, no. 145. Kildare was well enough to
sign routine warrants on 30 Apr.: BL, Add. MS 19,865, fo. 15.

been summoned to court to advise on negotiations for a peace treaty with Scotland, was arrested without warning at the conclusion of the peace and his property seized for the king.[110] Whether news of Dacre's fall encouraged Kildare to oppose the king's pleasure, we cannot now tell. Certainly the evidence of treasonable conspiracy against Dacre was less conclusive than that against Kildare, as became clear at Dacre's trial, and the earl may have felt that he had little more to lose by resistance. When his role in precipitating the rising led by his son in Ireland became clear, he was arrested and joined Dacre in the Tower on 29 June where on 2 September he died of his old wounds.[111] In Dacre's case the evidence of treason seems to have come chiefly from the charges made by the king's servant, Sir William Musgrave,[112] although the fact that the royal commissioners searched both Dacre's houses and Bishop Tunstall's for incriminating papers perhaps suggests that Dacre was also suspected of disloyalty on the divorce issue. None the less the king's suspicions clearly centred on Dacre's conduct of the recent Anglo-Scottish war and the nature of his dealings with the Scots. At first glance, the charges in his indictment look so far-fetched as to provide a convincing explanation for Dacre's unprecedented acquittal at his trial: no English peer would have become involved in such practices. The grand jury presented that Lord Dacre and his uncle, Sir Christopher, had in the last war adhered to the Scots, the king's enemies, aiding and abetting them by holding secret meetings and making private treaties with Lord Maxwell, the lairds of Buccleuch and Hempsfield, and the Scots of Liddesdale, to the destruction of the king's true lieges in Bewcastledale and the east and middle marches. He had 'made a wicked and treacherous agreement . . . with certain Scots . . . the king's enemies, inhabiting in a certain territory of Scotland called "Ledersdale", for surety against any acts of hostility, war, or invasion'. Allegedly, the aim had been to arrange mutual immunity from raids and invasions for the lands and tenants of each party, with the result that the east and middle marches under the earl of Northumberland and Bewcastledale, of which Sir William

---

[110] *L. & P. Hen. VIII*, vii, nos. 628, 647, 674, 676.

[111] Ellis, 'Tudor policy and the Kildare ascendancy', 257, 260; id., 'Thomas Cromwell and Ireland, 1532–1540', in *Hist. Jn.*, 23 (1980), 505.

[112] *L. & P. Hen. VIII*, vi, nos. 199, 876, vii, no. 281; James, *Society, politics and culture*, 100.

Musgrave was then captain, bore the brunt of the Scottish military effort.[113] Nevertheless, as we have seen, Dacre was, perhaps alone of the early-Tudor peers, a magnate whose connections with the Scottish court and Scottish border society were such that he could conceivably have made such treasonable arrangements. In other words, in Dacre's case the charges were inherently plausible.

Moreover, the circumstances of the 1532–4 war also lend credence to this argument. Unlike Henry VIII's previous wars with Scotland, in which 'the auld alliance' between Scotland and France had raised the prospect of a full-scale Franco-Scottish invasion of the English north, the 1532–4 war was essentially a localized border war. The *casus belli* was possession of the Debateable Land, a particularly ungracious doghole on the west march, and the war was prolonged by the English capture of an even less hospitable pele, the Cawmills, half a mile north of Berwick, which Henry VIII then refused to surrender. The military effort on both sides was half-hearted, with the French offering to mediate. And a feature of the war was the reluctance of some Scottish borderers to participate, while the Douglas earl of Angus fought on the English side.[114] Yet such military effort as was mounted on the English side was unevenly distributed. Although the Debateable Land lay north of Carlisle, Henry's first move was to increase the garrison on the east and middle marches from 1,000 to 2,500 men in early December 1532.[115] The west marches received very little additional support. In May 1532, with war looming, Dacre had reminded the king of the great decay of Carlisle castle, and also of Bewcastle, and he asked for the return of his cousin, Sir William Musgrave.[116] Henry sent £500 for repairs in September and reappointed Musgrave constable of Bewcastle; and in December he offered Dacre 300 men, either soldiers for garrisons or workmen to repair Carlisle.[117] Yet, by February, Dacre had only received another £500, to be employed to the utmost annoyance of the king's enemies. And when Cromwell wrote to ask why no 'great actes, excurses, and annoysaunces' had been done in the west, as

[113] Printed, *3rd Report of the Deputy Keeper of the Public Records* (London, 1842), app. ii, 234–6 (quotation, p. 234).

[114] *L. & P. Hen. VIII*, v, nos. 595, 1254, 1460, 1635.

[115] *L. & P. Hen. VIII*, v, nos. 1630, 1655, Add. i, nos. 801, 831.

[116] *L. & P. Hen. VIII*, v, no. 1054; Durham, H. of N. MS C/201/3; James, *Society, politics and culture*, 100.

[117] *L. & P. Hen. VIII*, v, no. 1370 (20), 1394, vi, nos. 107, 117.

elsewhere, Dacre replied that he had still not received any reinforcements and that, since the Scottish west march had been mustered against him, he feared that, if he invaded, he would suffer
more damage than he could do. He again requested troops and
artillery, without which he could not raze towers, and warned
Cromwell that unless reinforcements arrived, the marches were
like to go to ruin.[118] In fact, he got nothing more: by the time the
war petered out in June, following an abstinence agreed with the
Scots, military activities had cost the king £22,716. 13s. 9½d.,
mainly for 2,500 garrison troops, but Dacre's share of this had been
a mere £500.[119] And instead of thanks, he was reprimanded for his
recent, negligent defence of Bewcastledale and ordered to send
troops to help defend the east marches after the discharge of the
garrison.[120]

Thus Dacre was in effect forced to shift for himself during the
war, and in these circumstances it is hardly surprising that he
exploited his traditionally close links with Scottish border society
for border defence. The charges against Dacre do in fact broadly
correspond with what is known about Dacre's cross-border contacts immediately before the war. For instance, Dacre informed
the king in May 1532 of a secret visit by Robert Charteris, laird of
Hempsfield, to enquire on James V's behalf whether Dacre would
join Lord Maxwell, the Scottish warden, in destroying the inhabitants of the Debateable Land and whether he would agree not
to succour the inhabitants of Liddesdale if pursued by King James.
Charteris returned in June with a letter from James V, to which
Dacre replied, and sent Henry both the original letter and a copy
of his reply. The indictment alleged that Dacre had had secret
meetings with Charteris in time of war; and subsequently Dacre
confessed before the council that he had concealed a letter to him
from Charteris which presumably had been discovered at Naworth
by the royal commissioners.[121] Replying to Dacre in June 1532, the
king had ordered him to rebuff Charteris's approach, without it
appearing that he had had any specific answer from Henry, and

[118] *L. & P. Hen. VIII*, vi, nos. 117, 199, 299iv, 876.

[119] *L. & P. Hen. VIII*, vi, nos. 553, 664, 876.

[120] *L. & P. Hen. VIII*, vi, nos. 750, 876, 1152.

[121] *L. & P. Hen. VIII*, vi, nos. 1054, 1079, 1101, vii, no. 1270; *3rd rep. DKPR*, app.
ii, 234–6; *SP Hen. VIII*, iv. 608–9. Dacre had also cultivated good relations with the
Scottish court before the war. In July 1530, for instance, he sent James V a horse
worth £10: Durham, H. of N. MS C/201/2, m. 8d.

instead to 'entertain' the men of Liddesdale with a view to their
future service. Accordingly, Dacre gave Liddesdale a temporary
'special assurance', to be continued at the king's pleasure.[122] This
arrangement held after the outbreak of war, and in February an
army from Northumberland raiding Teviotdale issued a proclamation of assurance to the inhabitants of Liddesdale, on which
some of them offered their services.[123] The indictment charged
Dacre with making a private treaty of indemnity with the Scots of
Liddesdale, covering all within his wardenry except Sir William
Musgrave's followers, that he had issued a proclamation on 12
April forbidding any raid into Scotland not previously authorized
by himself, and that by reason of the indemnity the Liddesdale
men had on 1 July raided the king's lieges under Musgrave's
command in Bewcastledale without any reprisal.[124] In fact, Dacre
had on 2 July reported the raid on Bewcastledale as having been
made on 27 June by the Scots of west Teviotdale, who could only
have come in by Liddesdale. He alleged that his own tenants there
had also been robbed, and in response to the king's subsequent
charges of negligence, he replied that a reprisal raid had been made
on west Teviotdale, although far off, and that in any case responsibility for keeping a look-out against that quarter rested
in the first instance on the warden of the middle marches.[125]
Finally, in 1535 the Scottish government likewise indicted the
laird of Buccleuch for treasonable communications with Sir
Christopher Dacre and other Englishmen in wartime: he too was
acquitted.[126]

On the whole, therefore, what the evidence seems to suggest is
that Dacre had exploited in wartime his normal influence and
connections with Scottish borderers for the defence of his
wardenry; and that because he lacked a paid garrison with which to
take the offensive, he relied more on tacit understandings based on
his previously good relations with particular Scots in a primarily
defensive war. What was new in 1534 was that, exceptionally,
Henry VIII chose on this occasion to regard as treason, in line with
Musgrave's complaints, the contacts with Scots which Dacre had

---

[122] *SP Hen. VIII*, iv. 608–11; *L. & P. Hen. VIII*, v, nos. 1079, 1101, 1286.
[123] *L. & P. Hen. VIII*, v, no. 1460, vi, no. 125.
[124] *3rd rep. DKPR*, app. ii, 234–6.
[125] *SP Hen. VIII*, iv. 647; *L. & P. Hen. VIII*, vi, no. 876.
[126] *L. & P. Hen. VIII*, ix, nos. 64, 88; Rae, *Administration of the Scottish frontier*,
170–2.

normally maintained in wartime. Such contacts had always been technically treasonable, but hitherto the king had accepted them because they helped the English war effort and because Dacre's loyalty had been beyond question. In 1534, however, Henry VIII chose to think otherwise.

Yet, if Musgrave's charges were malicious, how was it that the matter was allowed to proceed so far? It has been suggested that behind the feud lay the development of a crown interest in the west marches, reflected in the appointment of Musgrave, a knight of the body, 'over Lord Dacre's head in 1531 as constable of Bewcastle, the isolated crown outpost on the western Border, an office which had been promised to Dacre'.[127] The position was, however, much more complicated than this, and was probably not caused by rivalry over Bewcastle. Sir John Musgrave and his son, Thomas, had been constables of Bewcastle for around forty years; and though William, Lord Dacre, was, exceptionally, given the reversion of the office in December 1527 when he recovered the wardenship, he appears never to have secured possession.[128] Moreover, Sir John, who had also been a knight of the body, and his son represented a junior branch of the family, not the senior line, of which Sir William's father, Sir Edward Musgrave of Edenhall, was then head. Both branches were Dacre followers, and until 1529–30 at least Sir William was Lord William's household servant.[129]

As we have seen, under Lord Thomas, both the Dacre tenants there, and also all the other inhabitants of Bewcastledale under their captain, had done suit at Dacre's court of Askerton.[130] Difficulties between the captain and warden were perhaps inevitable in the circumstances; but despite the strains, Dacre's relations remained good, both with Sir Edward, who held land of Dacre in Westmorland, and with Thomas Musgrave, the former constable,

---

[127] James, *Society, politics and culture*, 100.

[128] PRO, SP 1/141, fos. 248–51 (*L. & P. Hen. VIII*, xiii (ii), app. no. 36); *L. & P. Hen. VIII*, i (2nd edn.), no. 2684 (86), ii (i), no. 1084, iv (ii), nos. 3747 (6), 4134, 4531; *SP Hen. VIII*, iv. 502; *Cal. pat. rolls, 1485–94*, 429.

[129] PRO, SP 1/141, fos. 248–51 (*L. & P. Hen. VIII*, xiii (ii), app. no. 36); STAC 2/18/269, fos. 1, 2; STAC 2/30/74; STAC 2/33/60; Durham, H. of N. MSS C/201/2, mm 1, 4, 11d, 18, C/201/3; *Cal. pat. rolls, 1485–94*, 429; *Cal. close rolls, 1500–09*, nos. 582, 587; *A descriptive catalogue of ancient deeds in the Public Record Office*, iii. 497–8; *L. & P. Hen. VIII*, i (2nd edn.), no. 2684 (86), ii (i), no. 1084, iv (i), no. 2; James, *Society, politics and culture*, 100, 110, 112.

[130] See above, p. 96.

who in 1530 was Dacre's household retainer and forester of
Geltsdale in Gilsland.[131] In April 1528, Dacre had written to
Wolsey that Bewcastle had been spoiled and was uninhabitable,
but he offered an amicable agreement with Musgrave if the latter
would surrender his patent. The warden's main interest at this
time was in clearing the Armstrongs out of the Debateable Land,
an operation which required the co-operation both of the Scottish
warden and of a resident and active constable at Bewcastle.[132] And
by 1530 the office was being exercised by Sir William Musgrave,
with whom Thomas Musgrave was apparently joined.[133]

In principle, this was a sensible move, because Sir William, now
knight of the body, was better placed to control the Bewcastle
Musgraves. Yet Sir William was apparently a difficult man. In
1528 Dacre had arrested Richard Graham for march treason in
warning the Armstrongs of the warden's impending raid. Yet, to
Dacre's great annoyance, Sir William, then undersheriff to his
father, had permitted Graham to go at large in Carlisle castle, with
the result that he had escaped.[134] After receiving charge of
Bewcastle, Musgrave then disputed Dacre's right to particular
lands there. The matter was considered by the council in Star
Chamber in 1530, when Musgrave was ordered not to prevent
Dacre's tenants from paying their rents.[135] Moreover, as constable,
Sir William was no more willing to reside in Bewcastle than
Thomas Musgrave had been. Although appointed constable in his
own right in April 1531, he spent too much time at court, and his
deputy, John Musgrave, failed to control his kinsmen, who were at
feud with the Armstrongs.[136] With war looming, Dacre insisted on
Sir William's return, but the two subsequently quarrelled. The
circumstances are unclear, but the evidence is suggestive. Both
Dacre and Sir Edward were allied with the duke of Norfolk. Sir
William, however, had connections with Thomas Cromwell, who
no doubt encouraged an independent voice in the west marches.

[131] Durham, H. of N. MS C/201/2, mm 1, 4, 11d; James, *Society, politics and culture*, 100, 110, 112.
[132] *SP Hen. VIII*, iv. 488–95, 502; *L. & P. Hen. VIII*, iv (ii), nos. 3972, 4014, 4020, 4298.
[133] PRO, STAC 2/19/127. Sir William's father, Sir Edward Musgrave, and Thomas Musgrave were first cousins.
[134] *SP Hen. VIII*, iv. 488–95; *L. & P. Hen. VIII*, iv (ii), no. 4134.
[135] PRO, STAC 2/19/127.
[136] *L. & P. Hen. VIII*, iv (ii), no. 4531, (iii), no. 6135 (20), v, nos. 220 (9, 14), 477, xii (ii), no. 203.

Musgrave probably used these connections to bring charges against Dacre despite his father's wishes; and he later refused Norfolk's offer to arrange a marriage between his son and Dacre's daughter as a means of healing the feud.[137] Thus it looks as if the feud really began during the war, despite earlier difficulties between the two. Dacre would hardly have called for Musgrave's return if he had been 'a long-standing enemy of the family'.[138] Seemingly, in 1533–4 he was faced with an unexpected attack by someone he had considered an ally.

Overall, therefore, the fall of Dacre and Kildare in 1534 appears to reflect the interaction between two sets of forces. These were the growing influence of faction at court and the legacy of weakly supported attempts by the king in the 1520s to supplant the two lords as the ruling nobles in their respective regions: these earlier initiatives eroded the basis of mutual trust between crown and magnate which had been so central a feature of Tudor rule of the borderlands since the late 1490s, and they also encouraged a disastrous recrudescence of the faction and feuding between nobles which had characterized the fifteenth century—between the Dacres and Fitzgeralds on the one hand and their would-be successors, the Cliffords and Butlers respectively. Neither Dacre nor Kildare had strong ties with the Tudor court and, unlike other nobles who were thought to be disaffected, both held important military commands and controlled large numbers of troops. Thus in the charged atmosphere of 1534 the king may have been encouraged to strike against two magnates whose dubious associations and obstreperous conduct in the past encouraged him to believe that they now represented a threat to the Tudor dynasty.

Finally, what of the argument that under Dacre and Kildare the gradual decline of good order and English civility in the marches finally forced the government in the 1530s to adopt a vigorous programme of administrative reform? Taking a long-term view of developments since the 1450s, this was very probably the case in the far north because the military and financial resources available to Dacre as warden fell far short of what had been available to his Lancastrian predecessors. In Ireland, however, Kildare rule had undoubtedly strengthened the marches. The well-known reform

---

[137] *L. & P. Hen. VIII*, i (2nd edn.), no. 2246ii, v, nos. 1370 (20), 1375, 1394, vi, no. 1313, vii, nos. 281, 380, 829, 1647.
[138] Williams, *Tudor regime*, 445.

treatises emanating from some sections of Pale society could equally well reflect the region's increased stability as the political agenda moved on from the crisis of lordship—the focus of complaint in letters and petitions of the mid-fifteenth century—to the problem of degeneracy. In any case, the basic problem was not the shortcomings of the magnates but the crown's refusal to make adequate financial provision for the good rule and defence of these regions. It is of course easy to draw up an apparently damning indictment of Dacre and Kildare rule in the borderlands, based on the *ex parte* statements in the state papers of their political opponents; but there is no reliable evidence of any marked deterioration in the local standing of these magnates, nor of their capacity to rule the marches. For Ireland, large claims have been made for a revolutionary new policy of governmental reform by Cromwell, but the acid test of the importance and likely fate of any royal initiative there was the king's willingness to pay for troops to support it. In practice, in spring 1534 the new governor was to go armed with a mere 150 men and a high-sounding pamphlet, *Ordinances for the government of Ireland*, which, far from being a 'detailed blueprint for the overhaul of government', was simply a recapitulation of the terms of service to which all governors agreed when they took up office.[139] In the north, Dacre's successor, the luckless earl of Cumberland, was not even given this level of support, so that his failure as warden was almost a foregone conclusion.[140] Overall, therefore, the disgrace of Dacre and Kildare transformed what had been a distinctly secondary administrative problem into a major political crisis which had serious and long-term consequences for Tudor rule of the borders.

[139] Bradshaw, 'Cromwellian reform', 81–8 (quotation, p. 85); and see below, pp. 209–10. Ellis, 'Thomas Cromwell and Ireland', 502–4, provides a detailed refutation of these claims.
[140] Below, Ch. 8.

7

Confrontation
The Irish campaign of 1534–1535 and
its consequences

THE reorganization of royal government and the curbing of noble power which followed the crisis of 1534 have generally been portrayed by historians as a significant step in the establishment of a more broadly based and effective system of government. No doubt there is much truth in this, in that Tudor policy towards the borders was much more interventionist in the aftermath of the crisis than it had been before. Yet this was not necessarily an intended outcome, wholeheartedly welcomed by the king. And in many ways the crisis illustrated the mutual dependence of king and magnate for the good rule of the marches. This was particularly apparent in the events surrounding the military campaign of 1534–5 in Ireland which highlighted in an unusual way the respective strengths and weaknesses of royal authority and noble power. In both regions, moreover, the breach between crown and magnate had a destabilizing influence.

The lack of a standing army was a notorious weakness in the machinery for policy enforcement available to Tudor governments. It rendered the regime more vulnerable to popular uprisings, made it more dependent on great regional magnates like Dacre and Kildare for raising levies of their tenants, and it forced the crown to rely more on *ad hoc* administrative arrangements in equipping and supplying such armies as it put in the field. Not surprisingly, therefore, there remained in this sphere a particularly wide gap between planning and enforcement. Most notably, the difficulties of communication, of arranging adequate victualling, and of ensuring adequate training and equipment for the scratch levies commonly recruited meant that sickness, desertion, and demoralization were frequently more formidable foes than the enemy in the field. In consequence, Tudor armies functioned less than efficiently, although probably no less so than their continental counterparts.[1]

These remarks apply most immediately to the major campaigns of the period, in France and Scotland: serious internal disturbances, when royal armies were needed to crush rebellions like those in Norfolk and the West Country in 1549, rarely lasted long enough to expose the shortcomings of the administrative arrangements for transport and the supply of food and weapons. Yet neither expeditions to France nor to Scotland exposed the full range of the government's problems. Campaigns in France were of course a prestige event, offering the prospect of booty and military glory, and attracting leading courtiers and willing co-operation against the ancient adversary. And in the case of invasions of Scotland, where the terrain was more difficult and long sieges and set-piece battles were less likely, the campaigns were commonly extended border raids which could draw on standing arrangements for border defence. The government was assured of a ready supply of experienced border troops who could provide the necessary skills and local knowledge for the successful conduct of the kind of small-scale, low-intensity, marcher warfare which commonly characterized Scottish campaigns.[2] In Ireland in 1534, however, the government was unexpectedly faced with mounting a campaign in very different circumstances. Technically, the 1534–5 campaign was a response to an internal rebellion like those of 1549. Yet the lordship was geographically separate from England and, more importantly, the traditional structures for the defence of the region against the Gaelic Irish had in many cases been taken over by the rebels. Thus in 1534 the government was responding to what was, in effect, a worst-case scenario—the need to mount a hazardous and expensive amphibious expedition, which was totally unexpected, in a remote corner of the Tudor territories, with every prospect of encountering experienced English and Gaelic troops in an unfamiliar marcher terrain. In fact, the circumstances of the campaign very soon exposed the major weaknesses of Tudor policy, underlining the ultimate consequences of the failure to pursue a realistic strategy for the rule and defence of the border-

[1] See esp. Davies, 'Provisions for armies, 1509–50', 234–48; M. L. Bush, *The government policy of Protector Somerset* (London, 1975).

[2] See C. G. Cruickshank, *Army Royal: Henry VIII's invasion of France, 1513* (Oxford, 1969); Eaves, *Henry VIII's Scottish diplomacy*.

lands. And as the political situation in Ireland deteriorated in mid-century, what in 1534 had seemed an unusual range of problems was to become a recurring feature of Tudor campaigns there.

The lordship had always been a distinctly secondary concern to the Tudors, and such problems as arose were usually delegated to a local noble. Yet the 1534 rebellion was engineered by Gerald Fitzgerald, 9th earl of Kildare, the very lord who normally represented the crown as governor, and it was centred on the heart of the English interest in Ireland, the Pale. In addition, its leader, Thomas, Lord Offaly (who succeeded his father as 10th earl of Kildare in September) astutely represented the rising as a response to Henry VIII's ecclesiastical policies rather than the political reaction of a discontented noble which it actually was.[3] Ireland was of course too far from the centre of power to pose a serious direct challenge to the government, but there was a danger that some politically more important area might be encouraged to follow the lordship's lead. Thus the circumstances of the rebellion, occurring from an unexpected quarter at a critical time for general acceptance of the revolutionary changes associated with the Tudor Reformation, ruled out compromise and demanded a vigorous and speedy response. In other respects, however, the difficulties involved in organizing a relief army for Ireland did not initially appear too formidable. By 1534 the government was well aware that its policies were provoking widespread discontent, and it had taken steps to guard against popular rebellion or foreign invasion. *Inter alia* these included orders for repairing and putting in order the king's ships, ordnance and munitions, coastal fortresses and beacons, while measures were already in hand for the defence of the far north, Wales, and Ireland.[4] Thus, although the government was heavily committed in other respects, the Irish campaign was in fact a very fair test of the regime's military capacity and preparedness.

In the event, Lord Offaly's resignation as vice-deputy and formal defiance of the king at a meeting of the Irish council on 11 June marked the first act of rebellion. Yet it was only from mid-July, following the news of Earl Gerald's arrest in London on 29 June,

---

[3] Ellis, 'Kildare rebellion and the early Henrician Reformation', 807–30; id., 'Tudor policy and Kildare ascendancy', 235–71.

[4] See esp. *L. & P. Hen. VIII*, vi, nos. 1381–2, vii, no. 420; Elton, *Policy and police, passim.*

that the rebels made serious efforts to win control of the Pale.
These efforts culminated in the murder of Archbishop Alen of
Dublin on 27 July and the siege of the city.[5] In response to the first
reports of the rising, the government complacently continued its
preparations for the dispatch of Sir William Skeffington, the
governor-designate, with a retinue of 150 men. The Imperial ambassador, Eustace Chapuys, reported that it showed little urgency
in the matter. Skeffington's retinue of 100 mounted archers and 50
foot, although now grossly inadequate, was taken into pay from 19
July, and his ordnance was ready in London awaiting transport to
Chester.[6] At this point, however, the government belatedly realized the seriousness of the situation. The response was, as we shall
see, a more frenzied pursuit of the same policies of improvisation
and short-term expediency which had hitherto characterized the
king's conduct of Irish affairs. Events soon showed that, despite all
the preparations for war and talk of administrative reform, the
government was quite unprepared to meet the crisis. On 30 July,
Skeffington was appointed lord deputy of Ireland for life—clearly
a panic reaction and an extraordinary departure from early-Tudor
policy of curbing the autonomy of its officials in outlying parts.
A relief army of 1,500 men was decided on, and soon after
Skeffington departed for Wales to recruit troops.[7]

Further difficulties were soon identified. The rebels' establishment of military supremacy in the Pale and their seizure of the
king's ordnance raised the question of whether the relief army
would be able to land near Dublin, and therefore whether Chester
or north Wales were convenient points of embarkation. Moreover,
Skeffington's suitability as commander of the expedition was
called in question. There was no doubt about his qualifications: he
had already spent two years as deputy lieutenant of Ireland (1530–
2), and his office as master of the ordnance and his previous work
on the fortifications of the English Pale at Calais certainly
equipped him well for the post. Nor was there much competition
from other military men to lead an expedition to an impoverished

[5] Ellis, 'Tudor policy and Kildare ascendancy', 259–61; id., 'Thomas Cromwell
and Ireland', 504–5; Murray, 'Archbishop Alen, Tudor reform and the Kildare
rebellion', 1–2, 15.
[6] *L. & P. Hen. VIII*, vii, nos. 980, 1682; PRO, E 101/421/6, nos. 35, 36, 39.
[7] PRO, C 113/236, box 51 (I am grateful to Dr Margaret Condon for bringing this
document to my attention); *L. & P. Hen. VIII*, vii, nos. 1013–14, 1019, 1064; *Cal.
SP Spain, 1534–8*, pt. i, no. 84.

borderland from which, as Chapuys, expressed it, 'il ny a que gaigner que cops de bastons'. Skeffington probably owed his appointment to this lack of rivals as much as anything else, for he was 'scantily beloved' at court and over 70 years old. Chapuys reported that he was 'the most unfit for the command of that country that could be chosen', an assessment which subsequently proved accurate when his health broke down.[8]

Likewise, the selection of a suitable port of embarkation led to an unfortunate compromise. The original intention seems to have been that Skeffington's retinue should sail from Bristol for Waterford, and indeed a force assembling in the West Country was soon reinforced in response to appeals from the earl of Ossory for assistance in holding the south-east against the rebels.[9] Yet the need for experienced troops necessitated the recruitment of northern and Welsh troops who were more conveniently embarked at Chester, as was the ordnance since this could not easily be transported from Waterford to Dublin. Thus the relief army sailed in two parts, and this adversely affected its efficiency. Meanwhile the original complement of artillery was shipped independently to Waterford, leaving London on 23 August.[10]

The Bristol contingent had apparently been envisaged primarily as a garrison force; but as augmented it was in fact too large for this. It comprised 900 troops—600 foot from the West Country commanded by Sir John Saintlow and his brother, plus 200 Welsh foot raised by Sir Rhys Maunsell, a member of the council in the marches of Wales, and 100 horse under a Devonshire gentleman, John Kelway.[11] At Bristol, the main problem was the shortage of ships for transport. Chapuys reported in late July that in the Thames the king had only six seaworthy ships, but by mid-September ten ships, including embargoed Spanish and Flemish merchantmen, had been made ready at Bristol. Ships being

[8] PRO, PRO 31/18/3/1, fo. 127 (*Cal. SP Spain, 1534–8*, pt. i, no. 86); *Cal. SP Spain, 1534–8*, pt. i, no. 84 (quotation); *L. & P. Hen. VIII*, vii, no. 1014 (quotation); *Dictionary of National Biography*, *sub* Skeffington; Ellis, 'Thomas Cromwell and Ireland', 500–5.

[9] *Cal. SP Spain, 1534–8*, pt. i, nos. 86–7, 90; *L. & P. Hen. VIII*, vii, nos. 1019, 1161; *SP Hen. VIII*, ii. 201–2.

[10] PRO, E 101/421/6, no. 46; *Cal. SP Spain, 1534–8*, pt. i, nos. 75, 84.

[11] PRO, SP 65/1, no. 1 (*L. & P. Hen. VIII*, xi, no. 934). Cf. *L. & P. Hen. VIII*, vi, nos. 196 (8), 1481 (5, 29), vii, nos. 1026 (26), 1455. Kelway stayed on in Ireland after the rebellion, but was killed by the O'Tooles in 1538: see Ellis, 'Representations of the past in Ireland', 305–6.

prepared elsewhere were countermanded because of the difficulty,
through contrary winds, of getting them to Bristol. The king then
intervened to change two captains because he found others offering
to sail within six days, weather permitting, with an increased complement of troops. The force sailed at the end of the month and
reached Waterford without difficulty. Yet once the Chester contingent had arrived, most of the Waterford garrison were needed in
the Pale, but could not be moved until December when cavalry
was sent down to escort them north.[12] As a fighting force, therefore, the Bristol contingent was rather less formidable than its
actual numbers suggested.

The organization and composition of the Chester force underlined even more clearly the government's difficulties. The force
eventually comprised 1,600 men—250 Cheshire foot under Sir
William Brereton; 250 Welsh foot, led by John Salisbury, esquire
for the body and steward of the lordship of Denbigh; and 466
northern horse, under four Cumberland gentlemen. The remainder consisted of Skeffington's original retinue, plus 100 horse
under Edward Sutton, son of Lord Dudley, and a hastily recruited
Welsh force of 220 horse and 150 foot.[13] The backbone of the relief
army was thus the northerners. They consisted mainly of highly
prized spearmen, recruited from the west marches, who were well
accustomed to the kind of border warfare they would encounter in
Ireland and who, thanks to the recent Anglo-Scottish peace, could
now be spared for service in Ireland. Of their captains, Leonard
Musgrave was constable of the royal castle of Penrith, and had
served in Ireland twice before, under the earl of Surrey (1520–2)
and during Skeffington's previous deputyship (1530–2).[14] Edward
Aglionby was a gentleman of the household of William, Lord
Dacre, with modest possessions around Carlisle, who had been
licensed by the king in 1524 to retain a hundred men 'of your own
seruauntes and tenauntes', or of Dacre's tenants, for the defence of

---

[12] *L. & P. Hen. VIII*, vii, nos. 1181, 1186, xiv (ii), no. 194; *Cal. SP Spain, 1534–
8*, pt. i, nos. 75, 86, 90, 102; PRO, E 101/421/6, no. 43; *SP Hen. VIII*, ii. 202–3, 219–
20, 227.
[13] PRO, SP 65/1, no. 1 (*L. & P. Hen. VIII*, xi, no. 934); *SP Hen. VIII*, ii. 221,
233, 267. Cf. PRO, E 101/421/6, no. 43; *L. & P. Hen. VIII*, vi, nos. 615, 1379, vii,
nos. 674, 679, 895, 1498 (30), x, no. 1045, xii (ii), nos. 249–50, 696 (2), 712.
[14] *SP Hen. VIII*, ii. 32–3, 48, 61; *L. & P. Hen. VIII*, v, no. 398 (p. 318), vii, no.
1498 (30).

the west marches.[15] He had also served in Ireland under Skeffington in 1530–1, but was back in Cumberland by 1532 when Dacre, as receiver of the king's lands in Carlisle, made him a lease for a mill race at Aglionby. When Dacre was arrested for treason, Aglionby had immediately written to Cromwell begging to be remembered for a lease of Dacre's lands if they were forfeited.[16] It was no doubt this letter which ensured his return to Ireland four months later, along with Captain Thomas Dacre, newly released from the Tower, and Captain Laurence Hamerton.[17] Serving under them, presumably as petty captains, were Thomas Aglionby, perhaps a younger brother of Edward, and Richard Dacre, who was Lord Dacre's cousin.[18] Finally, there was John Musgrave, an illegitimate son of Dacre's erstwhile retainer and principal accuser in 1534, Sir William Musgrave, who acted as his deputy keeper of the royal outpost of Bewcastle. Thomas Dacre and John Musgrave had clashed during the recent Anglo-Scottish war, and Cromwell presumably thought the west marches would be quieter if their services were employed elsewhere.[19]

Thus even after Lord Dacre's disgrace, the king was still forced to depend on the Dacre connexion, since Dacre controlled one of the few sources of mounted spearmen in England. Overall, the captains included some experienced men, but few courtiers, and some like John Kelway who lacked both experience and connections. The account of the treasurer-at-war suggests that the total number of troops landed in the two forces was 2,502 men.[20] No doubt few of these troops had experience of Ireland, but significantly troops from the Welsh and northern marches had also

[15] CRO, Carlisle, MSS D/Ay/1/199 (this letter appears to be in the hand of William Brabazon, who in 1534 was appointed undertreasurer of Ireland); D/Ay/1/180; *L. & P. Hen. VIII*, iv, no. 2374.

[16] CRO, Carlisle, MS D/Ay/2/24; *L. & P. Hen. VIII*, vii, no. 895.

[17] PRO, SP 65/1, no. 1 (*L. & P. Hen. VIII*, xi, no. 934); *L. & P. Hen. VIII*, v, no. 1065 (17). Thomas Dacre later founded a junior branch of the Dacre family through his purchase of the priory of Lanercost: H. Whitehead, 'Church goods in Cumberland in 1552', in *C. & W.*, 8 (1886), 192 n.

[18] Ibid.; PRO, SP 60/3, fo. 6 (*L. & P. Hen. VIII*, x, no. 30); SP 1/112, fos. 153–4 (*L. & P. Hen. VIII*, xi, no. 332); SP 1/104, fos. 158, 160–5 (*L. & P. Hen. VIII*, x, nos. 1102–4); Bain (ed.), *Hamilton papers*, i, no. 289.

[19] PRO, SP 65/1, no. 1; *L. & P. Hen. VIII*, vii, no. 380 (i–iii); James, *Society, politics and culture*, 108–13.

[20] PRO, SP 65/1, no. 1; SP 60/2, fos. 100–1 (*L. & P. Hen. VIII*, viii, no. 449); *L. & P. Hen. VIII*, vii, no. 1366, xii (ii), no. 537.

formed the backbone of the English forces serving there under Surrey and Skeffington.[21] More disconcerting was the fact that for an Irish campaign, with mobility at a premium and few opportunities for a set-piece battle, the army was not a balanced force. The delays in sailing meant a winter campaign, in which the footmen could not be effectively deployed. In December a further 200 northern spearmen and 100 Welsh spearmen were requested in exchange for the Welsh foot (traditionally the lowest form of military life in English Ireland) who were to be discharged. The government later found horses for eighty of the footmen in order to use them as mounted archers, but the cavalry already included too large a proportion of mounted archers and not enough spearmen. In effect, the government was repeating the mistakes of Surrey's expedition in 1520 when the decorative but largely ineffective yeomen of the guard had been sent over.[22]

The army had also grown considerably from the 1,500 men envisaged in late July, partly no doubt because, with the splitting of the army into two forces, the Chester contingent was now deemed too small to operate as a field army. By the end of August, Skeffington, his retinue, and the bulk of the ordnance were at Chester awaiting the arrival of shipping and money. But as the political climate deteriorated with news of the growing storm in Ireland, the deputy sent his son back to London to plead for reinforcements, and then departed into Wales to raise more troops.[23] To pay the augmented force, the king appointed Cromwell's servant, William Brabazon, recently returned from the north, as undertreasurer and treasurer-at-war (26 August). Chapuys reported that the mounting of a major expedition under the duke of Suffolk or Norfolk was also canvassed at court, and inquiries were made about the possibility of recruiting 300 foreign mercenaries as arquebusiers.[24] Yet by the time the northerners were ready, the deputy's retinue had been depleted by desertions, horses were lacking, and Skeffington himself was still

[21] PRO, SP 65/1, no. 1; *SP Hen. VIII*, ii. 32–3, 48, 61; *L. & P. Hen. VIII*, v, no. 398 (p. 318).

[22] PRO, SP 65/1, no. 1; *SP Hen. VIII*, ii. 38, 48, 223, 293; *L. & P. Hen. VIII*, vii, no. 1574; Ellis, *Tudor Ireland*, 109.

[23] *L. & P. Hen. VIII*, vii, nos. 1019, 1102, 1186; *Cal. SP Spain, 1534–8*, pt. i, no. 87; PRO, SP 65/1, no. 1.

[24] *L. & P. Hen. VIII*, vii, nos. 1068 (12), 1291, 1368; PRO, E 101/421/6, no. 41; *Cal. SP Spain, 1534–8*, pt. i, nos. 86–7.

in Wales.[25] In fact the rebels had intercepted a ship laden with horses for the deputy and another had been stolen out of the Thames.[26] These losses followed a rebel decision to fit out ships to harass the invasion fleet, and in reaction the king was forced to mount coastal patrols.[27]

At Chester, Brabazon was now in charge and still awaiting the money which, contrary to Skeffington's instructions, had been sent to Bristol. A favourable wind had blown for over a week, and following receipt on 23 September of Cromwell's instructions, Brabazon had ordered the northern men aboard ship, intending to collect Skeffington's force at Holyhead. John Alen, master of the rolls in Ireland, was detailed to remain at Chester to receive the money and pay the ships for Brereton and Salisbury's retinues.[28] The deputy, however, was still at Beaumaris waiting for additional guns and artillery being transported from Conway castle, and on 4 October the northerners were still on board ship at Chester, now awaiting wind and weather, although Brereton's company had since arrived.[29] In excuse, Skeffington alleged the danger of sailing without an adequate force, but at the end of September the king, increasingly exasperated at the delays, sent him peremptory orders to sail by the first wind. Cromwell's agent, Stephen Vaughan, was also sent down to Chester to speed the preparations.[30] The fleet sailed up from Chester, and eventually left Graycourt Harbour for Ireland on 14 October, arriving off Lambay Island on the 15th.[31] Altogether, it had taken over two-and-a-half months to raise, equip, and transport a relatively small army to Ireland. And the operation, although occupying much of Cromwell's time, was

[25] PRO, SP 60/2, fo. 59 (*L. & P. Hen. VIII*, vii, no. 1186); *SP Hen. VIII*, ii. 202; *Cal. SP Spain, 1534–8*, pt. i, nos. 87, 257.
[26] *Cal. SP Spain, 1534–8*, pt. i, nos. 84, 90; *SP Hen. VIII*, ii. 228; Holinshed, *Chronicles*, vi. 299.
[27] PRO, E 101/421/6, nos. 45–6; *L. & P. Hen. VIII*, vii, nos. 1161, 1168, xiv (ii), no. 194; *Cal. SP Spain, 1534–8*, pt. i, no. 102. Cf. *SP Hen. VIII*, ii. 205, 225; *L. & P. Hen. VIII*, viii, nos. 193, 263. Perhaps a more permanent testimonial to the exploits of the Geraldine navy was the otherwise pointless re-enactment in 1536 of the Piracy Act of 1535, in which the word traitor was inserted in the description of pirates. See G. R. Elton, *Reform and renewal: Thomas Cromwell and the common weal* (Cambridge, 1973), 148 n. 51.
[28] *L. & P. Hen. VIII*, vii, no. 1186; PRO, E 101/421/6, no. 43.
[29] PRO, SP 65/1, no. 1; *SP Hen. VIII*, ii. 202–3.
[30] *Cal. SP Spain, 1534–8*, pt. i, nos. 102, 257; PRO, E 101/421/6, no. 45.
[31] *SP Hen. VIII*, ii. 203–5; PRO, SP 60/2, fo. 100 (*L. & P. Hen. VIII*, viii, no. 449).

evidently characterized more by improvisation than by proper planning.[32]

Skeffington's force landed, with difficulty, near Dublin over the period from 16 to 24 October, but even so, the government's difficulties were far from over. Upon arrival, it soon became apparent that the army was seriously short of weapons. Councillors later reported from Dublin that 'of 1,600 men being here at the landing of the same, ther were not 400 of them furnished with weapon'. The livery supplied from the Tower of London sufficed only for Skeffington's original retinue of 150 men, while the bows which came from Ludlow castle were useless, 'for many of them wold not holde the bendinge'.[33] Longbows could not be obtained in Ireland—supplies were normally imported from England—and from Waterford Sir John Saintlow reported a great shortage of handguns.[34] Moreover, many of the horses had died in passage because of the delays in sailing.[35] As late as the following February, John Alen was still complaining that 'this army want bowis and arows and stringes, and many other habylments of warr'.[36] In fact the supplies of weapons had in many cases not been increased from early estimates prepared in the ordnance office in late July, viz. 500 bows and 300 northern spears. An important exception were the very substantial pieces of artillery sent—two demi-cannon and two demi-culverins, with some smaller pieces. These followed reports (only partially correct) that the king's ordnance in Dublin castle had fallen into rebel hands. The 1534–5 campaign witnessed much the largest deployment of artillery in Ireland since its first introduction a half-century earlier, and the demi-cannons, firing 30 lb. shot, were three times the size of any field piece later available to Elizabeth's army there. Ironically, however, the other difficulties besetting the army meant that there was little opportunity to use them before the siege of Maynooth the following March.[37]

---

[32] *L. & P. Hen. VIII*, vii, nos. 1019, 1064, 1161, 1165, 1167–8, 1186.

[33] *SP Hen. VIII*, ii. 228 (where 'towne' should read 'towre' [of London]: *L. & P. Hen. VIII*, viii, no. 226), 267.

[34] *L. & P. Hen. VIII*, viii, nos. 287, 345; Ellis, *Reform and revival*, 127, 146.

[35] *SP Hen. VIII*, ii. 202, 206.   [36] Ibid., ii. 228.

[37] PRO, SP 2/Q, fo. 163 (*L. & P. Hen. VIII*, vii, no. 1682); *L. & P. Hen. VIII*, vii, no. 1681, Add. no. 936; Ellis, 'Indenture concerning the king's munitions', 100–3; Brian Trainor, 'Extracts from the Irish ordnance accounts, 1537–9', in *Ir. sword*, I (1952–3), 333 n. 3; Cyril Falls, *Elizabeth's Irish wars* (London, 1950), 38; G. A. Hayes-McCoy, 'The early history of guns in Ireland', in *Galway Archaeological Society Journal*, 18 (1938–9), 43–65.

As with campaigns in Scotland and for similar reasons, food was in short supply. Even without the additional burden of the army, the lordship commonly imported grain in years of poor harvest. Moreover, the rebels adopted a scorched-earth policy.[38] In this instance, however, the supply arrangements proved to be adequate. The deputy was authorized to appoint victuallers to purvey grain in England and there were no complaints about shortages of food.[39] Another perennial problem facing armies was sickness and disease. The 'death' (plague) had ravaged the English Pale shortly after Surrey's arrival in 1520, causing serious billeting difficulties, but the 'sickness' which affected the army between November 1534 and February 1535 was disruptive for different reasons, and during the summer of 1535 there was a resurgence of plague in the Pale. Forty men died in Salisbury's retinue from sweating sickness: altogether only a hundred men were affected, but these included Salisbury and Skeffington himself who lay ill and incapacitated for twelve weeks.[40] The deputy had recovered sufficiently by March to take the field, but his health was gone and he eventually died in December. In August, while sitting in council, he was said to be 'almost deade amonge them', and 'if he rise before 10 or 11 of the clocke, he is almost deade or none'.[41] During the winter of 1534–5 Skeffington's incapacity was a serious hindrance because there was no one else of sufficient seniority and experience to whom he dared to delegate command of a major expedition.[42]

The army's financial situation was also unsatisfactory. The lordship's internal revenues normally just covered administrative costs, and little money could be raised there by way of loans.[43] Once again, the initial delays set the pattern. Between July and October 1534 Cromwell disbursed £9,499. 14s. 8d. from the Jewel House for the war in Ireland, but over £2,500 of this had been spent before the deputy had even sailed.[44] By dint of leading a force of 300 cavalry to Waterford, Brabazon was able to bring up the rest

[38] Ellis, *Tudor Ireland*, 36; *SP Hen. VIII*, ii. 221. Cf. Davies, 'Provisions for armies', 236–7.

[39] *L. & P. Hen. VIII*, vii, no. 1497. Cf. ibid., vii, no. 1437, viii, no. 529: an army supply ship impounded at Cardiff.

[40] *SP Hen. VIII*, ii. 37–9, 232–3, 262, 280; *L. & P. Hen. VIII*, viii, no. 449.

[41] *SP Hen. VIII*, ii. 266–7, 302–3.

[42] PRO, SP 60/2, fos. 81–2 (*L. & P. Hen. VIII*, vii, no. 1574); *SP Hen. VIII*, ii. 227, 231, 233.

[43] *SP Hen. VIII*, ii. 225–6, 227.

[44] PRO, E 101/421/6, nos. 35–6, 39, 41–3, 45–6.

of the money there (and incidentally to escort back 500 footmen), and so had enough money for the army's pay-day in December. He scraped up sufficient in loans to pay most companies again in January, but from February army pay was usually in arrears.[45] Indeed, until new revenue began to come in from first fruits and tenths, the English government was itself pressed for money. A further £5,166. 13s. 4d. was sent at the end of January, but it took a month to arrive because the ship conveying it was 'with contrary wyend & evell weydryng broghet heder to the Hollehed agayne'.[46] In May a further £3,000 was dispatched, and £3,000 more in July, but the army was still a month in arrears after the July payment.[47] And by summer 1536, their pay was so far in arrears that the army mutinied.[48]

The cumulative effect of all these problems was a serious deterioration in army discipline, and consequently in military effectiveness. In default of a vigorous commander, the army spent much of November and December uselessly garrisoning Dublin and Drogheda, whilst the captains, who had been appointed to the privy council, democratically decided whether or not they would assent to any journey.[49] The army was not mustered before payment as required, and the captains enlisted others without licence to fill vacancies in the ranks. Some of the troops had gone missing, notably the northern men whose numbers were 'soore disminished, and withoute them no notable exploite can be doon'. Few had actually deserted to the rebels, although some of the captains were related to leading rebels and were reluctant to prosecute the war against them.[50] The wardens of the marches were required to search for soldiers absent without licence, and Alen vainly recommended the recruitment of two hundred more northern horse 'with some hardie capitayne' and to discharge some Welsh horse and foot.[51] Perhaps because they had been hurriedly

[45] *SP Hen. VIII*, ii. 219–20, 225, 227; *L. & P. Hen. VIII*, viii, no. 449.

[46] PRO, SP 60/2, fo. 87 (*L. & P. Hen. VIII*, viii, no. 193); E 101/421/6, no. 33; *L. & P. Hen. VIII*, ix, no. 234. Cf. G. R. Elton, *England under the Tudors* (2nd edn., London, 1974), 142–3.

[47] *L. & P. Hen. VIII*, viii, no. 653, ix, nos. 217, 513; *SP Hen. VIII*, ii, 243, 268.

[48] PRO, SP 60/3, fos. 99–100 (*L. & P. Hen. VIII*, x, no. 1224); Ellis, *Tudor Ireland*, 133.

[49] *SP Hen. VIII*, ii. 219–24, 227.

[50] Ibid., ii. 223, 225, 229, 242, 261–2, 291–2. Cf. *L. & P. Hen. VIII*, iii, nos. 1285 (p. 498), 1379 (25), v, no. 1715, vii, no. 1167.

[51] *SP Hen. VIII*, ii. 223, 225.

raised by an outsider who had no natural ties with their region, the
Welsh troops were particularly indisciplined, and Salisbury and
Brereton were lax in controlling their men. Alen urged the appointment of a marshal 'which may be no Walshman', for 'ther was
never army furder ought of order'. Lacking pay, 'they robbe bothe
frind and foo, and smaly regarde the deputie, and moch less any of
the counsaile'.[52] The appointment in January of William Pole, a
protégé of Cromwell, as provost-marshal and Thomas Paulet as
special commissioner temporarily checked this indiscipline. Paulet
brought instructions and a royal proclamation for reordering the
army, and also a commission for Sir John Saintlow as chief marshal.[53] Yet Saintlow remained in Waterford until mid-April,
having been delayed first by the non-payment of his troops and
then by the military situation; so Paulet stayed on to keep order,
taking musters of troops, forcing the captains to follow orders and
accept lower rates of pay for themselves, and restraining the
soldiers from robbery.[54]

Nevertheless, by June army discipline was worse than ever.
Everywhere there were complaints that the army 'pylle and extorte
the people'. Most of the footmen stayed in Dublin and 'snarle us
with lacke of money and wepon', while the horsemen would 'pay in
maner neither for horsemeit nor mannes meit, and the cuntrey
redie to fflee ffrom hus'. Not even the lands of loyalists were safe
from them: they pillaged three of the earl of Wiltshire's manors in
Co. Kildare and robbed his bailiff of a Co. Dublin manor. In
particular, the Welsh cavalry were almost uncontrollable and were
discharged in August.[55] Skeffington's debility was no doubt partly
responsible for the situation, but Saintlow was also sick at this
time. In July, therefore, the king tried a different tack. His replacement of Skeffington as military commander by a lord marshal
made good military sense, but politically too the man appointed to
take charge of the campaign was an astute choice: Lord Leonard
Grey, son of the marquis of Dorset, was the brother of the 9th earl
of Kildare's second wife. Grey quickly reached a political settle-

[52] Ibid., ii. 222–3, 229, 242–3.
[53] *SP Hen. VIII*, ii, 237–8, 240–1; *L. & P. Hen. VIII*, viii, nos. 45, 287.
[54] *SP Hen. VIII*, ii. 225, 227, 230 n., 235, 237–8, 241–3; *L. & P. Hen. VIII*, viii, nos. 287, 449, 574–5.
[55] PRO, SP 60/2, fo. 136 (*L. & P. Hen. VIII*, viii, no. 914), SP 65/1, no. 2 (*L. & P. Hen. VIII*, xii (ii), no. 1310); *SP Hen. VIII*, ii. 260–1, 267–8, 272; *L. & P. Hen. VIII*, Add., i, no. 982.

ment.[56] Overall, the revolt took fourteen months to suppress—an unprecedented length of time for a Tudor rebellion—but the reasons for this had much more to do with the shortcomings of the relief army and the inadequacies in military administration than the strength and determination of the rebels.

The story of the campaign itself may be more briefly told. Until the arrival of the king's army provided a focus of resistance in the Pale, even leading opponents of Kildare were forced to compromise with the rebels. With Skeffington's arrival, however, rebel support within the Englishry collapsed very quickly. When Offaly had gone to Dublin on 11 June to resign the governorship, he had brought with him a force of about 1,000 retainers. Leaving the bulk of his troops outside Dublin, he rode through the city to St Mary's abbey, where the council was meeting, with a strong company of horsemen who wore the silken fringes on their headpieces from which he received his name. This force was probably the largest readily available to Offaly without calling out his tenantry, and included the Kildare galloglass who, with the horsemen, were his best troops.[57] After news of Kildare's arrest, however, Offaly moved to seize military control of the Pale. He issued a proclamation that all those born in England should leave Ireland immediately on pain of death, denounced the king as a heretic, and instead required an oath of allegiance to himself, the pope, and the emperor.[58] After Offaly's resignation, the council had elected the veteran captain, Lord Delvin, as justiciar. Offaly countered their feeble efforts to organize resistance by burning the lands of his enemies in Co. Meath, exacting pledges from them, and imprisoning loyalists in Maynooth castle. The three English-born councillors, Archbishop Alen, Bishop Staples, and Prior Rawson, fled.[59]

[56] *SP Hen. VIII*, ii. 261, 264, 266–8; *L. & P. Hen. VIII*, viii, no. 1019, ix, no. 357; PRO, SP 65/1, no. 1.
[57] Archbishop Marsh's Library, Dublin, MS Z4 2 7, fo. 410; PRO, SP 60/2, fo. 109 (*L. & P. Hen. VIII*, viii, no. 695); TCD, MS 543/2, *s.a.* 1534; Holinshed, *Chronicles*, vi. 289–92; Ware, *Histories*, 89; T. Dowling, *Annales breves Hiberniae: Annals of Ireland*, ed. R. Butler (Dublin, 1849), *s.a.* 1534; Lambeth MS 602, fo. 138 (*Cal. Carew MSS, 1515–74*, no. 84).
[58] *Cal. SP Spain, 1534–8*, pt. i, nos. 70, 84, 86; *SP Hen. VIII*, ii. 198, 200, 228; *Stat. Ire.*, i, 28 Hen. VIII c. 1.
[59] *L. & P. Hen. VIII*, xii (ii), no. 1310 II 2; *SP Hen. VIII*, ii. 198, 200, 217; *Cal. Carew MSS, Bk. of Howth*, 193; *SP Hen. VIII*, ii. 200; Lambeth MS 602, fo. 138; Ware, *Histories*, 89; Holinshed, *Chronicles*, vi. 292, 294; Lambeth MS 602, fo. 139ᵛ; *Annála Uladh: Annals of Ulster*, *s.a.* 1534; *Annála Connacht: the Annals of Con-*

According to the annals of Connaught, 'mac an Iarla .i. Tomás do milled muinter Righ Saxa a ndigail a athar in gac ait a rabadar a nErinn. [The son of the earl, i.e. Thomas, destroyed the people of the king of England everywhere they were in Ireland in revenge for his father]'. Anyone born in England who fell into rebel hands—of whom Archbishop Alen was the most prominent—was summarily executed. At court news circulated that Offaly 'spareth not to put to deth man, woman or child which be borne in England, & so contynueth in as well tyrany & murtheryng the kynges subiectes'.[60]

By late July resistance within the Englishry was confined to the Co. Louth border, where Sir Walter Bellew of Roche held out against him, the city of Dublin and Finglas to the north, and the Butler territories of the south-east. Leaving Sir John Burnell to watch the city, Offaly assembled an army of about 2,500 men and marched north in late July to crush Bellew and to parley with O'Neill whose support he secured by ceding Greencastle, Co. Down, to him. Meanwhile, two rebel armies were operating in Cos. Wexford and Dublin. On 3 August Charles Bermingham, Norfolk's constable of Carlow castle, with Gerald Prendergast, MacMurrough, and 1,000 men attacked John Devereux of Balmagir.[61] The following day the citizens of Dublin were defeated by Burnell and the O'Tooles at Salcock Wood on 4 August while trying to defend Finglas, the city's granary. And on his return Offaly was able to negotiate a truce which allowed him to lay siege to the king's castle, where the justiciar and council still held out, from the city.[62] Leaving a small force to besiege the castle, Offaly then marched south to attack the Butlers who had been raiding the Kildare estates in Cos. Carlow and Kildare. He took Tullow castle after a five-day siege and then advanced down the Barrow valley as far as Great Island, where there was a skirmish with Ossory in mid-August. Offaly offered to cede half the country for Ossory's

---

nacht, s.a. 1534; *Annála ríoghacht Éireann: Annals of the kingdom of Ireland by the Four Masters*, s.a. 1535; *The annals of Loch Cé*, s.a. 1534.

[60] PRO, SP 3/14, fo. 41 (*L. & P. Hen. VIII*, vii, no. 1064); *Annála Connacht: the Annals of Connacht*, 684; Ellis, 'Tudor policy and Kildare ascendancy', 260–2; id., 'Kildare rebellion and Henrician Reformation', 814.

[61] Hore and Graves, *Southern & eastern cos.*, 43.

[62] TCD, MSS 543/2, s.a. 1534, 591, fos. 12ᵛ–13; Marsh, MS Z4 2 7, fos. 410–10ᵛ; Holinshed, *Chronicles*, vi. 293–5; Ware, *Histories*, 89; Lambeth MS 602, fos. 138, 140; *Annála ríoghachta Éireann: Annals of the kingdom of Ireland by the Four Masters*, s.a. 1535; Dowling, *Annals*, s.a. 1534.

support in the rebellion. The earl rejected this but agreed to a short
truce in order to defend Tipperary which the Munster Geraldines
under the earl of Desmond were raiding in his absence. The arrival
of O'Neill with reinforcements allowed Offaly to resume the offensive: the Butler estates were wasted as far south as Thomastown,
where Ossory was heavily defeated and Lord James Butler severely
wounded. Ossory retired to Waterford and Butler was besieged in
Kilkenny. In early September Offaly retained MacMurrough,
O'More, O'Connor, and O'Byrne and left them and the Kildare
gentry to guard the southern marches of his lordship against the
Butlers while he returned to Dublin where, on the king's orders,
the citizens had broken truce and captured many of his men.[63]

As lord deputy, Kildare had had control of the king's ordnance
in Ireland, and many of the artillery pieces had been removed from
Dublin castle in the months before the revolt, and so had passed
into rebel hands. With these, Earl Thomas had laid siege to
Dublin, which was a vital objective—politically because it was the
lordship's capital, but more importantly because the castle contained the chief store of powder and shot which he needed for his
artillery.[64] John Alen, writing from Chester, warned Cromwell that

the los of that citie and the castel were a playne subversion of the lande.
Also the rebell, which chieflie trusteth in his ordinaunce, which he hath of
the kinges, hath in effecte consumed all his shoote; and except he wynneth
the castell of Dublyn, he is destitute of shoote, which is a gret cumforte
and advantage for the kinges army.[65]

To this end, Offaly seemingly called up all the troops at his
disposal, and the city was besieged by an army of 15,000 men. The
chronicler, Richard Stanyhurst, records that many of the Pale
gentry, although forced to take part with their tenants in the siege,
simply shot headless arrows or messages into the city. Thus the
rebel army was nothing like so formidable as it seemed. The rebels
broke into the city at one point and did considerable damage, but
they were driven out again. The castle was also damaged but the
garrison of 50 gunners held out against the increasingly desperate

[63] Holinshed, *Chronicles*, vi. 293–6; *SP Hen. VIII*, ii. 250–1; *Stat. Ire.*, i, 28 Hen.
VIII c. 1; *Cal. SP Spain, 1534–8*, pt. i, no. 87; Dowling, *Annals, s.a.* 1534; BL, Add.
MS 4791, fos. 259–9ᵛ.
[64] An inventory of military stores in Dublin castle and elsewhere in Oct. 1532 is
printed in Ellis, 'Indenture concerning the king's munitions', 100–3.
[65] *SP Hen. VIII*, ii. 202.

attacks: one soldier, Francis Herbert, was said to have killed 24 rebels, including 20 on one day.[66]

Until Skeffington's arrival with the relief army, the rebels were very much in the ascendant, if not in full control of the lordship. From early August, they held the Pale, Cos. Carlow and Wexford, and probably parts of Co. Limerick. Desmond, O'Brien, and MacCarthy supported them in the south-west, as did most Gaelic chiefs elsewhere, and the Butlers were on the defensive in Cos. Kilkenny, Tipperary, and Waterford.[67] Beyond the Pale, the evidence is too slight to assess rebel support accurately, but the king's cause would probably have collapsed completely if Skeffington had delayed much longer. Yet the failure to capture Dublin marked a turning-point in the campaign. Realizing that his artillery was not sufficiently heavy to breach the walls and that he lacked the time to starve the city into surrender, Kildare (as Offaly now was since his father's death on 3 September) again took truce with the citizens and shifted his ordnance to Howth Head to try to oppose Skeffington's landing. The deputy was caught as he disembarked some Cumberland spears, and the fleet was driven off. The spearmen made for Dublin but were intercepted by 200 rebel cavalry at a bridge near Clontarf and 22 men, including Captains Leonard Musgrave and Laurence Hamerton, were killed and 18 taken prisoner. This, however, was Kildare's last major success. The following day Skeffington landed two forces at Skerries and Dublin (17 October) and himself disembarked with the rest of the troops at Dublin a week later.[68]

The reaction among Kildare's followers to Skeffington's arrival underlines the conditional nature of support among the Englishry for the earl, by contrast with the more personal nature of loyalties

[66] BL, Sloane MS 1449, fo. 154; Edward, Lord Herbert of Cherbury, *The life and raigne of King Henry the Eighth* (London, 1649), 387; Holinshed, *Chronicles*, vi. 297–8; *SP Hen. VIII*, ii. 203–4; PRO, SP 65/1, no. 2; SP 60/2, fo. 109 (*L. & P. Hen. VIII*, viii, no. 695).

[67] For Desmond, O'Brien, and the MacCarthies, see Ellis, 'Kildare rebellion and Henrician Reformation', 821–2; *SP Hen. VIII*, ii. 229, 251–2. In Tipperary, Kildare's castle of Knockgraffon provided a base for attacks on the Butlers: *SP Hen. VIII*, ii. 251. The revolt in Munster and south Leinster is discussed in S. G. Ellis, 'The Kildare rebellion, 1534', MA thesis, University of Manchester, 1974, 109–11, 123–30.

[68] *SP Hen. VIII*, ii. 203–5; PRO, SP 60/2, fos. 100–1 (*L. & P. Hen. VIII*, viii, no. 449); SP 1/86 (*L. & P. Hen. VIII*, vii, no. 1366); Holinshed, *Chronicles*, vi. 298–9; Lambeth MS 602, fo. 138; *Cal. Carew MSS, Bk. of Howth*, 194.

in Gaelic Ireland. Skeffington had Kildare proclaimed a traitor
from the High Cross at Drogheda, and summoned the gentry upon
their allegiance to attend him. Thereupon, all but the most com-
promised of Kildare's supporters within the Englishry defected to
the lord deputy.[69] Although Kildare had commanded the support
of the Palesmen as the king's deputy, after Skeffington's arrival
only a small minority were willing to bear arms against their
sovereign lord. Thus the earl was quickly reduced to reliance on
the few hundred Gaelic horsemen, galloglass, and kerne he normally retained, although many of Kildare's satellites among the
Gaelic chiefs continued to offer their support.[70] Kildare withdrew
to Maynooth, his principal castle, which had been prepared against
a siege, and began a scorched-earth policy in the Pale, 'wherby
he thinke to inforce this army to departe'.[71] During the winter
Skeffington's illness, and the army's own inactivity and inadequacies allowed the rebels to hold out, but in March the deputy
invested Maynooth, which fell after a ten-day siege. The army took
the basecourt by assault after an artillery bombardment, but the
constable was tricked into surrendering the great castle for a bribe.
The summary trial and execution of the garrison which followed
was widely seen in Ireland as a major breach of trust. And subsequently, during the Tudor conquest, 'the pardon of Maynooth',
as it was called, long served as a reminder to those in arms against
the crown of what they might expect if they refused to surrender
castles when summoned to do so.[72] After Maynooth, the army
quickly took control of the earl's castles and peles in Co. Kildare,
which were mostly yielded without a fight. Kildare retired first to
Lea castle, and then took refuge among the Irishry, from where he
initiated a series of raids on the Pale. In response, the army was
distributed into a chain of garrisons ringing the Pale, and the
campaign quickly subsided into the traditional kind of border
warfare between Englishry and Irishry. Kildare's raids were of
little military significance, but politically his continued activity
was a major embarrassment to the government, and the army
proved ill-suited to the task of hunting down rebels in the inde-

    [69] Ellis, 'Tudor policy and Kildare ascendancy', 268–70.
    [70] *SP Hen. VIII*, ii. 220–1, 234.
    [71] *SP Hen. VIII*, ii. 226; Ellis, 'Tudor policy and Kildare ascendancy', 266, 268.
    [72] *SP Hen. VIII*, ii. 236–8, 361–2; *L. & P. Hen. VIII*, viii, nos. 397, 449, 487;
Annála Uladh: Annals of Ulster, s.a. 1535; Ellis, 'Henry VIII, rebellion and the rule
of law', 518–19.

pendent Gaelic regions. Accordingly, Grey induced Kildare to surrender (24 August 1535) by a promise that his life would be spared. In the event, however, he was sent to the Tower, and was executed for treason at Tyburn (3 February 1537) after an interval which the government used to restore royal authority in the lordship.[73] Early in 1536, the earl's uncles were arrested on the king's orders and shipped to England; and despite the fact that Sir James and Richard Fitzgerald had done good service to Skeffington and had been pardoned by the king, they were all attainted and executed with Kildare.[74]

In one sense the outcome of the 1534–5 campaign was entirely predictable, revealing in the Irish theatre what Tudor magnates elsewhere had long believed to be the case. It demonstrated that, although Kildare's was still the dominant influence in the Pale at the start of the revolt, the administrative resources of the Tudor monarchy far outstripped anything available to even the most 'overmighty' of its subjects. It also showed that not even the strongest and most heavily defended medieval castle was proof against the heavy artillery now available to the crown. In this sense, then, the 1534–5 campaign was a striking demonstration of royal power and a crushing defeat for baronial autonomy in a region which had traditionally favoured the growth of aristocratic power. Yet because of the lordship's peripheral location in the Tudor state and the earl's ability to organize a guerrilla war by retreating into the Irishry, the revolt took far longer to suppress than a similar rising in lowland England. And considering the extent and longevity of the rising, the king's retribution was also comparatively mild. The seventy-five or so executions which followed were, however, more an indication of the government's difficulties and isolation in the aftermath of the revolt than of the king's desire for mercy. Quite simply, he could not afford a witchhunt of Kildare's supporters for fear of further alienating the support of the political community on which royal government depended.[75]

In other respects, too, the king found that the destruction of the Kildare interest created as many problems as it solved. The revolt

---

[73] *SP Hen. VIII*, ii. 247–8, 256, 262, 272; Ellis, 'Henry VIII, rebellion and the rule of law', 523–7.

[74] Ellis, 'Henry VIII, rebellion and the rule of law', 523–4.

[75] Ibid. 523–30.

reputedly cost £40,000 to suppress,[76] and it also did very serious damage to the lordship's economy and defences. Both Undertreasurer Brabazon's account for the later 1530s and the 1540–1 extents of crown lands (ancient demesne, monastic possessions, and forfeited estates of rebels) reveal numerous possessions, particularly in the Pale marches, which had been ravaged and destroyed at the time of the rebellion and which, in default of tenants, had lain waste, in whole or part, ever since.[77] Sometimes the record observes laconically that no one would live there for fear of the Irish nearby.[78] Moreover, although Brabazon accounted for IR£14,438. 11s. 3½d. for the three years to Michaelmas 1537, ominously IR£2,211. 7s. 9d. of this was in arrears, and a further IR£303. 0s. 6d. had been respited: three years later, only IR£431. 11s. 0½d. of these arrears had been collected.[79] And by 1542, when the Irish revenues amounted in theory to IR£7,450 per annum, only about IR£3,000 could actually be levied to meet the costs of government.[80]

The nature of the problem is even more apparent from an analysis of the fate of the Kildare estates after their seizure by the crown. For the year to Michaelmas 1535 the government managed to collect a derisory IR£674 from the earl's lands and virtually nothing from his other rights.[81] In August 1535 the council wrote to Cromwell asking him to make inquiries about how the earl's tributes on the Gaelic Irish could be levied and about his rental book, which was thought to be in the custody of his countess. A year later, the secretary was asked to examine Earl Thomas in the Tower concerning the whereabouts of the book. And councillors pointed out that many of Kildare's lands had been embezzled because his title deeds could not be found.[82] The earl's tributes from the Gaelic Irish were the financial expression of a military overlordship over the border chieftaincies: their disappearance spelled the collapse of the defensive arrangements whereby Kil-

---

[76] *L. & P. Hen. VIII*, x, no. 1051ii.

[77] PRO, SC 11/934–5, SP 65/1, no. 2, SP 65/3, no. 2; N. B. White (ed.), *Extents of Irish monastic possessions 1540–41* (Dublin, 1943).

[78] See also above, p. 29.

[79] PRO, SP 65/1, no. 2; *L. & P. Hen. VIII*, xvi, no. 777.

[80] *Cal. Carew MSS, 1515–74*, no. 176; *L. & P. Hen. VIII*, xviii (i), no. 553 (2).

[81] Calculated from PRO, SP 65/1, no. 2.

[82] PRO, SP 60/2, fo. 83 (*L. & P. Hen. VIII*, vii, no. 1211), SP 60/3, fos. 201–4 (*L. & P. Hen. VIII*, xi, no. 521), SP 60/3, fo. 162 (*L. & P. Hen. VIII*, xi, no. 709).

dare had protected tenants and extracted rents from many border estates. The effects were apparent even on one of the earl's principal estates, the manor of Kildare, which comprised the town and castle of Kildare, fourteen adjacent vills, and five outlying vills which were parcel of the manor. Before 1534, the manor had been worth IR£140 a year, with a further IR£39 allowed for the rent-free holdings of thirteen horsemen for defence: but destruction during the rebellion reduced its value to just IR£59. By 1540 rents had recovered to something like their former value, but in May a raid by O'Connor resulted in the burning of 44 cottages in the town (of which 32 were soon rebuilt) and 260½ acres of arable land there, the total destruction of 3 vills, and damage to 3 more. By then, 3 more vills were described as 'vastate et inoccupate eo quod iacent super confines patrie Hibernicorum vocatorum Dempsyes', the 13 horsemen had been reduced to 11, and the manor was worth no more than IR£77 a year.[83] By Michaelmas 1537 the total value to the crown of all the Kildare estates had recovered to IR£895 per annum, but this proved to be the limit of their value in crown hands. Over the next decade their yield stagnated, and arrears mounted steadily to reach IR£2,000 by the end of the reign.[84] The rest of the earl's landed income, together with his revenues from tributes, fees, and farms, simply vanished.

These are unmistakable signs of what might be called a crisis of lordship, or what was described in the Tudor north as 'the decay of the borders'. Quite simply, the collapse of the Kildare interest led to a partial power vacuum in the Pale marches, which the reconstructed Dublin administration proved unable to fill. The comparative peace and political stability provided by the Kildare ascendancy disappeared in the changed conditions after 1534, leading to higher levels of violence and disorder, and a consequent reduction in crown rents.[85] In the short term, of course, some such period of readjustment was inevitable. The events of the 1520s had demonstrated quite clearly that Kildare was the only magnate who could govern the lordship effectively without the need for financial or military subventions from England. Thus, with the attainder of

[83] *Crown surveys*, ed. Mac Niocaill, 148–52, 155–6; PRO, SP 65/1, no. 2: SP 60/5, fos. 148–9 (*L. & P. Hen. VIII*, xii (ii), no. 1317).
[84] Calculated from PRO, SP 65/1, no. 2; SP 65/4, nos. 1–2; SP 65/5, no. 1; SP 60/5, fos. 148–9; *Crown surveys*, ed. Mac Niocaill, *passim*.
[85] Ellis, 'Thomas Cromwell and Ireland', 514–18.

the man best placed to defend the English interest in Ireland, and the forfeiture of his estates, the crown was forced to fall back on the expensive strategy of appointing an outsider as governor, backed by a standing army to uphold royal authority. Hitherto, this strategy had only been followed for short periods of two or three years, particularly when some special effort was contemplated; but from 1534 the king's choice as governor of Ireland was always an English-born outsider. In turn the thrust of Tudor policy for Ireland necessarily altered. Where previously the central problem, viewed from London, had been how to persuade Kildare, if he were appointed governor, to govern acceptably, or, if another governor were appointed, to co-operate with him; now the Irish problem revolved around how to maintain an English-born deputy and a garrison without the lordship becoming a drain on royal finances.

In principle, a slimmed-down army supported out of the new revenues accruing from the king's ecclesiastical policies and the forfeited estates of leading rebels seemed to offer a solution to these difficulties. Shortly after Kildare's surrender, the army was disbanded save for a garrison of 700 men, and soon after debased 'coin of the harp' (nominally sterling groats, tariffed at 6d. Irish) were surreptitiously introduced to pay them—the first resort to a policy which was to have a disastrous impact throughout the Tudor state.[86] During the later 1530s, moreover, the Irish revenues exhibited a remarkable increase, from about IR£1,600 per annum before 1534 to between IR£3,000 and IR£4,500 in Henry VIII's later years.[87] Yet the administration soon ran into difficulties.

Militarily, English soldiers proved much less effective in the difficult terrain of Gaelic Ireland than in the open country of the Pale, and they were also more expensive to hire than Gaelic troops. Hitherto, Kildare's close contracts and marriages alliances with Gaelic chiefs like O'Neill and O'More had helped considerably to stabilize the Anglo-Gaelic frontier, and the earl had also maintained a permanent retinue of 120 galloglass and 120 kerne which could spearhead offensive operations in Gaelic Ireland.[88] The government soon learned the wisdom of maintaining a permanent retinue of Gaelic troops rather than hiring them for the occasional

[86] Ellis, *Tudor Ireland*, 132.
[87] Ellis, 'Thomas Cromwell and Ireland', 514–17.
[88] Ellis, *Reform and revival*, 54–5.

campaign, and the Kildare galloglass and kerne eventually passed into the service of the crown.[89] Yet Kildare's Gaelic alliances depended on personal contacts and loyalties which could only be built up by a resident magnate and could not be easily exercised by the new style of governor appointed after 1534.

Less tangibly, the 1534–5 campaign and its consequences led to an insidious militarization of government in Tudor Ireland. The conduct of warfare by both sides during the rebellion had at times exhibited a ruthlessness which was seldom seen in revolts in mainland England and which certainly departed from 'the rules of war' as practised in Anglo-French campaigns. In part this was because warfare as practised by Gaelic forces differed from English perceptions of what was permissible, but there is little doubt that the events of 1534–5 set the tone for the atrocities of Elizabethan Ireland.[90] Indeed, following experiments with the use of Gaelic kerne in France and Scotland in 1544, where their conduct distressed the French and appalled the Scots, Henry VIII decided to employ 2,000 of them in Scotland the following year, and gave instructions that they were to be recruited 'out of the most wild and savage sort of them there, whose absence should rather do good than hurt'.[91] In addition, the provision of a standing army for Ireland came to have a major impact on the character of royal government there. Traditionally, the unrestrained exercise of royal authority in the lordship had been tempered by the administration's heavy reliance on the nobles for border defence: unsupported, the power of the central government had been weak. Yet the crushing of the Kildare rebellion did little to alter the essential problems of ruling a half-conquered borderland; and as unrest and rebellion escalated, the government came increasingly to rely on

[89] *SP Hen. VIII*, ii. 266; Hore and Graves, *Southern & eastern cos.*, 152–3, 160–1; H. F. Hore, 'The Rental Book of Gerald Fitzgerald, 9th earl of Kildare', in *Journal of the Kilkenny Archaeological Society*, 2nd ser. 2 (1858–9), 266–80, 301–9; Nicholls, *Gaelic and gaelicised Ireland*, 86, 89.

[90] On Tudor perceptions of 'the rules of war', see Nicholas Canny, *The Elizabethan conquest of Ireland: a pattern established, 1565–1576* (Hassocks, 1976), chs. 6–7; C. S. L. Davies, 'Peasant revolt in France and England: a comparison', in *Agricultural History Review*, 21 (1973), 132–3; Ellis, 'Representations of the past in Ireland', 304–6. For a nationalist perspective on these developments, see Bradshaw, 'Nationalism and historical scholarship in modern Ireland', 338–9.

[91] D. G. White, 'Henry VIII's Irish kerne in France and Scotland, 1544–45', in *Ir. sword*, 3 (1957–8), 213–25 (quotation, p. 223); Ellis, 'Representations of the past in Ireland', 306.

the army to assist local officials in the execution of their duties.[92]
Thus began the practice of using the army in support of the civil
power which has remained a characteristically Irish contribution
to the development of English administrative structures down to
the present day.

In the longer term, the establishment of a standing army also led
to the growth of a distinct group of soldiers and military administrators who depended chiefly on the army for their living. True,
after a few years' service in Ireland, most of these soldier-
administrators departed to serve the king elsewhere, but for two
main reasons a significant minority stayed on in Ireland, and some
of them eventually came to establish themselves as part of the Irish
landowning élite. In the first place, apart from the garrisons at
Berwick-on-Tweed, Carlisle, and—until its loss in 1558—Calais,
service in Ireland constituted almost the only regular source of
employment to military men within the Tudor state. The intermittent wars with France and Scotland certainly offered more promising opportunities for fame and fortune while they lasted, but
under Elizabeth England enjoyed an unwonted period of peace
until 1585, whereas the gradual escalation of the wars in Ireland
provided steady and profitable, if unspectacular, employment to
Tudor adventurers.[93] Second, many of these adventurers were
younger sons of established gentry families, who inherited their
family's aristocratic outlook but not the estates to support it. Not
only did Ireland offer an outlet for military talents, but, beginning
with the estates of the earl of Kildare and the monasteries, the
periodic confiscation of land by the crown and its leasing or
regranting on favourable terms also provided the opportunity to
build up a landed inheritance.[94] Thus the changes of the mid-1530s
led to the establishment in Ireland of a new group of administrators, the New English, who had a much more aggressive, ac-
quisitive outlook on the government of Ireland than the lordship's
traditional ruling élite. The rivalry between New English and Old
English politicians, as they came to be called, was to cause serious

[92] Ellis, *Tudor Ireland*, ch. 6. Cf. Frame, *English lordship in Ireland*, ch. 3.
[93] Ellis, *Tudor Ireland*, 168–9, 245–6, 278–9; A. G. R. Smith, *The emergence of a nation state: the commonwealth of England 1529–1660* (London, 1984), pt. ii.
[94] Brendan Bradshaw, *The dissolution of the religious orders in Ireland under Henry VIII* (Cambridge, 1974), 191–5; Ellis, *Tudor Ireland*, 133–4.

complications for Tudor government in Ireland from the late 1540s onwards.

Financially, too, the government was soon in trouble. The Irish revenues fell well short of what was needed even to maintain a garrison of 700 men, let alone to cover other administrative expenses.[95] The administration gradually sank deeper into debt. Since they were relatively costly to maintain, and perhaps because they were needed at home, the Cumberland spears were soon discharged, even though they were the administration's best troops. By September 1535, only three companies were left, and Edward Aglionby's company was then disbanded—despite a proposal to settle 300 northern men in Co. Kildare and to send over 500 more northerners to make the land peaceful and profitable.[96] Captain Thomas Dacre and Richard Dacre were in trouble with the council during the autumn, and in June 1536 the remaining northern companies mutinied for lack of pay and were discharged soon after.[97] In September 1537 the king responded to the growing financial crisis by halving the garrison to 340 men, reducing army pay, and ordering other economies. Royal commissioners, sent over to investigate the lordship's government, calculated that the king should henceforth enjoy an outright surplus of 4,000 marks per annum: but this assumed that lands taken into the king's hand would continue to yield the same profits as they had in the hands of resident lords. In practice the changes still failed to balance the books, and the reduced garrison was now too weak even to defend the Pale properly. Two years later the garrison had to be increased again, and during the 1540s the government of Ireland cost the king about £4,000 a year.[98]

The changes of the 1530s were not a planned response to the problems faced by Tudor government in Ireland at the start of the decade. They did, however, underline the symbiotic nature of the relationship between crown and ruling magnate in border administration. Even the most overmighty subject proved no

---

[95] PRO, SP 65/1, no. 2; SC 11/934; *Cal. Carew MSS, 1515–74*, no. 111.

[96] PRO, SP 60/3, fo. 4 (*L. & P. Hen. VIII*, ix, no. 332: an undated letter which appears to be of Sept. 1535); SP 65/1, no. 1.

[97] PRO, SP 60/3, fo. 6 (*L. & P. Hen. VIII*, x, no. 30); SP 1/112, fos. 153–4 (*L. & P. Hen. VIII*, xi, no. 1249); SP 1/104, fos. 158, 160–5 (*L. & P. Hen. VIII*, x, nos. 1102–4); SP 60/3, fos. 99–100 (*L. & P. Hen. VIII*, x, no. 1224); SP 65/1, no. 1.

[98] Ellis, 'Thomas Cromwell and Ireland', 508–17.

match for the resources of the Tudor state, but the acquisition of the Kildare inheritance did not lead to a corresponding increase in the vigour of royal government: quite the opposite in fact, because royal authority rested in many ways on noble power. The destruction of the Kildare interest thus offered no real solution to the difficulties of ruling a remote borderland. Since the king remained basically uninterested in Ireland and very reluctant to spend money there, the changes of the mid-1530s had a pronounced destabilizing effect on the lordship. Within a few years, in fact, the needs of defence had forced the king to accept a new and more formalized method for managing Anglo-Gaelic relations ('surrender and regrant') to replace the old, unofficial alliances maintained by Kildare—though it is a fallacy to see the assimilation of Gaelic Ireland into the Tudor state as an inevitable consequence of these changes. Paradoxically, therefore, the destruction of the lordship's traditional power structures which the 1534–5 campaign brought about eventually forced Henry VIII to pursue and pay for the kind of interventionist policies for Ireland which Edward IV and Henry VII had always resisted. Thus, with hindsight, we may say that the campaign marked a major step towards the ending of Ireland's medieval partition and the establishment of Dublin castle as the headquarters of a united Ireland within a United Kingdom.

8

Submission and survival

Dacre fortunes in
Henry VIII's later years

BY contrast with Kildare, Lord Dacre was less disposed to contest the king's pleasure at the time of his arrest. His subsequent trial and unexpected acquittal for treason in July 1534 has received a good deal of attention from historians. It illustrates that an acquittal was still possible in a treason trial even though procedures were heavily weighted against the defendant. Perhaps equally important in a political context, however, were the consequences of that acquittal for the structure of power in the north-west. Despite the lord's disgrace and heavy fine, Dacre power remained a significant influence in the region throughout the mid-Tudor period.

The evidence concerning Dacre's trial has been ably reviewed by Helen Miller in her work on Henry VIII's relations with the nobility in England, and by Mervyn James in his outline of the factional alignments among the actors in Dacre's indictment.[1] Nevertheless, a few comments may be added. The charges in the indictment are very revealing of Dacre's cross-border connections. They are also reminiscent of the charges and countercharges made by the earls of Kildare and Ormond against each other in the 1520s concerning attempts to incite Gaelic raids on the English of Ireland.[2] Whether or not Dacre had made specific agreements and treaties with the Scots of Liddesdale, the lairds of Buccleuch and Hempsfield, and Lord Maxwell, as the indictments alleged, these figures were almost certainly part of the system of alliances by which Dacre normally defended the borders and with whom there would be, at the least, a tacit understanding about the targeting of

---

[1] Miller, *Henry VIII and the English nobility*, 51–7; James, *Society, politics and culture*, 108–11.

[2] Cf. *SP Hen. VIII*, ii. 121–4; PRO, SP 1/34, fos. 225–34 (*L. & P. Hen. VIII*, iv, no. 1352 (2)).

raids.[3] This is essentially the same system of alliances and understandings whose workings can be observed in more detail across the Anglo-Gaelic marches of Ireland.[4] And undoubtedly the government was generally aware of the nature of these contacts: but to obtain proof of treasonable conspiracy was another matter. In the 1520s, when charges had been made against the earl of Kildare for stirring up Gaelic resistance to Lord Lieutenant Surrey, a long investigation conducted by Wolsey produced 'oonly presumptions and uncertain conjectures'.[5]

In Dacre's case, Sir William Musgrave's detailed charges—coming as they did from a knight of the body who had been closely associated with the warden and had intimate knowledge of his practices and associations—must have offered a promising start to the government's investigation. Unfortunately they have not survived. The most conclusive method of substantiating them was of course to obtain documentary evidence, or the testimony of substantial men who were eyewitnesses, concerning treasonable dealings by Dacre with the Scots in wartime. Dacre was too careful to be seen openly with Scots enemies, but his castles were raided by the king's commissioners for incriminating letters. Either Dacre and his family had prudently not kept any such letters from Scots, however—or copies of their replies—or they had anticipated the raids and had destroyed the evidence. Thus when the commissioners arrived to seize and search Dacre's property, they were disappointed to discover only two letters from Sir Philip Dacre and the laird of Hempsfield which were in any way incriminating.[6]

Failing in this purpose, the government had to fall back on the testimony of witnesses. This was more problematic because Dacre was naturally cautious about whom he met and in whose company. Thus much depended on the lord's relations with his household. Dacre had to trust his own servants and retainers in this, and if some of them could be induced to testify against him, as happened at the trial of the duke of Buckingham, the crown's case would be much stronger. Sir William Musgrave evidently hoped for some co-operation: he warned Cromwell that those who were bound for Dacre's goods to the king would 'in nowise trust that he will have

[3] *3rd rep. DKPR*, app. ii, 234–6; *L. & P. Hen. VIII*, vii, no. 962. See also above, pp. 199–202.
[4] See above, Ch. 6.   [5] *SP Hen. VIII*, ii. 56.
[6] PRO, SP 2/Q, 14 (*L. & P. Hen. VIII*, vii, no. 1270).

any overthrow', but as soon as 'they see he shall go dowyn, I dowt not but they will say *Crucefige*'.[7] In the event, Dacre's trust in his servants and retainers proved justified, and there were no damaging defections. Cromwell instructed Musgrave to ensure that the indictments were fully substantiated, with the day and time specified. The commissioners appointed to inquire concerning treasons in Cumberland included Dacre's chief rivals, the earls of Northumberland and Cumberland, Sir Thomas Clifford, and Sir Thomas Wharton; and as an additional precaution two separate grand juries were empanelled to ensure that a true bill was found. One grand jury was, as Mervyn James observed, 'well packed with Wharton and Curwen kin, and with Percy and Clifford followers',[8] and was evidently trusted to find against Dacre. The other jury was composed chiefly of lesser gentry, including a few Dacre followers, and the commissioners may have hoped in this way to detach the lord's servants and secure their more active co-operation.

In the event, both juries dutifully found true bills, but the government apparently failed to secure any more hard evidence against Dacre.[9] Thus, at his trial, Dacre's chief accusers were Sir William Musgrave, Sir Ralph Fenwick, Northumberland's deputy lieutenant of the middle marches, and Sir Cuthbert Radcliffe.[10] More significantly, Lord Herbert of Cherbury (who had access to records not now extant) recorded that Fenwick and Musgrave produced as principal witnesses 'some mean and provoked Scottishmen' whose testimony, like that of Gaelic Irishmen, would presumably not have carried the same weight with the lords triers as that of the king's subjects.[11] The appointment of the duke of Norfolk, Dacre's patron at court, as lord high steward for the trial no doubt increased the chances of an acquittal; but perhaps crucial to the outcome was the fact that the only northern peers to be included among the lords triers were Thomas, Lord Darcy, himself a former warden, and Lord Talbot, Dacre's brother-in-

[7] PRO, SP 1/84, fo. 199 (*L. & P. Hen. VIII*, vii, no. 829). Cf. Harris, *Buckingham*, ch. 8.

[8] James, *Society, politics and culture*, 110–11; *L. & P. Hen. VIII*, vii, no. 962.

[9] *L. & P. Hen. VIII*, vii, no. 962. Cf. the list of Dacre's followers who signed the inventory of his goods in May 1534 (PRO, SP 1/84, fos. 33–50 (*L. & P. Hen. VIII*, vii, no. 676)) with the names of the grand jurors.

[10] *The reports of Sir John Spelman*, ed. J. H. Baker, i, Selden Society 93 (London, 1977), 54–5; *L. & P. Hen. VIII*, iv (ii), no. 5085.

[11] Herbert, *Henry the Eighth*, 379. Cf. R. W. Hoyle, 'Thomas Masters' Narrative of the Pilgrimage of Grace', in *Northern History*, 21 (1985), 53–79.

law.[12] If Darcy had in fact been plotting with Dacre against the king, then he had a strong vested interest in ensuring Dacre's acquittal. At any rate, the lords triers decided that the evidence of Dacre's chief accusers proceeded of malice and that the Scottish witnesses 'not only spoke maliciously, but might easily be suborned against [Dacre], who as one (having been warden of the marches) by frequent inroads had done much harme in that country'.[13] Accordingly, Dacre was found not guilty—the only nobleman to be acquitted by his peers during the reign of Henry VIII.

The verdict discredited those who had accused Dacre, and also reflected to some extent on the king and Cromwell. Despite this reverse, however, the government moved quickly to cripple Dacre's political influence by other means. There remained the two letters discovered by the commissioners from Sir Philip Dacre and the laird of Hempsfield, and following his acquittal on charges of treason Dacre was returned to the Tower for examination on charges of misprision of treason by his concealment of the letters. Eventually on 25 July he signed a confession to the charges 'of his mere and voluntarye will, without any maner of coaccion' and 'most humbly putteth him in mercy of the kinges highnes'. The price of the king's pardon was high. Dacre had to pay £10,000, to undertake not to go more than ten miles from London without the king's special licence in writing, not to molest anyone in connection with his recent trial, and to surrender before 20 October for cancellation any letters patent or leases he had of the king. And for the performance of these conditions and the payment of his fine, Dacre was bound by recognizance in 10,000 marks on 16 October. He was pardoned for his misprision on 2 December, and eventually licensed to leave London on 4 March, the day on which Sir Christopher Dacre was also finally pardoned, on condition that he return by 1 November.[14]

The conditions of Dacre's pardon were evidently intended to ensure that his influence in the west marches was much diminished. The earl of Cumberland was reappointed warden and cap-

[12] *3rd rep. DKPR*, app. ii, 234–6; *L. & P. Hen. VIII*, vii, no. 962.
[13] Herbert, *Henry the Eighth*, 379; *Reports of Sir John Spelman*, ed. Baker, i. 54–5.
[14] PRO, SP 2/Q, 14 (*L. & P. Hen. VIII*, vii, no. 1270); *L. & P. Hen. VIII*, vii, no. 1601 (1), viii, no. 481 (5), ix, app. no. 1.

tain of Carlisle in September, and he also recovered the steward-
ship and farms of the crown lands which traditionally went with
the wardenship.[15] Dacre's grip on the stewardships, farms, and
tithes of church lands in the region was not so quickly loosened,
but in November as part of an arbitration award by Cromwell
between Dacre and Cumberland, the new warden received the
stewardships and farms, while Dacre was granted the fees and
reserved rents.[16] By these means, the government calculated,
Dacre's *manraed* would be reduced and Clifford influence
enhanced.

Similarly, the heavy fine was intended to cripple Dacre
financially. The commissioners who seized Dacre's goods in May
1534 found plate and money worth altogether £4,066. 3s. 4d., of
which £2,668. 9s. 1d. was in ready money—an extraordinarily large
sum. Possibly Lord William maintained substantial reserves as a
contingency against the war with Scotland, but in March he had
sent home Roland Threlkeld, his receiver-general, to raise money
on his estates in Yorkshire and Durham.[17] Accordingly, the first
instalment of Dacre's fine was fixed at 7,000 marks, payable by 16
October 1534, which meant that Lord William had to raise a further £600. 10s. by then.[18] In fact his receiver-general's account for
the year to 11 November 1534 (Martinmas) reveals total receipts of
£6,413. 7s. 5⅛d., including the plate and money seized, so that
Dacre's usual revenues for that year, amounting to £2,347. 4s. 1⅛d.
comfortably covered the balance owing.[19] Of the remaining 8,000
marks of the fine, Dacre agreed to pay two instalments of 1,500
marks each by Michaelmas 1536, and then 1,000 marks per annum
until Michaelmas 1541 when the last instalment was due. In 1536
Dacre introduced some modest changes in his estate-management
policies, as we have seen, but his receiver-general's accounts for
the years after 1534 give no indication that Lord William was
particularly strapped for cash to pay his fine. Except for the year to
Martinmas 1536, when receipts fell to £1,927. 6s. 1d., perhaps
because of disruption caused by the Pilgrimage of Grace, Dacre's

[15] *L. & P. Hen. VIII*, vii, nos. 1018, 1217 (7–9).

[16] *L. & P. Hen. VIII*, vii, nos. 1365, 1549, viii, no. 1041.

[17] PRO, SP 1/84, fos. 33–50 (*L. & P. Hen. VIII*, vii, no. 676), fos. 62–2ᵛ (*L. & P. Hen. VIII*, vii, no. 679ii); *L. & P. Hen. VIII*, vii, no. 281, Add. i, no. 933.

[18] PRO, SP 2/Q, fo. 14 (*L. & P. Hen. VIII*, vii, no. 1270); *L. & P. Hen. VIII*, Add. i, no. 933.

[19] Durham, H. of N. MS C/201/3.

annual receipts usually amounted to about £2,300 for the rest of the reign.[20]

Finally, the condition in Dacre's recognizance that he should not leave London without the king's written permission seems to have been used as a means of licensing where Dacre might live. He was apparently allowed only brief visits to his estates around Naworth and Kirkoswald.[21] He was also removed from the commissions of the peace for Cumberland and Westmorland, so emulating his father's dismissal in 1525 and earning the Dacres the unhappy distinction of being the only peerage family to be removed from the commission twice over under Henry VIII.[22] For the most part Lord William had to reside east of the Pennines. Early in 1539 he wrote to Cromwell from Coniscliffe, Co. Durham, to move the king for licence to reside on his Yorkshire estates at Henderskelf, a few miles from the king's council at Sheriff Hutton, so that he would be able to do the king more service.[23] Since he was by then a member of the king's council and had been included on the peace commissions for the Yorkshire ridings, permission was granted.[24] In this way, therefore, Lord Dacre was reduced to a minor role in the wider government of the north.

Yet if Lord William paid a heavy price for his miscalculations in 1534, the price paid by the king for excluding Dacre from the west marches was perhaps equally heavy, measured in terms of its impact on the government of the region. Initially Henry had reappointed a reluctant earl of Cumberland as warden of the west marches, but the earl was no more successful in this office than he had been in 1525-7, and for much the same reasons. Although Dacre did not, apparently, blame Cumberland for his arrest and disgrace, initially relations between the two lords were, understandably, quite strained. There was a long dispute between them about rents and fees which Dacre claimed from the time of his wardenship and about sheep which Cumberland had seized at the

[20] PRO, SP 2/Q, fo. 14; Durham, H. of N. MS C/201/3; *L. & P. Hen. VIII*, xi, no. 477; above, pp. 87-90, 106.

[21] *L. & P. Hen. VIII*, x, no. 260, xi, nos. 477, 647, xiv (i), no. 750; Durham, H. of N. MS C/201/5, fo. 3.

[22] *L. & P. Hen. VIII*, viii, no. 149 (56, 82), xii (i), no. 795 (4), xii (ii), no. 1311 (29), xiii (i), no. 646 (41), xiv (i), no. 1354 (20); above, p. 163. Cf. Miller, *Henry VIII and the English nobility*, 204.

[23] *L. & P. Hen. VIII*, xiv (i), no. 134.

[24] *L. & P. Hen. VIII*, xiii (i), nos. 1269, 1519 (38-40), xiv (i), nos. 481, 1192 (26, 32), 1354 (18), xv, no. 612 (12, 14).

time of Dacre's arrest.[25] More seriously, Dacre's officers proved uncooperative, and even obstructive, to the new warden, and some of his tenants and followers stirred up further trouble.[26] Thus, since Cumberland continued to reside at Skipton castle and left much of the work to deputies, he exercised little real control over developments.[27] Fortunately for the new warden, the recent peace with Scotland held, but then in October 1536 the Pilgrimage of Grace burst upon the region.

In many ways, the events surrounding the Pilgrimage proved to be as much a watershed for Tudor rule of the northern marches as the Kildare rebellion did for Ireland. Dacre was not a central figure in the events leading up to the revolt, in the way that Kildare had been in Ireland; and the administrative reorganization which followed was on rather different lines. It would seem, however, that the rebels had counted on Dacre's support; and his conduct during the revolt was certainly central to its outcome in the north-west. In this respect then, the crisis of 1534 had a continuing influence on the politics and government of the region.

In the two years since the revolt in Ireland, the government had by 1536 moved much further in strengthening royal control of the provinces in response to the Reformation crisis. The suppression of the liberties and lesser monasteries, further restraints on noble power in the Statute of Uses, and the introduction of what seemed like taxation in peacetime (despite the wars in Ireland and with Scotland) had all followed the royal divorce and the supremacy. Thus rebel demands in the Pilgrimage reflected a similar combination of noble, regional, and religious grievances, but they were much more specific and broadly based than in Ireland. They demanded a parliament at York or Nottingham, for instance, to redress grievances and repeal unpopular legislation. And if the rebels failed to attract the active backing of any of the great regional magnates, neither did the government. Most of the magnates lay low, and without noble support the northern council proved powerless to contain rebellion.[28]

---

[25] *L. & P. Hen. VIII*, vii, no. 1549, viii, nos. 1030, 1041, xi, no. 477, xii (i), nos. 225, 372, xii (ii), no. 112; Hoyle, 'First earl of Cumberland', 93.

[26] *L. & P. Hen. VIII*, vii, nos. 1588–9, viii, nos. 310, 1030, 1046.

[27] *L. & P. Hen. VIII*, vii, no. 1589, ix, no. 844, x, nos. 160–1.

[28] There is an extensive literature concerning the Pilgrimage of Grace. Among the most recent works are Harrison, *Pilgrimage of Grace in the Lake Counties*; Elton, 'Politics and the Pilgrimage of Grace', 25–56; C. S. L. Davies, 'Popular religion and

Recent research on the Pilgrimage has stressed the extent of regional variation in what had once seemed a unified mass movement. Dacre's initial encounter with rebels was in south Yorkshire. His influence was much more discernible, however, on the course of the rising in the Lake Counties where, uniquely, estate management was a major source of unrest. A particular worry of the commons in the north-west was that the borders were so weak that the Scots would be encouraged to invade. The revolt was instigated by a letter circulating in the name of Captain Poverty, to which were attached articles of grievance. These demanded that entry-fines be abolished and seigneurial rents held at traditional levels. Behind these demands lay fears that arbitrary fines and enhanced rents were undermining the custom of border service, the obligation to do unpaid military service, and to keep horse and harness which was characteristic of tenant right. A rebel proclamation circulating in Cumberland asserted that the 'rulers of this country do not defend us against the Scots'.[29] The complaints about lack of defence should doubtless be seen as an indictment of early-Tudor policy in general, rather than simply as a reaction to recent events. It is hardly a coincidence, however, that they were voiced during Cumberland's wardenship, when the borders were particularly weak, lacking a resident lord to defend them, and when the rulers were so divided among themselves. It is also surely significant that the revolt, originating in Richmondshire on 14–15 October, spread northwards through Westmorland into south Cumberland:[30] that is, it began in those parts furthest from the border, in which landlords were more concerned with landed income than military service, not in northern Cumberland where Dacre influence was strongest.

From Henderskelf on 10 October Lord Dacre reported news of a rising at Beverley to the earl of Shrewsbury, his father-in-law and the king's lieutenant. Soon after, the rebels tried to persuade Dacre to join them, offering him assistance to revenge his injuries,

the Pilgrimage of Grace', in A. Fletcher and J. Stevenson (eds.), *Order and disorder in early modern England* (Cambridge, 1985), 58–91; Hoyle, 'Thomas Masters' Narrative', 53–79; M. L. Bush, 'Captain Poverty and the Pilgrimage of Grace', in *Historical Research*, 65 (1992), 17–36; id., 'The Richmondshire Uprising of October 1536 and the Pilgrimage of Grace', in *Northern History*, 29 (1993), 64–98.

[29] On all this, see now Bush, 'Captain Poverty', 17–36 (quotation, pp. 21–2).
[30] Ibid. 17–20.

but he refused.[31] Shrewsbury sent Dacre's letter on to the king, and Dacre was apparently ordered north to help stay the west marches.[32] The revolt in the north-west spread northwards along the Stainmore pass, reaching Brough and Kirkby Stephen on 16 October and Penrith on the 18th. The sheriff of Cumberland, Sir Thomas Wharton, fled as the rebels approached and did not re-emerge from hiding until January. Sir William Musgrave took refuge in Carlisle, on which, in late October, the rebels marched, intending to secure the city's support and to reinforce the defence of the border.[33] From Naworth, on 30 October, Dacre agreed with Lord Clifford, Cumberland's deputy in Carlisle, that each would assist the other if either were besieged.[34] And at Doncaster on the 28th, it was understood that Dacre was actually under siege.[35]

In fact, Lord Dacre and his uncle, Sir Christopher, were able to control the Dacre tenants in north Cumberland until well into November.[36] After news arrived of the truce taken with the duke of Norfolk at Doncaster on 27 October, the rebels were reluctant to disperse without taking Carlisle. Lord Clifford held the castle against them, but it was Sir Christopher Dacre who came under safe conduct and finally persuaded the rebels to disperse on 3 November, taking truce for a further ten days.[37] By then, however, Lord Dacre had secretly departed from Naworth, leaving his uncle in charge. His reasons are unknown: perhaps he felt that he would be more useful further south, or he may have feared that if he were implicated in treason a second time there would be no escape. In any event, lacking the king's confidence and on poor terms with the warden, he dared not take the initiative: his escape southwards was a safe move for himself but disastrous for the loyalists. He evaded the rebels and joined the king's forces south of Doncaster, and

---

[31] *L. & P. Hen. VIII*, xi, no. 647; Herbert, *Henry the Eighth*, 412; Hoyle, 'Thomas Masters' Narrative', 64.

[32] *L. & P. Hen. VIII*, xi, nos. 647, 673.

[33] *L. & P. Hen. VIII*, xii (i), no. 687 (1–2); Bush, 'Captain Poverty', 22; James, *Society, politics and culture*, 116–17.

[34] *L. & P. Hen. VIII*, xi, nos. 927, 1331.

[35] Hoyle, 'Thomas Masters' Narrative', 62, 71.

[36] *L. & P. Hen. VIII*, xi, no. 1331; Bush, 'Captain Poverty', 20; Fletcher, *Tudor rebellions*, 22.

[37] *L. & P. Hen. VIII*, xi, nos. 927, 1331, xii (i), no. 687 (1–2); Bush, 'Captain Poverty', 22.

wrote to inform the king of events in the north.[38] In his absence, events in Cumberland degenerated into private feuding. Richard Dacre came voluntarily to a rebel muster on 15 November and took upon himself to be grand captain of all Cumberland. The Dacre tenants of Gilsland and Burgh took the rebel oath at this time, but the aim was apparently to settle scores with Sir William Musgrave. None of the Dacres was among the rebel representatives nominated for the meeting at York. In their absence, however, Richard Dacre entered Carlisle with a company of Dacre tenants, and almost managed to assassinate Sir William Musgrave while also threatening Lord Clifford. Eventually, the mayor Edward Aglionby pacified them.[39] The king ordered Richard Dacre's arrest when reports of these feuds among the loyalists reached him. Too late, he realized the consequences of his actions in the west march. Dacre, Parr of Kendal and his nephew, Musgrave, and Clifford were summoned to court and, together with Cumberland *in absentia*, were peremptorily reconciled by the king and dispatched home, at Norfolk's urging, to restore order. Cumberland was informed of this in a long letter of rebuke from the king.[40]

The promise of the king's pardon in December brought only a temporary respite in Cumberland and Westmorland. By January there were more riots, unrest, and unlawful assemblies in west Cumberland and Westmorland. The gentry expected further trouble and appealed for help. Things were so bad around Cockermouth that in mid-January the sheriff, Sir Thomas Curwen, fled to Sheriff Hutton. Only in the north was an uneasy peace maintained.[41] Finally, the commons of Cumberland rose again on 12 February after Thomas Clifford, deputy captain of Carlisle, came to make two arrests at Kirkby Stephen and his retinue of border thieves began to spoil the town. Five thousand rebels marched on Carlisle, and Clifford and Sir John Lowther wrote urgently from Carlisle castle to Sir Christopher Dacre commanding him to bring assistance. As Norfolk hurried north from Richmond, raising reinforcements, and summoning further help

[38] *L. & P. Hen. VIII*, xi, nos. 1096, 1207, 1243, 1331.

[39] *L. & P. Hen. VIII*, v, no. 573, xi, nos. 1155, 1299, 1331; 'Letters of the Cliffords, lords Clifford and earls of Cumberland, c.1500–c.1565', ed. R. W. Hoyle in *Camden Miscellany*, 31 (1992), 60–1; James, *Society, politics and culture*, 113.

[40] *L. & P. Hen. VIII*, xii (i), nos. 225, 244, 336, 372; *SP Hen. VIII*, v. 64–5; 'Letters of the Cliffords', ed. Hoyle, 61–3.

[41] *L. & P. Hen. VIII*, xii (i), nos. 18, 71–2, 185, 318–19, 336, 362.

from Lord Dacre and his company, the fate of Carlisle rested on
Sir Christopher. Norfolk wrote him an animated letter, ordering
him to raise such a company as he could trust for the city's relief,
and recalling his old saying that

'Sir Christopher Dacre is a true knight to his sovereign lord, an hardy
knight, and a man of war.' Pinch now for no courtesy to shed blood of false
traitors; and be ye busy on the one side, and ye may be sure the duke of
Norfolk will come on the other. Finally, now, Sir Christopher, or never![42]

Lord Dacre learned of the new rising on reaching Doncaster on
the 19th, and the following evening he was in Carlisle. By then,
however, the danger was long past. As the rebels assaulted Carlisle,
they were routed by Sir Christopher Dacre with the men of
Gilsland, and the rebellion collapsed. Sir Christopher received a
personal letter of thanks from the king for this, and the Dacres
emerged from the Pilgrimage with their political credit much enhanced.[43]

The feud between the Dacres and Parrs on the one hand and the
Cliffords and Sir William Musgrave on the other was the chief
reason why the loyalists had done so poorly in the north-west.
Ironically, however, the most effective resistance to the revolt had
come from the Dacres, on whose support the rebels had probably
counted. Although the Pilgrims in the north-west shared some of
the religious grievances which characterized the movement elsewhere, resentment at the lords' estate-management policies were
far more prominent among rebel grievances there. Norfolk
thought that 'the only cause of this rebellion' was 'the gressing of
[the people] so marvellously sore in time past' and the 'increasing
of lords' rents by inclosings': and under questioning he implied
that the earl of Cumberland would have done better service had he
not been so greedy to get money from his tenants.[44] Subsequently,
John Leigh of Isel, a Dacre follower, responded to a charge of
inactivity during the revolt by placing the blame for failure to
organize resistance on the king's officers—the warden, the justices
of the peace, and the sheriffs—who had issued no orders, and
without whose commands he and others could not stir.[45] Thus,

[42] *L. & P. Hen. VIII*, xii (i), nos. 411, 419, 426 (quotation), 427.
[43] *L. & P. Hen. VIII*, xii (i), nos. 411, 419, 426–7, 439, 448, 479, 500, 687.
[44] *L. & P. Hen. VIII*, xii (i), nos. 478 (quotation), 919, 1214.
[45] *L. & P. Hen. VIII*, xii (i), no. 904; James, *Society, politics and culture*, 117, 142.

although the king may have felt more certain of Cumberland's loyalty, the reappointment of the earl as warden in 1534 did nothing to strengthen royal government in the region. Dacre influence, not Clifford as the king implied, was the decisive factor in the holding of Carlisle against the rebels, and the Dacres' more traditional estate-management policies probably explain why they were better able to control their tenants during the Pilgrimage.[46]

Even before the final insurrection in the north-west, however, the king had concluded that some other means would have to be found for the rule of the marches. In late January, Henry suddenly took the wardenship of the east and middle marches into his own hands and appointed two deputy wardens to rule in his absence. Shortly afterwards the council wrote to Cumberland that the king had advanced him to the Order of the Garter for services during the rebellion, and that he was not to exercise the wardenship of the west marches.[47] Instead, the king decided to appoint Sir Thomas Wharton as deputy warden. The adverse reaction of the duke of Norfolk to this scheme for ruling the marches through 'mean men', and his assertion that the borders could only be ruled effectively by noblemen, provoked Henry VIII's famous outburst that 'we woll not be bounde, of a necessitie, to be served there with lordes'.[48] The episode and its sequel have been carefully studied by Mervyn James and Michael Bush. Bush has convincingly revised in this respect James's illuminating survey of developments in the west marches.[49] Even so, it seems worth while considering Lord Dacre's continuing influence on the government of the west marches in Henry VIII's later years.

The new arrangements for the king's council in the north and the rule of the marches cost the king a total of £2,607. 6s. 8d. a year in fees. Since Sir Thomas Wharton had no great following, his appointment was accompanied by the feeing of thirty-three gentry of the west marches; and like previous wardens he also received a number of ecclesiastical stewardships which increased his *manraed*. The military establishment in Carlisle castle and the fees of the deputy warden's four commissioners were also increased. Thus, expenditure on the west marches, at £667. 6s. 8d. per

[46] *L. & P. Hen. VIII*, xii (i), no. 667.
[47] *L. & P. Hen. VIII*, xii (i), nos. 222–5, 372–3.   [48] *SP Hen. VIII*, i. 548.
[49] James, *Society, politics and culture*, ch. 3; Bush, 'Problem of the far north', 40–63.

annum, amounted to more than a quarter of the total.[50] Norfolk was initially very critical of the scheme. He recognized that Dacre could not be considered for the wardenship because of his recent disgrace, but he thought that Wharton 'will never serve the king well as warden', particularly since the Dacres and Musgraves both disliked him.[51] Cumberland, he thought, would do better, especially if he altered his estate-management policies, but he emphasized how vital it was to secure Dacre's assistance, particularly as regards his lordship of Gilsland, because 'this border is sore weked, and specially Westmoreland'.[52] The council frankly admitted that the king 'hath been much the worse served upon the west marches by reason of controversy and variance depending between the great men that lie upon the same', and felt that in order to secure co-operation from both Dacre and Cumberland, neither should be warden. The king relented, however, to the extent that Cumberland was allowed to retain the title of lord warden, without the power and perquisites, and he and Sir Edward Musgrave were ordered to reside nearer the border.[53]

The king's new-found willingness to subsidize the government of the region also opened up new possibilities. Upon Norfolk's recommendation, the new pensioners in the west marches included a number of Dacre followers like John Leigh, Thomas Salkeld, Cuthbert Hutton, Alexander Appleby, Lancelot Lancaster, Thomas Blennerhasset, and Christopher Threlkeld (and, revealingly, very few Clifford followers). The key appointment was that of Thomas Dacre, the lord's illegitimate half-brother, who was Wharton's cousin and whose fee of 20 marks was larger than any other pensioner there. Weighing his suitability for the office of keeper of Tynedale, for which Lord Dacre had been suggested and had emphatically declined ('he had rather loose one fynger of every hande then to medle therwith'), Norfolk wrote of him in September 1537 that he could command the power of Gilsland and had been brought up in the practices of the wild borderers, but that he was too poor to serve without a substantial fee.[54] Thus, although

---

[50] *L. & P. Hen. VIII*, xii (ii), nos. 191 (45, 51), 249–50, 914; James, *Society, politics and culture*, 133.

[51] Bush, 'Problem of the far north', 46 (quotation).

[52] *L. & P. Hen. VIII*, xii (i), nos. 478 (quotation), 919, xii (ii), nos. 203, 422, 696 (2), 772.

[53] Bush, 'Problem of the far north', 47–8 (quotation, p. 47).

[54] *L. & P. Hen. VIII*, xii (ii), no. 696, xv (i), no. 219, xvii, no. 1052; *SP Hen. VIII*,

Dacre—like Cumberland—was not personally well disposed to the deputy warden, these arrangements ensured that Wharton had some access to the Dacre *manraed*. Lord William himself received some recognition of his loyalty in the Pilgrimage by appointment as a member of the revitalized king's council in the north in June 1537, and the following year he was included on the commissions of the peace for the three Yorkshire ridings. He was still not allowed to reside in the west marches, however, although he intervened from time to time to assist the deputy warden.[55] As already mentioned, Lord Dacre was thus reduced to a minor role in the wider government of the north.

Initially, the new arrangements seemed to work well. Throughout 1538 and 1539 the government received a series of glowing reports from Sir Thomas Wharton about the establishment of good rule and royal authority, the readiness of the borderers to serve the king, and the co-operation of the Scottish warden.[56] The contrast between the peaceful and effective administration of the northern borders at this time and the renewed strife in Ireland was so striking, in fact, that the king's council in Ireland proposed its own system of fee'd retainers, and hoped to attract Thomas Dacre back to Ireland as second pensioner.[57] Conditions in the immediate aftermath of a major revolt, however, were quite exceptional: even the Irish lordship was quiet in 1535–6. Moreover, a fundamental difference was the comparatively firm peace with Scotland in the later 1530s. As this collapsed, the need to secure the co-operation of the borderers in the defence of the marches once again became an urgent priority, and in this traditional task Wharton was soon found wanting.

v. 108 (quotation); G. Duckett, 'Extracts from the Cottonian MSS relating to the border service', in *C. & W.*, 3 (1878), 207–13; James, *Society, politics and culture*, 133, 142–3.

[55] *L. & P. Hen. VIII*, xii (ii), nos. 102 (3, 4), 865, xiii (i), nos. 384 (23, 24), 1074, 1269, 1519 (19, 38–40), xiii (ii), nos. 720–1, 1129, xiv (ii), no. 203; Bush, 'Problem of the far north', 53.

[56] *L. & P. Hen. VIII*, xii (ii), no. 642, xiii (i), nos. 87, 128, 757, 1067, 1074, xiii (ii), nos. 63, 115–16, 547, 720–1, 777, 1101, 1145, xiv (ii), nos. 131, 279, 702; Bush, 'Problem of the far north', 53.

[57] *L. & P. Hen. VIII*, xvi, no. 265. The proposal was rejected by the privy council on the grounds that it was really a device for perpetuating the military order of St John of Jerusalem, but no doubt the additional expense was also a consideration: *L. & P. Hen. VIII*, xvi, no. 330.

As early as 1538 Wharton had become aware of the disdain in which he was held among the marcher lords and gentry,[58] and when Anglo-Scottish relations deteriorated in 1541 he reported that the baronies of Gilsland, Burgh and others were not so well horsed as they had been.[59] In late 1542 the government was faced with a winter of hostilities and no obvious candidate for the post of warden-general, now relinquished by the king, except the sick and elderly dukes of Norfolk and Suffolk or the ailing earl of Rutland, all of whom were desperate to be home for Christmas. Norfolk therefore made the suggestion that the young 2nd earl of Cumberland be appointed warden-general and Lord Dacre given permission to reside in Cumberland to assist the deputy warden there. The king, however, chose a complete outsider, Viscount Lisle, and would only allow that Cumberland, whom he thought too inexperienced, should attend the new warden.[60] Not surprisingly, when Wharton essayed a warden-rode into the Scottish west marches on the eve of Solway Moss, many of the Westmorland gentry who expected to garrison Northumberland with the earl of Cumberland did not appear, nor did some of Dacre's followers; and his stewards of Gilsland and Burgh, Thomas Dacre and John Leigh, brought only forty men.[61] The failure of this raid, however, only encouraged the Scots in their belief that the English west marches were unusually weak and divided, and this led directly to the rout of Solway Moss. In fact, the prospect of invasion by a powerful Scottish army concentrated minds and prompted a much more impressive turn-out by the Dacre affinity, Gilsland, and Burgh. Subsequently, Wharton took most of the credit for Solway Moss. His report of the battle made little mention of the activities of Dacre and Leigh, and was thought to be untrue. Dacre had to defend himself on charges that he and other borderers had given poor service (which was true of the preceding raid), but he wrote pointedly of the number of prisoners taken by his company. It is impossible to deny Wharton's courage and coolness in the face of the much larger Scottish army, and his ennoblement and pro-

---

[58] *L. & P. Hen. VIII*, xiii (i), nos. 115, 309, xiv (i), no. 50.

[59] *L. & P. Hen. VIII*, xv, no. 709, xvi, no. 1212.

[60] *L. & P. Hen. VIII*, xvii, nos. 1037, 1048, 1064; Bush, 'Problem of the far north', 51–2.

[61] *L. & P. Hen. VIII*, xvii, nos. 1119, 1121; Bain (ed.), *Hamilton papers*, i, p. lxxx.

motion as lord warden in recognition of his services was well earned.[62]

In practice, however, the events surrounding Solway Moss did nothing to ease tensions in the north-west. A kind of political stalemate ensued. Wharton's sensational stroke of luck confirmed the king's confidence in him as warden, just as his refusal to share the credit exacerbated tensions with the Dacre affinity on whose military support he depended. In June 1543 his proposal that the king acquire Lord Dacre's three baronies of Burgh, Gilsland, and Greystoke 'by exchayng or otherwisse', so that these lordships and their castles would be under the warden's control, was effectively an admission of failure.[63] In the years following, Wharton continued to complain about the lack of service, the decay of horsemen, the disobedience of Dacre's officers, and their disdain of Wharton, but to no avail.[64] In 1544, when the king required horsemen from the marches for service in France, only 200 could with great difficulty be scraped up from the west marches: Wharton's musters revealed that only 248 were available, of which Burgh could supply 67 and Gilsland a paltry 29. And to defend the west marches in their absence, 100 Gaelic kerne had to be deployed from Ireland.[65] Wharton reported in 1545 that the power of the west march was a mere 1,500 men, of whom only 200 were horsemen.[66] Even so, the king's lieutenant, the earl of Hertford, thought that the east and middle marches were far weaker than the west. For much of the 1540s, in fact, the king was forced to maintain a paid garrison of between 2,000 and 3,300 men on the borders. Thus, overall, the price which the king paid for excluding Lord Dacre from authority in the west marches was an enormous increase in administrative and military costs, coupled with a disastrous collapse in military preparedness. In the circumstances, it is hardly surprising that, after the death of Henry VIII, Protector Somerset took an early opportunity to rehabilitate Lord Dacre: in April 1549

[62] *L. & P. Hen. VIII*, xvii, nos. 1121, 1128, 1142, 1163, 1175, 1185, xviii (i), nos. 88, 592; Bain (ed.), *Hamilton papers*, i, pp. lxxxiii–xciii, xcvii–viii, nos. 240, 247, 252, 289, 393; James, *Society, politics and culture*, 125–6.

[63] *SP Hen. VIII*, v. 311–14.

[64] *L. & P. Hen. VIII*, xviii (ii), no. 173, xix (i), nos. 122, 331, 562, 621, xx (ii), no. 676; Bain (ed.), *Hamilton papers*, ii, nos. 30 (1), 170, 212; James, *Society, politics and culture*, 134–5; Bush, 'Problem of the far north', 53–5.

[65] *L. & P. Hen. VIII*, xix (i), nos. 227, 331, 562, 575.

[66] *L. & P. Hen. VIII*, xix (i), no. 575, xx (ii), no. 685; Bush, 'Problem of the far north', 55, 60.

Lord Wharton was dismissed and Dacre appointed warden in his place.[67]

The arrangements for the rule of the west marches after 1534, though very different from those for the government of Ireland, thus turned out to be no more successful. In both regions, the crown's strategy was an *ad hoc* response to an unexpected political crisis, not a preconceived policy of reducing noble power in favour of bureaucratic institutions. In retrospect of course, the arrangements for the government of Ireland appeared to mark a definitive change from the situation obtaining before the 1534 rebellion, in a way which was not the case in the far north. The government's reaction to the Kildare rebellion saw the razing to the ground of the traditional power structures in many parts of the lordship. In consequence, new structures had to be built on new foundations. By contrast, the changes in the far north, especially the system of gentlemen-pensioners, were broadly designed to shore up and adapt an existing structure at a time when its chief architect was unavailable for service. Thus when, after Henry VIII's death, the two lords were restored to favour, Lord Dacre effectively recovered command of a fortress—sadly neglected, certainly, and with its military foundations severely undermined—which was fundamentally unchanged from that from which he had been evicted fifteen years earlier. By contrast, the new earl of Kildare had to work with power structures which were quite different from those erected by his great-grandfather and grandfather a half-century before, and where there were now powerful vested interests against the restoration of the old order. He faced an uphill, and ultimately only partially successful, struggle even to recover the family estates, and he never achieved his ambition of becoming governor of Ireland.[68]

[67] Bush, 'Problem of the far north', 55; id., *Government policy of Protector Somerset*, 129, 141–2; James, *Society, politics and culture*, 134–5.

[68] On the career of the 11th earl, see now the important and illuminating study by Vincent Carey, 'Local elites and central authority: Gerald XI earl of Kildare and Tudor rule in Ireland, 1547–1586', Ph.D. thesis, State University of New York at Stony Brook, 1991.

❖

Conclusion
Tudor government and the transformation of
the Tudor state

THIS comparative study has been a good deal more difficult to write up than to research. For me, the fascination of the project lay chiefly in discovering how far the characteristics and problems of a marcher society in Ireland, on which I had worked extensively, were replicated in another borderland which is more normally compared with lowland England. At the same time, however, the study addresses an aspect of Tudor government which is usually divided between two different groups of historians and treated as two separate subjects. This has meant that, in historiographical terms, the project has been very demanding. The argument developed here is that this traditional division between England and Ireland is in many ways arbitrary, but the implications of these findings for English and Irish historiography need to be addressed separately, because the assumptions and methodology of historians working in the two fields are quite different.

The significance for Irish historiography of this comparative study is more briefly explained. In studying the lordship's development, historians have traditionally adopted a perspective which favours a 'vertical' approach to the subject. That is, they study change over time, measuring how the lordship's development during one period compares with the preceding or following phases of its history and, more generally, with the broad sweep of Irish history down to the present. A recent, overtly ideological, restatement of this approach, which advocated 'present-centred' history, has attempted to appropriate the *Gaedhil* and *Gaill* of sixteenth-century Ireland for modern Ireland's nationalist and republican tradition, but this is certainly an extreme position.[1] Admittedly,

---

[1] Bradshaw, 'Nationalism and historical scholarship', *passim*.

Irish historians have been reluctant to investigate the Tudor contribution to the making of Northern Ireland, and they have preferred a separate Irish focus for their writings over an archipelagic one, but they have generally been much more candid about the relationship between the past and Ireland's divided present. An alternative 'horizontal' frame of comparison which is frequently employed focuses on interaction with Gaelic Ireland, but this perspective too incorporates strong 'vertical' strands which are suggested by later developments, in particular the later assimilation of English and Gaelic society in Ireland after 1534.[2] By contrast, perspectives which extend outside the island of Ireland have been much less popular. For the early modern period, Professor David Quinn tentatively outlined an 'Atlantic world' perspective, which has been enthusiastically advanced by Professor Nicholas Canny.[3] Ireland's position in the developing European state system also needs more extended consideration. Yet the most obvious *lacuna* in terms of contemporary, 'horizontal' perspectives is surely one which relates politics and society in the lordship to the rest of the English state.

The argument elaborated here is a very simple one. The political community of the English Pale was English, as that term was generally understood under the early Tudors: as such, it also needs to be studied in conjunction with English communities in other border regions, and by historians trained in English history. The study also develops an alternative 'vertical' perspective which aims to relate developments in Ireland to the question of state formation throughout the British Isles. As we shall see, the pattern of the lordship's closer integration into the emerging Tudor state conditioned the nature and circumstances of Ireland's position within the later United Kingdom, and it continues to do so in Northern Ireland. Thus, viewed in its own terms, the historiographical ap-

---

[2] For a discussion of this distinction between 'horizontal' and 'vertical' perspectives with regard to Tudor–Stuart religious history, see Patrick Collinson, 'Towards a broader understanding of the early dissenting tradition', in id., *Godly people: essays on English Protestantism and Puritanism* (London, 1983), 527–62.

[3] See esp. D. B. Quinn, 'Ireland and sixteenth century European expansion', in *Historical Studies*, 1 (1958), 20–32; N. P. Canny, 'The ideology of English colonization: from Ireland to America', in *William and Mary Quarterly*, 3rd ser. 30 (1973), 575–98; id., *Kingdom and colony: Ireland in the Atlantic world, 1560–1800* (Baltimore, 1988). For a critique of this approach, see Hiram Morgan, 'Mid-Atlantic blues', in *Irish Review*, 11 (1991), 50–5.

proach underpinning the argument here is actually much more consonant with some interpretations of the English 'national myth' than with a 'revisionist' approach, even though historians whose starting-point is Ireland as a separate unit of study might wish to argue the contrary. The choice of perspective is in fact a much more fundamental issue than might appear from the rather minimal attention it has so far received in the Revisionist Debate in Irish historiography. Irish 'revisionists' might claim to debunk nationalist myths, but their choice of perspective can never be neutral. And there are surely other legitimate differences between English and Irish historians extending, for instance, to the way in which an Englishman and a British subject, as opposed to an Irishman and citizen of the Irish Republic, might empathize with a key figure in both English and Irish history like the earl of Kildare. Hiberno-centric presentations of the earl of Kildare as an essentially Irish figure, transcending the rival traditions of *Gaedhil* and *Gaill*, offer a fascinating commentary on the political ideas and aspirations of a more modern age, but they run counter to the most basic understanding of Tudor politics. The early Tudors were no more likely to appoint an Irishman as governor of Ireland than a Frenchman as governor of Calais. Thus, by marginalizing Kildare's English identity, traditional accounts obscure the fundamentals of English policy towards Ireland. Despite claims to the contrary, 'background and training' are important.[4]

None the less, the arguments developed here cut across much that has been written about medieval and early modern Ireland, and in conclusion it seems worth while to try to elaborate their implications for traditional 'vertical' perspectives on the making of modern Ireland. Irish specialists would readily accept that politics, society, and government in the medieval lordship of Ireland bore many striking resemblances to developments in England. This is hardly surprising since English institutions had been introduced to Ireland as part and parcel of English medieval settlement there, and afterwards much of crown policy was aimed at preserving the English character of the lordship. Despite these similarities, however, the burden of much historical writing on the late medieval lordship has been to suggest that different conditions in English Ireland, interaction and assimilation with Gaelic Ireland, and the

---

[4] Cf. Bradshaw, 'Nationalism and historical scholarship', 332–4.

slackening of ties with England all contributed to the growth of substantial differences between the English of Ireland and the English of England. Allegedly, the English of Ireland soon became 'a middle nation', so that their political ideas and loyalties were already intrinsically different from the English of England even before the Tudor phase of English conquest and settlement which began in 1534. As we have seen, moreover, the very different historiographical agenda of English historians seemed to lend credence to these arguments. Traditional surveys of nation and state in England had comparatively little to say about regionalism, marcher society, and the problems of cultural assimilation.

Even so, there is a certain circularity about these arguments based on contrasts, since the comparisons with conditions in England are generally based, not on primary sources, but on syntheses written by English historians; and as we have seen, English specialists traditionally exclude Ireland from their surveys and are equally unfamiliar with its source material. Accordingly, this study has attempted to test the general validity of these arguments by undertaking a more rigorous comparison over a range of themes between two regions and two leading magnates of the early-Tudor state, both of them drawn from the borderlands. Overall, Dacre and Kildare appear as essentially similar figures, whose careers bore striking resemblances. Both profited from their long occupation of sensitive provincial offices of a quasi-military nature to build up strong regional connexions based on consolidated landholdings, a loyal and martial tenantry, and estate-management policies which were geared chiefly to considerations of defence. Similarly, the influence of the border ensured that features which both contemporary English officials in Ireland and also modern Irish historians have regarded as peculiar to Gaelic or 'gaelicized' Ireland—clans and captaincies, joint responsibility and co-ownership of land, partible inheritance, and transhumance—were also characteristic, to a greater or lesser degree, of marcher society in the far north. In many ways, too, modern studies point to the existence of similar features in the marcher society of early-Tudor Wales.[5] Thus the conflicting pressures exerted on the two magnates by, on the one hand, the military exigencies of the border and

---

[5] See esp. Pugh (ed.) *Glamorgan County History*, iii, chs. 4–6, 11; Pugh, *Marcher lordships of south Wales, passim*; Williams, *Recovery, reorientation and Reformation*, pt. 1.

of marcher society and, on the other hand, by the demands of 'civil society' and the Tudor court led in both regions to the same kinds of clashes and tensions between crown, magnate, and community, which culminated in the crisis of 1534.

These comparisons are not of course intended to suggest that the cultures of Gaelic clans and northern surnames were almost identical, or that the king of Scots was really some superior Gaelic chief whose activities on the border presented Lord Dacre with problems which were simply on a larger scale than those faced by Kildare in Ireland. Clearly there were significant differences between the two regions. Along the western frontier of the Tudor state, the sharper contrasts between English and Gaelic culture imparted a somewhat different character to the phenomenon of cultural assimilation. And along the northern frontier Scottish kings were both more capable of upholding their claims to disputed territory, so that the actual border line was more stable, and also more able to control their own subjects, so that there was usually a single figure with whom the English warden could negotiate. Overall, however, the nature of the English administrative system and its weaknesses outside lowland England meant that the rule of the two borderlands presented very similar problems to the Tudor government. The departures from 'English civility' which Tudor administrators detected in marcher society also induced similar feelings of revulsion in the official mind and predisposed them to follow similar policies. Thus the problems presented by overmighty subjects, bastard feudalism, and marcher society in Ireland would not have appeared so overwhelming and unique to early-Tudor kings and officials as to preclude acceptance of English Ireland as another, somewhat disorderly, manifestation of English regional society. In addition to contemporary perceptions, moreover, a close comparative analysis of politics and society in English Ireland and the far north discloses a whole series of previously unsuspected parallels and similarities. These are such as to reduce very substantially the alleged differences between lordship and kingdom.

In view of the character of the recent Revisionist Debate, the conclusions to be drawn from this comparative study concerning Anglo-Irish relations and the growth of an Irish sense of identity need to be very carefully phrased. First, it is not denied that the descendants of the medieval Englishry eventually became es-

tranged from the crown and came to make common cause with the
Gaelic peoples of Ireland and to view themselves as an Irish nation. In arguing for some reconsideration by historians of these
traditional views about the building of a shared sense of Irish
national identity, my purpose is rather to question the causes and
timing of these changes, and their impact on Tudor politics. Undoubtedly, the lordship's unique position on the margins of the
English polity had led to the development of a shared sense of
identity among the political community of early-Tudor Ireland.
This sense of identity distinguished the Englishry of Ireland from
other communities in mainland England, as well as from the
Gaelic Irish. This study would, however, suggest that under the
early Tudors the distinguishing features of the English of Ireland
were not qualitatively different from those of other English regional communities, particularly of the far north: in other words,
these are regional differences within the one English nation and
emerging nation-state, not differences between two nations, and
they were perceived by contemporaries as such. Accordingly,
early-Tudor policy towards the lordship was broadly of a piece
with policy towards other peripheral regions, and it expected and
received a similar response from the political community there.
These regional differences were, however, important for the future. After 1534, and particularly after 1547, under the impact of
discriminatory policies pursued by the crown in connection with
the Tudor expansion into Gaelic Ireland, and then the relative
failure of the Tudor Reformation there, these differences sharpened. Tudor perceptions of the nature of the problem in Ireland
also began to change, although the reasons for this change also
need to be set within a Tudor context. Briefly, the successful
incorporation and assimilation of Wales and the impact of better
relations with Scotland on the far north (both surveyed below)
meant that Irish problems increasingly stood out. Eventually,
official acceptance of the English identity of the 'Old English'
was undermined, in part because Tudor perceptions of English
nationality narrowed and became more closely defined.[6] In the
north, tensions between crown and community exploded into
major rebellion on at least four occasions between 1489 and 1570,

[6] Ellis, 'Crown, community and government', *passim*; Guy, *Tudor England*, ch.
13.

and there were a number of other minor outbreaks; but these troubles were eventually contained. In Ireland, similar troubles eventually got out of hand. Overall, therefore, these findings suggest that in tracing the long-term process by which the descendants of Ireland's medieval Gaelic and English peoples developed a shared Irish sense of nationality, in opposition to English identity, rather more weight needs to be given to developments from *c*.1550 onwards and rather less to the medieval background.

Within a Tudor context, the obvious question arising from a comparative survey of two marcher lords and the borderlands which they ruled is how representative these magnates were; and how far the borderlands may be grouped together in this way so as to analyse the problems of Tudor government in terms of centre and periphery. Although the north and English Ireland were perhaps individually less important, collectively the borderlands (including the marches and principality of Wales) comprised over half the early-Tudor state. There is of course a well-known but controversial sociological study which analyses the development of the British Isles in these terms;[7] but Tudor specialists have hitherto inclined to regard the problems and characteristics of each particular borderland as unique to that region, believing that they had little in common. In many ways, this was certainly the case. The Celtic cultures of Wales and Ireland, for instance, had no counterpart in the north and also differed from each other in important respects. The Welsh marches were no longer an international frontier between independent nations, and their military significance was much reduced. Ireland was geographically separate from the English mainland, as was Calais, which, however, was little more than a military outpost. Thus each of these regions undoubtedly had particular features which set it apart from the other Tudor dominions and helped to shape its regional character.

Viewed in administrative terms, however, and in particular the range of problems which the borderlands presented to royal control, this study suggests that there is much to be said in favour of a collective approach. The borderlands were *ipso facto* distant from the centre of power, and they differed topographically from the

[7] Michael Hechter, *Internal colonialism: the Celtic fringe in British national development, 1536–1966* (London, 1975).

'core region'. They were regions wich contained a sizeable proportion of upland or boggy lowland, with poorer soils, and they
had a harsher climate than central and southern England. In consequence, the different patterns of land utilization in these areas,
in particular the emphasis on pasture farming, encouraged the
development of different structures of society there, with more
dispersed patterns of settlement and fewer towns. Necessarily,
therefore, the hold of the 'centre' on these regions was much
weaker. The problems of central control were also exacerbated by
particular deficiencies in the structure of English administration
itself. Quite simply, royal government was too rigid and centralized for the effective administration of these outlying areas. It was
admirably suited to the government of the heavily manorialized
regions of lowland England, with their small towns and nucleated
villages clustered around the parish church and manor house. But
the extension of English law and administration to these more
recent additions to the king's dominions was much less successful.
For instance, as the duties of the traditional English commissions
of the peace were extended under the Tudors, counties like
Cumberland and Kildare scarcely had the numbers of substantial
and resident county gentry needed for their effective operation.
The same difficulties recurred in Scotland after the introduction of
English-style JPs in 1609: their work was seriously hampered by
the small numbers of the justices and by the turbulence of Scottish
society.[8] Likewise, the work of other Tudor officials and resort to
the central courts was inhibited by the difficulties and dangers of
travel in the marches. Overall, then, traditional analyses of Tudor
government which purport to judge its effectiveness chiefly by the
control it exercised over lowland England seem rather like trying
to weigh the fortunes of the Conservative Party in a modern British
General Election by how many seats it wins across the south. The
real test of Tudor government was its ability to uphold law and
order in the borderlands.

   In the face of the problems posed by the marches, successive
English kings groped towards some kind of response which combined the effective devolution of authority with the retention of
overall central control. In Wales the marcher lords continued to

---

   [8] J. Irvine Smith, 'The transition to the modern law 1532–1660', in *An introduction to Scottish legal history*, The Stair Society, 20 (Edinburgh, 1958), 37–41.

exercise regalian rights within their lordships for 250 years after the original military justification for these institutions had disappeared; and the palatine liberties of Ireland and the north answered a similar need. The north had special wardens of the marches, and from the late fifteenth century another administrative tier was added there and in Wales, in the form of special regional councils to co-ordinate the government of the region. In Ireland the response was slightly different again: the maintenance of a complete but dependent administration, modelled on that for England, under the control of a viceroy. And in each region the weakness of royal government and the more disturbed conditions fostered the growth of a powerful, territorial nobility. Whether formally empowered to do so or not, the magnates generally exerted themselves to strengthen the rule of the marches through an extended system of seigneurial justice and private arbitration, but their distinctly military outlook could, in particular circumstances, also seem quite threatening to royal authority.

Nevertheless such combinations of centralized and devolved power and of royal and seigneurial authority could never hope to function as effectively as the developed system of English administration operating in the more favourable political environment of lowland England. The levels of public order and central control attainable in the borderlands would always fall short of what was possible in the south-east. And in these circumstances the Tudors were predisposed to a particular course of action by two further predilections of the official mind. From the reign of King Edward I at least, there was an influential body of opinion which held that the lands and dominions of the English crown ought to be governed by one law and system of administration. This attitude had, for instance, manifested itself in Edward's so-called Statute of Rhuddlan of 1284, by which aspects of English law and administration had been introduced for the government of post-conquest Wales; also by that king's refusal to accept the validity of Irish law; and by Edward III's ordinance of 1331 enjoining that 'una et eadem lex' should be in force as well among the Irish as among the English of Ireland.[9]

The desire for uniformity of law and administration may have been a particularly English one, but the second *idée fixe* of English

---

[9] Davies, *Age of conquest*, 368–70; Frame, *Colonial Ireland*, 106–10.

officials drew more on wider European habits of mind, and worked to ensure that the norms and values of the Tudor state should be chiefly those of lowland England. In part this was simply a reflection of the influence of the court and capital over the provinces: but it also reflected the idea that civilization resided chiefly in towns, or at least in the peaceful tenant villages of the arable lowlands rather than in the more turbulent communities of the wooded or pastoral uplands and marches. Thus in practice notions of 'English civility' reflected the norms and values of lowland England, even though, strictly, the indigenous population of Northumberland was no less English, and probably more so, than that of Worcestershire. In all, the interaction of these three sets of ideas—that the borderlands were at once uncivilized, unruly, and not fully English in their administrative structures—shaped both official perceptions of the nature of the problem, and also the direction of the government's response.

Tudor policy towards the marches went through two distinct phases, which were sharply divided by the crisis of 1534 and its aftermath. Initially, Henry VII had been much more concerned with the security of the new Tudor regime and the restoration of royal authority in lowland England than with the good rule of the marches. The financial and military resources available for border defence were deliberately cut back, partly to save money, but also to ensure that there would be no recurrence of 'overmighty subjects' like Richard, duke of York, and Richard Neville, earl of Salisbury, who could challenge the king's authority through their quasi-military offices and private armies in the borderlands. The rule of the marches through lesser nobles like Dacre and Kildare thus reflected the continuing early-Tudor appreciation of the dangers inherent in bolstering the power and authority of a great magnate. Instead, the king reduced the resources available to the deputy or warden to the point where they barely sufficed for the task in hand, and allowed him no opportunity for political interventions elsewhere.

The broad lines of this policy were continued after the accession of Henry VIII. By then, however, both nobles had exploited their extended occupation of key border offices to build up their local connexion and influence, so that they were less dependent on royal support. The new king, moreover, was generally less suspicious than his father of great accumulations of power and authority in the hands of the nobility, and he was less interested in exercising a close supervision of the borders. For over a decade, therefore, the rule of the marches continued to be entrusted to Dacre and Kildare with minimal supervision. On the other hand, when Henry VIII did finally stir himself, the demands which he made of his border officials were a good deal less realistic. He seems to have assumed, for instance, that individual magnates were expendable and that these offices could be exercised equally well by other nobles simply by issuing them with the king's commission. At times he refused to acknowledge the simple fact that the effective exercise of these offices on the reduced terms now offered was heavily dependent on a strong local following based on extensive landed possessions in the region. The chief recommendation of border magnates like Dacre and Kildare was that they could provide tolerably effective government cheaply, and so save the king the cost of a garrison. The lowland gentry might grumble about their dubious followers, cross-border alliances, and tolerance of border lawlessness, but 'good governance' and 'indifferent justice' cost money. Only in the 1530s, as memories of civil war faded and dangers of a different sort threatened, did Henry VIII decide that this was a price worth paying.

Overall, therefore, early-Tudor policy towards the borderlands was a minimalist one. Henry VII concentrated on dynastic security and the restoration of royal authority in lowland England; and under Henry VIII priority was given, until the 1530s, to the pursuit of an aggressive foreign policy which aimed at the recovery of Henry V's continental empire. Thus a major theme of early-Tudor government which requires far more attention from historians than it presently receives is the adverse impact of this strategy on the borderlands. Long periods of neglect were interspersed with sporadic attempts to adapt, at minimal cost, a centralized administrative system geared to lowland England for the government of outlying regions which had very different social structures. The result was more turbulent conditions, more consolidated patterns of landholding, strong landlord–tenant ties, and pronounced regional loyalties.

This indeed was the downside of Tudor policy as viewed from Westminster. It created a political environment which favoured the maintenance of seigneurial power at the expense of royal authority. Regional magnates like Kildare and Dacre prospered because, through their occupation of key offices in the borders, they could bridge the gap between the claims of royal government in the region and the realities of power there. They built up their influence so that Henry VIII came to depend heavily on their services and found it difficult to rule the borders without their support. In each case, the more disturbed conditions accentuated the importance of resident lordship, of the lord's *manraed*, and of the loyalty of his tenantry, and it encouraged the maintenance of traditional castles and peles rather than the building of country houses. Fundamentally, the relationship between crown and magnate was a symbiotic one. This indeed is the finding of much recent work on the nobility in England, but border conditions highlighted even more strikingly the reciprocal nature of the relationship. And increasingly, Henry VIII found quite irksome these restraints on the extension of royal authority. The political careers of Dacre and Kildare thus illustrate quite vividly the strains and tensions between the crown, the nobles, and the local communities generated by early-Tudor policy.

These findings concerning two of the most powerful and influential of the early-Tudor magnates are also very relevant to the debate about the changing role of the nobility in the Tudor state. The debate has focused on the relative power of the nobility *vis-à-vis* the crown, and the gradual transformation of the peerage through the decline of the ancient territorial magnates and the emergence of a Tudor service nobility. Unfortunately, the impact of much recent writing on the subject has been to stifle rather than to resolve an important and fruitful debate; and the full dimensions of the problem have also been obscured by the nationalist standpoint from which it has been approached.[10] By excluding from consideration the Irish peerage and the Anglo-Gaelic marches in Ireland, English specialists have created the impression that border barons like Lord Dacre were a feudal anachronism. Allegedly, Tudor nobles were typically rentier landowners, rather than warlords, who divided their time between supervising local government from their country houses and estates and frequent attendance at court or in parliament. In turn Irish specialists have

[10] The recent narrowing of perspectives on the nobility is epitomized by the editor's introduction to the latest collection of essays to appear on nobles in Tudor England (misleadingly titled, *The Tudor nobility* (ed. George Bernard; Manchester, 1992).

felt the need to explain why magnates like the Elizabethan earl of Desmond were unable to transform themselves into a service nobility of the kind which was increasingly typical of southern England.[11]

Dacre and Kildare, however, are examples of lesser nobles who were built up, with the active support of the early Tudors, into great territorial magnates. Necessarily, they played a major role in local defence as—until 1603 and the dismantling of the Tudor frontiers—did all nobles who had accumulations of marchland. And, in the main, the methods by which Dacre and Kildare performed these duties were quite traditional. Although they were perhaps the most powerful examples in the 1520s, they were otherwise typical of a class of Tudor marcher lord of which at different times the Butlers, the Nevilles, and the Percies were also prominent examples. In the marches, the more disturbed conditions reduced the value of money rents and enhanced the importance of service. And, necessarily, the ambitions and lifestyle of a noble whose income derived in large measure from holdings of marchland would be rather different from his southern English counterpart. Even an earl of Northumberland had to supervise the defence of his lordship. He needed to raise an army, and his estates were organized for that purpose. Thus it was not just a case of the crown curbing overmighty subjects and creating a new service nobility as the need and opportunity arose. The character of noble power was closely linked to the advance of 'civil society' and the persistence of the borderlands. The Tudor nobility should be viewed as a continuum, with marcher lords like Dacre or Kildare towards one end of the spectrum and a 'new noble' like Thomas, Lord Audley of Walden, at the other. The crown needed both, because Tudor government and society differed considerably from region to region.

It would be a mistake to exaggerate the differences between the territorial magnates of the borders and the new service nobility. Broadly, however, marcher lords had less interest in influencing policy-making at the centre; and an office in the royal household, entailing regular attendance at court, would have been a distinct liability. Office in their own 'country', however, was highly prized

---

[11] Cf. Ciaran Brady, 'Faction and the origins of the Desmond rebellion of 1579', in *IHS* 22 (1980–1), 289–312; Margaret MacCurtain, 'The fall of the house of Desmond', in *Kerry Archaeological Society Journal*, 8 (1975), 28–44.

for the local authority, influence, and *manraed* it conferred, rather
less so for the fees and perquisites which accompanied it. Indeed,
it is striking that Dacre and Kildare were both prepared to undertake provincial governorships entailing very heavy responsibilities
in return for salaries which were far less than those of their
Lancastrian predecessors. In part this eagerness to serve stemmed
from a juridical division between lordship of land and of men,
which indeed was a weakness of the English administrative system
in the borderlands. Territorial magnates had compact holdings of
land, but seigneurial authority over tenants, which was of heightened importance in the marches, was (in theory, at least) heavily
circumscribed by royal authority over subjects. In practice, until
1536 regalian rights were in many parts 'delegated' on a semi-
permanent basis to feudal magnates by the establishment of
liberties and palatinates; but elsewhere the magnates sought to
strengthen their tenurial lordship in their own countries by securing those particular offices which conferred royal authority over
the king's subjects. By contrast, nobles whose patrimony was
smaller and more scattered, and who had no pressing need to reside
on marchlands, accumulated offices and fees at court or in the
provinces as the opportunity arose. They needed to supplement
their more modest landed endowments. Thus, whereas the 5th earl
of Northumberland was only really interested in the wardenship of
the east and middle marches, and then on terms of his own choos-
ing, a new noble like Lord Darcy discharged a range of offices at
court, abroad, and throughout the north. He long resented his
removal from the wardenship of the east marches in 1511, but his
need for money made him a lot more biddable, from the crown's
point of view, than a long-established territorial magnate.[12]

In the case of the most powerful marcher lords, appointment to
high provincial office might entail regular trips to court, but it is
noticeable how much less frequently the northern nobility as a
whole attended the great state occasions of Henry VIII's reign
than their southern counterparts.[13] Some marcher lords, like
Henry VII's earl of Ormond or the 4th earl of Shrewsbury, might
choose to neglect their border estates in the hope of richer rewards

---

[12] For Darcy, see Miller, *Henry VIII and the English nobility, passim*; Gibbs *et al.*
(eds.), *Complete peerage*, iv. 73–4.
[13] This point is derived from the evidence assembled in Miller, *Henry VIII and
the English nobility*, esp. chs. 2–4.

at court.[14] Among the lesser nobility, however, there was much less reason to come to court. In fact, Robert, 5th Lord Ogle, opted to ignore the court altogether. It was unusual for Lord Ogle even to receive a writ of summons to parliament, let alone attend, and he never attended coronations or other great state occasions. Instead, he served the king all his life on the borders. In 1545, he made his will before invading Scotland, and he died soon after of wounds sustained in battle.[15] In the early-Tudor period, almost all the Irish peers were military men of this sort. From the Welsh marches, however, the Tudor court was much more accessible, and the absence of a military frontier in Wales meant that there was not quite the same premium there on resident lordship. Even so, Edward IV's Lord Herbert, Henry VII's Rhys ap Thomas (though not a peer), and under Henry VIII Henry Somerset, 2nd earl of Worcester, and Edward Grey, Lord Powis, seem to fall into this category of marcher lord.[16]

Thus taking the Tudor nobility as a whole, the evidence concerning the border magnates perhaps suggests that the debate about the relative power of the nobles needs to be conducted in rather different terms. In this context, there was a basic difference even among the great regional magnates—between the way in which Lord Dacre and, for instance, the earl of Shrewsbury wielded and consolidated their power, despite the intermarriage between the two families and the roughly similar level of their incomes. Shrewsbury had extensive possessions in the Anglo-Gaelic marches, where he was lord of the liberty of Wexford and earl of Waterford. These indeed offered considerable opportunities for the earl to build up his power as a marcher lord, but he showed no desire to emulate the Irish career of the 1st earl. In fact, his estates were so neglected that the king eventually confiscated them on the grounds of his perpetual absence.[17] Income alone, moreover, is a very crude indicator of the relative status and power of individual Tudor nobles. It tells us nothing about the strategic importance of their estates, and not much more about their extent.

[14] For Ormond, see above, pp. 42–3, 109; Bernard (ed.), *Tudor nobility*, 79, 153, 166. For Shrewsbury, see below.
[15] PRO, C 142/75, no. 16; Miller, *Henry VIII and the English nobility*, 10, 44, 99, 126, 159; Robson, *English highland clans*, 191–2.
[16] See Robinson, 'Patronage and hospitality in early Tudor Wales', 20–36.
[17] *Complete peerage*, xi. 706–9, xii. 419; Bernard, *Power of the early Tudor nobility*, 51, 140.

A border magnate was far more concerned about the size of his *manraed* than the level of his rents, and much more likely to spend his money on castles and peles. Nobles like Dacre and Kildare were militarily more powerful and had more extensive possessions than might appear simply from adding up their landed rents. In the circumstances, then, it is hardly surprising that historians' tables of noble income are dominated by southerners, with most northerners in the second division (and nobles in Ireland mostly disqualified for not having enough estates on the mainland). Yet the fact that, even on this basis, Dacre and Kildare should still have reached the Tudor top ten under Henry VIII, should prompt a fairly radical reappraisal of present assumptions concerning the nobility.

The 1530s saw the fall of a number of long-established regional magnates, and, in terms of numbers and political influence, this may well have tipped the balance in favour of a service nobility. In the following decade, however, 'surrender and regrant' in Ireland and later creations there added to the number of 'old-style', territorial magnates. The Dacres and Percies remained a force in the far north until 1570, and a recent study of the 11th earl of Kildare has highlighted the earl's crucial role in the defence of the Pale under Elizabeth.[18] By then, however, the growing acceptance in official circles of the lowland English model of a service nobility as the one true expression of aristocratic values was placing increasing strains on the crown's relations with the border magnates, who could not hope to answer the revised expectations of the state.[19] In continental Europe, a territorial nobility charged with the military defence of their lordships was still normal in the sixteenth century.[20] And throughout the British Isles, too, this remained a basic duty of the nobility until the dismantling of the frontiers after 1603. English historians have traditionally contrasted this continental pattern of territorial magnate with their own Tudor service nobility, but it should be noted that in Tudor times this emasculated breed of aristocrat was seldom sighted much outside lowland England.

[18] Carey, 'Local elites'.
[19] See, for instance, Canny, *Elizabethan conquest of Ireland*, esp. ch. 5.
[20] A useful survey which emphasizes the growing power of the European nobility in the 16th cent. is Richard Mackenney, *Sixteenth century Europe: expansion and conflict* (London, 1993), ch. 1.

The immediate circumstances which moved Henry VIII to break so radically with the policies inherited from his father were of course the crisis created by the Reformation and the royal divorce. The king's suspicions about the loyalty of his nobles prompted him to mount a pre-emptive strike against the two magnates who were, potentially at least, most capable of mounting a major military challenge to his policies. And the fall of Dacre and Kildare, and the major rebellions which ensued in the two regions, forced the king into a radical reorganization of Tudor government in the borderlands. The result of this reorganization was a considerable extension of royal authority and central control at the expense of seigneurial power. It involved the remodelling of the king's councils in Ireland, the north, and Wales; the destruction of the palatinates and marcher lordships, and the extension to these regions of standard English structures of local government; a reduction in the status and powers of the leading border officials; and a significant but very costly extension in the numbers of royal officials or pensioners in these regions.

By contrast with the earlier phase of Tudor policy, the changes which inaugurated this second phase have been closely studied by historians. They have been portrayed by Sir Geoffrey Elton, for instance, as a provincial extension of the Tudor revolution in government which, he claims, transformed the king's medieval dominions into a bureaucratic nation-state.[21] Undoubtedly, it makes good sense to view the reorganization in this way as part and parcel of change at the centre. Yet to focus too closely on a Westminster-centred view of events is perhaps to miss some of the character of the transformation of the Tudor state which occurred at this time. The watershed which the 1530s marked in relation to Tudor government was even more apparent in relation to the wider problem of the borderlands. The administrative changes of the mid-1530s considerably altered the traditional balance between centre and periphery. The 1536 Welsh 'act of union' led to the gradual extension to Wales of English norms and values, and in parts of the north too more intensive government by a remodelled king's council brought about a gradual extension of 'civil society' at the expense of the 'lineage society' of the marches.[22] Thus in

---

[21] See esp. his *Reform and Reformation*, ch. 9.
[22] Cf. James, *Family, lineage and civil society, passim*.

some regions the renewed emphasis on administrative uniformity and bureaucratic structures—where they were properly funded—did achieve results.

In the far north and Ireland, however, the analysis presented here of the transition from the early-Tudor phase of aristocratic delegation to a more centralized, interventionist style of government suggests that in both regions the new order had considerable shortcomings. The survival there of an international and military frontier posed an additional, more basic, problem than that presented by geographical remoteness alone, one which was not susceptible to the same bureaucratic solution. Quite simply, military considerations necessitated a devolution of power, and whether the preferred response were a great magnate, a chain of garrisons, a system of fee'd retainers supporting a gentleman-warden, or a combination of all three, each of the alternatives had associated disadvantages for royal government.

Overall, therefore, the reorganization of government in the mid-1530s failed to address the basic problem in the far north and Ireland, which indeed was insoluble by traditional Tudor methods. The reduction of the great magnates who had ruled the borders with royal support simply reduced the capacity of royal government in these regions and created more problems than it solved. For the remainder of his reign, in fact, Henry VIII sought unsuccessfully to devise some cheap and effective alternative to the appointment of a Dacre or Kildare to border office. This led to political instability and a pronounced discontinuity of policy as the government by turn tried some new strategy and counted the cost of its experiments. After Henry's death, Protector Somerset tried a different solution in both regions. This involved the establishment of garrisons in southern Scotland and the Irish midlands to protect the border. In other circumstances, this policy might have led in Scotland to the re-establishment of an English Pale, the dismantling of the existing border line, and eventual conquest, as it did in Ireland. In the north, however, the government drew back from this: the reappointment of William, Lord Dacre, as warden of the west marches in 1549 and then the disbanding of the garrisons in Scotland marked a return to the old order. And in the longer term the improved relations between the English and Scottish courts which developed from the advance of the Reformation meant that the policing and defence of the border was less of a problem. In Ireland, however, where the opposition to territorial expansion was weaker and more fragmented, experiments along the lines of the later 1540s continued: the earl of Kildare was pardoned and recovered many of his estates, but he was never reappointed to the deputyship.[23]

These changes were also important in the context of Tudor state formation and relations with the non-English territories in the archipelago. In the first place, they helped to focus attention more sharply on relations with the British territories outside the Tudor state, and so marked an important step towards the eventual unification of the British Isles. The continuing problems of dynastic security and royal control arising from the Reformation crisis ensured that the defence of these frontiers gradually came to be given a higher priority by the regime—at the expense of aggressive and costly campaigns in France which simply encouraged the French to repay the Tudors in kind on the Irish and Scottish borders.

More importantly, the reorganization of the 1530s had a major impact on the overall character of the Tudor state. It inaugurated a more interventionist, centralizing phase in relations between the crown and the provinces which effectively destroyed the traditional balance of power between centre and periphery. The marked reduction in seigneurial power which accompanied these changes saw the full force (and weaknesses) of the standard English system of government extended to the borderlands, regardless of its suitability to local conditions. Thus the traditional dominance of lowland England within the Tudor state was consolidated. Until 1603, the changes enjoyed only a partial success, away from the military frontiers: but the fact that they proved workable and indeed moderately successful in regions such as the Welsh marches, together with the traditional predilections of English administrators, encouraged the government to persevere with these policies. Tudor officials continued to believe that England

[23] Bush, *Government policy of Protector Somerset*, ch. 2; Ellis, *Tudor Ireland*, ch. 8; Carey, 'Local elites', *passim*. The arguments outlined here are developed in my 'Tudor state formation and the shaping of the British Isles', in id. and Sarah Barber (eds.), *Conquest and union: fashioning a British state, 1485–1725* (London, 1995), 40–63.

was an island, and that therefore neither a standing army nor the normal international frontier arrangements of continental Europe were really appropriate for Ireland or the far north. In these circumstances, the two regions were increasingly marginalized within the Tudor state. Tudor Ireland in fact gradually ceased to be governed by the normal methods of English administration, and was subjected to military conquest, colonization, and expropriation of the natives, with results which remain apparent down to the present.[24] The solution to the problem of the far north had even less to do with strategies of government: the Union of the Crowns in 1603 was a dynastic accident.

In the longer term, moreover, the problem of the borderlands exercised an unfortunate and enduring influence on the government's approach to the new problems created by dynastic union and conquest in 1603: how to turn the regal union of three kingdoms into a stable and unified British nation-state. Despite some flexibility with regard to means, the ultimate objectives of Tudor policy towards the north and Ireland had remained the same: the creation of a 'civil' English society, based on the norms and values of lowland England, and ruled by a centralized and uniform system of government. The government had not been brought to compromise on what constituted acceptable patterns of behaviour in a civil society. On the contrary, the government's strategy was shortly reinforced by centralizing interventionist policies in the religious sphere, which imposed on the borderlands a novel, bibliocentric presentation of Christianity geared chiefly to the more urbanized and literate south-east. And, in the short term, the changes of 1603 seemed to vindicate this stance: with the dismantling of the borders following dynastic union, the traditional problems of governing these regions seemed to disappear. March law was abolished on the Anglo-Scottish borders; Gaelic law was proscribed in Ireland. In practice of course, the government simply ran up against wider and even less tractable problems in its new relations with Scotland and Gaelic Ireland. So far as many English officials were concerned, these new territories presented King James with an old problem in a new guise: how to incorporate them into the existing English nation-state. And in Gaelic Ireland, which was now conquered territory, the government pressed blindly ahead with

---

[24] Ellis, *Tudor Ireland*, chs. 5–6, 8–9.

schemes to reduce the countryside to tillage and civility by plant-
ing English settlers in nucleated villages of English stone cottages,
regardless of the suitability of local conditions for these purposes.[25]
Scotland, as an independent sovereign kingdom, was of course
much less susceptible to such measures. The centralizing policies
of the 1530s thus exercised a continuing influence on state formation in the changed political situation after 1603, at a time when the
less intensive and more flexible and decentralized, early-Tudor
approach to the government of outlying provinces might have
offered a more acceptable solution. Thus, as the Tudors groped
towards the consolidation of a nation-state and the political unification of the British Isles, the problem of the borderlands was in
many ways a good deal more fundamental to the development of
British political culture and the Tudor state than the much more
familiar story of the struggle for power at court.

In writing about the peoples and societies of an earlier age, it is
customary for historians to approach the subject in two ways.
They seek to study these societies in their own terms, and they also
aim to trace the relationship between the past and the present. The
territories which provide the focus of this study were annexed to
the crown of England over 800 years ago. And with the addition
of Scotland after 1603 and the subtraction of twenty-six counties
in Ireland after 1922, they have been continuously ruled from
London right down to the present day. In the circumstances, one
might expect that historical perspectives on the Tudor borderlands
would address their central role both in the development of the
Tudor state and also in that process of state formation throughout
the archipelago which produced the United Kingdom in its modern and contemporary forms. As we have seen, the perspectives
traditionally favoured by historians of Ireland are rather better at
explaining the relationship between Tudor Ireland and the modern Irish Republic than in addressing Ireland's changing role in
the Tudor state. In the case of Tudor England, however, it is hard
to see how traditional perspectives advance our understanding of
either the contemporary Tudor or the modern British state. The
present crisis in Tudor studies is in fact neatly epitomized by the
perverse practice of, in effect, ignoring the wider problem of state

---

[25] Ellis, *Pale and the far north*, 26–7; Spence, 'Pacification of the Cumberland
borders', 99–122.

formation in relation to England and treating the sixteenth-century state as if it were a little England which had remained fundamentally unaltered in extent and national composition since Anglo-Saxon times and would so remain right down to the present day.

Bibliography

A. MANUSCRIPT SOURCES

Archbishop Marsh's Library, Dublin
 MS Z4 2 7

British Library, London
 Additional Charter 62,243
 Additional MSS 4787, 4791, 20030, 24,965 (Thomas Lord Dacre letter
  book, 1523–4)
 Caligula, MSS B. I, B. II, B. VI, B. VII
 Harleian MS 3756 (Rental book of Gerald, 9th earl of Kildare)
 Lansdowne MS I
 Royal MS 18C, XIV (Accounts of William Hattecliffe, undertreasurer
  of Ireland, 1495–6)
 Sloane MS 1449
 Titus MS B. XI
 Vespasian MS F. XIII

Castle Howard Archives, York
 A1
 F1/5/1–5

Cumbria Record Office, Carlisle
 D/Ay/1/180, 199, D/Ay/2/24
 D/HG/16, 18
 D/Lons/L LO.117

Durham University, Department of Palaeography and Diplomatic
 Howard of Naworth MSS

Lambeth Palace Library, London
 MSS 602 Carew manuscripts

National Library of Ireland, Dublin
 Ormond deeds

Public Record Office, Chancery Lane, London
 C54   Close rolls
 C66   Patent rolls
 C82   Warrants for the great seal, series II
 C113   Chancery, Masters exhibits

C142	Inquisitions *post mortem* (Chancery), series II
E30	Exchequer, Diplomatic documents
E36	Exchequer, Treasury of receipt, miscellaneous books
E40	Exchequer, ancient deeds
E101	Exchequer, King's remembrancer, accounts
E150	Inquisitions *post mortem* (Exchequer), series II
E375	Exchequer, sheriffs' proffers
E403	Exchequer of Receipt, Enrolments and registers of issues
E404	Exchequer of Receipt, writs and warrants for issues
E405	Exchequer of Receipt, rolls etc. of receipts and issues
PRO 31/18	Transcripts from Spanish archives
SC6	Ministers' accounts
SC11	Rentals and surveys
SP1	State Papers, Henry VIII
SP2	State Papers, Henry VIII, folio volumes
SP3	State Papers, Lisle papers
SP6	Theological tracts
SP60	State Papers, Ireland, Henry VIII
SP65	State Papers, Ireland, Henry VIII, folio volumes
STAC2	Star Chamber Proceedings, Henry VIII

Public Record Office of Ireland, Dublin

CH 1/1	Statute roll, 28–9 Henry VIII
EX 3/1	Controlment roll, estreats, Co. Meath
PRO 7/1	Transcript of parliament roll, 2–3 Richard III
RC 8	Record Commission, calendar of memoranda rolls
RC 13/8	Record Commission, transcript of parliament roll, 1 Richard III
1A 49 149	Ferguson repertory of memoranda roll extracts

Public Record Office of Northern Ireland, Belfast

D. 3078	Leinster MSS

St Peter's College, Wexford

Hore MS I   Transcripts of memoranda rolls

Trinity College, Dublin

MSS 543/2, 591, 1731

B. PRINTED SOURCES

Accounts of the Lord High Treasurer of Scotland, ed. Sir James Balfour, ii. *1500–04* (Edinburgh, 1900).

A descriptive catalogue of ancient deeds in the Public Record Office, iii (London, 1900).

'An accompt of the most considerable estates and families in the county of Cumberland. By John Denton', ed. R. S. Ferguson, in *C. & W. Tract Series*, 2 (1887).

Anglica Historia, ed. D. Hay (London, 1950).

Annála Connacht: the Annals of Connacht, A.D. 1224–1544, ed. A. M. Freeman (Dublin, 1944).

Annála ríoghachta Éireann: Annals of the kingdom of Ireland by the Four Masters, from the earliest period to the year 1616, ed. John O'Donovan, 7 vols. (Dublin, 1851).

Annála Uladh: Annals of Ulster . . . a chronicle of Irish affairs . . . 431 to 1541, ed. W. M. Hennessy, 4 vols. (Dublin, 1887–1901).

The annals of Loch Cé: a chronicle of Irish affairs, 1014–1590, ed. W. M. Hennessy, 2 vols. (London, 1871).

Bain, Joseph (ed.), *The Hamilton papers: letters and papers illustrating the political relations of England and Scotland in the XVI century*, i. (Edinburgh, 1890).

'The bills and statutes of the Irish parliaments of Henry VII and Henry VIII', ed. D. B. Quinn, in *Anal. Hib.*, 10 (1941).

British Library Harleian Manuscript 433, ed. R. Horrox and P. W. Hammond, 4 vols., Richard III society (London, 1979–83).

Calendar of ancient deeds and muniments preserved in the Pembroke Estate Office, Dublin (Dublin, 1891).

Calendar of Archbishop Alen's register, c.1172–1534, ed. C. McNeill (Dublin, 1950).

Calendar of close rolls, Henry VII, i. *1485–1500*, ii. *1500–09*. (London, 1954–63).

Calendar of documents relating to Scotland, ed. Joseph Bain, 5 vols. (Edinburgh, 1881–1987).

Calendar of inquisitions formerly in the office of the Chief Remembrancer, ed. M. C. Griffith, i. *Co. Dublin* (Dublin, 1991).

Calendar of inquisitions post mortem, Henry VII, 3 vols. (London, 1898–1956).

Calendar of Ormond deeds, 1172–1350 [etc.], ed. E. Curtis, 6 vols. (Dublin, 1932–43).

Calendar of patent rolls, 1232–47 [etc.] (London, 1906–).

Calendar of patent and close rolls of chancery in Ireland, Henry VIII to 18th Elizabeth, ed. J. Morrin (Dublin, 1861).

Calendar of state papers, etc. relating to negotiations between England and Spain, ed. G. A. Bergenroth *et al.* (London, 1862–1954).

Calendar of the Carew Manuscripts preserved in the archiepiscopal library at Lambeth, 1515–74 [etc.], 6 vols. (London, 1867–73).

'Calendar to Christ Church deeds, 1174–1684', ed. M. J. McEnery, in *Reports of the Deputy Keeper of the Public Record Office of Ireland, 20th report* (1888), *23rd* (1891), *24th* (1892), *27th* (1895).

Camden, William, *Britannia, a chorographical description* (trans. Philemon Holland, 1610).

Campbell, William (ed.), *Materials for a history of the reign of Henry VII*, 2 vols. (London, 1873, 1877).

Clifford letters of the sixteenth century, ed. A. G. Dickens, Surtees Society, clxxii (Durham, 1962).

Correspondence of Matthew Parker, D.D. Archbishop of Canterbury, ed. John Bruce and T. T. Perowne, Parker Society (Cambridge, 1853).

Court book of the liberty of St. Sepulchre, ed. Herbert Wood (Dublin, 1930).

Crown surveys of lands 1540–41, ed. Gearóid Mac Niocaill (Dublin, 1992).

Dowdall deeds, ed. Charles McNeill and A. J. Otway-Ruthven (Dublin, 1960).

Dowling, T., *Annales breves Hiberniae: Annals of Ireland*, ed. R. Butler (Dublin, 1849).

Ellis, Henry (ed.), *Original letters illustrative of English history*, 11 vols. in 3 ser. (London, 1824–6).

Gilbert, J. T. (ed.), *Calendar of ancient records of Dublin*, 18 vols. (Dublin, 1889–1922).

Hannay, R. K. (ed.), *Acts of the Lords of the Council in Public Affairs, 1501–1554* (Edinburgh, 1932).

Holinshed, R., *The . . . chronicles of England, Scotlande and Irelande*, ed. H. Ellis, 6 vols. (London, 1807–8).

Hore, H. F., and Graves, J. (eds.), *The social state of the southern and eastern counties of Ireland in the sixteenth century* (Dublin, 1870).

Inquisitions and assessments relating to Feudal Aids . . . 1284–1431, 4 vols. (London, 1899–1906).

Leges marchiarum, ed. William Nicolson (London, 1747).

Letters and papers, foreign and domestic, Henry VIII, 21 vols. (London, 1862–1932).

'Letters of the Cliffords, lords Clifford and earls of Cumberland, c.1500–c.1565', ed. R. W. Hoyle, in *Camden Miscellany*, 31 (1992).

The Loseley manuscripts, ed. A. J. Kempe (London, 1835).

Powicke, F. M., and Fryde, E. B. (eds.), *Handbook of British Chronology* (3rd edn., London, 1986).

D. B. Quinn (ed.), 'Guide to English financial records for Irish history, 1461–1558', in *Anal. Hib.*, 10 (1941).

The Red Book of the earls of Kildare, ed. G. Mac Niocaill (Dublin, 1964).

Register of the privy seal of Scotland, ed. M. Livingstone, i. *1488–1529* (Edinburgh, 1908).

Reports of the Deputy Keeper of the Public Records. 3rd Report (London, 1842).

The reports of Sir John Spelman, ed. J. H. Baker, i, Selden Society 93

(London, 1977).

Rotuli Scotiae, 1291–1516, ii. ed. D. Macpherson, Record Commissioner (London, 1819).

Rotulorum patentium et clausorum cancellariae Hiberniae calendarium, ed. Edward Tresham, i, part I. *Hen. II–Hen. VII*, Record Commissioners of Ireland (Dublin, 1828).

Selections from the household books of the Lord William Howard of Naworth castle, ed. George Ornsby, Surtees Society, lxviii (Durham, 1877).

State papers, Henry VIII, 11 vols. (London, 1830–52).

The statutes at large passed in the parliaments held in Ireland, 20 vols. (Dublin, 1786–1801).

The statutes of the realm, 11 vols. (London, 1810–28).

Statute rolls of the parliament of Ireland . . . reign of King Edward IV, ed. H. F. Berry and J. F. Morrissey, 2 vols. (Dublin, 1914–39).

Statute rolls of the parliament of Ireland, reign of King Henry VI, ed. H. F. Berry (Dublin, 1910).

Thorne, S. E. (ed.), *Prerogativa regis* (New Haven, Conn., 1949).

Valor Beneficiorum Ecclesiasticorum in Hibernia (Dublin, 1741).

Ware, Sir James, *The histories and antiquities of Ireland*, ed. R. Ware (Dublin, 1704).

White, N. B. (ed.), *Extents of Irish monastic possessions 1540–41* (Dublin, 1943).

C. SECONDARY WORKS

Barnes, Henry, 'Aikton church', in *C. & W.*, NS 13 (1913).

Barrow, G. W. S., *Feudal Britain* (London, 1956).

—— 'The Anglo-Scottish border', in *Northern History*, 1 (1966).

Bartlett, Robert, *The making of Europe: conquest, colonization and cultural change* (London, 1993).

—— and MacKay, Angus (eds.), *Medieval frontier societies* (Oxford, 1989).

Bean, J. M. W., 'The Percies and their estates in Scotland', in *Archaeologia Aeliana*, 4th ser. 35 (1957).

—— *The estates of the Percy family 1416–1537* (Oxford, 1958).

Bernard, G. W., *The power of the early Tudor nobility: a study of the fourth and fifth earls of Shrewsbury* (Brighton, 1985).

—— (ed.), *The Tudor nobility* (Manchester, 1992).

Blair, P. H., *An introduction to Anglo-Saxon England* (Cambridge, 1956).

Bliss, Alan, 'Language and literature', in J. F. Lydon (ed.), *The English in medieval Ireland* (Dublin, 1984).

Bouch C. M. L., and Jones, G. P., *A short economic and social history of the Lake Counties 1500–1830* (Manchester, 1961).

Bradshaw, Brendan, *The dissolution of the religious orders in Ireland under*

Henry VIII (Cambridge, 1974).

Bradshaw, Brendan, 'Cromwellian reform and the origins of the Kildare rebellion, 1533–4' in *TRHS* 5th ser. 27 (1977).

—— *The Irish constitutional revolution of the sixteenth century* (Cambridge, 1979).

—— 'Nationalism and historical scholarship in modern Ireland', in *IHS* 26 (1988–9).

Brady, Ciaran, 'Faction and the origins of the Desmond rebellion of 1579', in *IHS* 22 (1980–1).

Bryan, Donough, *Gerald FitzGerald, the Great Earl of Kildare, 1456–1513* (Dublin, 1933).

Bush, M. L., 'The problem of the far north: a study of the crisis of 1537 and its consequences', in *Northern History*, 6 (1971).

—— *The government policy of Protector Somerset* (London, 1975).

—— 'Captain Poverty and the Pilgrimage of Grace', in *Historical Research*, 65 (1992).

—— 'The Richmondshire Uprising of October 1536 and the Pilgrimage of Grace', in *Northern History*, 29 (1993).

Canny, Nicholas, 'The ideology of English colonization: from Ireland to America', in *William and Mary Quarterly*, 3rd ser. 30 (1973).

—— *The Elizabethan conquest of Ireland: a pattern established, 1565–1576* (Hassocks, 1976).

—— *Kingdom and colony: Ireland in the Atlantic world, 1560–1800* (Baltimore, 1988).

Carpenter, Christine, 'The Beauchamp affinity: a study of bastard feudalism at work', in *EHR* 95 (1980).

Chrimes, S. B., *Henry VII* (London, 1972).

Cockburn, J. S., *A history of English assizes 1558–1714* (Cambridge, 1972).

Collinson, Patrick, 'Towards a broader understanding of the early dissenting tradition', in id., *Godly people: essays on English Protestantism and Puritanism* (London, 1983).

Condon, Margaret, 'Ruling élites in the reign of Henry VII', in Charles Ross (ed.), *Patronage pedigree and power in later medieval England* (Gloucester, 1979).

Conway, Agnes, *Henry VII's relations with Scotland and Ireland, 1485–98* (Cambridge, 1932).

Cornwall, J. C. K., *Wealth and society in early sixteenth century England* (London, 1988).

Cosgrove, Art 'The execution of the earl of Desmond, 1468', in *Kerry Archaeological Society Journal*, 8 (1975).

—— 'Hiberniores ipsis Hibernis', in id. and Donal Macartney (eds.), *Studies in Irish history presented to R. Dudley Edwards* (Dublin, 1979).

—— *Late medieval Ireland, 1370–1541* (Dublin, 1981).

—— (ed.), *A new history of Ireland*, ii. *Medieval Ireland, 1169–1534*

(Oxford, 1987).

—— 'The writing of Irish medieval history', in *IHS* 27 (1990–1).

—— and Macartney, Donal (eds.), *Studies in Irish history presented to R. Dudley Edwards* (Dublin, 1979).

Coss, P. R., 'Bastard feudalism revised', in *Past and Present*, 125 (Nov. 1989).

Cruickshank, C. G., *Army Royal: Henry VIII's invasion of France, 1513* (Oxford, 1969).

Curtis, Edmund, *A history of medieval Ireland from 1086 to 1513* (London, 1938).

Curwen, J. F., 'Liddel Mote', in *C. & W.*; NS 10 (1910).

—— 'Isel Hall', in *C. & W.*, NS 11 (1911).

Davies, C. S. L., 'Provisions for armies, 1509–50; a study in the effectiveness of early Tudor government', in *Economic History Review*, 2nd ser. 17 (1964).

—— 'Peasant revolt in France and England: a comparison', in *Agricultural History Review*, 21 (1973).

—— 'Popular religion and the Pilgrimage of Grace', in A. Fletcher and J. Stevenson (eds.), *Order and disorder in early modern England* (Cambridge, 1985).

Davies, R. R., 'Frontier arrangements in fragmented societies: Ireland and Wales', in Robert Bartlett and Angus MacKay (eds.), *Medieval frontier societies* (Oxford, 1989), 77–100.

—— *Domination and conquest: the experience of Ireland, Scotland and Wales 1100–1300* (Cambridge, 1990).

—— *The age of conquest: Wales, 1063–1415* (Oxford, 1991).

Dawson, Jane, 'Two kingdoms or three? Ireland in Anglo-Scottish relations in the middle of the sixteenth century', in R. A. Mason (ed.), *Scotland and England 1286–1815* (Edinburgh, 1987).

—— 'The fifth earl of Argyle, Gaelic lordship and political power in sixteenth-century Scotland', in *SHR* 67 (1988).

Dixon, Philip, 'Towerhouses, pelehouses and border society', in *Archaeological Journal*, 136 (1979).

Duckett, G., 'Extracts from the Cottonian MSS relating to the border service', in *C. & W.*, 3 (1878).

Eaves, R. G., *Henry VIII's Scottish diplomacy 1513–1524: England's relations with the regency government of James V* (New York, 1971).

—— *Henry VIII and James V's regency 1524–1528: a study in Anglo-Scottish diplomacy* (Lanham, 1987).

Ellis, S. G., 'The Kildare rebellion and the early Henrician Reformation', in *Hist. Jn.*, 19 (1976).

—— 'Tudor policy and the Kildare ascendancy in the lordship of Ireland, 1496–1534', in *IHS* 20 (1976–7).

—— 'Taxation and defence in late medieval Ireland: the survival of scutage', in *RSAI Jn.*, 107 (1977).

Ellis, S. G., 'An indenture concerning the king's munitions in Ireland, 1532', in *Ir. Sword*, 14 (1980–1).

—— 'Thomas Cromwell and Ireland, 1532–1540', in *Hist. Jn.*, 23 (1980).

—— 'The destruction of the liberties: some further evidence', in *IHR Bull.*, 54 (1981).

—— 'England in the Tudor state', in *Hist. Jn.*, 26 (1983).

—— *Tudor Ireland: crown, community and the conflict of cultures, 1470–1603* (London, 1985).

—— 'Crown, community and government in the English territories, 1450–1575', in *History*, 71 (1986).

—— *Reform and revival: English government in Ireland, 1470–1534* (London, 1986).

—— 'Nationalist historiography and the English and Gaelic worlds in the late middle ages', in *IHS* 25 (1986–7).

—— ' "Not mere English": the British perspective, 1400–1650', in *History Today*, 28 (1988).

—— *The Pale and the far north: government and society in two early Tudor borderlands* (Galway, 1988).

—— 'Representations of the past in Ireland: whose past and whose present?', in *IHS* 27 (1990–1).

—— 'Tudor state formation and the shaping of the British Isles', in id. and Sarah Barber (eds.), *Conquest and union: fashioning a British state, 1485–1725* (London, 1995).

Elton, G. R., *The Tudor revolution in government* (Cambridge, 1953).

—— *Policy and police: the enforcement of the Reformation in the age of Thomas Cromwell* (Cambridge, 1972).

—— *Reform and renewal: Thomas Cromwell and the common weal* (Cambridge, 1973).

—— *England under the Tudors* (2nd edn., London, 1974).

—— *Reform and Reformation: England, 1509–1558* (London, 1977).

—— 'Politics and the Pilgrimage of Grace', in B. Malament (ed.), *After the Reformation* (New Haven, Conn., 1980).

—— *The Tudor constitution* (2nd edn., Cambridge, 1982).

Empey, C. A., 'The Butler lordship', in *Butler Society Journal*, 1 (1970–1).

—— 'From rags to riches: Piers Butler, earl of Ormond, 1515–39', in *Butler Society Journal*, 2:3 (1984).

—— and Simms, K., 'The ordinances of the White Earl and the problem of coign in the later middle ages', in *RIA Proc.*, 75 (1975), sect. C.

Falls, Cyril, *Elizabeth's Irish wars* (London, 1950).

Ferguson, C. J., 'Naworth castle', in *C. & W.*, 4 (1880).

Ferguson, R. S., 'Two border fortresses: Tryermain and Askerton castles', in *C. & W.*, 3 (1878).

—— 'The barony of Gilsland and its owners to the end of the sixteenth century', in *C. & W.*, 4 (1880).

——*History of Cumberland* (London, 1890).

Fernandez-Armesto, Felipe, *Before Columbus: exploration and colonisation from the Mediterranean to the Atlantic* (London, 1987).

Fitzgerald, Lord Walter, 'The manor and castle of Powerscourt . . . in the sixteenth century', in *Kildare Archaeological Society Journal*, 6 (1909–11).

Fletcher, Anthony, *Tudor rebellions* (3rd edn., London, 1983).

Frame, Robin, 'English officials and Irish chiefs in the fourteenth century', in *EHR* 90 (1975).

——'Power and society in the lordship of Ireland, 1272–1377', in *Past and Present*, 76 (Aug. 1977).

——*Colonial Ireland, 1169–1369* (Dublin, 1981).

——*English lordship in Ireland, 1318–1361* (Oxford, 1982).

——'War and peace in the medieval lordship of Ireland', in J. F. Lydon (ed.), *The English in medieval Ireland* (Dublin, 1984).

——*The political development of the British Isles 1100–1400* (Oxford, 1990).

——'Commissions of the peace in Ireland, 1302–1461', in *Anal. Hib.*, 35 (1992).

Gibbs, Vicary, *et al.* (eds.), *The Complete Peerage by G.E.C.*, 13 vols. (London, 1910–59).

Gillingham, John, *The Wars of the Roses* (London, 1981).

Goodman, Anthony, 'The Anglo-Scottish marches in the fifteenth century: a frontier society?', in R. A. Mason (ed.), *Scotland and England, 1286–1815* (Edinburgh, 1987).

——(ed.), *War and border societies in the middle ages* (Gloucester, 1992).

Graham, T. H. B., 'Six extinct Cumberland castles', in *C. & W.*, NS 9 (1909).

——'The border manors', in *C. & W.*, NS 11 (1911).

——'Extinct Cumberland castles. Part III', in *C. & W.*, NS 11 (1911).

——'The de Levingtons of Kirklinton', in *C. & W.*, NS 12 (1912).

——'The Debateable Land', in *C. & W.*, NS 12 (1912); 14 (1914).

——'The annals of Liddel', in *C. & W.*, NS 13 (1913).

——'The family of Denton', in *C. & W.*, NS 16 (1916).

——'The manor of Blakhale', in *C. & W.*, NS 18 (1918).

——'The eastern fells', in *C. & W.*, NS 19 (1919); 20 (1920).

——'The annals of Hayton', in *C. & W.*, NS 25 (1925).

——'The lords of Bewcastle', in *C. & W.*, NS 29 (1929).

Grant, Alexander, *Independence and nationhood: Scotland 1306–1469* (London, 1984).

Graves, M. A. R., *The Tudor parliaments: crown, lords and commons, 1485–1603* (London, 1985).

Gray, H. L., 'Incomes from land in England in 1436', in *EHR* 49 (1934).

Griffith, M. C., 'The Talbot–Ormond struggle for control of the Anglo-

Irish government', in *IHS* 2 (1940–1).

Griffiths, R. A., ' "*This royal throne of kings, this scept'red isle*"': the *English realm and nation in the later middle ages* (Swansea, 1983).

—— 'The English realm and dominions and the king's subjects in the later middle ages', in John Rowe (ed.), *Aspects of government and society in later medieval England: essays in honour of J. R. Lander* (Toronto, 1986).

Guy, J. A., *The Cardinal's Court: the impact of Thomas Wolsey in Star Chamber* (Hassocks, 1977).

—— 'Henry VIII and the praemunire manoeuvres of 1530–31', in *EHR* 97 (1982).

—— *Tudor England* (Oxford, 1988).

Gwyn, Peter, *The king's cardinal: the rise and fall of Thomas Wolsey* (London, 1990).

Harris, Barbara J., *Edward Stafford, 3rd duke of Buckingham* (Stanford, Calif., 1986).

—— 'Women and politics in early Tudor England', in *Hist. Jn.*, 33 (1990).

Harrison, S. M., *The Pilgrimage of Grace in the Lake Counties, 1536–7* (London, 1981).

Hartley, T. E., *Elizabeth's parliaments: queen, lords and commons 1559–1601* (Manchester, 1992).

Hayes-McCoy, G. A., 'The early history of guns in Ireland', in *Galway Archaeological Society Journal*, 18 (1938–9).

Hechter, Michael, *Internal colonialism: the Celtic fringe in British national development, 1536–1966* (London, 1975).

Herbert of Cherbury, Edward, Lord, *The life and raigne of King Henry the Eighth* (London, 1649).

Hodgson, John, *A history of Northumberland*, 3 parts in 7 vols. (Newcastle, 1820–5).

Hore, H. F., 'The Rental Book of Gerald Fitzgerald, 9th earl of Kildare', in *Journal of the Kilkenny Archaeological Society*, 2nd ser. 2 (1858–9).

Horrox, Rosemary, *Richard III: a study in service* (Cambridge, 1989).

Hoyle, R. W., 'Lords, tenants and tenant right in the sixteenth century: four studies', in *Northern History*, 20 (1984).

—— 'Thomas Masters' Narrative of the Pilgrimage of Grace', in *Northern History*, 21 (1985).

—— 'The first earl of Cumberland: a reputation re-assessed', in *Northern History*, 22 (1986).

—— 'An ancient and laudable custom: the definition and development of tenant right in north-western England in the sixteenth century', in *Past and Present*, 116 (Aug. 1987).

—— 'The Anglo-Scottish war of 1532–3', in *Camden Miscellany*, 31 (1992).

Huddleston, C. R., 'Cumberland and Westmorland feet of fines in the reign of Henry VII', in *C. & W.*, NS 66 (1966).

James, Mervyn, *Family, lineage and civil society: a study of society, politics, and mentality in the Durham region, 1500–1640* (Oxford, 1974).

——*Society, politics and culture: studies in early modern England* (Cambridge, 1986).

Kearney, Hugh, *The British Isles: a history of four nations* (Cambridge, 1989).

Kildare, marquis of, *The earls of Kildare and their ancestors* (3rd edn., Dublin, 1858).

Lander, J. R., *Crown and nobility 1450–1509* (London, 1976).

Leask, H. G., *Irish castles and castellated houses* (Dundalk, 1951).

Leerssen, J. Th., *Mere Irish & fíor-Ghael: studies in the idea of Irish nationality, its development and literary expression prior to the nineteenth century* (Amsterdam, 1986).

Loach, Jennifer, *Parliament under the Tudors* (Oxford, 1991).

López de Coca Castañer, José Enrique, 'Institutions on the Castilian–Granadan frontier', in Robert Bartlett and Angus MacKay (eds.), *Medieval frontier societies* (Oxford, 1989).

Loyn, H. R., *Anglo-Saxon England and the Norman conquest* (London, 1962).

Lydon, J. F., 'The problem of the frontier in medieval Ireland', in *Topic, 13* (Washington, DC, 1967).

——*Ireland in the later middle ages* (Dublin, 1972).

——*The lordship of Ireland in the middle ages* (Dublin, 1972).

——(ed.), *The English in medieval Ireland* (Dublin, 1984).

——'The middle nation', in id. (ed.), *The English in medieval Ireland* (Dublin, 1984).

MacCurtain, Margaret, 'The fall of the house of Desmond', in *Kerry Archaeological Society Journal*, 8 (1975).

McFarlane, K. B., *The nobility of late medieval England* (Oxford, 1973).

Mackenney, Richard, *Sixteenth century Europe: expansion and conflict* (London, 1993).

MacKenzie, W. MacKay, 'The Debateable Land', in *SHR* 30 (1951).

Mac Niocaill, Gearóid, 'The interaction of laws', in J. F. Lydon (ed.), *The English in medieval Ireland* (Dublin, 1984).

Mason, R. A., (ed.), *Scotland and England 1286–1815* (Edinburgh, 1987).

Miller, Helen, 'Subsidy assessments of the peerage in the sixteenth century', in *IHR Bull.*, 28 (1955).

——*Henry VIII and the English nobility* (Oxford, 1986).

Moody, T. W., Martin, F. X., and Byrne, F. J. (eds.), *A new history of Ireland*, iii. *Early modern Ireland, 1534–1691* (Oxford, 1976).

Morgan, Hiram, 'Mid-Atlantic blues' in *Irish Review*, 11 (1991).

Murray, James, 'Archbishop Alen, Tudor reform and the Kildare rebellion', in *RIA Proc.*, 89 (1989), sect. C.

Neville, C. J., 'Gaol delivery in the border counties, 1439–1459: some preliminary observations', in *Northern History*, 19 (1983).

Newton, Robert, 'The decay of the borders', in C. W. Chalklin and M. A. Havindon (eds.), *Rural change and urban growth 1500–1800* (London, 1974).

Nicholls, K. W., *Gaelic and gaelicised Ireland in the middle ages* (Dublin, 1972).

Nicholson, Ranald, *Scotland: the later middle ages* (Edinburgh, 1974).

Nicolson, J., and Burn, R., *The history and antiquities of the counties of Westmorland and Cumberland*, 2 vols. (London, 1777).

Ó Danachair, Caomhín, 'Irish tower houses and their regional distribution', in *Béaloideas*, 45–7 (1979).

Otway-Ruthven, A. J., 'The medieval county of Kildare', in *IHS* 11 (1959).

——*A history of medieval Ireland* (2nd edn., London, 1980).

Pollard, A. J., *North-eastern England during the Wars of the Roses* (Oxford, 1990).

Prestwich, Michael, 'Colonial Scotland: the English in Scotland under Edward I', in R. A. Mason (ed.), *Scotland and England 1286–1815* (Edinburgh, 1987).

——*Edward I* (London, 1988).

Price, L., 'Armed forces of the Irish chiefs in the early sixteenth century', in *RSAI Jn.*, 62 (1932).

Pugh, T. B. *The marcher lordships of south Wales, 1415–1536* (Cardiff, 1963).

——(ed.), *Glamorgan County History,* iii. *The Middle Ages* (Cardiff, 1971).

——'The magnates, knights and gentry', in S. B. Chrimes, C. D. Ross, and R. A. Griffiths (eds.), *Fifteenth-century England 1399–1509* (Manchester, 1972).

——and Ross, C. D., 'The English baronage and the income tax of 1436', in *IHR Bull.*, 26 (1953).

Quinn, D. B., 'Anglo-Irish Ulster in the early sixteenth century', in *Proceedings and reports of the Belfast Natural History and Philosophical Society*, 1933/4 (1935).

——'Henry Fitzroy, duke of Richmond, and his connexion with Ireland, 1529–30', in *IHR Bull.*, 12 (1935).

——'Ireland and sixteenth century European expansion', in *Historical Studies*, 1 (1958).

——'Henry VIII and Ireland, 1509–34', in *IHS* 12 (1960–1).

Rae, T. I., *The administration of the Scottish frontier, 1513–1603* (Edinburgh, 1966).

Ragg, F. W., 'Helton Flechan, Askham and Sandford of Askham', in *C. & W.*, NS 21 (1921).

Reid, R. R., *The king's council in the north* (London, 1921).

——'The office of warden of the marches: its origin and early history', in *EHR* 32 (1917).

Robinson, W. R. B., 'Patronage and hospitality in early Tudor Wales: the role of Henry earl of Worcester', in *IHR Bull.*, 51 (1978).

Robson, Ralph, *The rise and fall of the English highland clans: Tudor responses to a mediaeval problem* (Edinburgh, 1989).

Ross, Charles, *Edward IV* (London, 1974).

——*Richard III* (London, 1981).

Sahlins, Peter, *Boundaries: the making of France and Spain in the Pyrenees* (Berkeley, Calif., 1989).

Scarisbrick, J. J., *Henry VIII* (London, 1968).

Simms, Katharine, *From Kings to Warlords: the changing political structure of Gaelic Ireland in the later middle ages* (Woodbridge, 1987).

Smith, A. G. R., *The emergence of a nation state: the commonwealth of England 1529–1660* (London, 1984).

Smith, J. Irvine, 'The transition to the modern law 1532–1660', in *An introduction to Scottish legal history*, The Stair Society, 20 (Edinburgh, 1958).

Spence, R. T., 'The pacification of the Cumberland borders, 1593–1628', in *Northern History*, 13 (1977).

Storey, R. L., 'The wardens of the marches of England towards Scotland, 1377–1485', in *EHR* 72 (1957).

——*The reign of Henry VII* (London, 1968).

——*The end of the house of Lancaster* (2nd edn., Gloucester, 1986).

Summerson, Henry, 'Crime and society in medieval Cumberland', in *C. & W.*, 2nd ser. 82 (1982).

——'The early development of the laws of the Anglo-Scottish marches, 1249–1448', in W. M. Gordon (ed.), *Legal history in the making* (London, 1991).

——*Medieval Carlisle: the city and the borders from the late eleventh to mid-sixteenth century* (Carlisle, 1993), ii.

Taylor, M. W., 'Kirkoswald castle', in *C. & W.*, 2 (1876).

Thirsk, Joan (ed.), *The agrarian history of England and Wales.*, iv. *1500–1640* (Cambridge, 1967).

Thompson, M. W., *The decline of the castle* (Cambridge, 1987).

Thornley, Isabel, 'The destruction of sanctuary', in R. W. Seton-Watson (ed.), *Tudor studies* (London, 1924).

Tough, D. L. W., *The last years of a frontier: a history of the borders during the reign of Elizabeth* (Oxford, 1928).

Trainor, Brian, 'Extracts from the Irish ordnance accounts, 1537–9', in *Ir. sword*, 1 (1952–3).

Tuck, J. A., 'Richard II and the border magnates', in *Northern History*, 3 (1968).

——'Northumbrian society in the fourteenth century', in *Northern History*, 6 (1971).

Tuck, J. A., 'War and society in the medieval north', in *Northern History*, 21 (1985).

—— 'The emergence of a northern nobility, 1250–1400', in *Northern History*, 22 (1986).

The Victoria History of the Counties of England. A history of Cumberland, i–ii (London, 1901–5).

Watts, S. J., 'Tenant-right in early 17th-century Northumberland', in *Northern History*, 6 (1971).

—— *From border to middle shire: Northumberland 1586–1625* (Leicester, 1975).

Whelan, Kevin, 'Clio agus Caitlín Ní Uallacháin', in *Oghma 2* (Dublin, 1990).

White, D. G., 'Henry VIII's Irish kerne in France and Scotland, 1544–45', in *Ir. Sword*, 3 (1957–8).

Whitehead, H., 'Church goods in Cumberland in 1552', in *C. & W.*, 8 (1886).

Williams, Glanmor, *Recovery, reorientation and Reformation: Wales c.1415–1642* (Oxford, 1987).

—— *Wales and the Act of Union* (Bangor, 1992).

Williams, Penry, *The Tudor regime* (Oxford, 1979).

Winchester, A. J. L., *Landscape and society in medieval Cumbria* (Edinburgh, 1987).

Wormald, Jenny, *Court, kirk, and community: Scotland 1470–1625* (London, 1981).

—— *Lords and men in Scotland: bonds of manrent 1442–1603* (Edinburgh, 1985).

D. THESES

Carey, Vincent, 'Local elites and central authority: Gerald XI earl of Kildare and Tudor rule in Ireland, 1547–1586', Ph.D. thesis, State University of New York at Stony Brook, 1991.

Cott, Susan, 'The wardenship of Thomas Lord Dacre 1485–1525', MA thesis, University of Manchester, 1971.

Ellis, S. G., 'The Kildare rebellion, 1534', MA thesis, University of Manchester 1974.

Index